TRUE
TO
THEIR
SALT

TRUE TO THEIR SALT

THE BRITISH INDIAN ARMY AND AN ALTERNATIVE HISTORY OF DECOLONIZATION

RAVINDRA RATHEE

An Imprint of HarperCollins *Publishers*

First published in India by Fourth Estate 2022
An Imprint of HarperCollins *Publishers*
4th Floor, Tower A, Building No. 10, Phase II, DLF Cyber City,
Gurugram, Haryana – 122002
www.harpercollins.co.in

2 4 6 8 10 9 7 5 3 1

Copyright © Ravindra Rathee 2022

All images sourced from the British Library, London

P-ISBN: 978-93-5629-031-0
E-ISBN: 978-93-5629-039-6

The views and opinions expressed in this book are the author's own and the facts are as reported by him, and the publishers are not in any way liable for the same.

Ravindra Rathee asserts the moral right
to be identified as the author of this work.

For sale in the Indian subcontinent only.

All rights reserved. No part of this publication may be reproduced, stored in a retrieval system, or transmitted, in any form or by any means, electronic, mechanical, photocopying, recording or otherwise, without the prior permission of the publishers.

Typeset in 11.5/15.4 Stempel Garamond LT Std
Manipal Technologies Limited, Manipal

Printed and bound at
Thomson Press (India) Ltd

This book is produced from independently certified FSC® paper
to ensure responsible forest management.

To my grandparents, and countless men-at-arms and their families, who raised and destroyed empires and fortunes in this ancient land for millennia.

Contents

Introduction		ix
Chapter One	The Empire of Profit and Plunder	1
Chapter Two	An English Barrack in the Oriental Seas	8
Chapter Three	The Military Revolution in Hindustan	24
Chapter Four	The Grand Derangement	37
Chapter Five	True to Their Salt	63
Chapter Six	Pay, Batta and Pension	89
Chapter Seven	Trust Deficit	115
Chapter Eight	Colour before Honour	160
Chapter Nine	Defenders of the Faith	207
Chapter Ten	With Faith towards Freedom	258
Notes		301
Bibliography		329
Index		343
About the Author		361

Introduction

COLONIZATION AND ITS REVERSAL ARE STRATEGIC PHENOMENA. Eventually, colonization is about the domination of a population by an external or foreign power. It is achieved by force, and ends when the dominating force is not sufficient and the resistance is more powerful. The British Empire in India was no different. It was based on the foundations of military force, which predominantly comprised of Indians.

One cannot fully understand the British Empire without delving deeper into the instrument that enabled the Empire in the first place—the Indian Army and the sepoys that marched in its ranks. Colonization of India, and its rushed independence in 1947 are best understood by focusing on the Indian soldiers who were at the core of British (Company and later Crown) rule in India.

The Indian Army was also the global 'strategic reserve' for the Empire, and in many ways explains the 'exceptionalism' of Britain in world history. When reviewed in light of the small recruitment pool within the British Isles and the limited financial resources that, by necessity, had to be focused on the Navy, the critical role that the Indian Army played in Britain's predominant military position for almost a century and a half until the Second World War becomes clearer. This global military capability was achieved at very little additional cost to the British exchequer, as the Indian Army was paid for by Indian taxes, and Indian soldiers were grossly underpaid.

Indian soldiers made a pivotal contribution to the British Empire, and Great Britain's unlikely development into a dominant military and industrial power. This book aims to bridge the knowledge gap that exists about Indian soldiers' contribution to Britain's history and rise, by examining key themes in the history of the sepoy in British service, and looking beyond the well-trodden snapshot of the two world wars.

This book charts how the East India Company came to acquire this magnificent army in the first place, at a time when civil war in eighteenth-century India led to the breakdown of indigenous military command and control structures. By exploring the various mechanisms used by the Company and Crown to maintain control over Indian soldiers, we gain an insight into the role that insecurities of the Raj officials played on Indian and British history.

This book looks at the socio-cultural and emotional universe of the Indian soldiers who enlisted in the Company and Crown Armies in India, and the value system that drove them to serve with such dedication and loyalty. The service conditions, pay terms and discrimination suffered by Indian soldiers is reviewed in contrast to their contributions and motivations. A number of mutinies related to service terms are also reviewed, which were often resolved by temporary corrective measures. Nevertheless, the discrimination against Indian soldiers continued until the end of Raj.

This discrimination was not just limited to pay and service terms. The worst impact of discrimination became apparent during significant defeats that the British Indian Army suffered in campaigns outside India. It affected the life chances and recovery of the soldiers when the British imperial forces encountered a stronger adversary. The book reviews the Afghan disaster in 1839–42, the Mesopotamian campaign during the First World War and the Singapore defeat during the Second World War to review the tragic consequences for the Indian soldiers.

This book also examines the role of soldiers in maintaining the faith of their ancestors in India. The most severe of mutinies, including the rebellion of 1857, were a result of fears related to religious conversion. As a result, the British colonial rulers were forced to ban missionary activities in the Army and the wider Indian society to a point. The sepoys thus served as an effective control over the coercive powers of British rule in India, drawing a line in the sand over matters related to their faith that, though tested, were never breached.

Finally, as the ultimate proof of their critical importance to the maintenance of British rule, Indian soldiers also gained India's freedom from colonial rule after the Second World War. The history of decolonization as taught in Britain and India today lays too much emphasis on British 'voluntary withdrawal' or the nationalist popular movement in India. In fact, it was the growing doubt about Indian soldiers' continued loyalty to the British Raj that led to Independence. It was an attempt to punish the 'mutiny' of the Indian National Army (INA) soldiers—who fought against Britain during the Second World War—that undermined the loyalty of the Indian soldiers of the Raj.

The role of Indian soldiers in Indian independence has been underplayed (and in some ways forgotten), both within Indian and British national narratives. Imperial officers and British politicians did not want to admit that fear was the reason for their relinquishing of the 'jewel' of the British Empire—this did not suit the narrative of brave white men on a daring mission to civilize the world. It also did not suit the politicians who formed the new government of independent India, who preferred a narrative that emphasized the role of non-violent political movement, and therefore their own role, in achieving India's freedom.

Many new primary accounts by Indian soldiers have come to light in the past few decades, and need to be included for a better understanding of the Indian soldiers' contribution and thinking. This book is written with a focus on Indian soldiers and their experiences, without losing sight of the bigger political, historic and economic developments. It thus contextualizes a number of these first-hand Indian accounts spanning more than two centuries.

There is significant interest in Britain's colonial history today, and how we represent, mark and remember that history. Amid debates about decolonizing the UK curriculum and remembering all who contributed to Britain's past, present and future, it is important that students and citizens in the UK understand the critical contribution Indian soldiers made over two centuries to the prosperity of this country. I hope the book will serve as a correction to this collective amnesia and contribute to this dialogue. Instead of the negative, combative approach of denouncing characters and statues, this book suggests a more positive and perhaps more broad-reaching alternative: recognizing, celebrating and remembering the millions of Indian soldiers who served British interests over two centuries. The UK has an equal claim over these soldiers as India does, and maintaining their memory and history is of critical importance to harmonious race relations within the UK, as well as international relations with emerging countries.

As Britain exits the European Union and starts to build trade and cultural relationships with countries across the world, its diplomats, politicians and citizens should understand the special contribution of India and its soldiers to the Britain of today. The term 'special relationship' is taken to mean Britain's relationship with the USA, but it is from India that the past — and more importantly the future — of Britain has been and will perhaps be shaped.

However, empires, armies and decolonization are impersonal concepts. My drive behind this book is deeply personal. For millennia, my ancestors in north-west India (today's Haryana) had only two professions at their disposal: farming and soldiery. While my parents' generation, born around Independence, moved on to other occupations, as a family we were acutely aware of the profession of arms as the mainstay of our family history. In fact, both my grandfathers served in the army and the police, respectively. My maternal grandfather, Choudhary Raghbir Singh Sheoran, served in the British Indian Army during the Second World War in the Middle-East theatre.[1] My paternal grandfather, Choudhary Banwari Lal Rathee, was in charge of Sir Chhotu Ram's personal safety while serving in the Punjab police in pre-Partition Lahore during those perilous years.[2]

The stories that we hear as children from our parents and grandparents live and grow within us.

This book started as a personal research project. As a child, I heard stories from my grandfather of his experiences during the Second World War. After his death, I started researching his war service and realized that there is a much bigger story to tell. It then struck me that each year, my son celebrates Remembrance Day at school, and yet he and his school mates know very little about the contributions of Indian soldiers during the world wars, let alone the two preceding centuries. This must change. In a way, this book is as much for my son and his school mates as it is about my grandfather and his comrades.

The year 2022 is a particularly relevant year for the publication of this book. It is the seventy-fifth anniversary of Indian independence, to which Indian soldiers had a central contribution to make. It is also the 125th birth anniversary of Subhas Chandra Bose, the Indian national leader who lead the INA against Britain during the Second World War. Finally, and personally, it is an important year to me and my family as this is the 100th anniversary of the birth of my maternal grandfather.

I am deeply grateful to a number of individuals, without whose support this book would have never seen the light of day. My indomitable literary agent, Kanishka Gupta, did everything to ease my entry into publishing world. I thank my friend, Kaushik Barua, for connecting us. My editor at HarperCollins, Ujjaini Dasgupta, supported by Udayan Mitra, have been exceptional in their efforts. Connor Stait and Philip Dean at Amberley have made the book's journey a seamless one. Alex Hammond and Lydia Popiolek have been a great help with crafting the 'manuscript proposal' and proofreading.

Aliki-Anastasia Arkomani and Nicole Lofredi at the British Library have been extremely helpful and patient in answering my questions related to archive materials and images. I cannot thank Narayani Basu enough for reading through the whole manuscript and giving me extremely valuable comments. Squadron Leader R.T.S. Chhina (Retd) deserves my gratitude for reading through parts of an earlier version of the manuscript, for his helpful comments and for providing access to the library at the United Service Institution of India.

I am extremely grateful to Dr Shashi Tharoor for his recommendation to the publishers, and his endorsement. John Koshy deserves my thanks for connecting us. Amish Tripathi, director at the Nehru Centre, London, has been a fantastic support and guide.

I am very grateful to Smt Sangita and Sajjan Jindal for their continuous support and encouragement in all my professional and personal endeavours.

I cannot thank Naveen Jindal enough for his help to get the right support and treatment for my parents during the Covid pandemic, while I was in the final stage of writing this book. I also thank Dr Ajay Sharma, Abhishek Gulia and Jitender Rana for their help to my parents.

I am grateful to Sanjeev Sanyal and Sathnam Sanghera for their endorsements.

My friends and family have been supportive in whatever I have decided to do, and I consider myself fortunate that I have their love and affection. Amit Parmar, Akanksha Singh, Clare Brennan and Kusumanjali R. Shrikant have helped and cheered me on in numerous ways. Matthew O'Sullivan has been a constant source of encouragement throughout the past two years.

My sister Sarita and her family have been a source of immense support and love for all my efforts. The unconditional and deep love and affection from my parents—Smt. Krishna Devi and Jai Pal Singh Rathee—cannot be acknowledged in words. Without their sacrifices, I would be nothing.

Love and patient support from my wife Selene, who read the first draft of all chapters and gave helpful comments, made the journey of this book smoother. My son Aryaman is always a source of delight, who brightens up my days and life with his smile and enthusiasm. I hope he will enjoy reading the book.

The memory of my grandparents, to whom I dedicate this book, has been a source of strength and courage all through my life.

Finally, while everyone around me has made the effort to improve this book, any faults are my own.

Ravindra Rathee
London
July 2022

Chapter One

The Empire of Profit and Plunder

I

It doesn't appear that there is much in common between Niall Ferguson and William Wilberforce; one an agnostic with a utilitarian view of religion[1] and the other a die-hard Christian. Yet, despite the gulf of two centuries, and much water having flown down the Thames and Ganges, both appear to be singing from the same hymn sheet as far as extolling the benefits of the British Empire to the 'heathens' is concerned.[2] In between came Lord Macaulay, Charles Trevelyan, Bishop Heber, Rudyard Kipling and innumerable others to join the chorus with gusto. The founders, beneficiaries and apologists of the Empire continue to show the ungrateful former subjects the rich benefits of being subdued and governed by an 'enlightened' power. What is left unsaid is the flow of benefits—material and other—in the reverse direction, which is now being accounted for by historians and economists.[3]

Most imperial projects are driven by avarice, and the desire to dominate and project political power. The power is exercised for the economic gain of the ruling core at the cost of the periphery. Political power and economic gains go hand in hand. Most empires are profitable for the metropole, some more than others. The British Empire in India, more than any other, was an empire for profit.[4] The economic gains from India were so significant that the manner of acquisition, and maintenance of political domination, were dictated by the material considerations.

To begin with, the Indian dominion (the 'jewel in the crown') was acquired through the Trojan Horse of a trading company, seeking to profit from the lucrative trade with the East Indies.[5] The humble request from Queen Elizabeth I to 'Ackbursha' (Akbar the Great)—received by Akbar's son Jahangir in 1609— to allow 'our subjects to settle a factory there, like as we will do to yours if at any time it shall be requested of us…'[6] was initially denied. The persistence of the East India Company (EIC) servants paid off in 1613, when Jahangir relented and granted a firman[7] to Captain Thomas Best, permitting an English factory at Surat.[8] The principle of preponderance of profit was wisely noted by Sir Thomas Roe, first English Ambassador to the Court of Jahangir, in 1619: 'A war and traffic are incompatible … let this be received as a rule that if you will profit, seek it at sea and in quiet trade, for, without controversy, it is an error to effect garrisons and land wars in India.'[9]

As the whirlwind of events in the subcontinent unfolded over the next century and a half, this caution was thrown away. The acquisition of political power presented opportunities for gathering incalculable riches; an opportunity that was not missed by the alert EIC servants. From mid-eighteenth century onwards, political power in India was the fountainhead of untold economic and manpower resources, the most valuable of which was perhaps the British Indian Army of loyal sepoys.[10] This transformed England from a small island nation at the margins of Europe to a leading world power. The resources of the newly acquired Indian Empire enabled England to colonize a quarter of the known world, replace the lost empire in the North America with an even richer and longer-lasting one in Asia and Africa, and finance the industrial revolution in Britain and the white colonies. Britain exported surplus capital accumulated from imperial holdings in India to North America and Europe, which helped build their infrastructure. The opportunities for trade, employment and profit provided by the Empire also helped to cement England's union with Scotland. The well-oiled wheels of Empire smoothened the friction, and focused energies on acquiring wealth together in faraway lands, burying the hatchet.

II

The Empire allowed Britain to 'punch way above its weight' in the political affairs of the world, an advantage that it continues to exercise. A nation with less than 1 per cent of the world's population came to shape the destiny of millions across the world through the instrument of empire. The 'prestige' as the possessor of an empire allowed Britain to hold a seat at almost all the powerful global bodies and conferences that settled political matters over the last two and a half centuries. From the Congress of Vienna in 1814-15 to the Potsdam conference in 1945, and almost every other diplomatic congregation of significance in between, the UK as an imperial power has had the front seat. The advantages continue in the structural privileges gained in multilateral bodies such as the UK's permanent membership on the UN Security Council.

Within the Empire, it was the domain of India that was the envy of the other world powers and the 'jewel in the crown'. From Napoleon to the Czars, from the Kaiser to Hitler, it was a subject of envious awe, a sort of wonder that glorified Britain in the eyes of its adversaries. The fact that a vast geography at the other end of the world, inhabited by an ancient civilization, came under the direct rule of Britain, amazed both historians and political leaders alike. In this sense, India was unique among British colonial possessions in the Americas, Caribbean, Africa, and even Australia and New Zealand. In these domains, Britain either walked into uninhabited expanses and deserts or encountered civilizations that could not claim any superior history or present. India was different, as brilliantly summarized by the historian Alex von Tunzelmann:

> In the beginning, there were two nations. One was a vast, and magnificent empire, brilliantly organized and culturally unified, which dominated a massive swathe of the earth. The other was an undeveloped, semi-feudal realm, riven by religious factionalism and barely able to feed its illiterate, diseased and stinking masses. The first nation was India. The second was England.[11]

The leaders of the Empire were acutely aware of their unique privilege. 'As long as we rule India,' Lord Curzon wrote to Arthur Balfour in 1901, 'we are the greatest Power in the world. If we lose it, we shall drop straightaway to a third-rate Power.'[12] Winston Churchill knew that the loss of India would be a fatal blow to Britain's global dominance. It could not fail, he said, 'to be part of a process that would reduce us to the scale of a minor power.'[13] Whatever the apologists of Empire might say, the loss of India started a process of 'normalization' of Britain's political position in the comity of nations. The very slow, almost undiscernible pace of this decline over the last three-quarters of a century is a testament to the monumental historic privilege that the possession of the Indian dominion bestowed on Britain.

III

The perceived wisdom in British circles has been that the Empire was a rather 'expensive' affair. Except for the initial riches of 'nabobs'—the likes of Robert Clive, Warren Hastings, etc.—who made a fortune in the late eighteenth century in India, the established rule of the EIC and the Crown was a pompous but unprofitable venture. If anything, it was getting 'costly', and with the expenses of two world wars, the Empire supposedly had become an economic burden.

This narrative is based on the incorrect assumption that a significant amount of capital was channelled from Britain to India during the Raj, and that India's poverty is a historic unchanging fact. A poor country like India sucked in a lot of investment, and could not have been of any benefit to Britain in economic terms. Copious amounts of scholarship have gone into supporting these two views. Niall Ferguson talks about 'immense British investments in Indian infrastructure, irrigation and industry'.[14] He contrasts this with a very small drain of 1 per cent of the Indian net domestic product between 1868 and 1930—'a lot less than the Dutch drain of 7–10 per cent from Indonesia',[15] to be sure. He grudgingly concedes that 'the average Indian had not got much richer under British rule', but reminds us that 'things might conceivably have been worse under a restored Mughal regime'.[16]

It is now well established that India was a dominant global economy before the start of the British rule. While India accounted for approximately 25 per cent of global GDP in 1700, Britain accounted for approximately 3 per cent.[17] More importantly, even on a per capita basis, the difference between India and the UK in 1700 was not very significant. This, however, changed drastically over the next 250 years as colonial rule drained the immense wealth of India to enrich Britain.

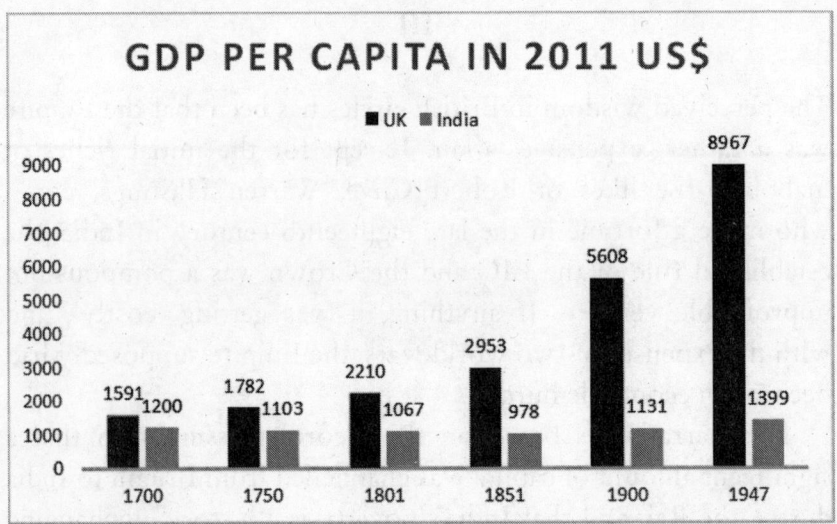

Source: Jutta Bolt et al., 'Rebasing "Maddison": New Income Comparisons and the Shape of Long-Run Economic Development', Maddison Project Working Paper, no. 10, Maddison Project Database, ver. 2018, www.ggdc.net/maddison.

Utsa Patnaik has quantified that Britain drained a total of nearly $45 trillion from India during the period 1765 to 1938.[18] This is visible in the six-fold jump in Britain's per capita income over this period, while Indian per capita income remained stagnant. This loot allowed Britain to finance its industrial revolution, pay for numerous imperial wars, and export surplus capital to Europe, North America and the new colonies of Australia and New Zealand. It was the wealth from imperial holdings in India that helped industrialize and enrich Britain, not the other way round. The institutional mechanism of this gross transfer of wealth is well explained by Patnaik, the details of which are beyond the scope of this book. In short, the control of the state as the revenue collector and sole purchaser of exports allowed Britain to pay for the products and exports of India from the revenue collected from the population. In essence, the proceeds from the export sale of

Indian goods ended up in the British treasury, without any cost. J. Terrine observed:

> From the opening of the 18th century, the Western World had been big with ideas, and the most world-changing was that of the use of steampower ... All that was lacking was the gold to fertilize it, and it was Clive who undammed the Yellow Stream ... Plassey appears as the midwife of the Industrial Revolution. And it was on this that the power of the British Empire itself rested for nearly two centuries.[19]

This institutional transfer of wealth is slowly coming to the light of people beyond the scholars researching the subject. This 'wealth transfer' is over and above the direct profits, dividends and inflated salaries and pensions paid to the British businessmen and British civil and military servants in India over two centuries. Shashi Tharoor rightly sums up:

> By the end of the nineteenth century, India was Britain's biggest source of revenue, the world's biggest purchaser of British exports and the source of highly paid employment for British civil servants and soldiers all at India's own expense. We literally paid for our own oppression.[20]

All this direct and indirect transfer of wealth from India enabled Britain to become the rich and prosperous nation it found itself to be in the middle of the twentieth century. Without the Indian Empire, it is not possible to imagine if this economic transformation could have been achieved in the space of less than two centuries, if it were to be achieved at all.

Chapter Two

An English Barrack in the Oriental Seas[1]

We don't want to fight,
But, by Jingo, if we do,
We won't go to the front ourselves,
We'll send the mild Hindoo.[2]

I

ESTABLISHMENT AND DEFENCE OF AN EMPIRE REQUIRES military force. No amount of diplomatic skulduggery or political chicanery can bring a subject people under the rule of a privileged few, especially when the rulers belong to an alien race. The British Empire was no exception.

There was one unique aspect to the British Empire, though. The size of the metropole (United Kingdom) was minuscule compared to the periphery (primarily India). They also remained distinct entities—culturally, religiously, geographically, racially—bound by a single military apparatus, and the imperial state structure.[3] The British Empire had the dual challenge of both subduing such a large and distinct population in India, while also protecting the vast and expansive Empire from its rivals.[4]

The sprawling Empire over almost one-third of humanity required immense military resources, especially when the metropole was barely 2-3 per cent of the global population. The sinews of war alone do not equip an army; it eventually needs men willing to fight and die for the cause. If a way can be found to hire and equip such men while spending less, the military advantage is supreme.

In India, the Empire found this unique combination of seemingly unlimited, and high-quality, military human resources at a fraction of the cost compared to the isles, or its adversaries in Europe. Eventually, it was the cost of frequent wars, both in terms of money and men, that brought the Napoleonic French, Russian and Ottoman Empires to heel. While its larger rivals exhausted themselves, Britain managed to outlast them, owing to its access to Indian military resources. That is, until at least the Second World War (WW2).

This was critical because Britain always fell short of quality fighting men from within the isles. The occupation of India balanced this deficit. As acknowledged by Ferguson:

> [India] gave Britain what for nearly two hundred years would be ... an inexhaustible reservoir of military manpower. India was much more than the 'jewel in the crown'. Literally, and metaphorically, it was a whole diamond mine.[5]

II

Amidst the pageantry and ceremony around armed forces in today's Britain, it is easy to forget that soldiering in the ranks was an extremely unpopular profession not so long ago. The image of the soldier and the army really changed with the first and second world wars in the twentieth century, when Britain found itself in an existential crisis. Conscription—standard in European nations in the previous century—had to be formally introduced during the world wars, and the wider British public finally experienced the impact of war in their personal lives.

Previously, the British Army had been in perennial shortage of manpower, especially in the ranks. The army was the last resort for the destitute, the drunkards and the dregs of society. Men preferred to remain unemployed than join the army. The criminal, the beggar, and the defaulter were coerced into enlistment frequently. Daniel Defoe noted the harsh options: 'In winter, the poor starve, thieve or turn soldier,'[6] most likely in that order of preference.

Wellington once remarked that his army was the 'scum of the earth ... fellows who have enlisted for drink—that is the plain fact', and we see Field Marshal Nicholson observing in 1906 that the army depended on the 'compulsion of destitution'.[7] Often, especially during major wars, destitution alone could not be relied upon to fill the ranks. We hear about 'crimpers' kidnapping men from the streets and then selling them on to the recruiting parties, during the Nine Years' War (1688–97)[8]. After 1695, in England, the convicts willing to 'volunteer' were freed from the prisons, and the criminals were sentenced to enlist in the army or were threatened with tougher sentences if they did not.[9] During the Spanish war of succession (1701–14), insolvent debtors (via special statutes), and then vagrants were added to the supply of convicts and criminals to the regiments.[10] This widespread social scorn and disapproval for the profession of arms continued unabated in society. Sometimes, even convicts and criminals preferred serving their sentence to enlistment, especially if the enlistment led them to the devastating climate of the West Indies and Africa.

A massive expansion drive for the army was launched when the American settlers rose in revolt. But the limits of the British pool of recruits was soon reached. The American War of Independence saw the raising of twenty-seven additional regiments between 1774 and 1776. Even these numbers proved insufficient in such a vast country. Britain lost its American colonies in 1781, for there weren't enough soldiers to hold them.

All previous conflicts that Britain had been involved in were dwarfed by the wars against revolutionary France between 1793 and 1815. The British Army increased from 40,000 at the outbreak of hostilities to 250,000 at their peak in 1813.[11] Even this massive increase was insufficient, and Britain had to resort to funding its allies and defensive wars. The capacity for offensive action was limited until France exhausted its resources. The size of the continental armies, in comparison, was huge. Napoleon's citizen army comprised almost a million men during its peak, and its European rivals—Russia and Austria—continued to fight a war of attrition, with their population as the cannon fodder. The Napoleonic war also forced Britain to expand the recruitment pool for its army. The home population reluctant and always insufficient, one-fifth of the British Army in 1813 composed of 'French royalists, Germans, Greeks, Corsicans and Negroes'.[12]

While victory over Napoleon in 1815 secured peace for Britain in Europe for almost a century, the sprawling Empire across the globe continued to require significant numbers of troops. The shortage of men in the British regiments continued, and the attitude of the British public towards soldiering as a profession did not improve. A number of large and small conflicts—Afghanistan, Sikh Wars, the Crimean War, the Indian rebellion, Jamaica, Sudan, South Africa, China, Ethiopia, New Zealand, Mauritius, Egypt, North America, Burma, etc.—throughout the nineteenth century required immense military personnel across the globe. As we shall see in the next chapters, this burden was bearable only with the help of sepoys recruited from India. In Britain, 'though the regular resort to "seduction, debauchery, and fraud" was persistently criticized, the traditional methods of inveigling "the foolish, the drunken, the ungodly, and the despairing" into the army were not abandoned until after 1867'.[13]

It was with this perennial shortage of fighting men from within the isles that Britain entered the twentieth century, and faced the existential crisis of two world wars. The indulgence of 'no conscription' afforded by the numerous troops from India, and the isolation of an island protected by its navy, finally came to an end. The total wars of the twentieth century required the total involvement of the nation. The country finally paid with its blood the price of freedom, a price it had managed so far to impose upon India.

III

The sepoys of the British Indian Army helped the EIC conquer India in the late eighteenth century, maintained British rule until the end of the Second World War, and served as a 'strategic imperial reserve' for the global defence of the British Empire.

E.W. Sheppard aptly said: 'An Army was built up from the people of India themselves, which in the end brought its own country under the sway of its foreign masters.'[14] Exactly how this miracle occurred is a subject that goes beyond the scope of this chapter. In essence, the civil war that followed the collapse of the Mughal Empire in eighteenth-century India created fertile ground for an organized foreign force to benefit. India had been a heavily militarized society since ancient times, and the profession of arms was widely practised on a full- or part-time basis. The EIC and other European trading companies (primarily French) had access to this military talent, and were able to employ a sufficiently large number of 'free lances and swords' during this tumultuous period. The French–British rivalry in Europe—occasioned by the Austrian War of Succession in the 1740s—provided further impetus to the arming of their trading companies in India. The performance of the sepoys surprised their foreign employers. Within a few short decades, the EIC emerged as one of the dominant powers in India, having defeated the French and their native allies decisively by the 1760s. Cornwallis, as the Governor-General, wrote to the Duke of York in 1787: 'A brigade of our sepoys can easily make anybody Emperor of Hindustan.'[15] An 'emperor' is eventually what the sepoys made the EIC in the next two or three decades in India, albeit the numbers required were more than a brigade.

Starting from the victories in the Carnatic Wars (in the 1740s), the sepoy army made the East India Company the de facto ruler of most of India by the end of the third Anglo–Maratha war in 1819. There was the Jat-held Fortress of Bharatpur to be breached in 1826, the Sikh state of Punjab to be annexed in the 1840s, and the sepoy-led rebellion of 1857 to be crushed. But by and large, India had come under EIC military and political control by the first quarter of the nineteenth century. The sepoy was the pillar of this military edifice that maintained the EIC's and, later, the Crown's rule over India.

The leaders of the Empire were acutely aware of their dependence on the sepoy for the defence and perpetuation of British rule in India. Sir Charles Metcalfe wrote in 1824: 'As long as our native army is faithful and we can pay enough for it, we can keep India in order by its instrumentality, but if the instruments should turn against us, where would be the British power? Echo answers, where?'[16]

The other key role of the Indian Army was a 'strategic imperial reserve', which was suitably located at the intersection of the Arabian Sea, Indian Ocean and the pathway to the Far East and Pacific. With a strong navy, the garrison in India could be deployed quickly to protect imperial interests, wherever threatened in the world. Philip Mason observes: 'The land masses whose shores those waters washed were all within reach of a small disciplined force which could be escorted from India ... It [the peace and defence of the British Empire] would not have been possible without a reservoir of troops in India.'[17] Niall Ferguson concludes the same: '[The British Raj's] foundation was military force. The army here was not just an imperial strategic reserve. It was also the guarantor of the internal stability of its Asian arsenal.'[18]

The role of the British Indian Army during the two world wars is relatively well known now. However, the numerous expeditions undertaken by the Indian Army outside India since the eighteenth century illustrate the significance of this 'English barrack in the Oriental Seas'.

The first recorded international expedition of the Indian Army was to Manila during 1762, where a 650-strong detachment of the erstwhile Madras Army was sent. Only a few soldiers survived this expedition and managed to return to India in 1767.[19] A large detachment of sepoys from the Bombay Army were sent to Egypt in 1801 to expel the French during the Napoleonic war.[20] Thereafter, sepoy expeditions to conquer, protect, police and evacuate across the globe became a regular feature. The Indian Army was deployed in the conquest of Java (1811); the Gurkha war (1814–16); Sri Lanka (1818); the Burma wars and rebellion (1824–26, 1852–53, 1885–95, 1930–32); the Afghan Wars (1838–42, 1878–80, 1919); the China Wars (1840–42, 1857–60, 1900–01); the Persian War (1856–57); the Bhutan campaign (1864–66); the Abyssinian campaign (1867–68); Malaya (1875); the garrison of Cyprus and Malta during the Russian crisis (1878); Egypt (1882, 1896); the Sudan wars (1884–85, 1896); the Somaliland campaign (1890, 1901–04); East Africa (1896–98); and the Tibet expedition (1903).[21] In addition, there was a recurring frontier war in the north-west against Pashtun tribes since the late nineteenth century.

The critical role of the Indian Army during the two world wars can't be described in a few pages. Even a summary would do no justice. The Indian Army played a central role in defeating the

Ottoman armies in Mesopotamia, and arrived in time to save the thinly held British and French lines on the Western Front during the First World War. Mason poignantly recognizes: 'The Indian Army sent an Army Corps to France in that crucial first period of 1914 when earth's foundations fled.'[22] Immediately after the First World War (WW1), there was a much stronger recognition of the contribution by Indian soldiers. It appears to fade away from British consciousness after the Second World War. While the memories of the war were fresh, the Duke of Connaught acknowledged in 1921, when laying the foundation for the Imperial Memorial in Delhi:

> Let us ... recapture once again that thrill that passed through us all when we first heard in those far off days of 1914 that the Indian troops had landed at Marseilles and were pressing towards our thinly held battle lines in France and Flanders ...[23]

The Prince of Wales, when unveiling the memorial to WW1 Indian soldiers in Brighton, said:

> It is befitting that we should remember, and that future generations should not forget, that our Indian comrades came when our need was highest—free men and voluntary soldiers who were true to their salt and gave their lives in a quarrel of which it was enough for them to know that the enemy were the foes of their sahibs, the Emperor and their King.[24]

By the end of WW1, Indian troops had fought in France and Belgium, in Gallipoli, Salonika and Palestine, in Egypt and the Sudan, in Mesopotamia, at Aden and in the Red Sea, in Somaliland, the Cameroons and East Africa, in North-West Persia and

Kurdistan, in Trans-Caspia, in the Persian Gulf, and in North China.[25] As many as 57,248 Indian soldiers died or were missing, according to the official estimate as on 31 December 1919.[26] Some estimate the number of Indian deaths to be between 50,000 and 70,000.[27]

The role of the Indian Army in WW2 was even more extensive. The Indian Army fought in almost every theatre of the war, including Dunkirk, Egypt, Somalia, Sudan, Eritria, Libya, Ethiopia, Iraq, Syria, Persia, Malaya, Singapore, Burma, Tunisia, Sicily, Italy and Thailand.[28] The Indian Army suffered 24,338 killed and 11,754 missing during the war.[29]

However, shortly after the Second World War, the last British Commander-in-Chief, Field Marshal Auchinleck, despaired:

> I think the English never cared; the English who lived in England, the politicians especially ... I think they used [the Indian Army] ... They couldn't have come through both wars if they hadn't had the Indian Army ... I think they never really understood it.[30]

IV

While the sheer magnitude of the Indian Army's contributions over the 200 years of the Raj is significant, what is remarkable is that it cost so little to Britain in comparative terms. This afforded Britain a massive advantage against its enemies, and allowed it to focus resources on enhancing their naval and technical capabilities. One would have thought that considering the 'cash cow' that the Indian dominion was for Britain, the instrument that enabled this possession—the Indian Army—would at least be paid from the British exchequer. Far from it. Leave aside the Indian soldiers of the British Indian Army, every British soldier posted to India had to be paid, equipped, fed and eventually pensioned from Indian revenues.[31]

The EIC, of course, paid for its Indian and European soldiers and officers from its revenue and profits, which were substantial, and included tax receipts from India. On transfer of power to the Crown in 1858, it was maintained that the army in India—both Indian and European soldiers and officers—were for the 'defence' of India. Therefore, Indian revenues would have to pay for this army. In reality, ever since the Madras contingent left for Manila in 1762, the Indian Army had served as a 'strategic reserve' for the defence of the Empire. The previous section summarized that with the exception of the Americas, the Indian Army had defended imperial interests across the globe. A force of this quality and number would have been impossible to afford from the resources of Britain, especially if its Indian soldiers were fairly paid. As it happened, Britain did not pay for this global force. Even when the army was funded by Indian revenues, the Indian soldier was paid less than his fair share compared to the Europeans in the Indian Army.

On the face of it, a policy charade was maintained that the army in India was solely for the internal stability and 'defence' of India from minor adversaries—like Afghanistan—in the neighbourhood. The Indian Army, on paper, was not expected to defend India from a 'first-rate power' like Russia. This was considered beyond the capabilities of the Indian garrison. According to this fictitious strategy, the Indian Army was to provide a first line of defence from a first-rate power's initial assault, until troops from Britain could come to their relief. This, of course, never occurred, except perhaps the brief rerouting of small European forces in Asia to India during the 1857 mutiny. In reality, it was the Indian troops who repeatedly came to the rescue of imperial territory and interests throughout the world.

The charade had a self-serving fiscal logic. By maintaining this on paper, it could be argued that the expenses of the Indian Army (including the white component) were to be borne entirely from Indian revenues. The British exchequer was not to be burdened with the cost of this huge imperial reserve, which ought to have been the case after a fair assessment of the Indian Army's role in imperial defence. This charade continued all the way up to the first and second world wars, when the Indian Army—paid for by Indian taxpayers—bled to preserve the freedom of Britain. Philip Mason admits:

> This [Indian Army solely for India's defence] was a matter on which London was adamant and it arose from parsimony; the men at the Treasury were not prepared to pay for a reserve held in India and they knew they would have to pay if the War Office admitted that in fact the Indian Army and British troops in India included an Imperial reserve ... The [first world] war underlined the hollowness of the arguments used by the War Office and Treasury; there was a reserve in India which ought to have been equipped and paid for by Britain in peace.[32]

The situation was no different in the period leading up to the Second World War. A complicated and muddled-up scheme was decided upon during WW2, but the essence remained unchanged.

The upside for Britain was that it made possible the maintenance of an army for cheap, allowing it to focus resources on a first-class navy, which dominated the seas. Almost two-thirds of the British standing army (325,000 men including the home and Indian armies) by the late nineteenth century was paid for by Indian taxes.[33] The Indian Army, paid for by Indian revenues, allowed the Empire to keep Britain's defence spending astonishingly low, while its capabilities and reach remained unrivalled until the Second World War. As late as 1900, during the Boxer Rebellion in China, the

German capability to equip and mobilize a force away from the homeland—compared to the British Indian contingent—was grossly inferior. The Indian Army could march into any conflict zone globally with an ease and flourish that was unmatched by any other European rival.

British defence spending—except during the time of conflicts with major European powers—stayed tiny while it possessed India. Defence spending was below 3 per cent of the net national product during most of the nineteenth century, and averaged little more than this figure between 1870 and 1913. This is not much higher than Britain's defence budget today (2.1 per cent of GDP in 2017), and far less than the equivalent percentage spent on defence during the Cold War. Ferguson points out:

> Between 1947 and 1987 British defence expenditure had amounted to 5.8 per cent of gross domestic product. A century before, the proportion had been a mere 2.6 per cent ... Perhaps the most remarkable thing about all this was how cheap it was to defend ... This was world domination on the cheap ... This was money well spent.[34]

Indeed, it was on the cheap because of the Indian sepoy, who was paid just above subsistence level, albeit regularly. Not only was the British Army short of able and willing men from the UK, but the men from the isles were far more expensive, and the mortality rate of white soldiers in India was very high. A standing army of this size could only be maintained by reliance on the Indian sepoy, who, as the icing on the cake, also cost less.

It was also cheap for Britain, because Indian taxpayers (mostly poor and starving peasants) paid through the nose. The residual and declining revenue—after its productive capacity was systematically destroyed through economic exploitation—collected from India was spent mainly on the maintenance of this defence edifice. Compared to the minuscule defence spending borne by the UK exchequer in 1930, a mere seventeen years before independence, military expenditure accounted for a little over 60 per cent of the Government of India's revenues.[35] The army in India absorbed 40–50 per cent of central government revenue, even in peacetime, under the Raj.[36] It seems the taxpayers of India existed primarily for the payment of this garrison for the British Empire's defence. This must have been a most expensive defence for Indians, if one can call a foreign occupation a defence. No wonder there was no money left to spend on basic health, education and public services, reducing India to a 'poster child for third-world poverty', as aptly remarked by Shashi Tharoor.

Ever since Clive recruited his 'Lal Paltan'[37] in 1757, which delivered him political control of the rich Bengal province, the number of Indian soldiers in the EIC army increased exponentially. Soon, the Indian sepoy was the mainstay of the British Indian Army. On a rough estimate, from the late eighteenth century until the 1857 rebellion, almost 60–65 per cent of soldiers fighting under the British standard (the home army, globally and the EIC army in India) were Indians. The ratio changed slightly as the number of white soldiers to Indian soldiers in India was increased after 1858. Even then, approximately 40–45 per cent of fighting men employed by the British Army (home, globally and India combined) were of Indian origin, until India's independence. There were exceptions to this ratio during grave conflicts, for example, during the continental war against Napoleon, and of course during the first and the second world wars. However, it is difficult to see where Britain would have found the men to defend and maintain its Empire, if it were not for the loyal service of the Indian sepoy.[38]

India raised the largest voluntary force the world has ever seen to defend the British Empire during the first and second world wars. Almost 1,096,013 Indians served outside India before November 1919 during WW1.[39] A total of 1,440,437 Indian combatants and non-combatants were recruited during the First World War, in addition to the 239,561 serving at the outbreak of the war.[40] The Indian Army expanded from 200,000 at the beginning of WW2 in 1939 to more than 2.5 million by 1945, all volunteers.[41]

The numbers, both of men employed, and how little it cost Britain, speak for themselves.

V

'The Indian Empire is a despotism, and the real backbone of the despotism is the Army,' remarked George Orwell in the early 1930s. 'Given the Army, the officials and the business men [white Britons in India] can rub along safely enough even if they are fools. And most of them are fools. A dull, decent people, cherishing and fortifying their dullness behind a quarter of a million bayonets.'[42] Two-thirds of the 'quarter of a million bayonets' were held by Indian sepoys. For two centuries, the sepoys underwrote the safety of the British in India, with the exception perhaps of the 1857 mutiny.

And what a fortification these bayonets provided to their employer. Unfazed by their treatment, so long as their faith was not disturbed, the loyalty of these soldiers was unflinching over two centuries. Except during the Bengal Army's rebellion and disintegration in 1857, the blame for which cannot be laid on the sepoys, they were the bedrock of the EIC rule and the Raj. The nationalist movement, the disgraceful break of promise for self-governance made to Indians during the First World War, wretched service conditions, discrimination—it seemed nothing could rupture the loyalty of the sepoy towards the Raj.

When the break did eventually come after the Second World War, the writing on the wall was for everyone to see. Thankfully, those in positions of responsibility understood that the limits of the sepoys' loyalty had been breached. The wisest thing to do was to withdraw in an organized fashion. Any other course would have invited bloodshed on a scale unseen before in the subcontinent.

Having understood this, the British authorities acted in time, and decided to leave India without jeopardizing the relationship between the sepoy, his officers and the Crown.

Approximately 45,000 soldiers of the British Indian Army in Singapore did respond to the call of Netaji Subhas Chandra Bose, and joined his Indian National Army (INA) to free India during the Second World War. The motivation and circumstances of this change of heart will be dealt with in subsequent chapters. However, this was sufficient to shake the confidence of the British Indian Army leadership. The botched attempts to try some of these INA soldiers after the end of the war at Delhi's Red Fort lead to the Naval Mutiny in 1946. More than the direct mutiny, it was the strain that this event was placing on the delicate relationship between the Indian soldiers, officers and the government that made the continuation of Raj in India impossible.

It was in this charged atmosphere that Choudhary Raghbir Singh Sheoran drew his weapon on his British officer in early 1946 at the Agra cantonment. Raghbir Singh enlisted at the tender age of seventeen in the 1st Battalion of the 19th Hyderabad Regiment in 1939, and transitioned into adulthood, far away from home, during the war. Raghbir Singh embarked for the Iraq theatre in 1941 as part of the PAI (Persia and Iran) force to defend the oil supplies, vital to the war effort. Married early, as was the custom in those days, he left his young bride to the care of his parents and extended family at his village, Khungai, in the Rohtak district of erstwhile Punjab, today Haryana. The young bride was not to hear from or of Raghbir Singh for the next three years, and like his family, assumed the worst. Raghbir Singh returned to India in 1944, with an Africa Star on his record. Not all Indian troops serving outside the Burma theatre were aware of the INA soldiers' attempts to fight against the Raj for their nation's freedom. However, through the course of 1945, stories and the surviving INA soldiers, now prisoners, started trickling in through the borders of India. The mood within the cantonments and barracks changed gradually. Where do you place the act of selfless soldiers fighting for their country's freedom on the scale of justice, even if it was technically a mutiny against their employer?

Decades later, Raghbir Singh recounted that fateful day when 'the dam of his patience burst'.[43] A young and inexperienced British officer made a snide remark about the loyalty of INA soldiers, calling their honour into question. An altercation followed, and the luck of the officer saved his life. Soldiers from the battalion intervened to calm the situation. The officer, aggrieved by this disciplinary breach, and seemingly distressed, vowed to have Raghbir Singh court-martialled and sentenced to 'life behind the bars, if he was lucky to escape the gallows'. Raghbir Singh retorted that the officer had better ensure the hangman did his job, else he would avenge any jail time with the officer's life, even if he were hiding in England. To avoid the incident escalating into something larger, senior officers intervened. Raghbir Singh was temporarily imprisoned, his battalion comrades intervened, and eventually the threatened disciplinary action could not be enforced. Raghbir Singh was immediately discharged from service, and went on to live for another fifty years to recount that fateful day to his grandchildren. It is very likely that many such small incidents of insubordination in the Indian Army occurred during that momentous year of 1946. The few major disturbances are documented, but a number were deliberately not brought to light by the authorities, for fear of a spiralling mutinous mood.

The British Empire in India rested on the loyalty of men like Raghbir Singh. The dilemma facing Raghbir Singh was widely shared within the Indian Army at the time. The authorities saw no sure way of ensuring discipline when loyalty was in doubt. The men who had gradually built and sustained the Empire over two centuries brought it to an equally swift end. Before talking about its end, let's see how it all started in the next chapter.

Chapter Three

The Military Revolution in Hindustan

I

THERE WERE AT LEAST FIVE TO SIX INDIAN SOLDIERS FOR EACH European soldier in the East India Company's Indian Army between 1794 and 1857.[1] The ratio of Indian soldiers was even higher before 1794, a critical period when the British Indian Army came into being. Very few white troops could be found at home to be sent to India. A large proportion of those who reached Indian shores perished due to heat and disease. The hire and maintenance of a European soldier also cost many times more than the native recruit. There was no alternative to the recruitment of Indian soldiers for any foreign military power in India.

The number of Indian soldiers hired by the EIC and other European trading companies did not exceed a few hundred until the 1740s. The 1740s were the turning point, and growth after that was explosive, with almost 154,500 sepoys in the EIC armies by 1808.[2]

How the EIC was able to initially hire these native soldiers, and eventually how it became the exclusive employer of the best military talent in Hindustan, lies at the core of the miraculous development and establishment of the British Indian Army and Empire. As we shall see, what happened in the mid-eighteenth century in India is nothing short of a military revolution in the profound impact it engendered in the military-political system, and the long-lasting consequences for not just India, but Britain and the world too.

Much is said about the 'military revolution' in Europe, believed to have occurred between the sixteenth and eighteenth centuries, as Europe came out of the Middle Ages. The first part of this revolution pertains to the training, equipment and tactical battlefield organization of a fighting unit. The second part relates to the command-and-control structure of an army. Let's review these two elements first, before we contrast them with developments in mid-eighteenth century India.

II

The very early modern European fighting soldiers were deployed either on horse or on foot. A battle would be carried by a dashing cavalry charge, followed by an infantry assault from foot soldiers. Numerical superiority counted for a lot, besides elements of surprise and courage. Over a period of time, firearms started to replace the sword and other sharp-edged weapons as the key offensive weapon for foot soldiers. Gradually, foot soldiers started to be organized in units able to deliver continuous fire, by way of a few lines standing in parallel. The back lines loaded their muskets, while the front line discharged the fire, and the lines continuously exchanged so that the unit continued to fire without stop. Maurice of Nassau (1567–1625), Prince of Orange, is credited with these first revolutionary changes in infantry tactics. Previously foot soldiers in open ground could be easily overwhelmed by a cavalry charge, but line infantry using firearms proved to have an edge over cavalry. The handheld firearm thus became a sustained weapon, and prevented the enemy cavalry from overrunning a small but disciplined force organized in such units. The infantry units developed extensive drill and manoeuvre tactics that enabled them to hold the field with a relatively small but well-trained force. Infantry organized in battalions or regiments thus became the most important part of European armies in the seventeenth and eighteenth centuries. The quality of firearms also improved significantly from a matchlock to a flintlock. Artillery, which was previously heavy siege weapons, slowly came to be incorporated in the field infantry units as light pieces. Artillery thus developed into a tactical infantry support unit, with lighter and more mobile small pieces that could be deployed quickly for targeted fire power. Swedish King Gustavus Adolphus is credited as the pioneer who attached four light guns to his infantry units, marking a decisive break with the tradition in the early seventeenth century.[3]

Thus, by the early eighteenth century, infantry units, supported by light artillery, gained primacy as the fighting unit within European armies. Cavalry still had a critical role due to mobility, shock and speed, but the infantry was now the primary fighting force.

The early modern European command structure was anchored around military entrepreneurs, who recruited the fighting units and offered their services for hire to kings and princes. These 'colonels' were paid a lump sum by their employers for the number of men they brought to a sovereign's assistance in wars. These mercenary entrepreneurs usually hired, armed, equipped, maintained and lead a few battalions, although some, like Count Albrecht von Wallenstein of Bohemia in the early seventeenth century, recruited, armed and commanded entire armies on the continent.[4] These were mercenaries, pure and simple. Hiring mercenaries had its advantages, as usually being 'outsiders', they were less prone to interfering in internal politics of the state. They could also be speedily hired in grave emergencies, while raising a standing army—even with conscription—would have been too late. However, they were prone to corruption and could not always be relied upon. The fighting soldiers in these armies were loyal to the leader who hired them and not to the sovereign whose cause they were supposed to defend. These hired armies were also prone to 'live off the land' more than usual. The 'colonel' saw looting as an efficient and cheaper way of supplying the army, each penny saved going to his pocket. According to a saying that gained currency during the Thirty Years' War, every soldier needed three peasants: 'One to provide his wife, one to give up his lodgings and one to take his place in hell'.[5] Of course, no peasant who had thus suffered would have much love left for the sovereign. Something had to be done to curb the 'colonels'.

The answer to these problems was the creation of a permanent standing army, under direct control of the state. This was not a new idea, as most princes had maintained units of personal bodyguards and household troops. However, their numbers were small, and mercenary armies rather than permanent forces were the norm till the mid-seventeenth century. The Thirty Years' War was the real watershed in this regard. After the Treaty of Westphalia in 1648, most European rulers decided to retain their mercenary armies— the armies that had devastated Europe for the last three decades— on a permanent basis. These were to be under the direct control of the rulers. The soldiers were to be paid by the state. Henceforth, the supply, equipment, weapons and ammunition were to be procured and distributed from a central command, the costs borne by the state exchequer. This was an attempt to reduce corruption and enhance efficiency but, most importantly, to create a standing army loyal to the sovereign. The integration of the feudal nobility into leadership roles within the standing army further enhanced the position of the ruler, and provided gainful employment to the restive nobility. Thus came into being European national armies: anchored around infantry, supported by cavalry and mobile artillery, commanded by professional leaders, supplied centrally and, most importantly, loyal to their sovereign. This greatly cemented the ruler's position against centrifugal forces from within, allowing him or her to deal with enemies from outside the state. Religious (and most often ethnic) uniformity were further glues that reinforced the ties of the sovereign, subjects, soldiers and nobles in a cohesive polity.

III

The situation in India at the time was in stark contrast. When the EIC dabbled in Indian military affairs in the mid-eighteenth century, the Marathas were the predominant military power in India. The once mighty Mughal Empire was a sorry skeleton of its former self, mostly overrun by Marathas, Jats and Sikhs. A few fragmented remnants were wrested by the regional Mughal viceroys, who had now become hereditary rulers and acted as independent rulers.

The command-and-control structure of both Maratha and Mughal armies was decentralized. Not only was the military command decentralized, the military command function was merged with tax collection. In this, the structure was even more defective than the mercenary band of 'colonels' in pre-Westphalia Europe. The Mughal and Maratha military commanders responsible for raising, equipping and leading soldiers—unlike their European counterparts in the pre-Westphalia era—were not paid directly by the state exchequer. They were instead awarded land grants (jagirs) to collect revenue for payment of their troops. This was a potentially dangerous combination of roles, as the ruler now relied on his commanders to maintain and provide the fighting soldiers. Conversely, the commander did not rely on the ruler to pay for such troops. The commander had an independent revenue base to pay for the army under his command, and hopefully generate sufficient surplus. The only obstacle in the commander's way from becoming a hereditary chief of his region was his need for the ruler to confirm the commander's position. So long as the ruler was able to rely on the competing jealousies of other commanders to bring a recalcitrant subordinate to heel, and the 'prestige' of the ruling house was high, this system worked well. When the position of the sovereign weakened and commanders started to league with the enemy, downfall was inevitable.

Battlefield tactics in India gave primacy to cavalry, with infantry in a supportive role. Artillery was more to intimidate than cause real damage to a mobile target. Artillery pieces were massive and moving them was a logistical challenge. Infantry undertook roles more akin to watchmen, performing tax collection and policing functions. The battlefield tactics centred around a cavalry charge with heavy artillery bombardment, relying more on 'shock and awe' tactics. This worked well against an enemy that was organized on similar principles, but an organized infantry battalion in line formation, supported with manoeuvrable light artillery pieces, would not be overwhelmed by a dashing cavalry charge alone.

Nevertheless, battlefield tactics were not the key differential that made European or Indian armies superior. A huge subcontinent like India was equally suited to the decisive advantage of a mobile cavalry for field offensive, and protecting and winning a land mass dotted with numerous fortifications. The enemy infantry could not match the speed of the cavalry. If no opportunity for open field combat was presented, a war of attrition often gave the edge to a superior cavalry force, which could easily destroy the long supply chains. Once the enemy was thus starved of supplies, area domination could subsequently be carried out by a mediocre infantry force, sallying forth from the forts and garrisons that dotted the subcontinent like a net.

The decisive edge for a European-led army in India was the command-and-control structure, not so much battlefield tactics or the skill or courage of the fighting men. The Indian command structure was the real weak spot, and as we shall see, it collapsed like a house of cards when the need was most critical.

A soldier needs effective leadership and confidence that his basic needs—and hopefully those of his loved ones left behind—will be looked after. Not much to ask for. A weak command structure could provide neither. The military revolution in Hindustan germinated from the quagmire of a fragmented polity, poor command structure and the internecine civil war that ensued over the corpse of the Mughal Empire during the early eighteenth century. The military talent was there; the skills of Indian soldiers were second to none. When combined with an improved command-and-control structure, the sepoys did wonders, and set their employers on the path to become the 'Emperors of Hindustan'. Let's now review how the Indian command-and-control structure—which was defective but had worked to date—collapsed in the late seventeenth and early eighteenth century.

IV

In 1658, Aurangzeb rose to the Mughal throne in Delhi, after imprisoning his father, executing two of his brothers and banishing the third brother to Burma to die. This was the beginning of the end for one of the richest and most powerful empires in the world. India was—as it is today—one of the most religiously and ethnically diverse societies in the world. While the ruling house of Mughals was Sunni Muslim, the majority of the subjects were non-Muslims, primarily Hindus. Conversions, either by force or inducements, which had worked well in Persia, Central Asia, Anatolia and North Africa, were not effective in inducing the majority of Indians to leave their forefathers' faith. Even when militarily cornered, the native ruling elite would reach a political accommodation, without giving up their faith. Aurangzeb's ancestors had accepted the strong moorings of the ancient Hindu faith within the native population. A tacit understanding led to the accommodation of some Hindus—mostly leading dynasties of Rajputana—in the imperial structure, and the rest were also allowed to practise their faith. This was far from perfect harmony but better than open confrontation between the rulers and the ruled.

Aurangzeb upset this careful balance of centuries with his bigotry and ambitious zeal to bring the inhabitants of Hindustan into Islam's fold. He destroyed numerous temples, imposed punitive taxes (jiziya) on non-Muslims, and overstretched himself in campaigns of conquest in the Deccan. He extended the Mughal Empire to its farthest limits, but made its foundations all the more brittle. The opposition to his tyranny sprang from the hardy peasant stock of the Marathas in the south, and from the indomitable Jat peasantry of the north. Marathas were employed in the military structure of the Deccan sultanates of Bijapur and Golconda, both of which were destroyed by Aurangzeb. The most famous of the Marathas, credited with leading the defiance of Mughal authority across Hindustan, was Shivaji Bhonsle. Shivaji was an able and dynamic leader, and his example inspired others chafing under the Mughal rule across Hindustan. When, in 1674, Shivaji declared himself the independent king of his domain, carved out of the southern parts of the Mughal Empire, he lit a ray of hope. The suffering masses came to believe that Mughal authority was as transient as numerous other preceding empires and kings in this ancient land.

During Aurangzeb's lifetime, the might of the Mughal military machine withstood the strains generated by his ambitions, blunders and follies. Cracks started to appear while he was alive, but it was upon his death in 1707 that all hell would break loose.

Meanwhile, with the world's largest army of a million men[6] under his command, Aurangzeb papered over the breaches in imperial authority, and tried to salvage the prestige of the House of Timur. But rebels kept springing up from the Maratha and Jat heartlands. As soon as he departed from an enemy fort just conquered, it was in flames or under siege by the rebels again. Edmund Burke's words regarding American colonists just as easily describe the situation in Aurangzeb's India: 'The use of force alone … may subdue for a moment, but it does not remove the necessity of subduing again; and a nation is not governed which is perpetually to be conquered.'[7]

The fire lit by Raje Shivaji would continue to burn for ages, despite his early death in 1680. Aurangzeb brutally revenged Shivaji's defiance of Mughal authority by publicly torturing and executing his son and successor, Sambhaji, in 1689. The peasant rebellion of Jats in the north was crushed by heavy artillery, personally commanded by Aurangzeb in 1669. The captured Jat rebel leader Gokula Singh was publicly tortured and executed at Agra. The Jats laid low for a few years, then regrouped under Gokula's successor Rajaram, the zamindar (chieftain) of Sinsini, and laid waste the land south of the capital. In 1688, the Jats raided the tomb of Akbar (Aurangzeb's great-grandfather), dug up his grave, and threw his bones on a bonfire in public.[8] Rajaram was killed by a Mughal musketeer shortly thereafter, affording a brief respite to Mughal authority in the north.

The ninth Guru of the Sikhs, Guru Teg Bahadur, courageously interceded on behalf of the hard-pressed Kashmiri Brahmins at the Mughal court in Delhi, but suffered retribution, and was publicly beheaded in 1675. The Mughal subahdar (governor) of Punjab bricked alive two of Teg Bahadur's grandsons in 1704, while the other two died as martyrs during the battle of Chamkaur the next year. Their father, the tenth Guru—Gobind Singh—did not get justice from Aurangzeb, who appeared to condone the brutality inflicted upon Gobind Singh's sons. While Gobind Singh was camping nearby at Nanded in the hope of justice, the tyrant Aurangzeb died on 20 February 1707, aged eighty-nine, near Ahmednagar. Facing death, he confessed the futility of his life to his son Azam in a sad letter:

> I came alone and I go as a stranger. The instant which has passed in power has left only sorrow behind it. I have not been the guardian and protector of the Empire. Life, so valuable, has been squandered in vain. God was in my heart but I could not see Him. Life is transient. The past is gone and there is no hope for the future. The whole Imperial army is like me: bewildered, perturbed, separated from God, quaking like quicksilver. I fear my punishment. Though I have a firm hope in God's grace, yet for my deeds anxiety ever remains with me.[9]

While his co-religionists remained aligned to the dynasty's cause during his life, Aurangzeb's death in 1707 started to unhinge Muslim subahdars from their allegiance to the Mughal throne. A chink in the armour of the Mughal dynasty was exposed by the continued defiance of the Marathas, Jats and Sikhs. Aurangzeb's victories over all three were pyrrhic, at best temporary. Within a few years of Aurangzeb's death, the Sikhs—supported by the Jat peasants of the north—overran the frontier province of Punjab under Banda Bahadur's leadership. Banda Bahadur, aided by the revenge-thirsty Jat and Sikh peasants of Punjab, razed the capital of Mughal subahdar Wazir Khan to the ground, and executed him on the battlefield in 1710. The persecution of Guru Gobind Singh's family was avenged.

Mughal authority was thus destroyed in a strategic area bordering external powers, viz. the Afghans and Persians, and this was to result in further damage in the coming decades. The Marathas wrested parts of the Deccan, and central and western India from the Mughals, and implanted themselves as independent rulers, with a nominal relationship with the Emperor in Delhi. While these gains were made at the cost of regional Muslim subahdars, the Jats in north India shocked the Mughal nobility by capturing significant territories around Delhi and Agra, much of which lay within the personal domain of the Emperor and his family. The Jat warlord Churaman Singh gained effective control of the most strategic piece of infrastructure within the country: the Agra–Delhi highway, and extorted tax from anyone treading upon it.

Another shock came during the battle of succession between Aurangzeb's sons at Jajau in 1707. Churaman Singh hovered around the battle scene, and looted both claimants' camps without partiality. This was a massive blow to the prestige of the ruling dynasty, and was unheard of in Hindustan to date. The tradition of nobles siding with one of the claimants, and later receiving favours or pardons—and sometimes punishment—was the norm. Churaman hit at the heart of the legitimacy of the House of Timur, disregarding the claims of both succeeding branches. Bahadur Shah, who won at Jajau, could not punish the Jat warlord for this egregious act, and grudgingly accepted him into the imperial fold. Churaman Singh repeated the display of his utter disregard for the Mughal dynasty during the next battle of succession in 1713, raiding the treasures of both Jahandar Shah and Farrukhsiyar. The victorious Emperor Farrukhsiyar did not dare to punish him. Such acts could not have escaped the notice of the amirs and nobles of the Empire, for soon they started to act to suit their independent interests.

The Mughal state was a massive but lumbering military machine. While the Marathas are rightly credited with smashing the spine of Mughal military power in India, the Jats and Sikhs went straight for the jugular. Thus, much before Nadir Shah of Persia publicly humiliated the Emperor of Hindustan in 1739 in Delhi and massacred its residents, the Timurid dynasty had lost its grip on the Mughal state and its military structure. The command-and-control structure was prone to centrifugal tendencies as explained earlier, and once the chink in the armour was exposed, it did not take long for the Empire to disintegrate into a situation of civil war.

This was the background to the momentous decade of the 1740s, when the European trading companies in India got involved in the ongoing military conflicts. The Marathas, under the leadership of the Peshwa in Pune, were the predominant power in Deccan, central and western India. The Jats under their redoubtable leader Suraj Mal had carved out a strategically located kingdom around the capital of the Mughals. The Sikhs, although divided into misls (tribal war bands), continued to jointly defy Mughal authority in Punjab, while hemmed in by the Afghans. The Afghans, by now, had declared independence from their Persian overlords. The new Afghan kingdom, founded by Ahmad Shah Durrani (Nadir Shah's generalissimo) with its capital in Kabul, had designs on Hindustan's wealth. Nevertheless, not all the Mughal nobles were finished. Three significant regional Mughal subahdars were in their place: the Nizam, the Viceroy in Deccan with his capital at Hyderabad; Alivardi Khan in Bengal with his capital at Murshidabad; and the Nawab Wazir Safdar Jung, with his capital at Faizabad in Awadh. All of them, and numerous other smaller powers, were involved in intrigue, conspiracy and outright conflicts against each other, moving allegiance and frontiers faster than one could keep account of. The same disunity and strife extended below each regional subahdar, with his subordinates playing the same games of intrigue and conflict, to the last military officer. Both the Nizam and the Nawab of Bengal were hard-pressed by Maratha raids, and were hanging on by a thread. These two remnant Mughal provinces would later prove to be fertile ground for the EIC, as we shall see later.

Even so, the affairs of European trading companies were minor concerns, as most Indian powers considered Ahmad Shah Abdali's Afghan hordes to be the most significant strategic threat to India. The Afghans raided India no less than eight times between 1748 to 1767. This precisely would be the time when the foundations of the EIC's military power were laid in India. The Afghan distraction was a big factor in the breathing space that European trading companies, especially the EIC, gained during these critical two decades. The once powerful Mughal Empire, embroiled in civil war and threatened by Afghan raiders from the north-west, was a perfect springboard for new empire builders, if they could hire dedicated soldiers.

Chapter Four

The Grand Derangement

I

To chart the course of the involvement of the East India Company in Indian affairs, we will have to move away from the high politics of Hindustan, centred in Delhi, to far-off Deccan. It was in the Carnatic, a feudatory principality of the Nizam of Hyderabad, in the south-east corner of India, that the EIC literally found its military feet.

During the course of the seventeenth century, the EIC had acquired a few 'factories' across India by way of grants from the local sovereigns. These were trading posts, which the EIC opportunistically tried to fortify, but kept getting rapped on knuckles for doing so. By the 1740s, the three most important EIC factories in India were at Madras, Calcutta and Bombay. Fort St. George garrisoned the Madras post, and Fort St. David, about 100 miles south, was the second fortification owned by the EIC in the Carnatic region. Fort William was erected on the banks of the Hooghly River to protect the Calcutta factory. The French

East India Company by that time had established its headquarters in Pondicherry, guarded by Fort Louis, menacingly located just over fifteen miles north of Fort St. David. Fort St. George, Fort Louis and Fort St. David were all three on the Coromandel coast. The second French trading post was at Chandarnagore, approximately twenty-five miles upriver from the English factory at Fort William.

For almost a century and a half, the EIC had carried on trade in compliance with the wishes of local rulers, and paid their taxes. The only noteworthy interaction for the mighty Mughals was the surgical abilities of the English. English surgeons helped cure Emperor Shah Jahan's daughter, Jahanara, from serious burns in 1644. Emperor Farrukhsiyar was also pleased with the English surgeon in 1716-17, for curing him of a painful disease. All these medical interventions were rewarded with favours, tax exemptions and grants for the EIC.[1]

Only once did the hubris of Sir Josiah Child, Director of the EIC in London, lead the EIC into open conflict against the Mughals, in 1686. On Child's incitement and the approval of King James II, a fleet of nineteen warships with 600 troops from England was sent to attack the Nawab of Bengal.[2] The expedition ended in disaster for the English, with landing parties swept away by Mughal soldiers, the English factors paraded in chains or kept in fetters, and all trade rights of the EIC extinguished. On repeated appeals, Aurangzeb allowed the EIC to resume in 1690, after it agreed to pay heavy compensation and make profuse apologies. The lesson was well learnt and for the next fifty years, the EIC stayed clear of any military pretensions in Hindustan, despite the chaos reigning across the Empire.

It was the French who goaded the English out of their military inertia in India during the 1740s in the Carnatic. Joseph Francoise Dupleix, the French trading company's Governor-General of India, was the mastermind of French initiatives. Ambitious, resourceful and resilient, as early as 1739 he had observed, before Nadir Shah reached Delhi:

> We are on the eve of a great revolution in this Empire. The weakness of Mogol government gives ample grounds to believe Nader may very soon be master of this Empire. This revolution if it takes place, can only cause a grand derangement to trade. However it can only be advantageous to Europeans.[3]

Based in Pondicherry from 1742, Dupleix was also the pioneer in realizing the value of locally raised troops. He took the initiative to train locally recruited Tamil-, Malayali- and Telugu-speaking soldiers in modern European infantry tactics. By 1746, he had raised, equipped, trained and paid two regiments of sepoys, and appointed the highly able Marquis de Bussy as his commander.[4] The English still maintained that Indian soldiers could not be disciplined, but events in the following months and years would prove them wrong. Very soon, the English would follow the French example in hiring and training native soldiers to assist in their conflict with the French and local princes.

Hostilities had been simmering between the English and French in India since 1744, when news of the declaration of war in Europe reached Madras. Britain had joined Austria in support of Maria Theresa's claim to the Habsburg throne, while France supported Prussia, Bavaria, Spain, Sweden and Saxony, who all opposed Maria Theresa. The English Navy was the first to attack French ships off the Coromandel coast in 1745. Some accounts suggest that Dupleix had personally invested in some of the ships and was stung by the loss. The French appealed to the Nawab of the Carnatic, Anwaruddin, who asked the English as well as the French not to disturb the peace. The English gave conciliatory answers, and in any event, their ships soon sailed away to Bengal, leaving Madras undefended from any retribution. The retribution was surely in the works.

Lacking sufficient naval capability, the ever-resourceful Dupleix asked for naval help from the French governor of Mauritius. Help arrived in 1746, and with it the French besieged Fort St. George and took it from the poorly organized defenders. It was now the turn of the English to appeal to the Nawab. The Nawab was furious at Dupleix for defying his prohibition, and sent a large force under the command of his elder son, Mahfuz Khan, to teach the French a lesson.

What happened next surprised all parties, and the event was a turning point in the military relations between foreign and native powers in India. A small French army of 230 French soldiers and 700 sepoys, under Captain Louis Paradis, a Swiss engineer officer in French service, attacked Mahfuz Khan's force across Adyar River. The organized French-commanded infantry, delivering a continuous fire, drove the enemy cavalry headlong from the field. The news sent shockwaves across south India.

The French decided to take the initiative further, and attacked Fort St. David the same year. The English situation was precarious in 1746, having lost Fort St. George earlier in the year. They appealed to the Nawab again. This time, the Nawab managed to salvage a shred of his prestige by sending his younger son, Muhammad Ali, to successfully defend Fort St. David against the French. Dupleix came to a temporary understanding with the Nawab by letting him fly the Mughal flag at Madras for a week, and the Nawab thought it best not to interfere in their fight further.

Something revolutionary had occurred in the year 1746. A foreign trading company had defied the orders of a Mughal official, and the foreigners could not be punished for this insubordination. The Nawab of the Carnatic, arguably, was not the most powerful or senior Mughal official. The responsibility for ensuring order lay with his overlord, the Nizam of Hyderabad, who was responsible for keeping order in this southern realm. The Nizam was unsettled by continuous attacks from the Marathas, who regularly raided his territories and inflicted crushing defeats. At the old age of seventy-five, the Nizam could not immediately assess and deal with this new threat to the Deccan from foreigners.

II

With the French and the Nawab in a temporary truce, the English stood alone. In this hour of supreme need, they now resorted to hiring Indian fighting men. With the French about to push the English into the Indian Ocean, and the Nawab temporarily unable and unwilling to help, Indian soldiers were the only hope. With their help, the English managed to defend Fort St. David against two further French attacks over the next eighteen months. The local levies of Indians were initially called 'peons'. These peons were dressed in a variety of clothes of their own and carried an equally varied assortment of arms—bows, arrows, spears, swords, bucklers and daggers—which they brought with them. Necessity pushed the English to emulate the French in raising local recruits and, by February 1747, there were 3,000 of these peons employed at Fort St. David, 900 of them armed with muskets.[5]

These levies were a far cry from the drilled sepoys of the French company, who, by now, were being put to devastating use across the Carnatic. This was to change soon, with the arrival of Major Stringer Lawrence in January 1748 at Fort St. David. Lawrence was a Captain in the King's Army, and had been appointed the 'Major of the Garrison'[6] of Fort St. George, though Fort St. George had fallen by the time he reached. So, he instead went on to the besieged Fort St. David.

Lawrence realized the precarious English position, and the value of the Indian fighting men to remedy it. The Major started to organize the 'peons' into regular companies of 100–200 each, trained and equipped in the English style, but still under

Indian officers. They were given proper uniforms, arms and the training of English soldiers, thus turning them from 'peons' into disciplined soldiers or 'sepoys'. Soon, these sepoys were to prove themselves the best infantry in India, laying the foundations of the Company's army and Indian Empire. The Indian infantry at Fort St. David stood at 1,000 in June 1748. The newly raised sepoys gave a good account of themselves, and repulsed repeated French assaults against Fort St. David. Major Lawrence seemed pleased with their performance, and wrote to the Council that 'the military both white and black as well as the *Sepoys* and peons ... behaved extremely well'.[7] The French siege of Fort St. David failed. Once fresh reinforcements arrived from England in 1748, and while Madras was still under French control, the EIC attempted, unsuccessfully, a naval blockade of Pondicherry. Eventually, Madras was restored to the British in early 1749 as part of the Treaty of Aix-la-Chapelle, which brought the war in Europe to a close.

Thus ends the first series of events that set the EIC on the path to become a significant military power. The French demonstrated that sepoys trained in European-style infantry tactics were a deadly instrument. Sepoys gave a good account of themselves, and were soon in demand by both the French and the English.

III

The end of war in Europe did not fully end the rivalry between the English and French companies in India. The French had an edge over the English in the first round in the Carnatic, but no permanent gain seemed to come out of it. Dupleix raised the stakes, and decided to play arbiter of the Deccan's volatile political landscape.

Chin Qilich Khan, also known as Nizam-ul-Mulk, was the most significant Mughal official in Deccan, with his capital at

Hyderabad. He was a loyal commander in Aurangzeb's army, but had independently established himself in the Deccan in 1724, paying a nominal allegiance to Aurangzeb's successors in Delhi. He was also the overlord of the Nawab of Carnatic, Anwaruddin, whose capital was at Arcot. In fact, Anwaruddin was personally appointed by the Nizam in 1744, after the Marathas killed the previous Nawab and took his family prisoner. One of the family members of the previous Nawab, who was captured by the Marathas was Chanda Sahib. Chanda Sahib begrudged Anwaruddin's Nawabi, and was waiting for an opportunity to take back what he believed was rightfully his.

In 1748, the Nizam-ul-Mulk died, just when Major Lawrence and his sepoys were deflecting French assaults on Fort St David. The Nizam's second son, Nasir Jung, succeeded the throne at Hyderabad, but Nasir's claim was disputed by his nephew, Muzaffar Jung, a grandson of Nizam-ul-Mulk from his favourite daughter. Thus, a succession dispute arose at Hyderabad—just the kind of opportunity Dupleix could not miss.

Confident of his military superiority, after repulsing the English naval blockade of Pondicherry, and previously holding Madras for more than two years by force, Dupleix decided to play kingmaker in the Deccan. Aware of Muzaffar Jung's revolt, and Chanda Sahib's designs, he created a grand alliance between the French, Muzaffar Jung and Chanda Sahib to back his Indian allies' claims in Hyderabad and Arcot respectively.

The year 1749 opened well for the French-backed alliance. Chanda Sahib, freed from Maratha imprisonment after paying ransom, and backed by Muzaffar Jung and the French, marched against Arcot, Anwaruddin's capital. Muzaffar Jung at this stage had little more than his name to add to the campaign, but Dupleix found it useful to have a potential claimant of the Nizam's throne in his alliance. In a decisive battle at Ambur, Anwaruddin was killed, and his elder son Mahfuz Khan taken prisoner. The younger son, Muhammad Ali, fled south to Tiruchirappalli (also called Trichinopoly), and declared himself Nawab of Carnatic, as his father's successor. The French, Muzaffar Jung and Chanda Sahib went in hot pursuit of Muhammad Ali, and laid siege to Tiruchirappalli. Muhammad Ali, desperately cornered, appealed to the English for help, and sent requests to his overlord, Nasir Jung in Hyderabad, to restore order.

The English were recovering from the shocks of the French capture of Madras and the Fort St. David siege. Aware that a French-installed Nawab of the Carnatic would be injurious to their trading and military interests, the English also joined the fray to help Muhammad Ali by sending a few troops to his aid at Tiruchirappalli. At the same time, news came of Nasir Jung's march against Pondicherry, the French capital, in aid of his subordinate, Muhammad Ali. The news of Nasir Jung marching in support of Muhammad Ali upset the French, Chanda Sahib and Muzaffar Jung's plans to crush their enemy. The French insisted on lifting the siege on Tiruchirappalli, and the grand alliance marched back to Pondicherry's defence.

Nasir Jung summoned Muhammad Ali and the English to come to his aid at Pondicherry at once. The English were relieved that their ally Muhammad Ali was out of imminent danger, and half-heartedly joined Nasir Jung at Pondicherry. Muhammad Ali also obeyed his overlord Nasir Jung, and joined him outside Pondicherry.

Nasir Jung decided to attack the French in earnest. Instead of waiting for the assault and lengthy siege, the French marched out of Pondicherry with Muzaffar Jung and Chanda Sahib to face Nasir Jung. The stage was set for a bloody and decisive battle. As it happened, a small event overshadowed the larger scheme of things. In the most critical moment, a mutiny occurred amongst the French officers. This collapsed the grand alliance's offensive, and both Chanda Sahib and the French retired back to the fort, instead of battling Nasir Jung. Muzaffar Jung's forces melted away on French withdrawal, and the young man hastily gave himself up to his uncle Nasir Jung, and begged for his mercy and protection. Nasir Jung wanted to continue the assault into the French garrison but the English prevaricated. A temporary truce was now agreed upon, between Nasir Jung and the French, and Nasir Jung departed for Arcot, with Muhammad Ali. He took his humbled nephew with him. Dupleix had suffered a temporary setback. His candidate for the Hyderabad throne was a captive of his enemy, and Muhammad Ali appeared set to regain Arcot. The English withdrew temporarily from the scene.

Instead of accepting the unfavourable turn of events, Dupleix took the initiative again. In 1750, the French captured the Fort of Gingee (situated approximately fifty miles south of Arcot, and thirty-seven miles northwest of Pondicherry), and defeated Muhammad Ali, who hovered around Arcot. Nasir Jung marched out of Arcot and attempted to recover Gingee. Dupleix at this stage hatched a conspiracy with the Pathan commanders of Nasir Jung's forces. In a surprise morning attack in December 1750, while French troops entered his camp, and Nasir Jung mounted an elephant to marshal his forces, he was shot dead by one of the treacherous Pathan commanders. Muzaffar Jung was taken out of his uncle's prison, and immediately raised as the new subahdar. What Dupleix had lost in battle, he secured in intrigue.

Thus, 1750 ended with great advantage to the French. When the news of Nasir Jung's death reached Pondicherry, Chanda Sahib ran through the streets to congratulate Dupleix. The newly minted Nizam, Muzaffar Jung, arrived in Pondicherry with fanfare, and appointed Chanda Sahib as his deputy and Nawab of Carnatic. With both the Subahdar of the Deccan and Nawab of Carnatic in his debt, Dupleix surveyed Deccan as its master. Dupleix asked De Bussy to escort Muzaffar Jung to his capital at

Hyderabad, where this able French commander was to stay for almost a decade.

Falling on hard times, Muhammad Ali again fled back to Tiruchirappalli in early 1751, on receipt of the shocking news of Nasir Jung's assassination. Chanda Sahib and the French pursued Muhammad Ali, determined to complete what was left unfinished two years before. They besieged Muhammad Ali at Tiruchirappalli, and his only hope was English help. Having invested so much in Muhammad Ali, who had aided them in saving Fort St. David in 1746 against the French, the English had no other option but to come to his aid.

A young Captain, named Robert Clive, suddenly appeared on the scene, and to his credit goes the surprising turn of English fortunes in the Carnatic in the following months. Instead of hurling all the EIC troops at the defence of Tiruchirappalli, Clive recommended a diversionary attack at Arcot, Chanda Sahib's capital in the north. It seems that Muhammad Ali was the first to propose this, and Clive agreed. With only 300 sepoys, 200 Europeans, and three small field guns, Clive marched towards Arcot. The Arcot garrison fled on Clive's arrival, and Clive strengthened the defences of the dilapidated fort, and collected supplies to withstand the siege that he expected Chanda Sahib to launch. Chanda Sahib sent his son Reza Sahib and 4,000 of his best troops from Tiruchirappalli to expel Clive and regain the contested capital city. Clive gained fame as the defender of Arcot against an overwhelmingly large force led by Reza Sahib in the next fifty days. While Clive and his sepoys doggedly defended Arcot, news came of Maratha and Mysore aid for the English, and Reza Sahib's siege of Arcot was soon over.

Clive then marched towards Tiruchirappalli to relieve Muhammad Ali, and on the way achieved a number of victories against the French and Chanda Sahib's forces. Clive's successful defence of Arcot and his subsequent victories were a turning point, marking British ascendancy in the Deccan.

One would wonder what the young Nizam, Muzaffar Jung, was doing all this while. Unfortunately, the Nizam's court was a hotbed of intrigue and machinations; a typical example of the collapse of the command-and-control structure of the Indian armies. Early in the year 1751, only a few months after his instalment as the Nizam, Muzaffar Jung was killed by Afghans in his court. Salabat Jung, the third son of the Nizam-ul-Mulk, succeeded as the subahdar. De Bussy immediately recognized Salabat Jung on Dupleix's advice, and the subahdar remained more or less aloof from the struggle for the Nawabi of Arcot. Salabat Jung had more serious threats from his eldest brother who was stationed in Delhi, and he also had the Marathas to contend with. Thus, the wider conflict within the empire and the collapse of the command structure prevented the Nizam, the Mughal official responsible for the Carnatic, from any further involvement in its affairs.

After sweeping the rest of the Carnatic, the English, led by Lawrence and Clive, with 1,100 sepoys and 400 Europeans under their command, reached Tiruchirappalli in April 1752 to relieve Muhammad Ali. They were joined by their allies: the Maratha, Mysore and Tanjore forces. The besiegers were now besieged. Chanda Sahib and his French allies were no match for the confederacy of the English, Marathas, Mysore and Tanjore. Chanda Sahib was defeated and executed. Finally, the French surrendered to the English in June 1752.

This was a crushing blow to Dupleix's ambition of becoming the lord of the Deccan. He tried to incite Mysore and the Marathas against Muhammad Ali, but failed. Muhammad Ali was now in control of most of his dominions in the Carnatic, and for this he owed everything to English support. He continued to finance the EIC troops stationed to defend his domain for the rest of his life, and was the first significant native prince to have come under the system of the English protective alliance. Eventually, Dupleix was recalled to France in 1754, and a treaty was signed between France and England, proclaiming the cessation of arms.

The English were clearly ascendant in the Carnatic by this time. This would not have been possible without the timely recruitment and dedicated service of the sepoys of the EIC Madras Army. By overplaying his hand, Dupleix lost this second round. The Nawab of Arcot was a grateful ally of the EIC, and the English held sway over the whole of the Carnatic. The French could console themselves by De Bussy's presence in Hyderabad, where he secured the Northern Circars as a grant from Salabat Jung, to defray the expenses of French troops. However, Salabat Jang was not such a committed ally, as we shall see; and, in fact, changed sides at the first available opportunity. The French were more or less on their own in the Deccan now.

IV

The French might have been subdued in the Deccan for the moment, but they were a great European power. The peace was temporary, and all parties expected war to break out in Europe again. De Bussy continued to be a menace to English interests in the Deccan while he was stationed at the Nizam's capital with his troops. The French were not very welcome at the Court of Salabat Jung in Hyderabad. A feeble attempt to dislodge De Bussy in 1756 by Salabat Jung collapsed, because the English help he expected did not arrive. The English had not betrayed Salabat Jung. Help could not be sent because of shocking developments in the Bengal province that seriously jeopardized the EIC interests in India. The matters in Bengal had to be dealt with urgently, and no resources could be spared to dislodge De Bussy from Hyderabad, at least for the moment.

Alivardi Khan, the subahdar of Bengal, Bihar and Orissa, died in 1756. From his capital at Murshidabad, he had been successful in repelling incessant Maratha attacks, but was hard-pressed. Like his counterpart in the Deccan, the Nizam-ul-Mulk, he paid nominal allegiance to the Mughal Emperor in Delhi. His grandson, Siraj-ud-Daulah, barely twenty-three years old, succeeded Alivardi Khan as the Nawab of Bengal upon his death. Siraj-ud-Daulah was a rash, intemperate and violent character. He was universally disliked—by his Muslim as well as Hindu courtiers, and the rich merchants of Bengal.

The EIC had secretly begun to fortify Fort William, anticipating imminent conflict with the French. The young Nawab had heard of the foreigners' intrigues in the Deccan, and after he did not receive a compliant response to his prohibition on fortifications, he decided to attack Fort William. Soon, the fort was occupied by the Nawab's forces, and the surviving English escaped down the river to Fulta, from where they sent appeals of help to Madras and Bombay. The English prisoners at Fort William were initially treated well, by the standards of their time. It changed when a drunk English soldier shot down one of the Nawab's troops. The remaining English were confined to a small cell overnight. Though it is clear that there was no bad intention, the lack of space, air and water led to the death of many prisoners. The most recent research suggests that out of sixty-four who entered the 'black hole'—as it was termed by subsequent English commentators—twenty-one survived. Nevertheless, the 'black hole' was used as one of the focal arguments of the barbarity and degeneracy of Indians, justifying English rule and oppression for more than two ensuing centuries. Using the incident to incite a howl of moral outrage, the English built a memorial at the site. The memorial was named after a survivor, John Holwell, who left a grossly exaggerated account of the brutality and death at the 'black hole'. This monument was to rile the Indian nationalists in the twentieth century. Indeed, it was a protest against this 'stain on the Nawab Siraj-ud-Daulah's honour' that led to Subhas Chandra Bose's arrest in July 1940.

When the appeal for help reached the Madras Council, the Presidency's legislative body, it was planning to aid Salabat Jung expel De Bussy from the Hyderabad Court. However, the crisis in Bengal was deemed critical, and it was decided that Hyderabad affairs could wait. Some records indicate that the Madras Council had a sizeable force by now: 10,000 sepoys and 2,000 European soldiers.[8] The sepoys appear to have not been organized into battalions at this time. In any event, the Council decided to send 900 European soldiers and 1,200 sepoys under the overall command of Admiral Watson, with Robert Clive as the commander of the land forces.[9] The force reached Fulta in December 1756 and, in a swift action, took Fort William back in January 1757. The Nawab was shocked by the swift response, and a temporary truce was agreed to, with an understanding that the trading privileges of the Company would be restored.

The news of the start of what would be the Seven Years' War in Europe now reached India. The situation was precarious as the French were on the right side of the Bengal Nawab so far. Clive took the precaution of raising the first battalion[10] of sepoys in Bengal. The battalion, also known as 'Lal Paltan', because of the redcoats worn by its members, was not raised from the natives of Bengal. Instead, it was raised from soldiers of various tribes of north India—Rohillas, Rajputs, Jats, Pathans and even some Brahmins—who were traditionally employed by Indian princes. Still under the shock of losing Fort William to Clive's sepoys, the Nawab panicked when he learnt that Afghans under Abdali were heading out from Delhi to plunder the rest of Hindustan. Abdali had already sacked Delhi, subdued the Mughal Emperor, and had just unleashed his murderous hordes against the Jat Raja Suraj Mal. The Nawab appealed for English help against the Afghans, and Clive exploited this opportunity to dislodge the French from the Nawab's favours, while making vague promises of help against the Afghans. Eventually, the valiant stand by the Jats and the spread of a cholera epidemic in his army, forced Abdali back to Afghanistan. Thus, Clive's promise of help to the Nawab remained untested. Meanwhile, Clive put the newly raised 'Lal Paltan' to good use by attacking and taking the French trading post of Chandarnagore, while the Nawab did not and could not explicitly forbid the English from preying upon the French. Thus far, everything seemed to have gone well for the EIC, and for Clive in his mission.

V

Soon, however, the stakes were going to get higher. The Nawab's 'prestige' had taken a severe blow due to recent reversals, and this started to strain the command structure in his army, right at the top. The setback suffered by the Nawab in the loss of Fort William at Calcutta and the destruction of the French post without his open consent emboldened his enemies at court. The English position, though much improved from the year before, did not appear fully secure. The remnants of the Chandarnagore French garrison, including its commander Jean Law de Lauriston, were still protected by the Nawab. There was also the fear of an imminent French attack in the Deccan, which would have inevitably required some troops to be diverted from Bengal.

In such circumstances of pervading suspicion, Clive started intriguing with the courtiers, especially Mir Jafar, the commander of the Nawab's forces, and the Jagat Seth family, who were rich bankers. In this, Clive was greatly aided by the capricious and violent nature of Siraj-ud-Daulah, who was reported to have struck the elder Jagat Seth in the face and threatened him with circumcision. Other men in high positions were spat upon or beaten. The Jagat Seths, Rai Durlabh (the Nawab's Diwan), Omichand (a merchant) and Mir Jafar, known to be already conspiring, were sounded out and a plot was set to overthrow and replace the Nawab.

When all the treacherous arrangements had been sealed, Clive marched out of Calcutta with 2,200 sepoys and 800 European soldiers against the Nawab. The Nawab was entrenched at Plassey with his large force, but had serious apprehensions by now. What followed could scarcely be called a 'battle' in the military sense, when the opposing forces made contact on 23 June 1757. The Nawab's faithful general, Mir Madan, led a dashing cavalry charge but was mortally wounded. Mir Madan's death created panic, and his troops started to fall back.

The Nawab's sole hope was in his commander Mir Jafar's battlefield leadership, whose loyalty had been recently doubted by the Nawab's closest advisers. Siraj-ud-Daulah sensed inaction from his commander, and feared it could cost him his life and kingdom. The wretched Nawab, in a desperate gesture, threw his turban at Mir Jafar's feet and begged him to defend with his life that emblem of his honour and sovereignty. It was too late. Mir Jafar bowed and withdrew, but other conspirators advised the Nawab to fly to safety. 'It was only when treason had done her work, when treason had driven the Nawab from the field, when treason had removed his army from its commanding position, that Clive was able to advance without the certainty of being annihilated.'[11] Irrespective of that, without the 2,200 sepoys under his command, it is doubtful Clive would have ever attempted to confront the Nawab at Plassey.

Thus ended the so called 'Battle of Plassey' when the EIC, with a small army of loyal sepoys, stood victorious over one of the most significant Mughal subahdars. Siraj-ud-Daulah was later captured and executed. Mir Jafar's treachery was rewarded by his proclamation as the new Nawab of Bengal. The ever prudent Clive now took the opportunity to raise the second battalion of sepoys in Bengal.

Soon the rumours surfaced that Raja Ram Narain, the Governor of Bihar and a subordinate of the Bengal Nawab, had allied himself with the neighbouring Nawab Wazir Shuja-ud-Daulah of Awadh, to eliminate Mir Jafar from Murshidabad. Clive and Mir Jafar had to march to Patna in a show of force, and although no fighting took place, Ram Narain was sufficiently intimidated for the moment. He accepted the Nawab's directive to be the deputy of Miran, Mir Jafar's son, at Patna. Clive took no chances, and raised the third battalion of Bengal sepoys from the Bhojpur district while on this mission.

It proved to be a wise move, for by the end of 1758, the news reached Bengal that Fort St. David had fallen to the French in June, and Madras was under siege. Clive was compelled to send two of his Bengal sepoy battalions, the troop of Madras sepoys, and 500 Europeans to the Northern Circars, under Colonel Forde's command. With most of his army on a mission to the south, Clive now raised the fourth battalion of the Bengal Army. In the same year, the Madras infantry was organized into sepoy battalions, and two battalions were formed in 1758 at Madras.

The year 1759 was a busy one for the Madras and Bengal armies. The Madras infantry was formed into six battalions during the year, while Clive raised a fifth battalion in Bengal.[12] Affairs in the south went in favour of the EIC. The French siege of Madras was lifted in February due to sustained vigorous action by forces under a native officer, Subedar Yusuf Khan, a pioneering EIC soldier about whom we will learn more later. More importantly, having taken their cue from the French, the EIC by now seemed to have invested much more successfully in native sepoys. The EIC sepoys were instrumental in English successes in the south. Even Lally, the French commander, lamented the superiority of English sepoys to his own. The difference, he said, 'is greater than that between a Nawab and a cooly. Theirs will even venture to attack white troops, while ours will not even look at their black ones.'[13] Short of cash, the French by now had fallen into the habit of Indian princes of not paying their soldiers regularly, while the EIC paid its sepoys on time. This would reflect in the quality of soldiers they could hire.

More astounding success was gained by Forde and his sepoys, who expelled the French from the Northern Circars. Salabat Jung—who was hovering around with a large force in the Northern Circars—was himself surprised at the fate of his French allies, and thought it best to turn the situation to his advantage. He signed a treaty with the EIC, undertaking to remove De Bussy and French troops from Hyderabad, and handed over part of the Northern Circars to the EIC. Barring occasional intrigues, like the one with Hyder Ali against the EIC in 1767, the 1759 treaty started a long and friendly alliance between the British and the Hyderabad state, which lasted until 1947.

VI

Events in Bengal proved to be more turbulent. Early in 1759, the Shahzada (Crown Prince) Shah Alam II had escaped the virtual prison in Delhi where he had been kept by the Vizier (Prime Minister) Imad-ul-Mulk, nephew of Salabat Jung and grandson of the illustrious Nizam-ul-Mulk. The Emperor and the Shahzada were under Imad's thumb, who had placed Alamgir II on the throne in 1754, after assassinating the previous incumbent. The Shahzada planned to revive his fortunes by invading and taking control of the rich province of Bengal. His scheme had the tacit support of the Nawab of Awadh, and some Bihar zamindars. The unpopularity of Mir Jafar in Bengal gave him hopes of success.

The Shahzada laid siege to Patna, and asked Ram Narain to surrender. Ram Narain gave conciliatory replies to buy time, and waited for Clive and Mir Jafar to come to his rescue. Mir Jafar and his English allies were able to repel this attack by the Shahzada, and forced him to retreat into the Awadh Nawab's territory. During the year, Clive suspected the Dutch of intriguing with Mir Jafar—he attacked and defeated them with swift action, thus putting an end to any Dutch pretensions in Hindustan. By the end of the year 1759, the Shahzada received the news of his father's murder by Imad-ul-Mulk. The Shahzada now declared himself Emperor, as Shah Alam II. More trouble lay ahead for those who did not acknowledge his suzerainty, which included the Bengal Nawab, his subordinate Raja Ram Narain at Patna, and the EIC.

The year 1760 was decisive in ending French military pretensions in India, when French forces under Lally were routed in the south at Wandiwash by Eyre Coote, who also recovered Fort St. David. Later that year, Pondicherry was also besieged, and surrendered to the EIC in January 1761. This was the end of French military power in India.

Despite the victories against the French in the south, the EIC now found itself embroiled in further intrigues and conflict in Bengal. Clive departed for England in February 1760, and was replaced by Henry Vansittrat. Within a few days of Clive's departure, the Emperor Shah Alam II crossed the Karmanasa river again, and attacked Ram Narain at Patna. Ram Narain was defeated, and fled back to his fort on his elephant. A Bengal Army contingent under Major Caillaud and Mir Jafar's son Miran came to relieve Ram Narain at Patna, and then it was Shah Alam II's turn to flee. The fleeing Emperor, in a bold move, made a dash towards Murshidabad, terrifying the Bengal Nawab and surprising the EIC forces. However, Shah Alam II was finally defeated in January 1761 at the Battle of Helsa, at the same time as the French surrendered Pondicherry in the south, and the Afghans inflicted a crushing defeat on the Marathas at Panipat. A few months before this battle, in October 1760, Vansittrat had fallen out with Mir Jafar, and replaced him with his son-in-law, Mir Kasim, as the Nawab of Bengal.

After the Battle of Helsa in early 1761, the Emperor was on the run, pursued by Major Carnac and his forces. Eventually, an agreement was reached, whereby both the EIC and Mir Kasim paid a token allegiance to Shah Alam II at a hastily scrambled throne in Patna. In return, Shah Alam II confirmed Mir Kasim as the Nawab of Bengal, and retired to Awadh in June 1761 as the guest of Shuja-ud-Daulah, whom he declared Nawab Vizier. The East India Company also raised the sixth and seventh battalions of Bengal sepoys during this year.

Mir Kasim turned out to be a man with a mind of his own, and by 1763 the EIC was at war with Mir Kasim. Mir Kasim lost the initial battles against the EIC. By the end of 1763, Mir Kasim retreated, and crossed the river Karmanasa to join Shah Alam II and the Nawab Vizier to live to fight another day. Mir Jafar, an opium addict by then, was restored as the Nawab once again. The number of sepoy battalions in the Bengal Army stood at ten by the end of 1763.

With the prospect of war with the confederacy of Emperor Shah Alam II, Nawab Vizier Shuja-ud-Daulah and Nawab Mir Kasim looming large in 1764, the Bengal Army sepoy battalion strength was raised to seventeen. The year also saw very significant mutinies in both the white as well as the native battalions. However, through a combination of tact and harsh measures, the mutinies were subdued before the decisive Battle of Buxar in October 1764.

In early 1764, Mir Kasim and Shuja-ud-Daulah launched an attack in the Emperor's name to take Patna, which failed. Thereafter, Shuja withdrew to an entrenched position near Buxar, across the Ganges, in Bihar territory. A force of 7,000 sepoys and 1,000 European soldiers under Major Hector Munro faced the Nawab Vizier's forces of 30,000 at Buxar.[14] Mir Kasim had by then fallen out with Shuja, who lost confidence in Mir Kasim after the failure to take Patna early in the year. As Mir Kasim was now unable to pay his troops, Shuja took them under his command. The Emperor Shah Alam II was in any event entirely dependent on

Shuja, and the reversal suffered at Patna dampened his enthusiasm for battling the EIC.

On 22 October 1764, Munro and his sepoys won the important and stubbornly fought Battle of Buxar. Shuja-ud-Daulah fled to Awadh and then to Rohilkhand. His last stand at Kora on 3 May 1765 ended in his defeat, and a treaty. This brought him and Awadh into the deadly embrace of the EIC, from which the state of Awadh could not ever escape. This also provided the EIC a fertile recruiting ground for the Bengal Army. Mir Kasim had disappeared into obscurity by then, and he died a pauper in Delhi years later.

Meanwhile, the Emperor Shah Alam II, representing himself as state prisoner of Shuja-ud-Daulah at Benares, sought British protection. Clive, who was now back in India, consented to his request, and installed him at Allahabad. In exchange, the Emperor bestowed upon the EIC the Diwani (revenue collection rights) for the Subah of Bengal. This was a momentous development, as with the Diwani, the whole administration of Bengal came under the Company's control. 'The Company became "Nabobs" in fact, if not in name, perhaps totally so without disguise.'[15] The same year, Nizam Ali Khan at Hyderabad entered into a treaty with the EIC for mutual defence.

The year 1765 marks the firm establishment of the EIC's dominion in India. The subahs of Bengal and the Carnatic were in the Company's grip, and Awadh and Hyderabad were subordinate allies. The French were crushed in the south as well as in Bengal. The EIC, with its sepoy battalions, was indeed on the way to be the masters of Hindustan.

From a few 'peons' in the 1740s, the EIC native army in 1765 stood at thirty-four sepoy battalions in Bengal and Madras alone, which would approximate to more than 27,000 sepoys, excluding Bombay.[16] Another estimate, including the Bombay garrison of 5,000, suggests there were 29,000 sepoys under EIC arms in 1765.[17] The Bombay Army was the smallest of the three presidencies, and while it had companies[18] of sepoys from 1760, the first two battalions were not raised until 1768.[19] This exponential growth within less than two decades was critical to the campaigns and victories described above. Clive now organized the Bengal Army into three brigades in 1765. Each brigade consisted of six sepoy battalions, one European infantry regiment, one troop of cavalry and one company of artillery. European troops were thus incorporated with native troops to guard against any potential insurrection. The signs of mistrust seemed to be visible as early as that.

VII

It is tempting to continue to write a chronological account of such exciting events. However, that is not the objective of this study. The two decades between 1746 and 1766 were of momentous import for the foundation of the British Indian Army. The events and circumstances illustrate the poor command-and-control structure that existed in India at the time. The Carnatic and Bengal Nawabs, the Nizam and the Awadh Nawab Vizier were at best second-rate powers in mid-eighteenth-century India. The Mughal Emperor was a mere symbol, with no resources or power at his command. Right from the Emperor's relations with the subahdars, and theirs with the subordinate commanders, opportunism, inaction and outright betrayal were the order of the day. The EIC, on the other hand, had a well-established command-and-control structure. This sound command structure—though burnished by strong leaders like Clive, Lawrence and Munro—was not susceptible to collapse without them. The corporate body provided a continuity of purpose and design, without excessive reliance on individuals. The Indian states and their armies, on the other hand, were fully dependent on the shifting priorities and loyalties of individual princes and their commanders. The sepoys rallied in strength to raise the Company's flag to victory. This was a relationship forged in crisis, and despite the strains, one that would endure for two centuries.

It is also worth noting that the initial successes gained by the EIC were at the expense of the Mughal Empire's weak regional subahdars. The more vigorous powers like the Marathas, Jats and Sikhs—which had in the first instance brought the Mughal military power to heel—would take another century to come under the Company's fold. The Mysore state was another example of what a strong command-and-control structure could achieve. Mysore was usurped by the able and ambitious Hyder Ali in 1761, while the Marathas were distracted confronting Abdali's Afghan hordes at Panipat. Once Hyder Ali declared himself the master of Mysore, it took the EIC four wars, with the support of the Nizam, and occasionally the Marathas, to defeat the Sultanate of Mysore in 1799.

In many ways, the chaos of the collapsing Mughal state was a golden age for 'military entrepreneurs'. Some, like Hyder Ali, succeeded in founding dynasties. Lesser known but numerous other military contractors were critical as the intermediaries in the military labour market of Hindustan. There were a large number of such 'jobber commanders', much like the European 'colonels' of the pre-Westphalia era. The sepoys came to enlist in small bands under their leader, usually known as 'jemadar' or 'subedar'. These jemadars and subedars hired, equipped, trained and paid the sepoys in their band, and received a lump sum for providing their service during the initial years of the Company's army. They also commanded the sepoys in action during the period surveyed above, and appeared to have done so admirably.

The first tactical unit that the native sepoys and their officers operated in was companies of varying sizes, ranging from 22 to 247 men in January 1749.[20] The subedars and jemadars often recruited men from their extended families and villages for their companies.

These were familial 'bands of brothers' bound by strong ties of family, honour and responsibility. In 1755, the Madras company structure was regularized and its strength was prescribed as one subedar, four jemadars, eight havildars, eight naiks, and eighty-four sepoys.[21] Thus, the jemadari war bands were brought closer in which to the European ideal of a 'company'. The incorporation of companies into battalions from 1757 onwards reduced the scope of native officers' leadership. As long as the company was the tactical unit of operation, the native officers had an independent sphere in which to operate. The battalions were officered by Europeans, and the subedars and jemadars leading companies were now effectively under the command and control of European officers. Even then, the number of European officers in the initial years was low, and each battalion had a 'black commandant' who was to take post in front of the battalion. As the EIC's military position appeared secure after defeating the French, the native officers' scope of leadership was reduced. The 'black commandant' position was abolished in the Madras Army in 1781, followed by the other two presidencies three years later. Thus, the importance of the native officer was progressively and systematically reduced as the EIC's army and empire grew.

In those early days, the sepoys gave yeoman service to the EIC against its enemies. One English officer provides a first-hand account of the sepoys in action against the French in 1752:

> Eight hundred of these sepoys were the very same who had made the resolute attempt to storm the breaches at Arcot …They [the sepoys] were a parcel of resolute fellows … These people [sepoys] being in the van never waited for the form of drawing up, but each company pressing for the honour of advancing their colours first, they set up a shout and ran at the French in the most daring manner, who had formed themselves in the front of their camp and

had begun to fire briskly upon them with their artillery, but they seemed to give very little attention to it, still running on in the same intrepid manner ... they fairly drove the French from their ground.[22]

VIII

Out of the mind-blowing set of characters and events in these years of transition, one man's story stands apart. Yusuf Khan, popularly called the 'Nellore Subedar', was appointed as the 'Commandant of all the Company's sepoys' in 1754, a position no one held before or after him. Tradition holds that he was born in a Hindu family, was of a rebellious nature as a child, and converted to Islam on his way to adulthood. He seemed to have met the English as enemies in 1751 as part of Reza Sahib's forces that laid siege to Arcot. When Clive repulsed the siege, and Reza Sahib fell back; Yusuf Khan, along with a number of other sepoys in Reza Sahib's army, had joined the EIC. 'Isouf Cawn', wrote Lawrence, 'had first a company of sepoys in his own service which were raised by himself. He is an excellent partisan, knows the country well, is brave and resolute ... He is a born soldier, and a better of his colour I never saw in the country.'[23]

Yusuf Khan soon endeared himself to the English commanders by his resolute action in the battles against the French and Chanda Sahib's forces across the Carnatic in 1752. 'Your Nellore sepoys are glorious fellows,' wrote an exuberant Captain Dalton to Clive, 'and their Subadar as good a man as ever breathed. He is my sole dependence.'[24] Yusuf Khan was sent to Madura and Tinnevelly in 1756, with independent command of a body of sepoys. He brought the revenue affairs of these territories in control over three years. He helped the EIC beat the French siege of Madras in 1758-59. When news of Lally's siege of Madras reached him in 1758, the Nellore Subedar immediately rode north from Madurai. He and his sepoys are credited with devastating French supply lines, cutting almost two months' worth of French supplies within a day, making the French siege untenable. The French Commander Lally lamented, 'They were like the flies, no sooner beat off from one part, they came to another.'[25] Yusuf Khan's guerrilla tactics finally compelled the French to lift the siege in 1759.

In 1759, while still at Madras, Yusuf Khan applied for the lease of the two southern districts that he pacified between 1756 and 1758. Nawab Muhammad Ali was suspicious but the EIC Council forced the Nawab to grant the lease to the Nellore Subedar. Once in Madurai as its effective governor, Yusuf Khan started to set himself up as an independent ruler. He collected a force of 6,000 sepoys and 300 horses, had French and African soldiers in his service, and was supplied by the Dutch and Danes. The EIC prevaricated, but finally decided to recall him in 1763. Nellore Subedar refused, and declared himself independent lord and master of Madurai. A series of negotiations failed, and he successfully repelled the Nawab and the EIC's initial joint expeditions against him. Finally, after a bitter struggle, there was a rising against him in the town. Thanks to treachery, he fell into the Nawab's hands, and was promptly hanged in 1764. Thus ended the meteoric career of a 'military entrepreneur' who at one point was the darling of the English Council and seemed on his way to be a second Hyder Ali in the Deccan at one stage.

It seems clear that sepoys and native officers who joined to fight under the English standard in these early years were eminently capable, and belonged to the same classes that native princes hired from. Most served their employers well, and steadily advanced their cause. What was the motivation, the belief system, the sociocultural mooring of these men that faithfully served a trading company with a dedication as firm as they gave to their native princes? The next chapter will try to look at the sepoy's emotional, spiritual and cultural world to answer some of these questions.

Chapter Five

True to Their Salt[1]

A sepoy's life is for some
And his death is for others
But all his discomforts and trials are his alone.[2]
    —Shah Wali Khan of the Ambala Cavalry Brigade

I

THE BRITISH LINES WERE HOLDING ON BY THE SKIN OF THEIR teeth in Flanders during the fateful month of October 1914. Numerically superior and better armed, the Germans were poised to smash through the British Expeditionary Force (BEF) and open a route to the coast. Two divisions (Lahore and Meerut) comprising 28,500 Indian troops[3] arrived to relieve the beleaguered BEF. Men born in the tropical climate of India suddenly faced European winters dressed in their khakis, meant for humid and hot Hindustan. Their rifles were of an unfamiliar pattern, and medical supplies and signalling equipment were short. The Germans had trench mortars, searchlights, hand grenades; the Indians had none of these, and were left to improvise grenades from jam tins.[4]

Within days of their arrival, the underequipped troops were fed piecemeal into the front line. Almost one-third of them would never return home, sacrificing their lives in the fields of Flanders. While British soldiers fought for their homes and families, the Indian soldiers fought for something vague but deeply ingrained in their psyche—honour. They held no grudge against the German as an enemy on a personal level, except that he threatened the interests of the sepoy's employer and the King-Emperor. This proved sufficient motivation for 8,000 of them to lay down their lives, 'blown apart by shell fire, choked by gas or buried alive in soggy collapsing trenches'.[5]

One man of these 8,000 was Dogra Jemadar Kapur Singh, the son of Jiwan from Ghagipur, Sialkot in Punjab in today's Pakistan. Not much is known about him, except for his deeds in Flanders. Aged twenty-six at his death, he is likely to have been married, and possibly a father too, going by the pattern of Indian family life of the time. On the fateful day of 31 October 1914, Jemadar Kapur Singh was defending the position at Messines from a furious German assault as part of the Dogra Company of the 57th Wilde's Rifles battalion. The German assault began at around 3 a.m. The Company of about eighty men was surrounded by nine German Grenadier battalions advancing at a 'jog-trot' and making 'raucous, guttural sounds'.[6] The Dogra Company's English commanding officer was badly wounded in the arm, and his men decided to evacuate him. Before leaving, he ordered the two surviving Indian officers to hold their position and under no circumstances to retire, unless the neighbouring units of British cavalry should do so first.

Taking their orders to heart, the two jemadars—Ram Singh and Kapur Singh—resolved to stand their ground. Unknown to them, the neighbouring British units were not as severely pressed by the German advance, and therefore did not withdraw. But the Dogras felt compelled to follow their orders to the letter. As night turned into morning, their position became increasingly desperate, and dangerous. All the men of the Dogra Company were killed one by one, leaving Kapur Singh as the last survivor. Eventually, by 8 a.m., the brave jemadar ran out of ammunition, except one bullet. Kapur Singh could not have been blamed if he now retired or decided to surrender. Standing in the trench without ammunition, and having lost all his comrades, he had fought as hard as any soldier could. His job was done; he had accounted for his 'salt'. However, the young Dogra saw matters in a different light. As the Germans approached, Jemadar Kapur Singh, commander of the post and the sole survivor of the Dogra Company, took his rifle and put his final bullet into his own brain. Merewether and Smith would later write:

> Even this war can present few more devoted pictures than the death of these noble-hearted Dogras and the heroic Indian officer who chose rather to follow his men than to surrender.[7]

Germans were known to have been kind to Indian soldiers taken prisoner, as they hoped to turn them against their masters. But Kapur Singh could not countenance a life as a surrendered prisoner, even if it meant death by his own hand. It is one thing to die in battle from enemy action, but it is quite another to value one's honour more than life. This final act of offering one's life, when there is nothing else left to give, is ingrained in the soldier's code that men like Kapur Singh undertook, as part of an Indian martial tradition. In his final act, Jemadar Kapur Singh was following the millennia-old traditions of 'saka' and 'jauhar'. This was the essence of a soldier's life, and there are numerous other examples to be found throughout the centuries of Indian history.

II

Turning back half a century, another moving incident captures the mentality of the Indian soldier serving his 'sirkar'. There are very few first-hand literary records from Indian soldiers during the two centuries of their employment in the British Indian Army. There are just two known accounts prior to the twentieth century, and a handful more during the last fifty years of the Raj. Subedar Sita Ram Pandey—one of the two from the nineteenth century—left an extensive account of his forty-eight years' service with the East India Company Army. The memoir, originally written in Awadhi, was translated into English by Lieutenant Colonel J.T. Norgate, Sita Ram's commanding officer.[8]

Born in 1797, Sita Ram enlisted in 1812 as a sepoy in the Bengal Infantry, and retired as a subedar in 1860, the highest rank an Indian could expect to reach in the British Indian Army. Sita Ram took part in the campaigns against Gurkhas, the second Anglo–Maratha war, the storming of Bharatpur, the first Afghan war and the Sikh wars. He remained loyal to the EIC during the 1857 rebellion. He was taken prisoner in Kabul after the disastrous expedition to place Shah Shuja on the Afghan throne, and managed to escape from captivity through his own efforts. A man of great experience, his account of his life throws some light on the thinking of a sepoy. He describes events beautifully in his book, and I will let him state his story wherever possible.

Sita Ram's first marriage was 'arranged' by his parents, while he was recuperating at home from a serious wound suffered during the Pindari war in 1817. When his leave ended, Sita Ram rejoined his unit, and went into action against Apa Sahib of Berar's forces during the 1818 Anglo–Maratha war. His unit was ordered to storm a village called Ahanpura, which was defended by Arab soldiers in Apa Sahib's pay. In this village, in the course of fierce fighting, Sita Ram found the love of his life:

> While running along a lane in the village, I came upon the enclosure of a house and entered it, expecting to find it deserted. However, I surprised an Arab in the very act of killing a girl who was kneeling at his feet and imploring him to spare her life. The moment he saw me he shouted out, 'Not yet!', and rushed at me like a tiger. He came so frantically that he transfixed himself on my bayonet before I could recover my surprise. I then fired my musket and blew a great hole in his chest, but even after this he managed in his dying struggles to give me a severe cut on my arm ... The girl threw herself at my feet and embraced my legs ... I asked her who she was, and where she came from, and where her friends and relations were. She told me she was the daughter of a Thakur in Bundelkhand, by name Mokum Singh. She had been carried off by the Pindaris who had sold her to this Arab, who had forced her to become his mistress. Her father had been killed, and many of her relations also, while defending their property. She also assured me that the survivors would never receive her back as she was disgraced beyond redemption, and she ended her sad story by telling me that I was her Lord and now her only protector.[9]

Sita Ram took the girl under his protection, and despite advice from his comrades to not encumber himself, managed to find a place for her in the unit follower's camp.

> This young creature rode my pony but remained in the care of the head follower. I saw her every day and my heart became inflamed with love, for she was beautiful to look on and always called me her protector. I am an old man now but never before nor since have I seen any woman like her, not even in Delhi.[10]

When the adjutant told Sita Ram that women were not permitted to accompany the forces, he wrote:

> [My mind] was filled with sadness and my heart became a target for the arrows of despair ... My uncle [who was in the same unit] strongly advised me to get rid of her as she would only bring disgrace on me. For the first time my uncle and I nearly had a quarrel. How true was the warning given me by the priest Duleep Ram: More men are entangled by the wiles of a woman than fish in the net of the most skilful fisherman. The arrows from their eyes wound more than the poisoned arrows of the Bhil.[11]

Sita Ram managed to convince his officers to let him keep the young Thakurain (Thakur woman) with him until the end of the war. He was injured, and the Thakurain looked after him. Finally, Sita Ram 'spent a lot of money in order that the Thakurain could regain her caste, and [he] was married to her by the ceremony called Gardab.[12] While [they] were at Meerut "a joy of the world" was born to [him]—a son!'[13] This would have been around 1820.

This 'joy of the world' became a fine young man, and was enlisted into Sita Ram's corps around 1837, as was the tradition in the army units of the time, where sons and relatives would follow their fathers and elders. While Sita Ram was a prisoner in Kabul, his son transferred to another regiment. After his escape, Sita Ram frequently complained of not hearing from his son for years. Given the distances involved, the father and son did not see each other for nearly two decades.

In 1857, the sepoys of the Bengal Army rose against the East India Company. The war divided the regiments and companies. Much blood was shed. Sita Ram, however, remained loyal to the EIC during the conflict. The mutineers considered him to be a traitor and carried him off to Lucknow to be put to death. Luckily, he was rescued by a roving party of British troopers, and he joined a new unit. Here, the sword of fate smote this old soldier's heart in a way no one ought to ever suffer. He faced a dilemma, and his thoughts and actions illustrate much that was the core of a loyal soldier's character.

By now, the EIC army was winning over the rebels, and it was time for retribution. As jemadar, Sita Ram was asked to command a firing party to execute the captured rebel sepoys.

> I asked the prisoners their names and their regiments. After hearing some five or six, one sepoy said he belonged to a certain regiment which was my son's. I naturally enquired whether he had known my son, Ananti Ram, of the Light Company. He answered that that was his own name. However, this is a very common name, and because I had always imagined that my son must have died from the Sind fever, since I had never heard from him, it did not at first strike me. But when he told me that he came from Tilowee [Sita Ram's village], my heart leapt in my mouth. Could he be my long-lost son? There was no doubt about it, for he gave my name as his father, and fell down at my feet imploring my pardon. He had mutinied with the rest of his regiment and gone to Lucknow ... The prisoners were to be shot at four o'clock in the afternoon and I must be my son's executioner! Such is fate![14]

This 'joy of the world', whom Sita Ram doted on as a child, was about to end his life as a rebel. Sita Ram at this stage broke down, and asked his commanding officer, a major, that he be excused from this duty, as one of the rebels was his son. The major initially did not believe him, and accused him of sympathizing with the rebels, until he interviewed Ananti Ram personally to establish the truth.

Sita Ram was excused from the task of commanding the firing party, but at no stage did he make an effort to seek pardon for his son, even if such clemency had been in his major's power to grant. Sita Ram's thoughts around the subject reveal much:

> I shall never forget this terrible scene. Not for one moment did I consider requesting that his life should be spared — that he did not deserve. I went to my tent bowed down with grief which was made worse by the gibes and taunts of the Sikhs who declared I was a renegade. In a short time, I heard a volley. My son had received the reward for mutiny! He showed no fear but I would much rather that he had been killed in battle ... Through the kindness of the Major I was allowed to perform the funeral rites over my misguided son. He was the only one of the prisoners over whom it was performed, for the remainder were all thrown to the jackals and the vultures. I had not heard from my son since just after my return from slavery [in Kabul]. I had not seen him since I went to Kabul, and thus I met him again, untrue to his salt, and in open rebellion against the master who had fed his father and himself ... The Major told me later that he was much blamed by the other officers for allowing the funeral rites to be performed on a rebel but if good deeds wipe away sins, then his sins will be very white. Bad luck never waits upon the merciful! May my Major soon become a General.[15]

Sita Ram did not lack courage by any means. He was wounded seven times, was awarded six medals, and when taken prisoner in Kabul, he escaped to return to duty. In any event, he was at the twilight of his life when this incident occurred, and it could not have been fear of death or love of life that guided his actions. What sense of duty prevented him from pleading for his son's life, let alone make any effort to rescue him?

It is interesting to note the ideas that mattered most to him when this incident occurred. He believed that service to his employer was sacred. His sense of shame at the taunts he received from the Sikhs is palpable. He makes the point that his son did not show any fear facing death, which seems important to him. His regret is that his son could not die on the field of battle. His gratitude to the major for allowing him to perform the funeral rites shows how important his religious and spiritual values were to him. His sadness that his son rebelled against the government, whose salt both he and his son had eaten, is poignant.

Any father can draw his own conclusions about the motivations and system of belief of the old subedar. This belief system, however, was widely shared by the sepoys. It connected their lives and professions to a deeper meaning. It provided the anchor necessary to perform a service where sacrifice and devotion were key. Jemadar Kapur Singh and Subedar Sita Ram Pandey are just two surviving stories from countless forgotten lives, which illustrate the sepoy's inner world.

III

If such were the thoughts of the sepoy at the end of his life, let's survey what motivations brought him to the profession of arms in the first place. Fortunately, we have one more personal account of an EIC soldier from late eighteenth-century India. Dean Mahomet, born in Bihar, joined the EIC as a 'camp follower' at the tender age of ten. He later migrated first to Cork, Ireland, and then England, where he died in 1851. His autobiography, which was initially published as a newspaper series, gives very interesting insights into the life of an Indian soldier in eighteenth-century India.[16]

Dean Mahomet was born in 1759 in Patna.[17] Dean's father was a subedar in the 3rd Battalion of the Bengal Army.[18] In 1769, Dean's father commanded a company of sepoys of the 3rd Battalion sent to enforce a revenue demanded by Raja Shitab Rai.

Dean's father, unfortunately, was killed during this campaign. Having lost his father at such a tender age, Dean was left in his mother's care, who had some means to look after them due to their close ties to the family of the Nawab of Murshidabad.

The pull of the profession of arms played on the young mind of Dean Mahomet. While in Patna, he observed the army officers, and their high status in the court of Raja Shitab Rai. Impressed with what he saw, and despite losing his father in service, he was determined to be a soldier from a young age. His mother, of course, had serious reservations. However, she could only suffer in silence as her son was drawn by the charms of the uniform. Dean recounts:

> My mother's house was not far from the Raja's palace; and the number of Officers passing by our door on their way thither, attracted my notice, and excited the ambition I already had of entering on a military life … Nothing could exceed my ambition of leading a soldier's life: the notion of carrying arms, and living in a camp, could not be easily removed: my fond mother's entreaties were of no avail: I grew anxious for the moment that would bring the military Officers by our door. Whenever I perceived their route, I instantly followed them.[19]

At a tennis party in Patna, the eleven-year-old Dean Mahomet caught the eye of his future patron, Godfrey Evan Baker. Baker was a newly appointed Irish cadet, assigned to the European Regiment of the Third Brigade in the Bengal Army. Underaged, Dean Mahomet's only option was to join as a 'camp follower' attached to Baker's entourage. The number of camp followers in each unit was two to three times that of fighting sepoys. Some were formally employed by the Company, and the rest informally by the officers and soldiers. Camp followers set up camp, transported baggage and equipment, and handled supply distribution, besides serving their individual employers. Baker offered Dean a place as his camp follower, which Dean immediately accepted as 'it flattered [his] hopes beyond expression.'[20] Dean was to remain attached with Baker, until both of them left India in 1784. While there was no formal place for Dean in a European battalion, when Baker was promoted to captain in command of two sepoy battalions in 1781, he appointed Dean as jemadar out of turn.

But in 1769, ten-year-old Dean's mother's apprehensions came true when the young Dean sneaked out of Patna with his new patron, Mr Baker. Dean writes in his memoir:

> My mother, observing some alteration in my conduct, since I first saw Mr. Baker, naturally supposed that I was meditating a separation from her. She knew I spoke to him; and apprehensive that I would go with him, she did everything in her power to frustrate my intentions. Notwithstanding all her vigilance, I found means to join my new master, with whom I went early the next morning to Bankeepore [Bankipur], leaving my mother to lament my departure.[21]

A mother's heart is not so easily deterred, however. Unable to bear parting from her young son, she caught up with Baker and Dean after a few months. She urged Baker to return her son. Their final interaction could scarcely shake Dean's resolution, though it broke his mother's heart. Baker agreed to let the young boy go, if he so wished, but Dean chose to stay:

I was extremely affected at her presence, yet my deep sense of gratitude to a sincere friend conquered my duty to an affectionate parent, and made me determine in favour of the former: I would not go, I told her—I would stay in the camp; her disappointment smote my soul—she stood silent—yet I could perceive some tears succeed each other, stealing down her cheeks—my hurt was wrung—at length, seeing my resolution fixed as fate, she dragged herself away, and returned home in a state of mind beyond my power to describe.[22]

The fate of Sita Ram Pandey's mother was not much different. The profession of arms in a militarized society like India in the eighteenth century was very risky. That did not deter the sepoys, though inevitably their mothers suffered in silence, knowing very well what fate might hold for their sons.

Sita Ram's maternal uncle, Hanuman, was a jemadar in an infantry battalion of the Bengal Army. It was during one of his uncle's visits to their village that young Sita Ram 'imbibed a strong desire to enter the world, and try the fortune of a soldier'.[23] Sita Ram, like Dean Mahomet, was fascinated by the prospect of becoming a soldier:

Nothing else could I think of, day or night. The rank of Jemadar I looked on as quite equal to that of Ghazidin Hydar, the Kind of Awadh himself ... My uncle had observed how attentive I was to all his stories, and how military ardour had inflamed my breast, and certainly he did all in his power to encourage me. He never said anything about it before my father and mother, or the priest ... How I longed to mention this to my mother, but dared not for I well knew her dearest wish was for me to become a priest. However, one day when I had been reading with

Duleep Ram [the priest and Sita Ram's tutor] about the mighty battles fought by the Gods, I fairly told him my wish to become a soldier. How horrified he seemed! How he reproached me, declaring that all the instruction he had so laboured to impart me was thrown away, and that half the stories my uncle had told me were false; that I might be flogged, and certainly should be defiled by entering the Company's service. A hundred other terrors he conjured up, but these had no effect on me.[24]

When Sita Ram's mother found out about his plans,

[She] wept, scolded, entreated, and threatened [him], ending by imploring [him] to give up the idea, and abused [his] father for not preventing such a catastrophe ... [Sita Ram] had to sustain the united attacks of the priest and [his] mother. They tried every inducement to make [him] give up the idea. [His] mother even cursed the day her brother had set foot in [their] house.[25]

Despite all their efforts, Sita Ram became more and more determined to follow his uncle.

When his uncle visited them next time, he 'in a measure succeeded in bringing [his] mother to think it was [his] destiny to be a soldier, and her fate to part with her son.'[26] Sita Ram's mother reluctantly let her son join the Company's Army, but could not hide her pain when Sita Ram left with his uncle on 10 October 1812. Sita Ram remembered:

Just before starting, my mother violently kissed me, and gave me six gold mohurs sewn in a cloth bag, but being convinced that it was her fate to part with me, she uttered no words but moaned piteously.[27]

It is no coincidence that the only two known detailed first-hand accounts by sepoys from the late eighteenth to early nineteenth century show how irresistible the charm of the profession of arms was to the local recruits. The sepoys belonged to privileged families and good social rank, and were by no means joining the army under any financial compulsion. This is in stark contrast to the pool of recruits the Company had access to back home in England and Europe. In 1768, a year before Dean joined the service, the Commander-in-Chief of the Bengal Army wrote about the latest crop of European recruits:

> They are exceedingly bad ... the refuse of our metropolis ... The Company are at a great expence [sic] to send abroad annually a number of soldiers when in fact, instead of recruiting our army, they only serve to increase our Hospitals ... [A]t present our European Regiments compared to a Batallion of Sepoys appear like a Regiment of Dwarfs.[28]

IV

The attraction of the profession of arms seen above should not come as a surprise to those acquainted with the ancient traditions of India. In the segmented societal order, the right to bear arms carried a degree of sanctity with it. This sanctity came from the expectation of conducting oneself according to 'dharma', a code of righteous conduct. Those who had the good fortune to bear arms did so to protect and nurture dharma, and hence were obliged to follow the righteous path. The soldier thus had to follow a complex, uncoded set of behaviours suitable to his status as the protector of dharma.

Many authors have tried to describe the soldier's conduct in terms of notions of honour, shame, duty, righteousness, etc. No doubt these were all important traits. However, the overarching trait underlining the ancient soldier's behaviour and code of conduct was renunciation. The act and symbolism of renunciation is the core of virtues defined for collective as well as individual actions in the ancient texts of India. The ability to renounce, to discard and walk away, is the source of the power of the yogi, the king and the kshatriya—the soldier—alike.

The power of a 'yogi' is derived from his ability to renounce the material word and its pleasures. The one who has no value for the matter is considered enlightened, and on the path to 'moksha' or liberation. The yogi has the highest status in the societal order per ancient scriptures. An ordinary person too moves through the four 'ashramas' (stages) in life, which are progressively geared towards renunciation, the last ashram being of 'vanvas' (hermit or forest dweller). This material renunciation is the background, path and preparation for the hopeful spiritual renunciation: moksha or freedom from the cycle of rebirth. The biggest yogi is Lord Shiva himself, who renounced the world and lives like a hermit in the barren Himalaya mountains or in graveyards. Lord Rama—considered to be an avatar of Lord Vishnu—is revered as an ideal man for his ability to renounce his kingdom for fourteen years to honour his father's word, while suffering the life of a hermit in the forests.

A soldier, in this worldview, has to be prepared to renounce his greatest possession—his life—in the righteous path of dharma (roughly translated in this context as duty). The king is the epitome of an ideal kshatriya: the soldier. The soldier has to be prepared to give the final gift—this life and the world—when his other worldly acts are insufficient to uphold dharma.

Dharma has different implications in different contexts, but fulfilling one's duty is one of its key aspects. It is a soldier's duty to follow his leader, and serve according to the righteous path set out for him. This normative paradigm has continued to inform the spirit and culture of warrior classes in India since antiquity. The skills of a warrior were held in high esteem, and the ruling classes justified their claims based on their military capabilities, which were essential to carrying out their duties. Military valour and arms training were coveted skills, and separated the kshatriyas from the rest. This kshatriya tradition was imbibed by the Rajputs, and subsequently other fighting classes like Marathas, Jats, Sikhs, Gurkhas, and even Muslim soldiers, many of whom remembered their Rajput and Jat ancestors after conversion.

The skilled warrior Arjun in the epic Mahabharata wavers before the final war as he sees his relatives arrayed against him on the battlefield. His charioteer, who is no less than Lord Krishna himself, reminds him of his duty as a kshatriya in these words:

> Considering your specific duty as a kshatriya, you should know that there is no better engagement for you than fighting on principles; and so there is no need for hesitation. O Partha, happy are the kshatriyas to whom such fighting opportunities come unsought, opening for them the doors of heavenly planets. If, however, you do not perform your religious duty of fighting, then you will certainly incur sins for neglecting your duties and thus lose your reputation as a fighter. People will always speak of your infamy, and for a respectable person, dishonour is worse than death.[29]

The classic 'kshatriya' battle fought 'fairly' was a contest between skilled warriors in an almost ritualistic observance of the code and formalities. There is an illustrative description of such a combat, quoted by Norman Ziegler from a sixteenth-century Rajput court epic:

> Then Kumbho got down [from his horse] ... went into the camp and bowed to Hemo. Hemo said, 'Very fine,

Kumbho!' Then Hemo said, 'Kumbho! You inflict a wound.' Kumbho said, 'Hemoji! You inflict a wound.' Hemo said, 'Kumbho! You are a boy. I have had nim leaves bandaged on many [a wound].' Then Kumbho was saying, 'Hemoji! You inflict a wound.' Hemo said, 'Kumbho! Your body has yet felt no sword; you are a boy. You inflict a wound. I am an elder; why should I inflict the [first] wound?' Kumbho said, 'Hemoji! In years you are elder, but in rank I am senior. You have taken my grain in the hem of your clothes; you are my military servant [and] therefore, I am senior; you inflict [the first] wound.' Then Hemo said, 'What should I do? You allow me no choice.' Then Hemo wounded Kumbho. The blow [of his sword] severed Kumbho's helmet, split [his] skull [as though smashing] a clay bowl, sliced between his eyebrows and lodged [itself] at the top of his ear. Kumbho inflicted a wound; [he] cut Hemo in two parts. Hemo fell down. Then Kumbho drew his dagger and stabbed [it] into Hemo's chest.[30]

Such elaborate and exaggerated politeness shown by two combatants might be doubtful. However, this story sets an example of the conduct to be followed by warriors, as part of their ethos. Personal bravery and an absence of fear of death were virtues expected of all warriors. Equally important was the loyalty and the patron–client relationship. Loyalty to the master was considered a sacred obligation by a warrior.

In the south, when Tanjavur ruler Vijayvarghava's son was cut down before his own eyes by overwhelming Madurai forces in 1673, Vijayvarghava realized he himself was doomed. When Madurai matchlock men attacked him, he called out to the Madurai ruler: 'You must order your men not to shoot their guns but to fight only with swords and spears. Do you want to know why? Because if one dies from some lousy bullet shot from a distance, he fails to enter heaven—that is nothing like a warrior's death. Don't you know all this yourself?'[31] The wish was granted and the Tanjavur ruler rushed at his opponents, sword in hand, and attained the right kind of death in the right kind of fighting.

The supreme manifestation of this culture of renunciation of the ascetic warrior was the custom of 'saka' and 'jauhar'. When faced with an overwhelming enemy and certain defeat, the defending warriors would ride out or rush at their opponents, sword in hand, facing almost certain death. This final ritual charge of the warrior is the ultimate act of renunciation, and was frequently adopted during many conflicts in India. While men performed this ritual saka, the unarmed women would consign themselves to the eternal flame, in the ritual of jauhar, to escape torture, rape and dishonour at the hand of the victorious foe.

One poignant event, well documented by medieval historians, illustrates this perfectly. In 1531, Bahadur Shah, the Sultan of Gujarat, destroyed the Malwa sultanate of Sultan Mahmud II, with the help of a Purbiya Rajput warlord, Silhadi. The victory celebrations were barely over before Silhadi and Bahadur Shah fell out. The dispute was over the issue of the Muslim women in Silhadi's household. The ulemas goaded Bahadur Shah to take remedial action, and he proposed that Silhadi either convert or surrender the Muslim women from his household. Silhadi prevaricated for some time before showing signs of reconciliation by telling the Sultan 'he wished to be dignified with the nobility of Islam'. Silhadi then moved back to the Fort of Raisen, where his home and relations were stationed.

At Raisen, his wife Durgavati put an end to Silhadi's dilemmas by clearly outlining the path of the Rajput: 'The right way of bravery is this, that we should perform "jauhar" of our women and children, and should ourselves fight and be slain; and there should be no further longing left in our hearts.'[32] Silhadi was moved by her steadfast conduct, and realized that she truly embraced the meaning and value of life for a kshatriya. When Bahadur Shah sent a Muslim amir to coerce and counsel Silhadi, he replied:

> Every day one 'kror' of betel leaves, and some 'seers' of camphor are consumed in my house, and every day three hundred women put on new garments. If we are killed with our women and children, what honour and what glory.[33]

This seemingly irrelevant statement, irrational as it is, reflects the inner turmoil of the hard-pressed kshatriya. After all, he lists the material wealth he has built up over a lifetime. However, earning honour by renouncing life and its pleasures is the kshatriya's code, and Silhadi followed it to the end.

Having conveyed their decision firmly, Rani Durgavati, taking her daughter-in-law[34] and her two children by the hand, walked into the jauhar. Silhadi, his brother Lakshman, Taj Khan, and other warriors then armed themselves, and died in a ritual battle with the Sultan's infantry at the foot of the fort.

Note that the Muslim relative of Silhadi, Taj Khan, who likely had converted recently, joined his family in this final act of saka and jauhar. The code of righteous and honourable conduct, as demanded of a kshatriya, stayed with him through the conversion. In fact, the military ethos of the Muslim soldiers of India continued to draw upon this Indian tradition across centuries. The practice of jauhar and saka had percolated in the military ethos of Muslim soldiers as much as Hindus during the medieval period.

In 1617, the recalcitrant ex-Governor of Bengal, Qasim Khan, was in a fort near Dhaka, surrounded by the Mughal imperial forces led by Ibrahim Khan. When Ibrahim Khan ordered his troops to attack the fort, his officers replied: 'Qasim Khan has taken the oath of committing "jawhar", and as soon as the fort is broken into, will kill all his people. God forbid, if such a thing happens, who is going to answer imperial investigations?'[35]

A few years later, Mirza Nathan, the Mughal commander, sent to chastise the rebellious Assamese, had to issue this order to his subordinate in a perilous moment: 'As soon as you hear that I have attained martyrdom in the field, perform the rites of "jawhar", with all the inmates of the mahal, big and small, and take your journey to the Kingdom of Heaven with eternal honour.'[36]

Eventually, Qasim Khan did not, and Mirza Nathan did not have to carry through the ritual to its conclusion by offering their lives, but, sadly, about fifty to a hundred women and soldiers did end their lives by friendly sword in both episodes. The ethos and vocabulary of renunciation had seeped into the soldiery of all faiths of India.

There is some parallel in the elaborate martial code of conduct that existed in Japanese samurai culture in medieval Japan. Loyalty to the master and to the right course of action, placing the value of life below that of righteous conduct, and the final rituals of saka and hara kiri, offer some pertinent resemblances in this respect between Indian and Japanese ancient martial cultures.

V

Over a period of time, the soldier's moral code came to centre around three elements: his religious duty, his sacred obligation to his king as the employer, and finally his duty to protect and enhance the honour of his family and his tribe or ethnic group.

In the First World War, the greatest deployment of Indian troops was in Mesopotamia—almost 600,000 sepoys were sent against the Ottoman armies. The proportion of Indians to European soldiers in the makeup of British forces in Mesopotamia was heavily skewed towards Indians, almost the reverse of the situation on the Western Front. Poorly armed and equipped— much worse than their comrades in Europe—Indian troops suffered horrendous casualties. They were considered expendable by the bumbling authorities. The official inquiries later confirmed the callousness with which the Indian soldiers were sent to battle, and it is unlikely that an army predominantly of white soldiers would have been thrust so inadequately equipped into action in a theatre that was deemed to be of secondary importance. In Mesopotamia, the sepoys suffered starvation, adverse climate and disease comparable to the disastrous retreat from Kabul during the first Anglo–Afghan war in 1839–42.

In such adverse circumstances, the battalion of 117th Mahrattas (Marathas) acquitted themselves well enough that a British commander congratulated a British regiment on being brigaded with them.[37] During their march, the Turks dropped Hindi pamphlets on them, telling them that England was starving and would not be able to feed or clothe them soon. The Mahrattas wrote a reply that they asked to be dropped on the enemy:

> We have never been fed and clothed so well but prisoners taken from you are in rags … We will never cease to fight for the King Emperor Jarj Panjam [George V] until the evil Kaiser is utterly trodden into the mud, as was the ten-headed demon Rawan by Ramchandraji.[38]

It is difficult to know what the Kaiser, Sultan or indeed their soldiers would have made of it. However, the parallel drawn with their ancient gods says much about the moral universe of the sepoys. It was a sacred duty to their faith and to their employer that they were there to discharge, and they would do so even at significant personal cost.

In stark contrast to earlier periods of the British Indian Army, the Indian soldiers' letters from the Western Front and Mesopotamia are plentiful. We are fortunate in hearing some of the sepoy voices, their motivations, fears and hopes first-hand in these letters. A survey of these letters will help us enhance our understanding of the soldiers' motivations.

Many soldiers thought that sacrificing their lives in battle would liberate their souls, and they would attain heaven in the afterlife. A wounded Garhwali wrote from England in February 1915 to a friend:

> It is a noble fate for us to be allowed to sacrifice our bodies for our King. If our ancestors help us and God shows us favour, if we die on the battlefield in the service of our King, this is equal to entering heaven … Although I am in hospital, yet my spirit yearns for the battlefield.[39]

British officers were well aware of this streak in their sepoys, and they exploited it to the hilt for motivation. Jemadar Chur Singh of the 47th Sikh Regiment met his death in a fit of rage when his religious duty was invoked by his British officer. A sepoy who witnessed Chur Singh's last moments later wrote to a friend from Brighton Hospital in December 1915:

> The 47th Sikhs were charging. [The] Sahib said, 'Chur Singh, you are not a Sikh of Guru Gobind Singh, [you] who sit in fear inside the trench!' Chur Singh was very angry. Chur Singh gave [the] order to his company to charge. He drew his sword and went forward. A bullet came from the enemy and hit him in the mouth. So did our brother Chur Singh become a martyr. No other man was like Jemadar Chur Singh.[40]

Sepoy Mansa Ram of the 107th Jat Pioneers wrote from Brighton Hospital in April 1915 to his friend: 'Don't you be anxious about me, because it is fitting for anyone who has eaten the salt of the Government to die.'[41] The soldiers felt obliged to risk their lives on the battlefield to defend the interest of their employer, the King-Emperor, to whom they were intensely loyal. Prabhu Dayal (Dogra) wrote to his friend in 1915 from Brighton Hospital:

> To run away or try and hide is the work of a coward, for it is the Rajput's duty to fight. I have been born once, of my mother, and in this world I cannot get another birth. I am always praying that my master and King may be victorious, or that death may be my lot. I cannot fight for anyone else, for I have taken up service for my King and whether I am spared to serve him faithfully, or whether I die on the battlefield, I shall go straight to Heaven. We must be true to our salt and he who is faithful will win Paradise for his parents as well as for himself. The faithless man will disgrace his parents ... Do not be anxious and worried. I will come back when the King wins the war, and we will destroy the evil Germans.[42]

The soldiers' morale is described as very high on account of the chance they receive to 'exalt the name of race, country, ancestors, parents, village and brothers, and to prove our loyalty to the Government'.[43] Signaller Kartar Singh (Sikh, 6th Cavalry) wrote from France in 1916 to Kunar Khan, describing their march to the battlefield thus:

> When we go to the trenches we go in such spirits as to the wedding of a younger brother, or like boys to the fair ... We go singing as we march and care nothing that we are going to die.[44]

Jemadar Ganda Singh (Jat, 6th Cavalry) wrote from France in April 1916 to an acquaintance in Punjab, describing the familial link with the King-Emperor, which many soldiers felt. Ganda

Singh is excited about the prospect of the 'privilege of bearing back unfurled to India the Royal Standard fluttering in the gentle breeze. It is that Royal Standard under which we risaldars and sirdars march joyfully forward. It is we and we alone who will have the privilege of unfurling that flag in India because we are, in a way, near relations of King George V.'[45]

Finally, the competitive pugnacity to uphold the honour and prestige of one's caste, tribe or regional group was an equally strong motivation. The honour of the family and ancestors was enhanced by one's brave deeds. Equally, anyone deserting would bring shame upon his extended family and village members, as the news would certainly travel back home through other compatriots. A Gurkha wrote to his friend in France in 1915: 'If you die, you will make a name up to seven forefathers and will go straight to paradise. You will become as famous as the sun. Bravo! Bravo!'[46]

Sowar Dawak Ram (Jat) wrote from France in 1915 to his friend Dafadar Gordhan Singh (16th Cavalry, Persia):

> And what you say in your letter, that you are doing business with the sword, is quite true—but what can I do here? I get no opportunity of fighting with the sword, although I came here for that very purpose ... You talk as if you were a very great hero, but what are you in comparison with us? We have come from India like lions, and are still as lions. As yet we have had no opportunity [to fight with the sword] but we hope most surely to get the opportunity.[47]

Dawak Ram is jealous of his friend who got the chance to fight with the sword against the Turks; the right manner of combat for a brave man. The Indian cavalry in Europe did eventually get the opportunity to charge on horseback, but had to wait a long time for it.

Gulab Singh (16th Rajputs) wrote from a hospital in England to his comrade in France:

> This is the first occasion on which our quivering arm is showing to a tyrannous enemy on the fields of Europe the jewel of real Rajput blood ... The time is at hand that our reputation will be exalted. It is a good opportunity to obey the behest of our superiors and to pray to God, from whom alone comes justice.[48]

Shiv Ram (Jat) wrote from England to Shri Dutt of Beri village in the Rohtak district during 1915:

> And brother, day and night I think of this—that the Divine Being may give victory to the Government, and that our fame may remain in accordance with the work which we have done. There is only one regiment of Jats [in France], but it has won renown, and there is no doubt that there is a [glorious] race of Jats. Now the people who talk say that it is a very brave race, and has done very well; and they know that those who have suffered heavy losses have done good work.[49]

Jemadar Sultan Khan (Punjabi Muslim, 18th Lancers) wrote from France to Malik Fateh Mahomed Khan in June 1917:

> Our caste is very low down in the scale, just because we do not serve in the Army. Every one knows I am an officer, but no one knows who the Buranas are ... Just look at the Biloch caste. Who used to know anything about them, and now, how do they stand? We get our livelihood here all right, but what about our izzat [honour]? The whole object

of military service is to raise the reputation of one's caste, and that is what we have to do.[50]

Most soldiers were equally concerned about the reputation of their families, and the tribe that they belonged to. Their motivations were complex, and sprang from the deepest impulses within their moral universe. The obligation of faith, loyalty to the King-Emperor, and reputation of one's family and ethnic group were the foundation of a sepoy's motivation.

One would expect that the material returns for their service would correspond to the heart-and-soul effort these soldiers brought to their job. Sadly, however, this was far from the case. The real contrast is the pay gulf between the sepoy and white officers and soldiers, and this was rationalized as compensation for white soldiers serving far from home. When the sepoys were sent abroad, however, this argument crumbled, as we shall see.

Chapter Six

Pay, Batta and Pension

I

THE MATERIAL REWARDS OF SERVICE FOR THE SEPOY WERE nothing to brag about. The actual pay was just above subsistence level. However, though the pay might have been low, it was regular and certain. But disparity between sepoys, and white officers and soldiers, extended beyond pay and included equipment, training, health, accommodation and uniform.

Despite that, military service was in high demand by native soldiers, and remained so throughout British rule. Viscount Gough said before the select committee of the Parliament in 1852, 'the military service in India [was] a very popular service'.[1] Bentinck observed in 1830 that there was no other country in the world in which men could be recruited 'with such facility and at such trifling expenses as that of the native army of the Bengal Presidency'.[2]

The earliest mentions of a sepoy's pay during the early eighteenth century fix it at four rupees.[3] The earliest Madras Presidency order prescribing the strength and pay of a company of Indian sepoys was issued in 1755, after English victories over the French and Chanda Sahib. The pay per month was Rs 6 for a sepoy, Rs 8 for a naik, Rs 10 for a havildar, Rs 16 for a jemadar and Rs 60 for a subedar.[4] The Bengal Army framed the payscale in 1779 at exactly the same rates as in Madras's 1755 order. The pay of sepoys during the critical decades of the 1750s, '60s and '70s was likely to have been the same.

The pay of a sepoy was slightly improved to Rs 7 per month in 1796,[5] and it would stay at this rate for almost a century. During this century, the GDP per head in Britain multiplied by three times. In 1895, the pay of a sepoy was raised by two rupees to Rs 9 per month.[6] This seems to have inched up to Rs 11 per month in the run-up to the First World War, also referred to as the Great War.[7] This amount was increased to Rs 18 per month for active service during the war.[8] Yasmin Khan reports the pay of a sepoy before the Second World War (WW2) to have been Rs 16 per month, which finally increased to Rs 37 per month in 1944.[9]

Even this less-than-princely sum was not straightforwardly delivered to the sepoy. During the EIC years, there were a number of deductions applied to the sepoy's pay. For many years, he literally worked for dal and roti. When the Commander-in-Chief Edward Paget recommended in 1824 to the EIC Court of Directors that the sepoy should be supplied some articles of his dress at public expense, the Court did not approve. Instead, it passed orders that a sepoy should pay for three white linen ungahs (garments similar to tunics, worn by sepoys when they are off-duty), three pairs of white linen trousers, one pair of coloured trousers, one set of beads with clasps, one pair of shoes, one kamar-band with buckle and band, one turban and cover, one knapsack and greatcoat, to be supplied to him by the quartermaster of the regiment. But 'to make the economic condition of the sepoy easy', the Court asked the Bengal Government that 'not more than five rupees per annum might be deducted as stoppages from the pay of the Bengal infantry sepoys'.[10] This practice of deductions remained in place up to the year 1852. In addition, the sepoy was required to pay for the services of a washerman, barber and sweeper. To make matters worse, from 1845 onwards, sepoys had to pay for the service of a ghanty pandy (the man appointed to strike the bell at every hour for denoting the time), too.[11] This was after the sepoy had already spent at least a month's pay on building a hut for himself as a new recruit, as no government accommodation was provided to him. During the early years of the EIC rule, there was also corruption by the British officers that directly impacted the sepoys: false musters, pocketing the pay of sepoys on furlough, illegal stoppages from their wages, etc.[12]

After all these deductions, there was very little cash left for the sepoy to live on or transfer to his family. The Court order limiting annual deduction at Rs 5 seems to have been abused by EIC local authorities. A clerk in the commissariat of the Bengal Army noted in 1847 that after clearing all dues, the sepoy often actually received only one rupee eight annas, or even as little as one anna, in cash per month. Indeed, sometimes he received nothing, and had to be content that his dues were being settled.[13] Captain Briggs stated: 'Their [sepoys'] pay ... yields them little more than a day labourer and less than many menial servants.'[14]

In comparison, the domestic servants of Europeans earned between Rs 4 to Rs 20 per month, and palankeen (palanquin) bearers Rs 7 to Rs 8 per month.[15] In 1831, Raja Ram Mohan Roy deposed before the select committee of the House of Commons on the material and moral conditions in India under the Company's administration: 'At Calcutta artisans such as blacksmiths and carpenters (if good workmen) get from Rs 10 to Rs 12 a month; common workers who do inferior plain work 5 or 6 rupees; masons from 5 to 7 rupees a month; common labourers about 3.5 and some 4 rupees a month and palanquin bearers the same.'[16] Henry Lawrence highlighted the underpayment in the native army:

> Also we should expect the Soobedar and Jemadar to be content with 67 and 24 rupees a month respectively while in the Civil Department their fellows, ten and twenty years younger enjoy 500, 600 and even 1,000 rupees and while they themselves if under a native ruler would be Generals if not Rajahs or Nawabs.[17]

It should be added that a sepoy had other advantages including promotion prospects, rations in the field, prize money in action or 'batta', and of course the coveted pension. These, along with his desire to maintain the status that went with a soldier's profession, perhaps counterweighed the monetary disadvantages compared to other professions.

However, no such redeeming incentives were available when comparing the sepoy's pay and benefits to that of white officers and even soldiers. After deductions and stoppages (much fewer than a sepoy's), a white soldier was paid Rs 9 per month in the mid-nineteenth century.[18] Besides, there were a number of other advantages and benefits available to the white soldier. Even 'a private in India cannot draw his own water, nor cook his own victuals, nor could he, till lately, clean his own boots, nor shave his chin'.[19] The cost of employing a white soldier in India was four times that of employing a sepoy. While this higher cost might not have been paid out directly in salary, it did reflect itself in other facilities, including accommodation, health, entertainment, equipment, pension, etc. In 1921, Commander-in-Chief Henry Rawlinson pointed out that 6,000 British soldiers cost the Government of India the same as 25,000 Indian soldiers.[20] V. Longer estimates that the average annual cost of maintaining a British soldier was Rs 2,500 per annum compared to Rs 631 per annum for an Indian sepoy in the 1920s.[21] Moreover, as a retired officer observed, 'The European corps take no share in the rough ordinary duties of the service ... They are lodged, fed, and paid in a manner unknown to other soldiers.'[22]

The disparity was not entirely unnoticed by the sepoys. In 1886, the 3rd Gurkha Regiment was discontented and made demands for equal pay with British troops. Those daring to ask for equal pay were tried by a court martial. After trial, four men were sentenced to hard labour.[23]

If there was a glaring disparity between the pay and incentives of white soldiers compared to sepoys, the gulf between them and the white officers was obscene. This gulf was acutely felt by Indians because only white Britons were allowed to be officers in the Army. In 1855, even an ensign in the infantry was paid Rs 203 per month as basic salary, a captain Rs 415, and a colonel Rs 1,295; compared to the 7 rupees per month of a sepoy.[24] A white officer started at a base pay twenty-nine times that of a sepoy. We have already seen that the white private was paid better and enjoyed a more comfortable lifestyle than his Indian peer, with four times as much being spent on the white troops. However, the base salary was a very small part of the perks of a white officer in India. John Jacob lampooned the junior officer of the Bengal Army in 1857 thus:

> He must not go out in the sunshine, he must travel in a palki instead of on horseback, he must be punkaed, and tattied, and God knows what else; he must have a khansamaun, a kidmutgar, a sirdar bearer and bearers, and a host of other servants, one for his pipe, another for his umbrella, another for his bottle, another for his chair, etc., all to do the work of one man.[25]

Dr Gerald Bryant estimates that in 1766 a Bengal captain on campaign was entitled to allowances worth Rs 520 over and above his basic pay of Rs 120 per month.[26]

This disparity was felt particularly acutely as no native soldier could attain a rank higher than that of a British ensign, no matter the length of service. Holmes observes:

> Though he [the sepoy] might give signs of the military genius of a Hyder, he knew that he could never attain the pay of an English subaltern, and that the rank to which he might attain, after some thirty years of faithful service, would not protect him from the insolent dictation of an ensign fresh from England.[27]

A retired officer noted, 'The entire army of India amounts to 315,520 men costing £9,802,235. Out of this sum no less than £5,668,110 are expended on 51,316 European officers and soldiers.'[28] In 1859, the 1,000 sepoys of an Indian battalion at full strength received between them Rs 7,000 a month, whereas its twenty-six European officers earned a total of Rs 9,861.[29]

Paltry though his pay from the EIC might be, in one respect it marked a positive departure from the prevailing practice in the eighteenth century. It was paid—barring some exigencies—regularly by the EIC. Indian princes often kept their troops in arrears, sometimes as security to avoid defection. For a peasant soldier, who could combine farming with a career in the army, it might work well to be paid for part of the year. For standing troops, it was a source of friction, and often put them in conflict against their employers. The minor improvement by the EIC of paying its sepoys regularly had a revolutionary impact on the military labour market of Hindustan.

It should be noted that barring Raje Shivaji, who paid his troops regularly, almost all native powers kept their soldiery in arrears. It perhaps explains the meteoric successes that Shivaji experienced in his short career. It also accounts for the failure of his successors to extend the nascent state he founded into a sustainable indigenous polity that could have replaced the Mughal rule. Eventually, the task fell on a foreign trading company, which filled the vacuum left by the native powers in the military labour market.

An infantry soldier in Raje Shivaji's army were paid between Rs 9 and Rs 13 during the seventeenth century, depending on their seniority.[30] The Mughal infantry sepoy during the eighteenth century earned between Rs 6 and 8 annas, to Rs 10 per month.[31] The Sikh sepoy, under Ranjit Singh's rule in the early nineteenth century, received between Rs 7, and Rs 8 and 8 annas per month.[32] When it came to the regularity of pay, the EIC trumped the native powers, far and wide. William Irvine in his study of the Mughal Army states that 'this [soldiers' pay in arrears] was the case in the very best of times.'[33] Similarly, Surendra Nath Sen observes that the pay of the Maratha soldier 'was allowed to fall in arrears in the Peshwa days'.[34] Besides, the Mughal soldiers were regularly deprived of one or two months' pay in a year, similar to the case of the soldiers under Ranjit Singh, to whom 'monthly payments were not regularly made; …they were normally paid five times a year.'[35]

In 1838, Captain Osborne, Governor-General Auckland's nephew and military secretary, visited Maharaja Ranjit Singh's court at Lahore. Captain Osborne observes:

> But the vice of old age, avarice, is fast creeping upon him [Ranjit Singh]; and at this moment, two out of three of his regular infantry regiments at Peshowar are in a state of open mutiny for want of their pay, one of them being eighteen, and the other twenty-two months in arrears. With six millions sterling in his treasury at Amritsir, such is his love of money, that he will risk the loss of his kingdom rather than open his hoards, and disgusts his people and army by this ill-timed and cruel parsimony; at a time, too, when his most bitter enemies, Dost Mahommed Khan and

the Afghans, are only watching for the first favourable opportunity to attempt his destruction.[36]

There might be some exaggeration, but the import of regular pay, and the absence of it in the most significant native power left in Hindustan, is very clear.

In contrast, as early as 1785, the EIC directors emphasized the vital importance to the Company of its reputation as a good paymaster. They laid it down that 'the leading principle of the Company's Government should be that the pay of the soldier ought never to be in arrear; while there was a rupee in the treasury, he was to be paid, every other article of expenditure being postponed to that consideration.'[37] Thus, the Company's sepoys felt the advantage of enjoying a regular payment each and every month.

Besides regular payment, there was one more novel feature of EIC employment that endeared itself to the sepoys: the pension. 'The pension is our great hold on India',[38] said Viscount Gough before the select committee of 1852 on the governance of Indian territories. This was no mere boast. The formal pension was a favour previously unknown to an Indian soldier, where before there had only been a rudimentary system of benefits for soldiers who died or were invalided in the service of Indian princes. Irvine mentions that the Mughal Emperor Humayun provided for the dependants of his soldiers who fell in service, but is otherwise silent on the issue.[39] Wounded soldiers of the Maratha army received a special allowance according to the nature of their wounds, while orphans of soldiers who died in active service were awarded a pension—called Balparveshi—by the state.[40] Under Ranjit Singh, there was a 'kind of allowance' sometimes granted to the families of the dead and wounded.[41]

The East India Company instituted a regular system of pensions, which proved to be very popular with the potential recruits and sepoys. Initially, Robert Clive used a gift of Rs 5 lakh, bequeathed to him by Mir Jafar in 1765, to set up the Lord Clive's Fund. The fund excluded sepoys, and provided for the relief of disabled white officers and men and widows.[42] Over time, the pension as a benefit was extended to the sepoys and their families. Under EIC rules, every native soldier was allowed to enjoy a pension of Rs 3 per month, provided he had served for a minimum of twenty years. A jagir system of pension was also in vogue between 1782 to 1811, by which land grants were made. New regulations in 1837 permitted a pension of Rs 4 per month after fifteen years' service, and a higher rate of Rs 7 per month after forty years of service.[43]

On his part, the sepoy remained loyal to his employer, knowing the overall intention of the Company was to keep faith. Even when, on some occasions, his pay and emoluments were delayed, the sepoy proved that he was not just a mercenary changing sides on the first instance to the highest bidder. During the Anglo-Mysore war of 1781–84, the payment to sepoys was delayed for months. Lt. Col. Wilson observes:

> It is worthy of remark that while the British soldiers were always paid up to date, or nearly so, the native army, serving alien masters, was kept constantly in arrears for several consecutive years, notwithstanding which, and the extreme severity of the service, it steadily resisted, with few exceptions, the numerous offers conveyed by the commissaries of Hyder and Tipu. Such fidelity, under similar circumstances, is without parallel in the military history of any nation.[44]

After escaping with his life during the expedition against Chet Singh of Banaras in 1781, Warren Hastings observed:

On my arrival at Chunar I found myself in great and immediate distress for want of money. The troops were some four and other five months in arrears; [but I have] however great pleasure in testifying that distressed as the sepoys were for the want of money, they never manifested the least symptoms of discontent.[45]

II

There were two other elements of monetary compensation a sepoy received. The first was batta, loosely translated as incentive pay or hardship pay. This was in addition to the base salary, and was meant to compensate for hardships during active service, and especially service beyond the borders of the sepoy's native territory. The second was prize money or booty, which was more prevalent during the early part of the EIC rule. Both these elements were available to both white officers and troops as well as sepoys. In fact, the rates for white officers were extremely rich, and often the sepoy was discriminated against in favour of the white troops.

These two pay elements were often a bone of contention with the officers and soldiers alike. The disparity often caused much heartburn to the sepoys, and on occasion led to mutinies and threatened the EIC's government in Hindustan. Since there was a greater level of discretion involved in their grant, the discrimination on these items stung more than the known and understood difference in the basic pay scale. These often discretionary incentives were prevalent during the EIC's rule, and were done away with during the late nineteenth century, when the Crown took over. The exception was the allowance on overseas expeditions, which continued but was better laid in policy, and made less discretionary.

The reader will recall that in 1763 a war had broken out in Bengal between the EIC and the Nawab Mir Kasim. Mir Jafar was restored as the Nawab while the Bengal Army chased Mir Kasim to Awadh by the end of 1763. On his restoration, the beleaguered the Nawab Mir Jafar had promised a donation to the troops upon their victory against Mir Kasim. The promised award was not distributed to the troops until early 1764, despite their success. The European troops of the Company's field force at Sawant mutinied in February 1764, and it was learnt that the 'French portion of these mutineers intended to join the army of the Nawab of Awadh and to make themselves the masters of the country'.[46] Captain Jennings, the commander at Sawant, with great difficulty and the promise of the early distribution of prize money, managed to convince the European troops to return to their quarters, and summoned the Nawab for prompt payment of the donation. Sepoy units so far were loyal, and were in fact marched against the white troops to bring them to heel.

Nawab Mir Jafar sent one lakh rupees as earnest money, which was immediately distributed, but now it was the turn of the sepoys to be disgruntled. Each European sergeant received Rs 80, each corporal Rs 60, and each private Rs 40; the sepoy sergeants (havildars) were offered only Rs 12 each, the corporals (naiks) Rs 9 each and the sepoys only Rs 6 each.[47] The sepoys registered their protest against this discrimination, and like their European comrades, decided to stand against the authorities. The European soldiers tried to intimidate the sepoys because they did not want to share their spoils. Fortunately, Captain Jennings seemed to have averted escalation by improving the prize for havildar, naik, and sepoys to Rs 40, 30 and 20 respectively.

A few months passed, and the initial assault by the forces of Awadh and Mir Kasim on Patna was repelled. Major Hector Munro now took command of the EIC forces in Bengal on 13 August 1764. While the enemy forces were hovering around Buxar, signs of sepoy discontent were discovered in the Patna station. The immediate cause was the reduction of their batta to half. Major Pemble, the commander at Patna, reported that his predecessor had promised the sepoys that 'on their achieving victory their *cartouche* [cartridge] boxes would be filled with money reward'.[48] Not only were they disappointed at the delay of and discrimination over the prize money payment, the batta seemed to have been reduced while inflation was high in the war-torn province of Bihar and Bengal. Major Pemble managed to restore the batta to the full amount, but on the issue of less prize money, the Council in Calcutta observed, 'Prize money was an indulgence that none had a right to ask and it had been divided according to the approbation of the Nawab who gave it [and hence it could admit] of no alteration.'[49] This, of course, was a lie. The Nawab was a puppet of the Council, and if they had insisted, they could have increased the sepoys' prize money to match the European soldiers. No such thing was done. There is no conclusive evidence that the slight improvement in prize money that the sepoys of the field force at Sawant achieved under Captain Jennings in February was implemented across all the sepoy battalions in Bengal. It is very possible that the sepoys in Patna and other stations were still protesting against the Rs 6 each, and could have been satisfied with the increase to twenty rupees each, even if it was half of what was given to a European private.

In the absence of redress for their genuine grievances, the sepoys' insubordination spread. The 1st Sepoy Battalion at Monier had seized their arms and imprisoned their officers on 8th September. This was the first serious mutiny of Indian sepoys. The sepoys released their officers the next day, who at once left for Chupra, the closest station with EIC troops. The sepoys clearly did not intend to harm their officers, and had expected to follow the example of their white compatriots in achieving their objective of fair distribution of prize money. A sepoy battalion and detachment of marines promptly marched from Chupra, and apprehended the mutinous sepoys at Monier, where they were surprised and arrested. The arrested sepoys were stripped of their arms and marched back to Chupra.

The disarmed mutineers were paraded in front of all the troops at the Chupra parade ground, who were fully armed and accompanied with field guns, on 13 September. The commanding officer of the mutinous battalion was asked to identify the twenty-four ringleaders. On identification, they were tried by a general court martial, constituted of the officers of the two native battalions, one of which arrested the mutineers. Major Munro took care to warn the court that 'if proper sentence was not passed, no regard would be paid to the same and proper notice would be taken of them'.[50] The court did not disappoint Major Munro, and sentenced the guilty soldiers 'to be blown away from the guns'.

There were four six-pounder guns on the parade ground at Chupra. On Major Munro's confirmation of the court's order, four of the condemned men were tied to the guns with their bodies over the muzzles. As the men were being bound, four tall, stately grenadiers stepped forward from among the ill-fated twenty-four and 'represented that, as they had always held the post of honour in life, it was due to them that they should take precedence in death'. Their plea was accepted; the four men from companies of line were untied and the four grenadiers took their place. At a signal from the commander, the matches were put to the touchholes and the four guns were fired, scattering fragments of their bodies over the plain. Seeing their comrades' bodies blown to smithereens, horror gripped the audience. This did not prevent Major Munro from blowing up sixteen more men, four at a time. Four were reserved to suffer the same fate in the presence of another battalion at a nearby station, which had shown signs of insubordination.

The sword of discipline was particularly harsh upon the sepoys. While the white mutineers only a few months ago had improved their share in prize money, a different fate awaited the sepoys.

Perhaps they had gone too far when they imprisoned the officers, but negotiating with their employer over pay arrears and grievances was usual in India at the time. As most native princes kept their soldiers in arrears, when the war bells tolled, it occasioned a parley between the commander and the soldiers. The latter would often collectively refuse to march until their dues were settled. Some settlement would be reached before the army set itself to the task of confronting the enemy. In this milieu, negotiating over pay and benefits was not understood to be a crime deserving such severe punishment. The sepoys of 1st Battalion suddenly realized that a code of conduct which was alien to them would be exactly enforced. Despite the shock, they met their fate with moving composure.

The Company, on its part, employed the most brutal form of execution which had been the hallmark of Mughal oppression. No European soldier was ever blown by the gun, neither by the English nor the French in India. What is more, no European had been executed in India since 1674 by the Company.[51] However, the existential fear that mutiny by Indian sepoys created in the British officers' minds meant that any outbreaks by native sepoys would be brutally crushed, while the white troops were treated with kid gloves.

The flare-ups over batta and pay arrears continued to burst out occasionally. At Arcot in 1784, Madras infantry and artillerymen lost patience with long overdue pay arrears while the men were starving. Two men were blown from guns. The same year, at Arni, the cavalry that was recently transferred from the Nawab of Arcot to Company service mutinied because the Nawab had not cleared their dues, and their families were starving. A subedar and a trooper were blown from guns. In 1798, the 27th Madras Infantry Battalion mutinied at Guntur against the non-payment of a promised allowance. The alleged ringleader was blown away by a gun. The 1815 mutiny in far-away Java was partially driven by non-payment of the men's family allotments for four years. Seventeen men were shot, and fifty put in irons for transportation.[52]

All these injustices and follies of the Company officials pale into insignificance when we come across the happenings in the Bengal Army in Sind in 1844. The disaster of the first expedition to Afghanistan (1839–42) was fresh in the Bengal Army's mind. General Pollock's Army of Retribution managed to salvage a few shreds of the Company's prestige in late 1842. As soon as the Company extricated itself from Afghan affairs, the war in Sind broke out. After the Afghan defeat, the Company unfairly took its anger out on Sind's Amir, and annexed Sind in August 1843. The Commander-in-Chief then decided that Sind should be garrisoned by the 4th, 34th, 64th and 69th battalions of the Bengal Army.

For the Awadh and Bihar sepoy, Sind was a foreign country, beyond the Indus. While the EIC faced grave difficulties, its Bombay Army troops operating in the Sind enjoyed full batta and allowances until mid-1843. The Sind climate was inhospitable, the marches long, and being populated by Muslims, there would have been no reason in the ordinary way for a Hindu sepoy to venture out that far from his home base in Awadh. All in all, in his mind, Sind was as foreign as Afghanistan or Bukhara.

The Company—frugal and cost-conscious—had permitted the extra allowances and batta so as to tide over the crisis period of 1842-43. When the war in Sind ended in mid-1843, the batta and allowances were withdrawn. The Bombay Army, which was involved in the Sind war, was replaced by the Bengal Army for post-war occupation. The Bengal Army had no inkling that the batta had been withdrawn. The army authorities did not advertise the withdrawal of the batta, as clearly it was not news that would please the Bengal sepoys who were to replace the Bombay Army.

Thus, when the four Bengal Army battalions were asked to march to Sind, they felt fully entitled to the batta and allowances. If any of the sepoys were uncertain of the batta situation, they sought to clarify it with their commanding officers. Instead of being upfront, the commanding officers assured some of the battalions that the batta was in place. From a sepoy's perspective, the scrapping of batta on the grounds that Sind was now part of the Company's Empire appeared 'a piece of legal casuistry he [the sepoy] could not understand. The Indus was still there, life in Sind was as hard as it had been in 1842, and, if his claim was legitimate in 1842, how could it lose its validity in 1844.'[53]

The 64th battalion, therefore, refused to accept pay without the expected Sind batta in June 1844, after an arduous march to Shikarpur from Ambala. The disgrace of it all was that even the Commander-in-Chief (C-in-C) was complicit in keeping the battalion under the impression that batta would be granted when they reached Sind. The Governor-General had already informed the C-in-C in March that batta could no longer be allowed. The C-in-C did not communicate this firm decision to the Commanding Officer of the battalion Lieutenant-Colonel Moseley, who continued to state that the batta would be paid. Incidentally, the Division Commander Major-General Hunter was also at Shikarpur for inspection, when the 64th refused to accept pay.

Feeling utterly betrayed, the sepoys 'in an instant were off to their lines making use of most abusive language and declaring they had been deceived.'[54] The Major-General had the good sense not to force the issue, and continued to urge the sepoys to remain calm on the promise that although he did not have the power to grant batta, he would represent their grievances to the government. Finally, he realized that the men had been deceived, and removed Moseley from the command of the battalion and granted him leave of absence. The C-in-C, himself being complicit in this deception, criticized the righteous action of Hunter against Moseley for misleading the sepoys. The battalion had been in turmoil since October 1843 on the batta issue, and Moseley as the commanding officer had the ultimate responsibility to be upfront with them as he was aware that the future of batta was uncertain, whereas he kept assuring them to the contrary.

Hunter's tactful handling of the situation saved the day, and finally he managed to identify thirty-nine ringleaders, and put them under arrest. The battalion was not was allowed to be disbanded, because two other native regiments were recently disbanded. So, a middle path was chosen, and the battalion allowed to continue service. The court martial was held on 22 July 1844. Moseley was accused by Hunter of being 'of an imperious and abusive nature'. He also added, 'Either by way of pleasantry or in ridicule, [Moseley] had often called the men of his regiment the black goralog (a word used to describe white Europeans by natives) which displeased the sepoys very much.'[55]

The court sentenced six of the thirty-nine to be immediately executed; the rest received imprisonment sentences of various lengths, and only one was acquitted.[56] Lieutenant-Colonel Moseley managed to escape with the relatively lenient sentence of being cashiered.

The 34th Infantry Battalion had reached Ferozepore from Meerut in early February. On 9 February, this battalion too refused to march to Sukkur, unless they received the full batta and allowances. There ensued a frantic exchange of communication between the Commanding Officer Major Wheeler, the Commander at Ferozepore Major-General Vincent, the C-in-C Gough, and Governor-General Ellenborough. The purport of the exchanges was the same as for the 64th battalion. The C-in-C and Vincent requested for allowances to be restored, and the Governor-General refused outright. The battalion refused to give in, and was marched back to Meerut in March 1844. The battalion was disbanded at Meerut parade ground on 26 March.

The disbanding of the 34th didn't stem the tide, and two more battalions now got infected with the mutinous spirit over the same grievance. The 69th and 4th Infantry had been marching from Shahjahanpur and Bareilly respectively towards Ferozepore in February, when the 34th had turned openly mutinous. Efforts were made to halt these two battalions at some intermediate point, to prevent their encountering men of the mutinous 34th. However, there was no available station with sufficient supplies, and both these battalions reached Ferozepore much before the 34th was dispersed. Therefore, they were all well aware of the dispute, and were equally anxious.

The 69th refused to march to Sukkur unless batta was assured. An olive branch was proffered to the sepoys, in the form of a reassurance that their officers were remonstrating with the C-in-C, and after much discussion and cajolery, the majority agreed to march. Ninety dissidents were immediately paid up and discharged, as any attempts to discipline them would have reignited discontent in the remaining battalion. Finally, the 69th sailed for Sukkur in April.

The 4th Infantry would experience more turbulence before departing for Sind. On their arrival at Ferozepore, they were fully aware of the uncertainty around batta. The battalion did not unload their bullock-carts on arrival. The Commanding Officer Major Caley let the brash Lieutenant Young into the situation, which he was ill-equipped to handle. When Young forcefully ordered the sepoys to unload the bullock-carts, Davedeen Singh, one of the sepoys, asked: 'How could four files [a number of troops drawn up in a column] unload a hackery when it took 120 men to do it?'[57] Young struck Davedeen Singh on the face with his bayonet. The trouble started, and the men surrounded Young 'all at once in a threatening manner'.[58] The regiment immediately was up in arms and in a state of open mutiny. Captain Goldney, the commander of 9th Company, demanded one of the men to hand over his musket and took it. However, soon 'the man wrested it back'. Goldney drew his sword at this insubordination.

Caley then realized the disaster into which he had allowed the regiment to drift by allowing junior officers to thus openly offend the sepoys. He immediately withdrew his order to unload the bullock-carts, and temporary peace was restored in the lines.

During a court of enquiry, Young admitted having struck Davedeen Singh and Ram Singh and medical certificates showed both Davedeen Singh and Ram Singh 'had a slight puncture of the skin on the right cheek'.[59] Goldney was acquitted, but Young was held guilty and placed under arrest. He was later released with an admonition to have greater restraint on his temper in the future, and temporarily removed from command. Given his infringements, he escaped lightly.

The tense stalemate continued for a few days. On learning that the 69th had submitted, most of the battalion finally agreed to march, except for 190 sepoys and one naik. Caley breathed a sigh of relief, and instead of putting them to court martial, prudently discharged all the 190 sepoys and the naik. The C-in-C was much incensed at the decision of both the commanding officers of the 69th and 4th for not showing the courage to discipline the mutinous sepoys. However, the same prudence required him to swallow his pride, and be content with the disbanding of the 34th and the court martial of the ringleaders of the 64th. The 4th and 69th battalions went scot-free.

The Court of Directors in London, from a far distance, were critical of the Governor-General for acting so imprudently and risking a mutiny in the Bengal Army on such a wide scale. *The Friend of India* wrote that it was impossible 'to deny that the men had reason and equity on their side however objectionable might be the mode in which they had forced their claims on the notice of Government'.[60] The *Bombay Times* said: 'If the Company was not in a position to pay their troops on such a scale as to secure their service let them contract the boundaries of their empire and limit the strength of their army.'[61]

The same story was repeated in 1849, when the Bengal Army sepoys defeated the Khalsa Army after a fierce fight. Punjab, previously a foreign territory, was now annexed and batta removed for the garrison stationed in the restive province. The anxiety and heartburn it caused led to mutiny in various regiments. The 66th Infantry Battalion had to be disbanded and forty-six men were imprisoned, some being assigned to 'chain gangs'; forty-nine men were dismissed from service.

In 1886, the 3rd Gurkha Regiment had a 'tumultuous' gathering at Almora because of proposed cuts in 'dearness allowance' for rice. We also notice that one of their demands was equal pay with the British troops, which most sepoys from Hindustan had grudgingly accepted as unachievable.

While in India, the white soldier claimed higher pay on account of the distance from his home, and the associated hardship. While not perfect, this had come to be accepted as it was by most sepoys and the authorities. The challenge arose when both the sepoy and the white soldier served outside India and England, jointly in the cause of the Company or the Empire. As it happened, the disparity and the discrimination experienced by the sepoy remained on overseas service.

During WW1, a British private was paid one shilling a day, which roughly translated to Rs 22 per month,[62] compared to the Rs 16 per month paid to the sepoy. The disparity was applied not just to the regular pay. About 6,500 Indian and 2,750 British soldiers were taken as prisoners by the Ottoman Army after the disastrous British surrender at Kut-al-Amara during WW1.[63] In captivity, the Indian sepoys could not escape the imperial hierarchy, in such a mundane matter as the POW (prisoner of war) compensation according to the laws of war. Sisir Sarbadhikari, a Bengali medical assistant, who was part of the garrison taken prisoner at Kut, left a moving account of their travails. He remarks on 12 February 1917 that money was distributed to the prisoners: 'Five liras for the whites, four for the Russians and three liras for us. The money comes from British or Indian POW funds, but still the Russians get more than us. Not only are we a defeated race, we're black on top of that.'[64] Sarbadhikari adds in July 1918:

> Some funds have arrived for us from the Red Cross Society—3 liras for the British, and one and a half liras for us. We all refused it ... [But] after much persuasion ... we agreed to take the one and a half liras. What we said when we refused the money was that white soldiers are paid higher salaries in India (bharatvarsha) because they are serving in a foreign country and therefore have extra expenses ... But that argument doesn't work in this instance. Turkey is not our country, just as it is not theirs ... The differences and distinctions that have been created between whites and blacks in all things is deeply insulting to us. A Hindustani sepoy receives half the pay that a white soldier gets; his clothing and uniform is different too—the white's is better. But the white Tommy and the black sepoy both put aside their love of life to go to war, they both suffer equally—yet in the midst of shared hardship, everything possible is done to make things better for Tommy. Even his rations are different—Tommy drinks his tea with sugar, we drink it with jaggery. And what tea it is! Sacks of it lie in front of the store; people walk over it with their boots. If there's a canteen then we aren't allowed into it: only whites can buy from them ... A lot can be written about this.[65]

The pay of a British private in WW2 (who was paid the lowest of all the Allied armies) was approximately Rs 40 per month;[66] compare this to the Rs 16 paid to the sepoy. The sepoy's pay was increased to Rs 37 per month in 1944, with the British private's pay rising to Rs 60 per month.[67] Niall Ferguson gives a starker difference of

Rs 75 per month for a British soldier, Rs 18 for an Indian.[68] Even in the midst of the desperation of WW2, the disparity between the white and Indian troops remained. Troops at the Signals Training Centre at Jubbulpore, in February 1946, demanded parity with British troops. The matter was dealt with 'administratively'; a euphemism for no disciplinary action. We will turn to the details of what happened later in 1946. The sepoy in that year felt that over the course of two centuries he had more than discharged his duty to the British Empire.

III

Beyond monetary compensation, the provision of accommodation, healthcare and diet was sub-optimal, at least in the early years of the Company rule. Unlike for the white troops, the Company did not provide barracks accommodation for the sepoy. They were allotted some land to build their huts, at their own expense in the Bengal Army, and with hutting allowance in the Madras and Bombay Armies. The furniture and fixtures in a sepoy's hut consisted of a charpoy, a dhurrie and a few cooking vessels. The inadequacy and unfairness of the accommodation for sepoys was visible, and commented upon by the press of the time. The authorities were asked to do away with the unmilitary system of wretched huts—'relics of barbarism'—and build barracks for the sepoys at public expense.[69]

Florence Nightingale, while dissatisfied with the conditions of the barracks for the white soldiers in India, had this to say about the sepoy's accommodation:

> But all these conditions paled before what was endured by native troops. The native troops had no barracks, no lavatories, no baths, no kitchens, no sanitary supervision of any kind. They used the ground round them as privies

without hindrance and left cleansing to the rains. The squalor of their huts was indescribable, bodies of animals and of human beings were left unburied for days; the water they drank was stinking. Consequently, though temperate, the Bengal native soldiers were decimated by disease.[70]

The sepoys had to build their own huts as late as the eve of the Great War, and it was not until the 1930s that sepoys were housed in barracks.[71]

Any hospitalized native soldiers had to pay for medical service. Even as late as 1859, 'The native hospitals were almost altogether in a hopeless state. They were lacking in means of cleanliness or bathing, in water supply and drainage.'[72] As for food, the sepoy had to purchase his own provisions from the regimental bazaar. With his limited pay, the sepoy could only afford chapati and dal—fish, meat and vegetables being too expensive. Only when on foreign service did the sepoy receive rations from the government. The rations on foreign service might be provided by the government, but the discrimination in the quality of provisions, compared to white troops, continued. The inadequacy and discrimination in rations for sepoys in foreign service is repeatedly commented upon during the Afghan campaign and the Mesopotamia theatre during WW1.

Indian soldiers frequently received smaller rations during the critical Mesopotamia campaign in the Great War. British soldiers received fairly large quantities of meat, bread and either potatoes or green vegetables, along with smaller amounts of butter, jam and tea. The Indian diet consisted primarily of atta, or chickpea flour, which was made into chapatis, supplemented by milk, lentils, vegetables and assorted condiments and spices. Those who ate meat were given goat meat. It was no coincidence that by the last six months of 1916, more than 11,000 Indian soldiers succumbed to scurvy.[73]

Until the Great War, there were no hospitals for the Indian troops.[74] As late as WW2, healthcare for Indian soldiers was pitiful compared to the white soldiers. During WW2 in the Burma theatre, the English nurses saw and commented upon the poor state of health facilities for the Indian soldiers. There were six times more nurses per patient in British hospitals compared to Indian general and military hospitals.[75] When Nurse Lilian Pert raised with British authorities the shocking neglect and deficiencies, she also remarked, 'By the tone of their remarks [I] might almost have made an improper suggestion by saying that English women should nurse Indian soldiers!'[76] More about the British obsession on keeping the white women away from Indians, even within the tragic settings of Brighton hospital in WW1, and elsewhere, later. Suffice it to say that the imperial attitudes did no justice to the sepoy's health.

Great pomp and show accompanied the King-Emperor opening one of his palaces' gates for the treatment of wounded Indian soldiers from the Western Front during WW1. This palace at Brighton was, in fact, a municipal property, long since transferred to the local authorities. However, the propaganda was used to the hilt. The postcards showed photos of recuperating sepoys with the oriental domes of the Brighton pavilion in the background. The postcards and letters sent to their families by Indian soldiers mention this gracious act of the King-Emperor and his concern for his Indian 'sipahis'. Inside the Brighton pavilion, the hierarchies of the Empire were no less stifling. The English female nurses were banned from providing care to the Indian sepoys. The sepoys were not allowed to freely move about in Brighton town. The resentments came out at the Kitchener Hospital in Brighton when an Indian sub-assistant surgeon fired at the commander of the Hospital, Col. Bruce Seton. The colonel survived thanks to the timely intervention of another Indian soldier, who wrote about the event: 'By the grace of God the revolver missed fire and I immediately caught hold of the man.'[77]

While the sepoys on the Western Front benefitted from being too close to Britain to be neglected without it becoming public knowledge, no such luck was afforded to more than half a million sepoys engaged against the Turks in Mesopotamia. It was in Mesopotamia that a disaster of unimaginable scale unfolded, where the medical facilities available for the sepoys were grossly inadequate, almost non-existent. The tragedy began in late 1915, when General Townshend extended supply lines in a vainglorious attempt to take Baghdad for British 'prestige'. More about this disaster later, but such was the situation at the Battle of Ctesiphon in November 1915:

> Hospital ships with accommodation for five hundred had been made ready at Lajj, but these were soon filled with casualties which came trickling back over the desert ... when on the night of the 22nd the battle casualties began to arrive, their thin clothing soaked through, and their bodies almost flayed by the bitter wind which was blowing, no room could be found for them. These men, jolted over the rough desert in the springless, cushionless Army Transport Carts which had been improvised as ambulances—ambulances so ineffective that wounded men with broken limbs threw themselves out and crawled across the desert on hands and knees rather than endure the agony of the shaking, or used dead bodies as cushions between them and the bottom of the carts—these men arrived to be stuffed into a ship, closer than hounds are packed into a hound-van, there to endure the voyage to Basra.[78]

The situation was no better in January next year, when a relief under General Aylmer was smashed by the Turks:

Men lay out all night in pitiless, icy rain, dying from exposure because the medical personnel—heroic in its efforts—was hopelessly inadequate to succour them. In the morning, many sepoys were found dead without a mark upon them … Still later, men arrived at Amara with wounds which for eight days had remained untended—wounds which were putrefying, gangrenous and full of maggots.[79]

Their misery did not seem to end when Townshend finally surrendered at Kut on 29 April 1916. Sisir Sarbadhikari notes the discrimination suffered by the sepoys even in such dreadful conditions, while the defeated garrison—taken prisoner at Kut—was being transferred to Baghdad on 12 May:

The whites are sitting in comfort in the lower deck, every one of them has space to sleep. We're on the upper deck—there's no roof over our heads, and we scarcely have enough space to sit.[80]

The service conditions of the sepoys were inferior to those of the white soldiers. Not just pay and allowances; the disparity continued in basic facilities like accommodation and healthcare. Even on active foreign service, and during the world wars, the hierarchies of the Empire remained. Some efforts were made to reverse this by the end of the Second World War. However, that would prove to be too late.

Chapter Seven

Trust Deficit

France has its Arab Generals and Russia has many Asiatic Generals, but Liberal England restricts its best native officers to posts subordinate to that of sergeant-major.[1]
—*The Tribune*, 1914

I

THE BRITISH RAJ RESTED ON A FUNDAMENTAL CONTRADICTION. The British Indian Army was the guarantor of the British rule in India, and by extension was also the biggest risk to the foundation of the Raj. What if the very foundation on which the British rule was built crumbled? After all, the foundation rested as much in the minds of the Indian sepoys, who stayed loyal to the British Raj out of their personal convictions. What if that loyalty was tampered with, or couldn't be guaranteed? This was a dilemma for which the leaders of the Empire had no solution. It, however, meant that there was a degree of distrust towards the native soldier from the beginning to the end of the Raj. Their utter and absolute dependence on the sepoys also made British leaders suspicious of them. This suspicion could not be removed from the minds of the officers, civil servants and politicians, no matter how much the sepoy proved his worth with his toil and blood. From this perspective, the British Empire in India—which lasted almost two centuries—is a wonder.

Beneath the surface, the military leaders of Raj frequently revealed their anxieties:

> We are trying an experiment never yet tried in the world, maintaining a foreign dominion by means of a native army ... Even if all India could be brought under the British dominion, it is very questionable whether such a change ought to be desired ... the Indian Army, having no longer any war-like neighbours to control, would gradually lose its military habits and discipline and the native troops would have leisure to feel their own strength and for want of other employment, to turn it against their European masters.[2]

Governor General Bentinck concluded that the Raj was indeed always in danger when:

> ... one hundred millions of people are under the control of a Government which has no hold whatever on their affections, when out of this population is formed that army on the fidelity of which we rely principally for our preservation, when our European troops, of whose support alone we are sure under all circumstances, are so exceedingly limited in number and efficiency as to be of little avail against any extensive plan of insurrection.'[3]

Mistrust lingering in the background, the leaders of the Raj employed a number of devices to mitigate the risk of the sepoy losing his fidelity. Not all these measures were laudatory, but they did succeed in maintaining the Indian Army's loyalty to the Raj, broadly speaking. Barring the rebellion of 1857, it was only during WW2 that the Indian sepoy finally became unsure of the future course of action. The sepoy's loyalty remained unfazed despite the broken promise of self-government after WW1, and the nationalist movement within the civilian population.

The Raj employed three tools to deal with the doubts about its Indian soldiers' loyalty: firstly, the religious, cultural and social differences between various groups of soldiers were accentuated to keep them from working as a united force; secondly, the weapons and training of the native sepoy were always kept inferior to that of the white soldier; and finally, the command and control of the army was kept in the hands of the British officers. During the 1857 rebellion, the Bengal Army sepoys overcame the first handicap by uniting Hindus and Muslims. The disadvantage in weapons was partially compensated by their motivation, and by helping themselves to the government armoury. It was the third barrier—lack of effective leadership and field command experience—that the Bengal Army sepoys could not overcome. Their rebellion was, therefore, eventually quelled, but not without the help of a new class of Indian soldiers, hired from Punjab. It would be only during WW2 that all three limitations were effectively overcome, with a number of experienced Indian commissioned officers in the army having fought across the world, capable of leading an insurrection across India.

II

The foundations of British military power in India were laid during the internecine civil war raging between the remnants of the Mughal Empire and among the vigorous powers that rose against Aurangzeb's tyranny. The EIC had been in India since 1600, and for 150 years they were patient traders and law-abiding residents and visitors. No magical improvement in English arms had occurred suddenly in the mid-eighteenth century, when the EIC found itself the military master of a large swathe of Hindustan. They happened to be at the right place at the right time, when the Mughal state apparatus was being dismembered. If one surveys mid-eighteenth century India, Marathas, Jats and Sikhs had wrested control of most of the Mughal provinces, with the notable exception of Hyderabad, Bengal and Awadh. It was in Hyderabad and Bengal that the English had notable initial successes. The subahdars of both these provinces were hard-pressed by Maratha invasions. However, before the Marathas could overrun these provinces, they passed under the security umbrella of the EIC. A country the size of Europe, thus divided in its government structure, was equally divided in its soldiery, who belonged to different faiths, communities and ethnic groups.

These divisions and differences often broke out even within the same army commanded by a prince. As early as 1632-33, the English traveller Peter Mundy, travelling between Surat, Agra and Patna, hired 440 Jats, Baluchis, carters and cameleers, who were all armed, in his caravan.[4] Mundy seemed to have had a tough time controlling his small army. At some stage, the Baluchis and camel-drivers, who were Muslims, clashed with the Jats and carters, who were Hindus. One Baluchi was killed in this clash. This made Mundy think that it is too explosive to take both Jats and Baluchis, and both carters and cameleers, in one force. Later, Mundy reports that even the carters and Jats fought with each other. The differences between the men, if not appropriately and sensitively managed, often led to conflicts. As a corollary, if a compartmentalized system of class- and community-based organization of the army were achieved, each unit could act as an effective control on the other, belonging to a distinct class. This is precisely what the EIC designed for its Indian Army.

Robert Clive, fine strategist as he was, understood the value of religious differences as a potential bulwark against the unity of the Company's Indian Army, should it turn against its employer. When he organized the Bengal Army into three brigades in 1765, after the Company emerged as de facto ruler of Bengal from the Battle of Buxar, he laid out the process to achieve internal security. Clive proposed that the sepoys of each brigade should comprise equal numbers of 'Gentoos[5] and Mussalmans' and that a rivalry in the standard of discipline between them should be encouraged.[6] The Committee of Secrecy appointed by the House of Commons on EIC affairs in India approved and said:

> If it were only on the principle of 'Divide et impera', the Moormen and Gentoos should be separated into distinct companies. Besides the obvious reasons, other advantages might result from it, by detaching all Mussalmans or all Gentoos, into any particular country, as might be expedient in war or to conciliate their affection by rendering it more satisfactory to the inhabitants in times of peace.[7]

This ideal division of 'Gentoos and Moormen' could not always be achieved as, over the next fifty years, the Bengal Army came to be dominated by Hindu sepoys from Bihar and Awadh. But the Company's officers did not lose sight of the imbalance, and even in 1830 the Bengal Government observed: 'an unusually large number of Brahmins has of late entered service, [and] it would be desirable, to follow the proportion which formerly prevailed by giving a decided preference to the Rajputs and to the Mahomedans.'[8]

After their defeat in the second Anglo–Sikh war in 1849, the Sikhs were recruited and embedded in the Bengal Infantry battalions, as a counterpoise to the 'purabiya'[9] sepoys, who were lately showing signs of discontent. This strategy paid off during the 1857 rebellion when the Sikhs, both of the Bengal regiments as well as of the newly raised battalions in Punjab, helped the British re-conquer Delhi first, and subsequently the rest of Hindustan. To an outsider, the Sikhs' support of the EIC to re-establish its power might appear incongruous with their valiant fight against it just eight years earlier. However, the Sikhs were in fact defeated by an army comprised predominantly of purabiya sepoys, with a smaller European element. There was an undercurrent of disdain towards each other. The Sikhs had little time for the ritualistic puritan approach of the purabiya soldier, while the purabiya sepoy thought the burly Sikh was uncouth with his long hair and rough approach. Sita Ram Pandey, as we read in an earlier chapter, mentions that Sikh soldiers in fact chided him about his loyalty, after his son's execution.

The Company's administration in Punjab after defeating the Sikh kingdom was particularly mild, with low taxes, and an almost complete employment for the remnants of the Khalsa army. If anything, the Sikhs in the Company's army thought 1857 was an opportunity to teach a lesson to the purabiya sepoys, whom they held responsible for bringing about the end of the Sikh kingdom.

The committee that took evidence on points related to the reorganization of the Indian Army in London in 1858, grappled with the issue of immense diversity within the Indian Army. It suggested: 'Different nationalities and castes should be mixed promiscuously through each regiment.'[10] But these were men in London with little on-the-ground experience. As it happened, this observation was never followed in India. The EIC Army in India never recruited battalions across the citizenry as would be the case in European states. The Bengal Army prior to the Mutiny comprised regiments of homogeneous class (based on faith, caste, community, etc.). The new model settled on homogeneous companies within a regiment, while the regiment would have more than one class. By the end of the century, things came back full circle as the one-class regiments again gained popularity. The Punjab Committee's observations were more apt:

> As we cannot do without a large native Army in India ... next to the grand counterpoise of a sufficient European force, comes the counterpoise of natives against natives. At first sight, it might be thought that the best way to secure this would be to mix up all the available military races of India in each and every regiment, and to make them all general service corps. But excellent as this theory seems, it does not bear the test of practice. It is found that different races mixed together do not long preserve their distinctiveness, their corners and angles, and feeling and prejudice get rubbed off, till at last they assimilate, and the object of their association to a considerable extent is lost.[11]

Insecure, and having always to watch over their shoulders after the 1857 Mutiny, the Raj's military leadership developed its own coping mechanisms. One of the more widely known was the 'martial races' theory. This theory said that most of the Indian population was unfit or unsuitable for military service. Either they were physically weak or did not have the character and fibre to be a soldier. Predictably developed after the Mutiny, the theory lionized the new classes that came to British aid during that struggle. Gurkhas, Sikhs, Jats, Rajputs, select Muslims and Dogras were considered 'martial'. Lord Roberts was one of the greatest proponents of this theory, on which a treatise was also written by George McMunn in 1935, titled 'The Martial Races of India'. This strategy limited recruitment to the 'martial races', and shifted the recruitment ground to north-west India, Punjab in particular. This meant that at the start of the Great War, out of a population of 350 million, the military recruitment base was restricted to 35 million.

Out of this 35 million, those in the age bracket for recruitment (males between twenty to thirty-five years) were about 3 million. It restricted the pool of recruitment, but having concentrated the recruitment base, this also created an army that was different from the majority of the Indian population. The provinces from where the recruitment was done could now be given particular favours to buy their support. The inhabitants in Punjab rightly felt the positive impacts of the 'canal colonies' established under the Raj, when ex-soldiers and their relatives were settled with large land grants. The peasant of Punjab indeed had some reason to think that the government was, if not benevolent, at least just and considerate.

The observations of Lord Roberts, who was appointed Commander-in-Chief of the Bengal Army in 1885 with supervisory power over Madras and Bombay, make interesting reading:

> I made long tours in order to acquaint myself with the needs and capabilities of the Madras Army. I tried hard to discover in them those fighting qualities which had distinguished their forefathers during the wars of the last and the beginning of the present century ... and I was forced to the conclusion that the ancient military spirit had died in them as it had died in the ordinary Hindostani of Bengal and the Mahratta of Bombay, and that they could no longer with safety be pitted against warlike races or employed outside the limits of Southern India ... It was with extreme reluctance that I formed this opinion.[12] ... No comparison can be made between the martial value of a regiment recruited amongst the Gurkhas of Nepal or the warlike races of northern India and of one recruited among the effeminate races of the South.[13]

MacMunn writes that without British control the martial peoples of the north would 'eat up' the south. The British officers of the respective regiments gleefully noted and encouraged the contempt of one class against the other: the Gurkhas for the inhabitants of India, the dislike of the Sikh for the easterner, and so on. Sir Walter Lawrence adoringly and emotionally recounts a conversation with Sir Pratab Singh, regent and uncle of the Jodhpur Maharaja: 'And here was Sir Pratab, my brother by adoption, the great and courteous Rajput gentleman, telling me with terrible truthfulness that now he had only two things to live for, to fall leading a charge of cavalry against the foes of the King Emperor ... and to wipe out the Moslems from India.'[14] How much of this is what Sir Lawrence would have liked to have heard is an open question, but such competitive pugnacity was encouraged, and not too quietly, across the Army.

The fact that the three presidency armies continued as separate units until 1895, despite clear inefficiencies, is another example of how divide-and-rule thinking impacted the basic Army structure. The Bombay and Madras Armies existed as separate units because of the theory of 'watertight compartments': two compartments would keep the ship afloat even if one out of three sprang a leak. This was not entirely baseless, as during 1857, the Madras and Bombay Armies had broadly remained loyal.

All this was a matter of fine balance, for when trust is in short supply, one wrong step or excess on the scale could easily rock the boat. The divisions, helpful so long as they didn't let the Army unite for its components' own purposes, could also impact the efficacy and discipline of the force. One British officer thus observed: 'In war, under stress, there is no one like the Sikh; work him almost to death and he is magnificent. But relax, give him leisure and a chance to recuperate, and he will start to intrigue—Jat against Khattri, Manjha against Malwa or village against village—he will find some way of making allies and enemies and trying to get promotion of favour.'[15] No one can say the task of an imperial army officer was an easy one.

These exclusive strategies came under stress during the Great War, when more than a million men were required from India to serve. However, as soon as the Great War was over, the doors opened for other classes were shut again, only to be broken by the needs of WW2. The 2.5 million men could not have been found amongst the Punjab peasantry or the 'martial classes'. The recruitment had to be broad-based, and the Indian Army came close to representing a 'national' army. The results would change the destiny of India, within months of the end of the war.

III

A grand committee was constituted in 1858 in London to examine the disaster of the 1857 Mutiny, its causes and what changes ought to be implemented. Before that committee, Sir Bartle Frere, member of Lord Canning's executive council, former Chief Commissioner of Sind, made an impassioned plea:

> Indian troops must be trusted if they were to be any use at all. They could not be half-trusted. They must be armed with the most efficient weapons available, just as British soldiers must. To give them weapons inferior to the British soldier—muskets instead of rifles, as many witnesses suggested—was to underline mistrust ... And it was inefficient and wasteful. Why have two sepoys with muskets (or three with clubs) when one with a rifle can do what is needed better? If sepoys are incurably untrustworthy—which I do not believe—why have three traitors instead of one? There should be better weapons and better organization for the Indian troops—though it is as much as a man's sanity is worth to urge this truth at present.[16]

He was in a clear minority, and his words fell on deaf ears. On the issue of arms, equipment and training, the Indian sepoy was always kept inferior to the British. It would continue to be so, even at great cost, as was realized during the two world wars. In numbers, British soldiers could never match the native sepoys in the Indian Army. It was thought that the superior weapons, artillery and equipment for the British would level the playing field, in the event of a widespread mutiny by the native sepoys. This was an article of faith, and seems to have been implemented early in the development of the Company's army in India. One of the first orders from the Directors received by Major Stringer Lawrence on his arrival at Madras in 1748 was that 'no Indian, black, or person of a mixed breed, nor any Roman Catholic, of what nation so ever'[17] was permitted to be associated with any of the artillery units. The compulsions of economy made sure that this was not strictly enforced. However, the intent was clear from the very beginning.

The economic rationale favoured employing natives in artillery units, but the Court of Directors in London continued to forbid it. The Directors were clear that the native soldier could not be trusted with such a decisive weapon as artillery. However, the cash-strapped EIC Army in India did not always fully implement the wishes of the Directors. In 1771, a policy was laid down in Madras that 'natives ought to be kept as ignorant as possible of the theory and practice of gunnery,'[18] and guns attached to sepoy battalions were withdrawn. Despite the policy, up to 1784, there was one native artillery unit alongside a European unit in the Madras Army.[19] The native artillery unit was broken up the following year, with the native companies attached to the European companies as assistant native gunners to the Europeans. However, this also did not seem satisfactory. So, in 1786, very clear orders came from the Court of Directors, forbidding the entertainment of any 'native artillery or golandauz'. The native gunners and their officers already employed in the hybrid unit were asked to either transfer to the infantry units or to be employed as 'lascars' in the European companies. Lascars were not supposed to aim and fire the guns, and were considered inferior to 'golandauz'. The Directors ordered: 'None of the natives from the interior of Hindostan shall henceforth be taught the exercise of artillery.'[20] Despite the orders, in 1819 we find a battalion of native gunners had been raised again in Madras, although counterbalanced with two European battalions by then.

By the eve of the 1857 Mutiny, there were some native artillery units, but while the ratio of natives to European was five to one in the infantry, in the artillery the ratio was reversed. The few native artillery units were swept away by the changes made after the Mutiny. Ironically, the Indian gunners who mutinied gave a very good account of their skills and effectiveness. Any lingering doubts about leaving such devastating weaponry in Indian hands were thrown away. Lord Elphinstone, the Governor of Bombay, while deposing in front of the Peel Commission in 1858, said that '[it was] not judicious to train any natives of India to the use of guns. They make excellent artillerymen, and they attach great value and importance to guns, but these very circumstances make it dangerous to place them in their hands.'[21]

From 1861 onwards, there were no Indian gunners except small mountain batteries, whose guns were carried on mules. All other artillery, henceforth, was firmly in European hands. The Indian gunners either transferred to cavalry or infantry, or were pensioned off or discharged. The Indian mountain batteries were used for the frontier operations against restive tribes on the Afghan borders. One of these units was present in Dunkirk during WW2, and while chaos reigned all around them, they maintained their discipline, and were evacuated to Britain. Artillery was tightly regulated in the forces of Indian states in subsidiary alliance to the

Raj. The Eden Commission in 1879 made sure to recommend that 'on no account should arms of precision be given to the troops of Native States, that their field artillery should be kept within the smallest possible limits'.[22] It would be another three-quarters of a century before an Indian artillery unit made its appearance in 1935 in Bangalore.

Prior to Major Lawrence's organization of native infantry in companies during 1749, the native soldiers in the Company's pay were armed 'with matchlocks, bows and arrows, spears, swords, bucklers, daggers, or any other weapon they could get'.[23] Only about 900 of the 2,000 'peons' assembled at Fort St. David in early 1747 were provided with muskets. In 1754, on Major Lawrence's request, the Fort St. George Council authorized 500 buccaneer and trading guns to be sent to him for arming newly raised sepoys. Buccaneer and French pieces took longer to reload than the military muskets but were also cheaper and lighter in weight, albeit less reliable than military muskets made for European markets. Thus, the frequent issue of buccaneer pieces in large quantities suggests that the sepoy was primarily expected to provide little more than a disciplined volume of fire.[24] Their performance at Plassey, Buxar and subsequent battles proved this to be an underestimation of their capability.

The Mutiny widened the gulf between the quality of arms supplied to the sepoy and that of his European counterpart. The standard 'Brown Bess' flintlock musket of the European soldier until the mid-nineteenth century was replaced by the Minié muzzle-loading rifle during the Crimean war. The Minié rifle, in its turn, was replaced by the Enfield, first introduced in 1853-54. About 10,000 of these Enfield rifles were delivered to the European troops in India before 1857. The sepoy was armed with the 'Brown Bess' at the time. It seems to have been the intention of the Company to issue the new Enfield rifles to the sepoys too. However, the grease used in its cartridges threatened ritual pollution to Hindu as well as Muslim sepoys, as it allegedly contained cow and pig fat.

More on the cartridges and Mutiny in a later chapter, but it suffices to note here that the convulsions of 1857 served as a sufficient excuse to implement an official policy to provide the native troops with firearms of lesser lethality than those in the hands of the British soldiers. Thus, in 1857, the Inspector General of Ordnance and Magazines in India writes to the Military Department Secretary:

> The experience acquired within the last three months may have excited some doubt as to the prudence of giving such powerful pieces as the Enfield Rifles to every description of Sepoys and it may be thought advisable to arm the greater part of them with common Musquets or Fuzils.[25]

The Inspector General asked for a decision on the matter, and within a day the answer came: 'I am directed to acquaint you that for the present Enfield Rifles are not to be issued to any native corps.'[26]

After the Mutiny, the Indian soldier was issued with an improved weapon, only after the British soldier had discarded the same for an even better version. Never again would the sepoy be equipped with a weapon of the same fighting quality as that of the British. While the British soldier was armed with the Enfield rifle, the sepoy received an identical weapon without rifling, a smooth-bore Enfield musket, with less range and accuracy than the rifle. The Snider breech-loading rifle was issued to British units in 1866, and the Indians were handed the discarded Enfield rifles from the British. When the Martini-Henry rifle reached British units in 1874, the Sniders were transferred to the Indian units. In 1892, the bolt-action Lee-Metford rifle was supplied to British soldiers, and the Martini was given to Indian troops. In 1905, it seems that Lee-Metford and Lee-Enfield rifles started to be issued to Indian troops.

The British troops were already transitioning to Lee-Enfield rifles. However, the determination to issue an inferior weapon to Indian troops persisted. Even as late as 1911, when the British infantry standard weapon was the short magazine Lee-Enfield, a special model was designed as a single-shot, non-magazine weapon for the Indian troops. This, however, seems to have not been issued, and finally the compulsions of the Great War forced a degree of parity in the arms held by Indian and British soldiers.[27]

IV

'The grandsons of the Gauls, who opposed Caesar, were senators of Rome and the Jye Singhs and Jeswant Singhs led the Mughal armies, but it cannot be said that it was to any such liberality the empire of either Rome or Delhi owed its fall.'[28] These were the words of Sir Henry Lawrence in an essay in 1844 on the reduced authority and absence of command and promotion prospects for the Indian officers in the Company Army. Whether or not his statement was correct, the British Raj took no chances. The most senior Indian officer rank was that of a subedar aged over fifty, which was junior to an English ensign aged less than twenty. The native officer was allowed real command only when it was a military compulsion at the beginning of the EIC rule in the eighteenth century. Once the Company felt more settled and confident in maintaining its military hold over its dominion, one of the first casualties was the authority of the native subedars and jemadars.

The rapid and unplanned growth of the Company Army during the 1740s and 1750s occurred in response to the emerging crisis faced by the Madras and Bengal Presidencies. In an hour of crisis, the native officers led a number of expeditions, and were clearly in command of their 'war bands'. The situation changed slightly during the 1750s, when the sepoys were organized in companies, with a complement of English officers. Finally, when the battalions were formed, the command of the sepoy battalions was firmly in the hands of Europeans, the subedar restricted to the level of leading a company. There was a post of 'black commandant' that was attached to each battalion until the 1780s, that gave a ceremonial role to a native officer. The reorganization of 1796 increased the number of European officers manifold at the battalion level, and was the last in a series of changes that effectively reduced the native officers to a position inferior to a European sergeant. The grievances of the native officers multiplied during and after this period, and was considered one of the key reasons behind the 1857 Mutiny of the Bengal Army.

During the tumultuous decade of the 1750s, a number of native officers are mentioned to have commanded sizeable troops in active combat. The 'war bands' recruited by the subedars would usually comprise trusted men from their extended families and villages. It was natural for these native officers to lead their troops in action.

Thus, we hear of Subedar Jemaul Sahib, 'an officer of some reputation', who led a thousand sepoys in combat in 1756 at Tinnavelly. Subedar Jemaul Sahib is again mentioned during the defence of Fort St. George in 1758-59, when the French laid siege. Jemaul Sahib is mentioned to have led several hundred sepoys in a sortie against enemy positions.[29] Another native officer mentioned is Keser Singh, who led the Madras sepoys in an overland march to support Clive's expedition to Bengal in 1756.[30]

The repute of 'Nellore Subedar' Yusuf Khan rises above all others, and some contemporary commentators have even compared him to Clive and Lawrence. Sir John Malcolm observes: 'The name of this hero, for such he was, occurs almost as often in the page of the English historian [Robert Orme] as that of Lawrence or Clive.'[31] We have already seen in previous chapters the role played by Yusuf Khan as the 'commandant over all sepoys of the Company'. There is plenty of evidence that Subedar Yusuf Khan had independence of command, and often sparred with his fellow British officers, who sometimes found him too hard to handle.

In 1755, he accompanied Colonel Alexander Heron on an expedition, and Heron frequently clashed with Yusuf Khan. Heron was resentful and hostile of Yusuf Khan's independent attitude, and complained that Yusuf Khan was 'a brave man but by no means fit for an independent command'.[32] Heron was proved wrong and was soon disgraced, while the Nellore Subedar continued to rise to significant commands in future expeditions. In those early days, we even see the evidence of European sergeants and gunners under the command of the Nellore Subedar. Thus, when Yusuf Khan rode out from Madurai to aid the besieged garrison at Madras in 1758-59, the Madras Council ordered that 'the gunners and sergeants that command the sepoy companies must be strictly enjoined to yield entire obedience to the orders of Yusuf Khan', adding that they shall 'severely resent a contrary behaviour'.[33]

Yusuf Khan's rebellion in 1763 is often cited as the reason why the native officer's independence was curtailed. However, this seems like an excuse, as the trend of reducing the native officer's authority seems to have started much earlier. Men like Yusuf Khan rose to status and command because of the absolute necessity to rely upon native officers and men during the decade of crisis in the Madras Presidency. The existential crisis, limited resources and experience of the Company, and hostility of the French and their local allies meant the Company had to make the best use of available resources. On this matter, like many others, Robert Clive laid the foundations of the command structure that started to subordinate native officers to Europeans. Clive reports that soon after the abortive siege of Pondicherry in 1748, Lieutenant Bulkley was appointed 'commander of sepoys'.[34] It is not very clear, though, whether Bulkley's role extended beyond a general supervision. It is likely that while sepoy companies were under the command of native officers at that stage, Bulkley might have been responsible for the overall supervision. By the mid-1750s, the European officers were embedded with sepoy companies, at least in the Madras Presidency.

Nevertheless, as the examples of Keser Singh, Jemaul Sahib and many others illustrate, the native officer still had a very important role at the company level, and often held independent command. In fact, the sepoy companies were invariably identified by the name of their subedar, and this practice persisted even after the regularization of sepoy companies in 1755. Besides, the subedar had an important role, as the early British officers did not all speak the native languages. The subedar, therefore, performed the function of an interlocutor, as much as a tactical unit leader.

The watershed in the position of native officers came with the establishment of battalions in the Bengal and Madras Armies during 1757–59. The early Bengal battalion had a European captain, lieutenant and ensign assisted by a sergeant major and a few sergeants—all of them Europeans. The sepoys in the battalion were organized into ten companies, each comprising one subedar, three jemadars, five havildars, four naiks, two drummers, one trumpeter and seventy sepoys. The Madras Army had a similar structure with slight variations in the numbers. Besides, each battalion had a 'black commandant' who was to take post in front of the battalion, and was subordinate to the European commissioned officers. The Bombay Army battalions organized in 1768 were on similar lines. This greatly diluted the authority of the native officers, as the company was no longer the tactical unit where the subedar perhaps was subordinated to just one European officer. The company now would be one of the nine or ten units of the battalion, which had now become the tactical unit, reducing the autonomy of a company. The subedar was now subordinated to a number of British officers at the battalion level, and the European control of sepoys increased manifold.

The sepoys and their native officers secured a stunning victory for the Company in the Battle of Buxar in 1764. The province of Bengal was now firmly in the hands of the Company. Unfortunately, the reward for the native officer was a reduction in his authority, as the number of European officers in each sepoy battalion increased during the next year's reorganization of the Bengal Army. There would be eleven European officers for each battalion now. The Madras Army followed with similar changes in 1766. An English visitor, Mrs Kindersley, observed regarding the Bengal Army in September 1767 that she heard no instance 'of an European soldier being under a black man, for the sergeants are superior in command to even the first black officer of the army; the natives are most numerous, but the power and command is vested entirely in the Europeans'.[35]

The 'black commandant' position survived the 1765 Bengal Army reorganization, but not for long. In 1781, the Madras Army abolished the post, followed by the Bengal and Bombay Armies three years later. In one stroke, the company abolished the highest office available to a native officer in its service, even if it had been ceremonial to some extent. The number of European officers in the sepoy battalions continued to grow. By 1780, a European subaltern was in command of a sepoy company in all three presidency armies. In 1785, a European sergeant was added to the subaltern to command each company.

By the last decade of the eighteenth century, the sepoy had given ample proof of his loyalty and skills to his employer. After the Battle of Buxar, three wars with the Mysore state of Hyder Ali and Tipu, the first Anglo–Maratha war, the reduction of Chet Singh of Benares, and many other small actions entrenched the EIC's army as a formidable force in India. Despite this, the position of the native officer only continued to deteriorate. Lord Cornwallis, the Governor-General of India, submitted his elaborate plan to reorganize the Indian Army of the Company in 1794. Most of his recommendations were accepted, and the implementation started in 1796, although they were not completed until 1804. The 1796 reorganization effectively reduced the native officer to a figurehead liaison function between the European officers and the sepoys. The regimental system in all three armies now provided for forty-eight European officers per regiment. Each regiment consisted of two battalions, so the number of European officers in each battalion more than doubled from eleven to twenty-four. There was now an exclusive European chain of command for the sepoy units. The emasculation of the native officer was almost complete, and it did not escape notice, or consequences. T. Rice Holmes comments:

> But the very successes which the sepoys helped their masters to gain paved the way for their own depression ... [The English showed a] growing tendency to add to the number of their officers with each battalion and to concentrate power in their hands ... But in 1796, a further change took place ... [and] the increase in the number of European officers still further lowered the already fallen position of their native comrades. Thenceforward, there was nothing to stimulate the ambition of a sepoy ... But, for a few years, nothing occurred to show the authors of these changes how disastrous they were to prove ... It was not until the excitement of conquest, which had diverted [the sepoy's] mind, subsided, that they began to brood over their grievances.[36]

V

The days of Keser Singh, Jemaul Sahib and Yusuf Khan were long gone. The subedars and jemadars, who led their troops in battle, often held command over European soldiers and acted in camaraderie with the European commissioned officers, were a thing of the past. When new recruits joined, they would now interface with the English sergeants in the company, and not the trusted subedars of yore. Sita Ram Pandey complained about the sergeant of his company, on joining in 1814, that he was 'continually finding fault and getting me punished'.[37] He then revealed that it was because he did not give the usual 'present' (euphemism for bribe) of sixteen rupees to the drill havildar, of which five or six were to go to the sergeant. Sita Ram complained further that some sergeants 'resorted to low abuse. Numerous complaints were made to the Adjutant, but he nearly always took the side of the European sergeant, and we could obtain very little or no redress'.[38] Thus, a chain of command where the native officers were sidelined, and grievances of the ordinary sepoys were almost always under the judgement of Europeans, did not bode well.

A ceremonial position of subedar-major was created for the native officers in 1818, for each native infantry battalion. This was just a bit of eyewash, as the subedar-major continued to be subservient to even the most junior European commissioned officer. The subedar-major rank was not even comparable to the 'black commandant' position that was abolished during 1781–84. The new rank had higher pay and pension attached to it, but no command responsibility. The 1824 reorganization retained the high number of European officers in each sepoy battalion, while doing away with the regimental system introduced in 1796. The position of the native officers did not see any change. Wise statesmen such as Sir Henry Lawrence considered this arrangement both unjust and dangerous. He noted in an essay during 1844:

> There are many commandants in the Maratta and Seikh service, who were privates in our army. General Dhokul Singh, now at Lahore, was a drill naik in one of our sepoy corps; and Raja Buktawar Singh, one of the richest and

most powerful men at Oude, was a Havildar in our cavalry. But is it not absurd that the rank of Subedar and Russaldar Major is the highest that a native can attain in a native army of nearly three hundred thousand men, in a land too that above all others have been accustomed to see its military merit rewarded and to witness the successive rise of families from the lowest conditions, owing to gallantry in the field?[39]

Sir Henry followed up with another essay in 1856, where he wrote:

The minds of Subedars and Rissaldars, sepoys and sowars, can no more with safety be forever cramped, trammelled and restricted as at present, than can a twenty-foot embankment restrain the Atlantic. It is simply a question of time. The question is only whether justice is to be gracefully conceded or violently seized. Ten or twenty years must settle the point.[40]

It took one year before the Mutiny in the Bengal Army broke out, and in an ironic twist of events, Sir Henry Lawrence was killed during the siege of the Lucknow Residency in 1857. However, the views of men like Sir Henry, Malcolm and Munro were in the minority, and the native officers would remain in a subordinate position until the early twentieth century, when with great reluctance, the Raj had to admit some natives into commissioned ranks.

Not only was the highest rank available to native officers subordinate to all Europeans, no native could attain it before his old age. Sita Ram Pandey was promoted to the rank of subedar in 1862, after forty-eight years of service, aged sixty-five. He rightly complained:

[I] would have been much better fitted for this position thirty years earlier. What could I do now at the head of my Company? How could I double-march, or perform Light Infantry drill? But I was expected to be as active as ever and no allowance was made for my forty-eight years' service. No one bothered to remember that I had carried a musket for thirty years and had been present in as many battles as most of the officers had lived years. I was shouted at by the Adjutant as if I was a bullock, and he a mere boy, young enough to be my grandson. I was abused by the Commanding Officer, and called a fool, a donkey, and an old woman! ... The time it took to become a Subedar was far too long for most sepoys to aspire to, for this promotion was seldom given until after forty years' service.[41]

Thus, the instrument of the Raj was kept in British control by excluding Indians from officer ranks. The policy was driven by fear and mistrust, not so much by prejudice, at least at the start. In the beginning, the move to keep Indians excluded from command does not seem to be inspired by the sense of racial superiority that gradually seeped into the British psyche in India later. The initial policy was a practical tactic to ensure the safety and stability of the Company's rule in India. As time progressed, it appears that racial prejudices came to inform the views of the British, which suggested that Indians were not 'fit for command'. The Indian sepoy and officer did not seem to notice initially the far-reaching impact the degradation of the native officer's position caused. When the sepoys came to realize this, resentment started to build. However, the Company did not yield on this point. As a consequence, while this was one of the reasons leading to the Mutiny of 1857, the absence of native officers with command and field experience also was a huge limiting factor in the ability of the mutinous sepoys and their rebellion. The policy that generated so much resentment had its rationale without doubt, and despite the huge cost of the Mutiny, it did succeed in containing the ability of the Bengal Army's mutinous sepoys to overthrow the Company's rule.

Nothing illustrates the paucity of trained and experienced leadership during the Mutiny better than the dilemma of Emperor Bahadur Shah Zafar in appointing a Commander-in-Chief of his Army in Delhi. First, Prince Mirza Moghul, who had no military experience, was appointed as the Commander-in-Chief. Mirza Moghul was found deficient in the role. Finally, the hapless Emperor appointed Bakht Khan, the commander of the Bareilly troops of the Bengal Army, who had made their way to Delhi in July 1857 after mutinying. Bakht Khan, well past his prime, was an artillery subedar of forty years' experience. He rode his horse with difficulty, and could barely control his troops from looting the shopkeepers in the city. Captain Waddy said that Bakht Khan was 'a very bad rider owing to large stomach and round thighs, but clever,'[42] while another officer described him as 'a big fat man, obsequious … [a] dreadful hypocrite'.[43] Even if we discount the disdain that English must have felt for a rebel commander, the rebel military leadership cannot be absolved from the subsequent events in their camp, and the collapse of order in the city and discipline in their army.

The Indians, both within and outside the Army, came to realize that self-government was only feasible if the Army was officered by Indians. As long as the Army was exclusively commanded by British officers, no reliance could be placed on its fidelity to a native administration. The lesson was reinforced by the shambolic track record of expensive European (mainly French, but also Italians, Swiss, Austrians and at least one American) commanders that Scindia, Holkar, Jawahir Singh of Bharatpur, Ranjit Singh of Lahore and other native powers had employed in their Armies.

The European commanders melted away on the first contact with the EIC armies during the second Anglo–Maratha War.

Raja Ram Mohan Roy seems to have made the first official representation to senior levels of the British Government on the subject. In 1833, when the House of Commons was considering the renewal of the EIC charter, Raja Ram Mohan Roy gave evidence before the Select Committee, appealing for the Indianization of the British Indian Army. Of course, no one took the suggestion seriously.

VI

In 1858, Queen Victoria generously proclaimed:

> And it is our further will that, so far as may be, Our subjects, of whatever Race or Creed, be freely and impartially admitted to Offices in our Service, the Duties of which they may be qualified, by their education, ability and integrity, duly to discharge.[44]

It turned out to be a false promise, as far as officer ranks in the Indian Army were concerned. Her Government in India did not contemplate any steps to induct Indians into commissioned officer ranks for another half a century.

The Indian Civil Service (ICS) was the body of selected bureaucrats that administered India under the Raj. While during the first half of the nineteenth century the members were exclusively drawn from the British population, the service became open 'in principle' to admit Indians from 1854, when a competitive examination was accepted as the basis for selection by the British Parliament. The first Indian—Satyendra Nath Tagore—was selected for the ICS as early as 1864. Thereafter, the debate was about the number and proportion of Indians in the ICS, and bargaining around the selection criteria: weight apportioned to Indian languages that aided Indian candidates; the age bar and location of exams in the UK, which favoured the British. But the principle of admitting Indians to the most senior level of civil service was accepted. Not so for the army. Every concession demanded was turned down, every citadel of privilege jealously guarded, every concession bitterly contested. If there was ever any evidence needed to prove the true foundation of the Raj lay in its control of the Indian Army, the reluctance in admitting Indians to officer ranks proves this beyond doubt.

Nevertheless, politically conscious Indians could clearly see that the path to self-governance of any form was only feasible if the Army was Indianized: that is, Indians were allowed into the officer ranks. After the Mutiny, the commissioned officers of the Indian Army were known as King's Commissioned Officers (KCOs). Trained at Sandhurst or Woolwich, only white Britons were allowed to attain the KCO rank. The Indian officers—subedars and jemadars—were called Viceroy's Commissioned Officers (VCOs). In reality, they were not really commissioned officers as they did not hold command, and were subordinate to the KCOs and British non-commissioned officers (NCOs). Thus, the issue of Indianization was the Indians' demand that they should also be inducted into KCO ranks and Indian officers allowed to command troops in the army. The barriers were twofold: first, to be able to command *any* troops at all in the officer capacity, and second, to command white troops. Even if Indians could be permitted to command Indian troops as commissioned officers, the racial hierarchy would be upset if Indians were allowed the right to command white soldiers and officers. The last barrier was the elevation of Indian officers to the field command, which would have enabled Indians to entirely replace their white officers.

Before the twentieth century, the only armies where Indians could attain a 'proper' officer rank were in the forces of Indian princes: 500 or so principalities that owed their allegiance to the British Raj. Their forces were under the supervision of British officers, and except for large states like Scindia and the Nizam, not very efficient or professionally organized or trained. Nevertheless, they did provide some degree of autonomy to an Indian, at least in commanding the troops included in their rolls, and in ceremonial leadership.

The Indian National Congress (INC) was founded in 1885, and one of its first demands was the Indianization of the army. In 1887, the INC passed a resolution asking for an Indian military college to be established in India to train Indians for higher commissions. Of course, no note was taken of such a profoundly radical idea. Lord Roberts was the Commander-in-Chief, and he had no time for such absurd demands. A firm believer in the racial superiority of Europeans as 'officer material', he did not think Indians had it in them to be officers, no matter how brave they might be as individuals. At least this was the stated pretence, though it was a convenient way to hide British discomfort in allowing Indians to take such a critical role in the administration of the Raj, which would eventually undermine its authority. Lord Roberts also maintained that British soldiers and officers would not want to serve under Indians. This probably was a correct assessment, but it is not clear why the views of British soldiers and officers should be more important than their counterparts in the civil services, where at least some Indians were permitted to be superior to whites. Somehow, the idea of a British soldier taking orders from an Indian was deemed to be far more dangerous to the Raj's authority than a British civilian subordinated to an Indian civil servant, even in very limited roles. The task of those seeking the elevation of Indians to officer roles thus had to go through three levels of changes: Indians to be allowed official command at least over other Indians; Indians to be permitted to command British troops and officers; and finally Indians to be allowed to senior military roles with field command opportunities. The last two of these did not occur until the emergency of WW2 left no option for the British authorities, due to the extreme shortage of British officers and the gigantic expansion of the Indian Army to almost 2.5 million, serving across the most critical sectors of the war against the Nazis and the Japanese.

VII

Returning to the last decade of the nineteenth century, the INC demands had no impact on the British authorities. Finally, an appeal was submitted by the Raja of Cooch-Behar in 1897 to the India Secretary[45] in London to allow the possibility of his son taking up a regular commission after training at Sandhurst. The objections from the War Office and Colonial Office did not permit the Maharaja's request, but the authorities also found it difficult to ignore it completely. In the imperial hierarchy, the native princes came somewhere close to be considered 'socially acceptable', if not 'equal', as brother officers. Given the strong support by the Indian princes during the Boer and China wars, India Secretary Lord George Hamilton was keen to 'soften the racial bar ... which exist[ed] in the Army'.[46] His views were shared by the Viceroy, Lord George Curzon. Curzon, as an aristocrat himself, strongly believed that the local princes were the only true allies of the British Raj in India; 'the only class in India who are bound to us by every tie of self-interest, if not of loyalty'.[47]

They came up with the anodyne Imperial Cadet Corps (ICC) scheme, which would allow twenty to thirty candidates of princely lineage to undergo a two-year rudimentary military training scheme. A select few of the 'cadets' who completed the two-year training would be allowed a third year of training, before being offered officer's commissions. However, these would not be King's Commissions allowing them to command troops in the Indian Army. These would be commissions in the pompously named Her Majesty's Native Indian Land Forces (HMNILF), but without any authority to command Indian or white troops of the Indian Army. These officers would be restricted to ceremonial 'extra regimental billets': posts on the staff of some European generals in India.

Twenty-one cadets joined in January 1902, but only four of those who joined completed the training. The intake continued to decline, and those who did complete the training were unhappy over their limited career prospects. After much discussion, the Imperial State Troops (ISTs)—the forces of Indian princes—were allowed to employ the ICC graduates. By 1912, it was apparent to all that the scheme had failed. The scheme allowed 'unimportant posts that did not give … [the ICC graduates] … meaningful professional military experience—and they knew it'.[48]

One of the twenty-one cadets who joined the ICC's first batch in January 1902 was Amar Singh, a Rajput heir from the minor principality of Kanota, twelve miles east of Jaipur. Amar Singh was also one of the four who completed the training in 1905 and was commissioned in the HMNILF. Prior to joining the ICC, Amar Singh had served in the Jodhpur Lancers—Jodhpur State's Imperial Service Troops—which saw service in China during 1900-01 to crush the Boxer Rebellion. The British Army was hard-pressed in the Boer War already, and the Indian Army and Imperial State Troops were deployed to deal with the Boxer Rebellion in China. Amar Singh, born in 1878, quite unlike other Indian military officers, wrote an extensive diary for almost forty-four years from 1898 till his death in 1942. His diary gives a unique insight into the mind of an Indian military man, subordinated to the British Raj. The concerns, the discrimination, the frustrations that he outlines in his diary are illustrative of the challenges that Indians faced in the military establishment of the British Raj in India. He writes lucidly, and it would serve our purpose to survey his thoughts on the subject of the Indian officer's status in British Raj's forces.

The Jodhpur Lancers—where Amar Singh served—was founded in 1888 by Sir Pratap Singh, the Regent of Jodhpur, who was one of the most honoured Indo-Victorians in the British establishment, almost the 'beau ideal' of the Indian prince. Besides aiding the Empire in China, the Jodhpur Lancers also fought during WW1 on the Western Front and in the Middle-East. In 1900, the Jodhpur Lancers were drafted to assist the British Raj in subduing the Boxer Rebellion in China. An interesting situation developed during this expedition that mirrored the insecurities of the Raj in allowing Indians to operate in senior military roles—even if the said Indians were members of Imperial State Troops, that is, not directly employed by the Indian Army.

Sir Pratap Singh was the honorary commandant of the Jodhpur Lancers, and was told that he would be leading the Jodhpur Lancers in the mission. In parallel, Major Turner, a British Indian Army Officer, was deputed to 'inspect' Jodhpur Lancers in 1898, and to 'direct them in the field'. Hurjee Singh and Jasji Singh were the colonel and subedar-major of the Jodhpur Lancers, all appointed by the Jodhpur State. Major Turner and other British officers were used to treating the VCOs in the Indian Army (subedar major, subedar and jemadar) as equivalent to non-commissioned sergeants. Sir Pratap, Amar Singh and the Indian officers considered Jodhpur ranks as equivalent to the British ranks: Hurjee to be a colonel, Jasji to be a major, etc. Amar Singh himself was a rissaldar, which the Jodhpur officers considered to be equivalent to lieutenant in rank.

A political tug-of-war ensued between Sir Pratap Singh, who was in the 'general command' of the regiment, and Major Turner, who was supposed to 'direct and control' the regiment. The division of authority was opaque at best, and Sir Pratap Singh's status as a royal overrode Major Turner's as a middle-class professional officer. On the other hand, Major Turner assumed to himself tasks like discipline and reprimand of native officers, which Amar Singh thought ought to have been left to Sir Pratap. Eventually, while the mission in China was successful, the experience of Amar Singh left him disillusioned about the British Army, and he vowed never to be a 'coolie' in the Indian Army, preferring to remain in the Imperial State Troops, even if the career prospects in Jodhpur were extremely limited.

The first point of contention was the dining and transport arrangements. Amar Singh was put in charge of staff work and arranged for the mess at Mathura rail station in August 1900, from where the contingent departed for Calcutta to board their ship to China. Amar Singh was at a loss to understand Major Turner's behaviour, and was bothered to find that the Major 'wanted that none of the other officers [Jodhpur Rajputs] should dine in it [the mess table], except we few who have eaten with him, and even in this he wanted to have two separate parts in which one was to consist of himself, Capt. Hughes, Sarkar [Sir Pratap Singh] and Hurjee … while the rest of the officers were to have their separate mess.'[49]

The exasperation continued in relation to the travel arrangements on board ship. Amar Singh found that Major Turner's opinion was 'that only the staff [white officers, Sir Pratap and Hurjee] would be in the first class while the other officers … were to be in the second class.'[50] Somehow, Sir Pratap intervened and managed to have his way as Amar Singh recorded: 'All this arrangement of his [Major Tuner's mess and travel hierarchies] was dismissed, I don't know by what authority.'[51]

The regiment reached China in September, and while most of the fighting against the Boxer rebels was over in August, the troops were deployed in a few mop-up operations and guard duties. The tussle between Major Turner and Sir Pratap Singh reached a stage where others started to get embroiled. Major Turner attempted to undermine Sir Pratap's authority by directly intermediating with Jasjee, who, as subedar-major, was the commandant of the unit.

Major Turner used the excuse that Sir Pratap was the general officer commanding, and most mundane regiment-related functions, for example, parade ground roll, etc., ought to be done by Jasjee as the commandant.

Matters came to a head over the disciplining of the commandant Jasjee by Captain Hughes, who, in the eyes of Amar Singh, was junior in rank to Jasjee (Amar Singh insists on the subedar-major rank to be equal to a major). It appears that Jasjee, the regiment commandant, had some drink while on the march. Captain Hughes took away Jasjee's sword to discipline him. The Indian officers found it a great insult to be deprived of their sword. Sir Pratap again intervened to stop the matter escalating further. Amar Singh's observations by this time become quite bitter. In July 1901, Amar Singh writes:

> The Indians are looked upon as inferiors in the scale of humanity. The British are better treated, supplied, fed, clothed, and paid than the Indians. Even they are better armed ... No Indian can rise above the rank of a rissaldar or subadar major, and however young or junior a British officer may be he always looks down upon the other as an ignorant fellow, even though he may be much [more] experienced and possessed of [a] better head ... Captain Hughes always considered himself much more senior to Jasjee [subedar-major and commandant of the regiment] and even went so far as to take away his sword without any trial. Hughes is merely a captain while Jasjee is a major ... The taking away of Jasjee's sword is a great blow to our pride ... He had no doubt drunk a little, which every other British officer does ... Nowhere, either in the British or foreign armies, a junior can punish a senior. Then what business Hughes had? If Jasjee is not to be considered a major why does the government allow or empower the

states [princely states like Jodhpur] to confer these ranks in the Imperial Service Forces?—Hurjee would never be considered on the same footing as a British colonel or I as a lieutenant. Whatever may happen, I for myself will never serve in the army except in imperial service [meaning the princely state forces, which were commanded by Indian officers]. Even if anyone offered me a direct rissaldar majorship in the British Indian Army, I would straight away reject. I would not like to be treated like a coolie ... British sergeants and soldiers never salute Indian officers, no, not even ... Sarkar [Sir Pratap]. They look as if they expect the others to salute them ... It is a mark of great favour on the part of the sergeant or soldier if he even condescends to say good morning. Now if an Indian officer did not salute a British officer there would be a hell of a row and the Indian would be punished for his impunity ... I do not blame the French soldiers for calling the Indians coolies, considering the way British treat them ... British make a great row when they hear the foreigners calling Indian soldiers and officers coolies, though they do not mind treating them as such themselves.[52]

The Jodhpur Lancers and Amar Singh returned to India in July 1901. Although Amar Singh was quite disillusioned with the prospect of serving in the British Indian Army, he joined the ICC's first batch at Meerut in January 1902 at the initiative of his patron Sir Pratap Singh. The ICC was Curzon's baby, who had devised the scheme with very few people within the British establishment half-heartedly agreeing to it. Even Curzon was certain that the ICC would not lead to a commission in the Indian Army—'for that would or might involve a black man commanding a white man, which no one will look at'.[53] The uncertainty of the future of cadets continued throughout the training period; even the British officers who were in charge of the training had little clue what eventually would be the fate of the cadets. No wonder that most of the cadets dropped out, and only four, including Amar Singh, managed to graduate in 1905. On 16 May 1903, Amar Singh notes:

> Nearly every Englishman who knows me has asked as to what is to be done with us at the end of the course. They do not know and we do not know ... we are not going to get any commission in the British or native army ... The reason is that no Britisher would ever like to be under a native's command at present. It will require some generations before this feeling of the conquerors and the conquered, the ruler and the ruled, and of blacks and whites would fall away.[54]

Amar Singh again speculates in April 1904: 'They are going to give us regular commissions with all the pay, promotion and privileges of a British officer though we shall never be made to command them.'[55]

Eventually, the only roles open for the four graduates were in the Imperial State Troops or as a staff officer, that is, without command authority in the Indian Army. Amar Singh could not secure a role within the Jaipur State forces due to a dispute his family had with the Maharaja of Jaipur. He spent his next nine years quietly as a staff officer—and the only Indian in the British officer's mess—in Mhow under General O'Moore Creagh, then commander of the 5th Division, Western Army. In 1914, WW1 erupted, and Amar Singh was despatched to the Western Front in Europe as aide-de-camp (ADC) to the commanding officer, Sirhind Brigade, Lahore Division. Around the same time, the limping ICC scheme was shut down.

The sacrifices and contributions by Indian soldiers in defending the thinly held Western Front during the opening years of the war temporarily softened British hearts. The British authorities felt a sense of remorse tinged with the strategic urgency of tightening their bonds with the Indian soldier. The Secretary of State Chamberlain wrote to the Viceroy on 18 November 1915:

> On Imperial grounds early action seems to me desirable in order to mark the part played by Indian troops in the war and refute the colour bar theory. I would propose selection of a few officers ... for commission in Indian regiments. The selection ... would have the advantage of giving concessions as act of grace and not in response to agitation ... I should like to make the announcement on January 1st.[56]

The deadline of 1 January came and went, and no announcement was made. The Indians continued to shed their blood in the imperial cause, first in Europe, and then in Mesopotamia and a number of other theatres. On the Western Front, the Indian sepoy could not fail to notice how differently the French colonial subjects like the Algerians and Moroccans were treated by their colonial masters. The French colonial subjects were eligible for, and served as, commissioned officers, equivalent to French officers. There was a much higher degree of fraternity and even-handed treatment of the French colonial subjects, compared to the Indians. The British were also aware of this, and taking no chances, they sent all the injured soldiers (only those who had very strong chances of recovering and being able to go back to the front) back to the UK, instead of risking them being treated in French hospitals, where they would have faced the truth of their inferior comparative treatment by their colonial masters. By 1917, the impulse that drove Chamberlain gained further momentum, and nationalist agitators in India added further weight to the demands of Indianizing the army.

On 20 August 1917, the Montagu–Chelmsford duo made the 'momentous declaration' committing Britain to 'responsible government' in India. Five days later, King's Commissions were offered to Amar Singh and eight other former ICC cadets in response to the 'powerful and increasing demand for a greater share by Indians in the administration of the country'.[57] It was later proven that this was an overzealous step by the imperial authorities under war pressure. Neither the promise of 'responsible government' nor that of 'greater share in administration'—as far as military leadership was concerned—were kept. It was always a case of one step forward, and two back.

The British military and civil administration in India used bureaucratic hurdles to undermine the policy initiatives aimed at elevating a minuscule number of Indians to ranks equal to the British officers in the army. The Indian Army's first counter was to offer inferior terms to the newly minted King's Commissioned Indian Officers (KCIOs); terms that would force them to refuse the commissions. The offerees were told that their years as officers in the HMNILF would not count towards future promotion and pension as KCIOs. Amar Singh, who was made captain in July 1914 in the ICC, and was due for promotion to Major in July 1920, was told in 1917 that as a KCIO gazetted captain he would not be able to achieve the major rank before 1927. Some, like Zorawar Singh, a close friend of Amar Singh at the Cadet Corps, resigned in protest. Amar Singh filed a protest while within service, and managed to retain the pension service length from the date of his commission into the ICC in 1905. The promotion to major was too far away in the future, and in any event, Amar Singh did not survive in the Indian Army that long, having been forced to leave in 1921 under unhappy circumstances.

The 1917 announcement was part of the euphoria felt by some of the British on India's contribution, and for others a convenient wartime expedient. The enthusiasm to get Indians into commissioned ranks evaporated with the end of the war. The happy status quo, which excluded Indians from commissioned officer ranks as much as possible, was maintained. To pay lip service to the 1917 announcement, on paper at least, the scheme of including Indians was not reversed. Instead, the bar was now further raised: the only way for Indians to gain King's Commission now was by training at Sandhurst, where, from 1918, ten seats each year were reserved for Indians. Leaving aside the expense and difficulties for an Indian family to send their son to Sandhurst, even if ten officers got commissioned each year, the Indianization of the Indian Army was 300–500 years away.[58]

VIII

It is hard to believe today that an army of 200,000 with almost 4,000 commissioned officers was struggling to digest ten to twenty Indian commissioned officers. However, it was not simply a matter of number; a bigger principle was at stake. It was one thing for a white civil servant to be subordinated to a pen-wielding Indian; it was totally different when a white soldier or officer might have to take orders from an armed Indian. The sword arm of the Raj was the Indian Army, and its control by the white British was the only security of the Empire. In hindsight, the surprising achievement of the imperial officers and politicians was to keep the demand for Indianization at bay for two more decades, until the WW2 emergency forced a different course.

While some cadets started going to Sandhurst to be trained as officers, many unsuccessfully, the few who had already been commissioned were having a difficult time. Amar Singh participated in the third Afghan war as captain, but encountered the insubordination of a junior white officer in 1919. The experience made him bitter, and reinforced his views of not wanting to be a 'coolie' in the Indian Army. While he joined as a

King's Commissioned Indian Officer, not as a VCO, he could not escape the systemic barriers and racism that prevented him from having a satisfying career. In 1921, he exchanged 'hot words' with his regimental commander Colonel Mears, and resigned without revealing the reasons to his diary. His career in the Indian Army, twelve years as a non-commanding staff officer, and four years as a commanding officer, was cut short. He managed to have a much happier time as commandant of the Jaipur State force, which he joined in 1922, and retired from in 1936. Amar Singh's career is emblematic of the confused, double-faced policy of British Army authority, with high-sounding principles, but obstructing any real progress in letting an armed Indian command troops.

By mid-1923, only fourteen out of twenty-eight Indian cadets successfully passed Sandhurst and were granted a King's Commission. The rest either dropped out or died. Two resigned, and one had it cancelled because he was 'late in reporting for duty'.[59] The trickle of Indians who managed to graduate from Sandhurst continued to face discrimination in the regiments where they were posted, similar to the barriers experienced by Amar Singh. This had an adverse effect on the morale of Indian officers. The social contact continued to be minimal between the handful of Indian KCIOs and other British officers. Some Indian officers recall in their memoirs that they were never once invited to the homes of the British commanding officers for even so much as a cup of tea. One of them wrote that KCIOs lived in 'virtual isolation' from their British counterparts.[60]

In typical bureaucratic fashion, a number of commissions and committees exercised immense intellectual jugglery to devise schemes that could slow down the pace of Indianization, while appearing to advance it. The Esher Committee, Cobbe Scheme, Rawlinson Committee, Skeen Committee and the numerous debates and resolutions in the Indian Central Legislative Assembly (CLA) confound any reader with the sheer amount of paperwork generated on this subject between the two wars. Their essence is the same: obfuscate, pretend to concede, withdraw a few steps, cite obstructions from VCOs and British officers, lack of leadership capabilities of Indians, disunity of Indians, degeneracy of babus, and so on. We will just survey the essence of what occurred, and the intentions of the British authorities. For the intention on Indianization provides a mirror to what the British really thought about how long they expected their Indian Empire to last: it was simply as long as the Indian Army was under British command.

One committee under Commander-in-Chief Rawlinson proposed in 1922 what the British thought was entirely radical: complete Indianization, albeit by 1967. It would proceed in three stages of fourteen years each, starting in 1925. In Stage 1, twenty-seven units would be Indianized; in Stage 2, forty-seven; and in Stage 3, forty-one. Indian officers would start at the most junior rank, and slowly elevate as older British officers retired, making sure no British officer ever served under an Indian. Such a radical scheme was immediately rejected by London. The year 1967 was felt to be too early a date to end the Empire. Lord Curzon (the Foreign Secretary) felt the scheme 'was probably doomed to failure from the beginning; if it succeeded, it would almost certainly endanger our rule in India'.[61] Any doubt on this count was cleared by the Prime Minister Lloyd George: 'There was no question of a withdrawal of the British government from India … let everybody know that it was the fixed and irrevocable intention of His Majesty's Government to see that British ascendancy and British rule in India are maintained.'[62] The subject of Indianization was inextricably linked to decolonization, and the most senior British leaders and politicians understood it as such. The existential threat that the Indianization of the army posed in the British mind is in stark contrast to the concessions allowed for Indian participation in legislative bodies established in 1921 and the civil service from the 1860s.

Despite wholesale rejection of the idea of Indianization at any foreseeable point in future, some concession had to be made in light of the promises made in 1917, and the agitations launched by the nationalist leaders since 1919. So, it was grudgingly decided to Indianize eight units—six infantry and two cavalry units—as an experiment from 1923 onward. Each unit would take about fifteen years to Indianize, and no British officer would have to serve under an Indian. So far so good, as at this pace, the Indian Army would be fully Indianized in another two centuries. So, the anxieties of ending the Raj in the current and following generations would not plague its proponents. From now on, all KCIOs from Sandhurst would be posted exclusively to the Indianizing units. Everyone could see that this would lead to segregation, and both British and Indian officers started to see these units as inferior.

The Skeen Committee submitted its report in 1926, and it contended that *if* the measures recommended were implemented, approximately half of the Indian Army officer cadre could be Indianized by 1952. Implying full Indianization by 1978, this again was thought to be too fast. Most of the recommendations were rejected, but to appease sentiments, the number of Indians at Sandhurst was increased from ten to twenty-five per year, and small numbers were allowed to Woolwich and the RAF academy at Cranwell.[63] Increasing the places for Indians at Sandhurst soon started to create an oversupply of Indian officers, as the experimental eight units were not sufficient to absorb them. The obvious solution would have been to extend the number of Indianizing units from the meagre eight. However, some within the British Raj spotted an opportunity—why not replace the old VCOs with KCIOs, and pit the classes from which VCOs came against the wider background of KCIOs? The VCOs came from the 'martial classes' which traditionally did not focus so much on western education. The KCIOs, by now, were drawing men from among educated middle-class Indians, where nationalist ideas were most prevalent. The Indian units of the army were officered by nineteen to twenty VCOs and twelve to fourteen KCOs/KCIOs up to that time. British units, of course, had no VCOs, and were officered by twenty-three to twenty-eight KCOs.

In the new arrangement, with Indian officers entering Indian units, they (KCIOs) were first placed in VCO positions and then worked their way up. The rationale put forward was that as Indians, KCIOs did not need VCOs as 'intermediaries', which were required for British KCOs in Indian units. In reality, the intent was to undermine the KCIOs' promotion prospects. Stepping into VCO shoes, a newly minted KCIO lieutenant would command only a platoon, whereas a new British KCO would start as second-in-command of a company at his initial posting, well ahead of his Indian peers. The KCIOs would now take much longer for promotion to regiment-level posts, having to spend a large part of their initial careers in junior command roles earlier filled by VCOs. The scheme also caused some anxiety to the VCOs, who were to soon become extinct in the Indianizing units, with promotion to VCO formally stopping from 1935 in such units.

In 1931, the Indianization scheme was extended from eight units to a full division, comprising twelve infantry battalions and three cavalry units. This was a minor incremental change, for complete Indianization would still be a century away, unless more units were brought into the scheme before the experimental units were Indianized fully. The other features of the scheme—ensuring no Indian had command over a white officer, gradual replacement of VCOs and slow promotion—continued to be in place.

Meanwhile, the Indian cadets at Sandhurst continued to have a tough time, far away from their familiar environment. It was made difficult by the British officers and establishment who were not sympathetic to the Indians strolling about at Sandhurst. By 1932, excluding the 41 still training, 21 of the 121 cadets who joined since

1919 had either failed or resigned.[64] Of the 101 commissioned since 1919, 72 were still employed in the eight units that were earmarked for Indianization in 1923, with a handful serving in the seven newly Indianizing units.[65] The eight units had Indianized only by 50 per cent over nine years,[66] and the original plan of Indianizing the earmarked units within fifteen years appeared ambitious.

There had been recurring demands for an Indian Sandhurst since the 1920s. In 1932, The Indian Military Academy (IMA) opened at Dehradun in December 1932, with an annual intake of eighty cadets, only thirty of whom were through open competition.[67] Of the remaining fifty, thirty were VCOs recommended by their officers and twenty came from the princely state forces. With the opening of the IMA, no more Indians were allowed to enter Sandhurst or Woolwich, the last Indians entering in 1932, and graduating by 1934. From 1935 onwards, the cadets graduating from IMA were commissioned as Indian Commissioned Officers (ICOs) in the Indianizing units, marking them as distinct from the Indians who trained at Sandhurst and were known as KCIOs. The pay and allowances of ICOs were inferior to the white KCOs and Indian KCIOs. The latter received two or three times the pay and allowances of the ICOs. The rationale given was that serving in their own country, the ICOs did not need the extra incentive required to compensate expatriate British officers serving in India. In truth, this was plain and simple discrimination. We remember the Indian soldiers serving during WW1 outside India were not paid 'extra incentive' to serve outside their home country. In fact, they were paid less than British soldiers serving in the same theatres. The KCIOs did continue to receive similar pay as the British KCOs, but that seemed to fly in face of the 'extra incentive' argument. Irrespective of pay, both ICOs and KCIOs continued to the face limited promotion prospects because they were limited to the fifteen Indianizing units, and had almost no field command experience. The ICOs trained at Dehradun were not given much staff training either, and were instead focused on platoon-level tactical leadership and skills development.

The initial enthusiasm shown by Indians in applying for IMA eroded as the discrimination on pay, promotion and training became apparent. In 1932, 274 Indians competed for entry to the IMA and by 1938 only 128 came forward. At the start of WW2, there were just 300 Indian commissioned officers (KCIOs and ICOs) in the Indian Army, which had a peace-time officer strength of 5,000.[68] This meagre number of Indian officers was the fruit of forty years of schemes and committees, various proclamations by British Prime Ministers, establishment of training institutions at Meerut, Dehradun and Indore, and of course training at Sandhurst. Indian public opinion and the nationalist leaders by that time had realized that the so-called 'Indianization' scheme was actually fraudulent and the intentions behind the announcements and efforts were never sincere. Much like the empty promises of self-government or dominion status, the efforts to Indianize the officer cadre were more for public consumption.

One more committee was appointed in 1939 to perhaps repeat the same obfuscation and delay. However, the emergency of WW2 forced a change that was irreversible. As more units were raised, they needed more officers. Attempts to find white officers in Britain and even Australia for the Indian Army failed. There was no alternative but to train and hire more Indian officers to face the German and Japanese onslaught. Yielding to the inevitable, the Indian Government announced on 17 June 1940 that the ICOs would be 'available for posting throughout the Indian Army, where their services can best be used'.[69] Finally, in their darkest hour, the British Raj allowed Indian officers to train and serve alongside white officers, and removed the bar from an Indian commanding a white soldier or officer. Indianization, debated, talked and written about for so long, since the times of Raja Ram Mohan Roy a century earlier, finally started in earnest. The trickle would turn into a flood, and by the end of WW2, there would be 15,000 Indian commissioned officers compared to approximately 30,000 British officers in the Indian Army, which had swelled to 2.5 million by 1945.[70] Many of the Indian officers commanded battalions and gained significant field experience. The proportion of Indian officers had risen from 5 per cent at the start to almost 33 per cent by the end of the war. Moreover, all Indian officers were volunteers, committed to stay, whereas most British officers were enlisted for hostilities-only service, and keen to go back to their civilian lives. This was no less than a 'revolution'; as much as the EIC's ability to hire and train Indian sepoys officered by Europeans was in the 1740s and 1750s. The impact of such drastic changes would be profound.

The Raj tried as hard as it could to defend the last bastion of privilege—the white officer commanding Indian soldiers. The modern war, and its need for Indian manpower and resources, left no option but to discard this jealously guarded privilege during WW2. However, in Indian eyes, this was too late. The sepoy had loyally served his employer for almost two centuries, and bled for the Empire during WW1, in the hope that the promise of self-government made in 1917 would be honoured. With hindsight, that would have been the appropriate time for the British Raj to end amicably in India. The fact that the fifteen-unit scheme would have taken almost a century to complete Indianization was clear evidence of the British intention to not leave India in the foreseeable future. So, when the changes occurred during the war, it was not seen as voluntary. General Claude Auchinleck wrote pithily in October 1940:

> We [the British] have been playing a losing hand from the start in this matter of 'Indianization'. The Indian has always thought, rightly or wrongly, that we never intended the scheme to succeed and expected it to fail. Colour has been lent to this view by the way in which each new step

has had to be wrested from us instead of being freely given. Now that we have given the lot, we get no credit because there was little grace in our giving.[71]

There is no better summary on the subject of Indianization. The story of British dominance in India is also a story of wresting military leadership from Indian hands, and its end would also lie in the restoration of that leadership, aided by the compulsions of total war.

Chapter Eight

Colour before Honour

I

As helpless Afghan civilians allied with the US and British forces crept towards Kabul airport in August 2021 in hope of rescue and asylum, the Western soldiers made their exit in warplanes. The world's moral outrage, sparked by the betrayal of Afghan allies of the Western forces, reached a fever pitch seeing young children and women left to the mercy of the Taliban. Most British citizens howling over social media assumed this was a unique failure of British foreign and defence policy on overseas expeditions.

The truth is this was a fairly regular experience for British imperial allies when crisis hit. Indian soldiers were the biggest ally of the British Empire, and they were abandoned outside India during grave defeats, of which there were three: the 1842 rout in Afghanistan, the surrender at Kut-al-Amara to the Ottoman Army in 1916, and the surrender to the Japanese Army at Singapore in 1942. The Singapore defeat will be covered in the last chapter of the book. This chapter will review the experiences of Indian soldiers in Afghanistan and Mesopotamia, and how imperial hierarchies valued their lives less than their white comrades'. Finally, we will also review the bonds developed between the Armenian victims of the Ottoman genocide and the Indian prisoners of war in Mesopotamia during WW1. As the underdogs of two imperial systems, a sympathetic relationship emerged, where the Indian soldiers tried their best to help Armenian survivors. This speaks of the humanity of these men, who, while caught up in their inferior position and difficult circumstances, did not lose that fundamental bond between humans across cultures and faiths.

The discrimination in pay and terms of service, though abhorrent, were clear for all to see, especially to the soldiers, before they enlisted. The discrimination in matters of life and death revealed the inequity and unjust hierarchy of the Empire, despite all the propaganda surrounding its notions of honour, fair play and justice. The response of the imperial authorities to these crises reveals the true nature of imperialism.

II

At the high noon of the Victorian era in 1898, fifty-six years after the actual events, William Barns Wollen painted 'The Last Stand at Gandamuck'. The painting shows the final battle of the surviving soldiers of the 44th Infantry Regiment at Gandamak, Afghanistan, in 1842 against the Afghans. The painting has come to depict the stoic fortitude of the British soldiers faced with overwhelming odds, in service of the Empire. The painting does not show any Indian soldiers, leave aside the numerous camp followers. The Afghans look more like the Sudanese followers of the Mahdi, perhaps reflecting the contemporary impression of the Sudanese campaign of the last decade of the nineteenth century.

The valorization of the action of the sole European regiment that was part of the disastrous retreat from Kabul in 1842 needs to be understood in context of the experiences of their Indian comrades, and numerous camp followers. A different picture starts to emerge when we review some of the first-hand accounts of this unfortunate campaign. The retreating army of predominantly Indian soldiers, their families and camp followers were mercilessly slaughtered by the Afghans in the treacherous mountain passes. While this disaster unfolded, the survivors of the 44th Regiment, who were supposed to be the advance guards, were last seen at Gandamak, while their charge of 15,000 Indian camp followers were butchered to the last woman and child, with the more unfortunate ones sold as slaves.

To understand this inglorious end of the Afghan campaign, we will review the events from the war's beginning in 1838. The invasion of Afghanistan by the government of the EIC was an act of imperial hubris. We can analyse the various characters involved, the motivations of British officials, and the actions of the Afghans and Persians. However, in the end it appears to be an inevitable act of aggressive expansion that all empires are wont to conduct, until an opposing force restrains it. Having conquered most of India after the fall of Bharatpur in 1826, the imperialists forgot to account for the differences in Afghanistan. Afghanistan is a country united by a single faith, and the mountainous terrain was ill-suited to the manoeuvres of the line infantry regiments and field artillery, which had proved to be a devastating success against Indian foes when fighting on more-or-less plain ground.

The northern frontier of the Indian Empire was protected by the Himalayas and the sturdy Gurkhas, the southern flanks by the Arabian, Indian and Bengal Seas. The Burmese were defeated in 1826, which only left the north-western frontier for expansion. The Sikh state of Ranjit Singh on the north-west border of India maintained a formidable army, and was tied to the EIC via a treaty of mutual friendship since 1809. The bogey of a Russian threat and the personal ambitions of various civil and military officials of the EIC led to the decision to invade Afghanistan, ostensibly in alliance with the Sikhs. The immediate excuse was the Persian siege of Herat in Afghanistan near its western border and the perceived risk to British domains. Additionally, the British wanted to replace the Afghan ruler with their own favourite. However, before the campaign started, the Persians had withdrawn. The momentum to invade had gathered by then, forces mobilized were not withdrawn, and the invasion went ahead anyway.

Ranjit Singh was a shrewd diplomat, and while on the surface he encouraged the plans, in substance he contributed very little. Eventually, he even denied the movement of EIC troops across Punjab to enter Afghanistan through the usual route of the Khyber Pass. This meant that the ornamentally titled 'Grand Army of the Indus' had to march through a circuitous and treacherous route from Ferozepore in Punjab via Sind and finally the Bolan and Khojak passes to Kandahar, almost 1,000 miles through desert, as long as a march from London to Venice.

The composition of the 'Army of the Indus' was predominantly Indian: approximately 15,000[1] Indian sepoys in the Company Army, and an additional 6,000 in Shah Shuja's contingent, whom the EIC wanted to install as the King of Kabul to replace Dost Mohammad Khan. In addition, approximately 40,000 camp followers and families of the sepoys accompanied the army. The European troops and officers numbered between 1,000 and 2,000 at most. At any rate, more than 90 per cent of the fighting men and more than 95 per cent of the Army, including followers, were made up of Indians. The main body of the force was made up of Bengal Army regiments, with an additional brigade from the Bombay Army. Shah Shuja's contingent had been recruited from the upper Hindustan, and included Sita Ram Pandey.[2]

It had been the custom for the EIC's Madras Army sepoys to march with their families during the eighteenth and early nineteenth centuries, while within the confines of Hindustan.

Not so for the Bombay Army, and certainly not for the Bengal Army sepoys. The European soldiers and officers never encumbered themselves with their families, for obvious reasons of the safety of their loved ones. Families joining the soldiers was a much older Indian tradition on long campaigns, but the Company managed to eliminate it in the Bengal and Bombay Armies in the eighteenth century.

In a highly unusual decision, the Indian sepoys were allowed to take their families with them on this campaign. The oddity of this decision did not escape Lady Sale's observation, who had joined her husband—Brigadier Sale—in Kabul during the summer of 1841. By 1841, the British garrison in Kabul was taking a more permanent appearance, and many officers and a few European soldiers asked their families to join them through the familiar Khyber Pass route. In the adversity of the Afghan winter of 1841, the details of which we will survey later, Lady Sale observed:

> The garrison were encumbered with [sepoys'] wives and children, who had been encouraged to come up from Hindostan in great numbers. It is affirmed that they did so by permission of Lord Auckland, it being supposed that they would have no wish to quit the country with their families settled along with them. The not being allowed to bring up their families even at their own expence, was always considered as a heavy grievance by the European [soldiers]; but, in their instance, the wisdom of the refusal has been proved.[3]

Just why was it permitted for sepoys to endanger their wives and children, in what was clearly a dangerous expedition from the start and included a treacherous march across Sind, is a question to ponder. However, the 1838 Punjab winter at Ferozepur was not the scene for such serious questions. The heady excitement of a fresh campaign, with visions of battle honours, promotions and prize money, swept along the soldiers and officers. Just before the expedition, a young British officer sang:

> The valour of our Sepoy sires lives in us o'er again
> The British banner in our keep has never met with stain—
> And as we stood by stout old Lake, hurrah!
> We'll stand by Fane![4]

The same officer commented on the 'invincible character of an army knit together by the invisible bonds of brotherhood'.[5] Sadly, we will see these fraternal bonds melted away under the heat of Afghan blades.

III

The over encumbered Army of the Indus had a harrowing march through Sind and Baluchistan on the way to the Bolan pass. The heat of the desert and lack of drinking water was made all the more intolerable by attacks from Baluchi brigands, who would murder the camp followers, and steal camels and supplies. Sita Ram records:

> The water in the few wells was bitter ... The Baluchis now began to harass us by night attacks and drove off long strings of our camels ... the heat was such that ... one day thirty-five men fell victim to it ... Everyone passing through these hills is robbed and attacked, no matter friend or foe ... The country we came through [into Afghanistan] must surely have been on the confines of hell! It was a land of stones with nothing green except the camel-thorn, and no birds apart from the vultures that feasted on the carcasses of our baggage animals, and on the bodies of our comrades we

were unable to bury ... There was no wood with which to perform the funeral rites when a Hindu died, and he was far from holy Benares and the pure Ganges. His fate was unhappy for he was conveyed about in diverse places in the bellies of hungry jackals! Now I understood why it was forbidden to cross the Indus.[6]

As supplies dwindled, the sepoys' ration was reduced to half, pushing them to the point of starvation. The European soldiers, by contrast, had a pound of meat each served daily, though officially their ration was also reduced to half.[7] Since most of the sepoys were Hindus, meat was not an option, except for a small number of Muslim sepoys. The starvation, the Baluchi knives, and heat and thirst started to take its toll on the camp followers and sepoys' families. A young infantry officer, Thomas Seaton, described one family's ordeal:

> One of the native officers in camp had with him a little girl, his only child, whose mother was dead. She was a pretty, lively, prattling thing of about six years of age, the delight of everybody. I used to see her every day chattering to her father, helping him light the fire, and cook their food; and her pretty little ways were a delight to witness. I saw her at ten o'clock all well, and at 3 p.m. she was dead and laid out for burial.[8]

The exhausted Army of the Indus eventually entered Afghanistan, and took Kandahar and Ghazni in quick succession. The morale of the army recovered slightly, and the sepoys appeared resolute, as Sita Ram noted on the storming of Ghazni: 'Some companies of Europeans were driven back and two companies of sepoys charged and carried the gateway. The Europeans were so pleased by this that they shook hands with every man of that regiment.'[9] They particularly pleased Brigadier Nott, who said: 'I would at any time lead one thousand Bengal sepoys against five thousand Afghans.'[10] Nott proved himself as the rare capable British commander in Afghanistan over the next three years. Leaving a garrison at Kandahar under Brigadier Nott, the rest of the army moved to Kabul, and successfully installed Shah Shuja in his capital on 7 August 1839. Dost Mohammad fled north with his small band of retainers. The Bombay Army left Kabul in September 1839 for India, but the Bengal Army encamped in Kabul to prop up Shah Shuja.

It soon became apparent that Shah Shuja was not liked by the Afghans. Sita Ram records:

> Soon, however, the Afghans began to chafe at the occupation of their country by the English. They complained that the English were not adhering to 'Lad Macnaten' sahib's promise that the army would return to Hindustan as soon as Shah Shujah was secured on his throne. They pointed out that the king had been restored, and yet the foreigners still remained.[11]

The surrender by Dost Mohammad in November 1840 gave momentary respite, but the British situation was becoming increasingly tenuous. Although Dost Mohammad and his harem were exiled to India, it was apparent that Shah Shuja would be dislodged as soon as the Bengal Army left. At the same time, the garrison in Kabul made the British presence more unpopular, besides adding to the expense. The expense to keep such a large force in a country with very little revenue or resources was exorbitant, and continued to mount. Lord Macnaghten, the British Envoy, adopted a policy of bribing the various disparate Afghan tribes to keep the Khyber Pass and supply lines clear. Nevertheless, feelings continued to simmer as the foreigners made themselves comfortable in Kabul, some of them a bit too much, including liaisons with Afghan women. 'By the autumn of 1841 the country was seething with rebellion and intrigue.'[12] The Governor-General in India ordered Macnaghten to economize, and tried to stop some payments to the Ghilzai chiefs who controlled the strategic Khyber Pass to Punjab and thence to India.

As part of the cuts, a brigade under Robert Sale, husband of Lady Sale, was ordered to retire to India in early October, when reinforcements should have been moving in the other direction. Before Sale's brigade could reach Jalalabad, Sir Alexander Burns, Macnaghten's deputy, was murdered on 2 November in Kabul and his faithful sepoy guard massacred; an open revolt broke out in Kabul. The British political and military leadership dithered, but Shah Shuja, their ally, did send a 'Hindostanee regiment into the city ... who maintained an arduous conflict for some time ... but being wholly unsupported ... the greater part of them were cut to pieces.'[13]

IV

The very next day, Macnaghten realized the gravity of the situation, and asked Sale to return to Kabul, and Nott to send reinforcements up from Kandahar. Sale prevaricated, and marched off to Jalalabad. Nott reluctantly despatched three regiments to Kabul but they were blocked by snow and returned to Kandahar after losing some of the baggage animals in the severe cold.

This left the Kabul garrison to look after its own defence, just when thousands of Afghans started to pour into Kabul from the countryside, laying siege to the city and the cantonment. The British garrison had approximately 5,000 fighting men, of which just about 700 were Europeans, the rest being Indians. There were about 15,000 camp followers and families of the sepoys, and a few hundred or so wives and children of European officers and soldiers.

The diplomatic head of the British mission, William Macnaghten, had recently been offered the governorship of Bombay, so he was keen to get out of Afghanistan, and was delusional about British prospects of keeping Shuja in power. The general who led the garrison, Elphinstone, was a seventy-year-old gout patient, incapacitated, and was desperate to hand over command to Nott, if he could arrive from Kandahar, or anyone capable and willing to take over. His deputy, Brigadier Shelton, strongly disliked Indian sepoys; was obstructive at worst and unresponsive at best; he pretended to be asleep in his quilt on the floor during evening military meetings called by Elphinstone.

The pusillanimity of British leadership was frustrating Lady Sale, who recorded on 2 and 3 November:

> In cantonments all was confusion and indecision. The Envoy mounted his horse and rode to the gateway, and then rode back again ... No military steps have been taken to suppress the insurrection, nor even to protect our only means of subsistence (the Godowns), in the event of a siege. The King, Envoy, and General appear perfectly paralysed by this sudden outbreak.[14]

The Deputy Envoy was murdered next to the garrison of 5,000 soldiers, and nothing was done. This emboldened the rebellion, and Afghans started to attack the surrounding posts of the cantonment, which were hopelessly exposed on open ground. The suggestion to march out to Bala Hisar Fort, where they could have withstood siege until relief arrived, was turned down by Brigadier Shelton. So, the doomed garrison stumbled to its dark fate. Sadly, most of the group comprised helpless Indian children and women as camp followers. It must have been heartbreaking for the sepoys, whose families were exposed to the elements of the weather, now in the shadow of Afghan knives, and their leadership incapable of a decisive break-out.

Soon, the Commissariat Fort was stormed and taken by Afghans, and thus the garrison lost twelve months' worth of supplies. They were now reliant on diminishing supplies, and under-equipped to fight and survive in the treacherous winter. The rations were soon cut, and the worst sufferers again were the camp followers and sepoys' families: 'Our camp followers have for the past two days had nothing to eat except the carcasses of our camels and horses that have died from want of food.'[15]

The morale and physical capability of the men deteriorated. Sita Ram noted: 'There was fighting every day, and because there was no good food for the European soldiers, they lost spirit and did not fight as well as they used to do.' Seeing the food for their wives and children being stolen by Afghans in broad daylight, putting their families' lives at risk, the sepoys agitated to act, despite their own desperate situation. Lady Sale noted the sepoys' desperation when the European regiment (the 44th) retreated from a last effort to salvage the Commissariat Fort:

> When the 44th retreated from Mahommed Shureef's fort [opposite the Commissariat], all were in amazement; the [sepoys of] 37th asked leave to go and take it, but were not permitted to do so. The sipahees are grumbling at short allowance, and not being allowed to do anything. The 37th [sepoys] were anxious to be employed in recovering the Commissariat fort, though no actual proposition to that effect was officially made to the General.[16]

Seeing that the British garrison's supplies were running out, the Afghans sharpened their knives. While the European 44th Regiment lost the motivation to fight, the sepoys continued to give a good account of themselves, albeit circumscribed due to hunger and cold. Sita Ram complained, 'Men lost the use of their fingers and toes which fell off after great suffering.'[17] While sepoys were losing their limbs to the cold, the beleaguered Shah Shuja sent 'each sahib [European officer] a warm silk rezai [duvet] and a pillow. Which were very acceptable, as they were all starving [sic] with cold.'[18]

A sepoy and a havildar were the first into the same fort the next day, when it was stormed, despite being part of the rear company. Another sepoy was at the forefront in having taken the flag from the enemy, waved it on the crest of the breach, and was promoted for the act.[19] On 10 November, in severe fighting for the Rikabashees' fort at Bibi Mahru, six Afghans were killed by a sepoy, for which he was promoted.[20] However, watching the same battle from the cantonment, Lady Sale despaired about the European soldiers: 'Major Scott in vain tried to rally the 44th: excited to tears, he called for volunteers to follow him, when a private, named Stuart, was the only man who offered to go, and for which ... he was ... promoted sergeant.'[21]

After the despair of the last few days, Lady Sale finally had something to celebrate, and she doesn't mince words: 'The conduct of the 37th [sepoys] is highly spoken of: they drove the enemy (who had got on the top of a bastion) with their bayonets clean over the side, where they were received on the bayonets of the 44th.'[22]

In another action on 13 November, the Europeans of the 44th fled from the field, exposing the sepoys of the 37th, who were forced to retire 'when [they] saw the Europeans run, and knew [they] should not be supported'.[23] The Envoy despaired at the conduct of the 44th: 'They are behaving like a pack of despicable cowards.'[24] Sir Moon remarks that the behaviour of the 44th foot was so bad that the '37th Native Infantry refused to act with them, saying that they retreated on their ranks and threw them into confusion'.[25]

The loss of spirit was not limited to soldiers; there was much 'croaking going on' amongst officers, notes Lady Sale: 'Talk of retreat, and consequent desertion of our Mussulman troops ... All this makes a bad impression on the men. Our soldiery like to see the officers bear their part in privation; it makes them more cheerful.'[26] One colonel, when informed that his troops had brought grain from a foraging sortie, replied: 'It was needless, for they would never live to eat it.'[27]

The sense of despondence was such that on 23 November, despite repeated urging from the officers, the men would not advance against a party of Afghan Ghazees, numbering no more than 150. Lady Sale notes, 'Our men would not advance ... At length one of the Ghazees rushed forward, waving his sword over his head: a Sipahee of the 37th darted forth and met him with his bayonet ... and they both fell, and both rose again. Both were killed eventually ... It was very like the scenes depicted in the battles of the Crusaders.'[28] When Captain Mackenzie asked for volunteers to capture the enemy's flags, a havildar of the 37th alone came forward. The 37th Native Infantry had eighty men killed that day; the 44th reported no deaths. Despite this, Brigadier Shelton 'tries to lay all the blame on the Sipahees. He says they are timid, and that makes Europeans timid also; but he has been told some home truths.'[29] After that day, no more military initiatives were taken by the British against their enemies.

In the meantime, Mohammad Akbar Khan, son of the exiled Dost Mohammad Khan, arrived in Kabul with 6,000 Uzbek retainers on 25 November. The noose around the British cantonment tightened further, and attacks became bolder, severe and frequent. The camp followers were now at the brink of starvation; many were surviving on the carcasses of dead animals, which perished due to starvation in the first place. Another skirmish took place, involving the 44th, and after a poor show, the 44th Regiment asked for a court of inquiry to exonerate them and shift the blame to the sepoys. However, Lady Sale, as witness to all ongoings, was clear in her judgement: 'There is too much evidence to prove that the Europeans were the first to run away from the Captured fort.'[30]

Finally, on 11 December, an agreement was reached between the Envoy and Akbar Khan for the British to evacuate the garrison and march back to India, an English officer to be given as hostage, the Afghans ensuring safe passage of the garrison to Peshawar, and supplies on advance payment. The EIC government undertook never to send their army to Afghanistan unless invited, and to restore Dost Mohammad Khan to his throne. They treacherously agreed that Shah Shuja was to evacuate Bala Hisar, either to return to India or stay as a private citizen in Afghanistan.

The agreement nullified all the British efforts to that date, and was a death sentence for Shah Shuja and his immediate family. However, the primary concern of the Envoy and his advisers was for the English to retire to India quickly and safely, with little regard for their allies. Shah Shuja remonstrated: 'Did you bring us back to this country only to hand us over to our enemies?' Shah Shuja was not alone in his despair. Sita Ram remarked:

> At this time a circumstance occurred which I have never seen or heard of before. The Sirdars [Afghan leaders] sent [a] message dictating terms to the Sirkar's [British government's] army ... Nevertheless it would have been better to have died fighting than massacred in the retreat which followed. Wisdom seems to have departed from everyone. The usual energy of the English officers had vanished.[31]

The designated date for the departure of the Army of the Indus, 14 December, came and went. No supplies were received from

Akbar Khan, despite some payments. While the camp followers were scrounging garbage and fodder to get some nourishment, the top British officials now started to curry favour with their enemy, Akbar Khan. This did not escape Lady Sale's notice, who mentions that 'Brigadier Shelton wrote privately to Akbar Khan for forage for his own use, and obtained ten loads of bhoosa [dry grass].'[32] When the Envoy, Macnaghten, discovered the episode, he admonished Shelton for writing to the Afghan chief directly. When General Elphinstone heard about the story, instead of getting angry with his subordinate, he chose not to be left behind in ingratiating himself with Akbar Khan, and asked the Envoy 'if he also could not obtain forage from Akbar direct'.[33] The Envoy forbade direct correspondence between his senior military officials and Akbar Khan but—lo and behold—added that: 'He was in expectation of obtaining some [supplies] for himself, of which he would permit Gen. Elphinstone to have a part'.[34] This shameful and cowardly behaviour on the part of the senior British officials to establish a rapport with the untrustworthy Akbar Khan was to prove destructive to the hapless Indian women and children in the next few weeks.

In the absence of supplies, Macnaghten now foolishly got involved in the Afghan chiefs' intrigues and tried to 'outdiplomatize' the Afghans via a strategy of divide and rule. However, he was exposed and finally murdered by Akbar Khan in plain view of the British cantonment on 23 December. His body was mutilated and his mangled remains left on the streets as a warning to the foreigners. Despite this, Shelton 'again had recourse to Mahommed Akbar; and obtained carriage from him'[35] as late as 29 December.

V

The death march of the Kabul garrison, disguised as a retreat under the treaty, started on 6 January 1842. By that date, the

Afghans had extracted a lot more money and hostages from the British officials, without delivering anything substantial in terms of supplies. All in all, about 4,500 fighting men, and 14,000 women, children and other camp followers departed Kabul on that fateful day. Six British officers were given hostage; sick and wounded British officers and their families were also allowed to remain behind. Lady Macnaghten, Lady Sale and a few other officers' wives and children chose to leave with the army. For those curious about the fate of the sepoys' wives and children, Patrick Macrory comments: 'No one supposed for a moment that he [the General] was referring to any but the British wives and children, nor was any plea put in for the far more numerous wives and children of the sepoys and camp followers … these were native and expendable.'[36]

The Afghan attacks started on the flanks soon, and became sharper and deeper. The biting cold of the winter claimed its own victims. The safe passage promised by Akbar Khan was a ruse. Despite their enfeebled state, the sepoys of the 54th Regiment, part of the rear guard, fought back against the Afghans who had burst into the cantonment before the garrison could depart, and fifty sepoys perished on the first day. Amidst the stampede, a British officer

> [R] remembered as one of the most heart-rending sights of that humiliating day, fixing his eyes by chance on a little Hindustani child, perfectly naked, sitting on the snow, with no mother or father near it. It was a beautiful little girl about two years old … hair curling in waving locks around the soft little throat, and her great black eyes, dilated to twice their normal size, fixed on the armed men, the passing cavalry, and all the strange sights that met her gaze.[37]

The way was littered with children, women and men left on the roadside to perish in the snow.

On the second day, the advance guard, composed of the 44th Regiment, 'moved off—no order given—no bugle sounded'.[38] The Afghans now captured all the guns, and the 44th, whose duty it was to guard them, 'very precipitately made themselves scarce'.[39] The unfortunate column straggled along the treacherous Afghan countryside, with Afghans slaughtering the innocent children, women and men at will. Akbar Khan continued to hover at the tail of the garrison, claiming he was unable to restrain his countrymen.

The nights claimed even more lives: 'Many frozen corpses lay on the ground. Sipahees burnt their accoutrements, and clothes to keep themselves warm.'[40] When a sepoy's tent was used by the few British ladies and their husbands to sleep, 'the Sipahees and camp followers, half frozen, tried to force their way, not only into the tent, but actually into our beds ... Many poor wretches died round the tent in the night.'[41]

When the desperate and dying stragglers reached Khord Kabul Pass, surrounded by Ghilzai tribes with their jezails, 'The scene of slaughter was dreadful ... The enemy ... poured in a murderous fire ... descended into the Pass and slew man, woman and child. The whole road for a distance of 5 miles was covered with dead and dying. The 37th Native Infantry lost more than half its men.'[42]

The Afghans now started to strip and plunder the defenceless camp followers, and took young children and women to be sold as slaves. An English officer who was accompanying Akbar Khan as a hostage saw: 'One miscreant [Afghan] had a little Indian girl seated on his horse behind him,'[43] and reported nothing further on her.

On 9 January, General Elphinstone handed all the English women and children to Akbar Khan for their safety, including Lady Sale. Again, no thought was given to the safety of the Indian women and children. When Lady Sale marched with Akbar Khan to the rear of the column, she saw: 'The road covered with awfully mangled bodies, all naked ... Numbers of camp followers, still

The storming of Seringapatam depicted by John Vendramini, 1802.

An Indian Army column marching through a French village as locals watch, 1915.

The Indian cavalry marching through a French village, Estrée Blanche, 25 July 1915.

Wrestling matches, Jats at play, near Merville, France, with an audience of 6th Jats, 26 July 1915.

A group of off-duty soldiers from 6th Jats smoking and relaxing outside their billets near Merville, France. 26 July 1915.

Sikhs and French villagers in Le Sart, France, 24 July 1915.

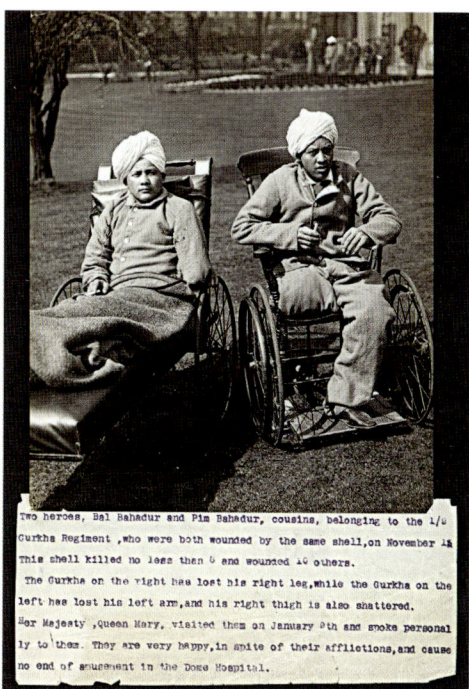

Two heroes, Bal Bahadur and Pim Bahadur, in the Dome Hospital in Brighton, 1915.

A sepoy, probably of the Madras Native Infantry, on the march. The sepoy is in undress, carrying a sword, and is preceded by his wife and two children mounted on a white bullock. A man carrying a stick and a bundle leads the way. Created c. 1800.

The East offering its riches to Britannia, by Spiridione Roma, 1778.

Panorama of a durbar procession of Akbar II, the Emperor of Delhi, 1806–37, probably on the occasion of Eid or after Ramadan. Created c. 1815.

A postcard, c. 1905–18.

The passage of River Chumbal by the British Indian Army, by Dickinson & Co., Young, Charles Becher, London, c. 1850.

A coffee party after a parade at a military station in India, by Michael Hanhart and Nicholas Hanhart, c. 1850.

Mutinous sepoys, by George Francklin Atkinson, London, 1859.

Reinforcements proceeding to Delhi, by George Francklin Atkinson, London, 1859.

The advance of the siege train, by George Francklin Atkinson, London, 1859.

An assemblage of Gurkhas, by James Baillie Fraser and Robert Havell, London, 1820.

A crowd and procession of elephants at the Delhi durbar event to celebrate Queen Victoria taking the title 'Empress of India', 1 January 1877.

Naik Darwen Singh Negi depicted in an action for which he was awarded the Victoria Cross, 1915.

The Kurukshetra battle: Lord Krishna explaining the duties of a warrior to Arjun, 1753.

'Terrible disaster in Afghanistan. Great slaughter of British troops', in *The Illustrated Police News*, London, 1880.

'Nanga', a naked ascetic. This particular one is associated with the 'Vairagis' and is armed with a spear, gun and tulwar. Created by Anon., 1825.

alive, frost bitten and starving, some perfectly out of their senses and idiotic ... the smell of blood sickening; and the corpses lay so thick it was impossible to look from them, as it required care to guide my horse so as not to tread upon the bodies.'[44]

By the next morning, 10 January, an English officer recorded: 'We had now not a single sepoy remaining of the whole of the Kabul Force.'[45] That same evening, the General and his surviving British troops tried to quietly sneak away from the camp followers to Jagdalak. At this stage, the usually empathetic Lady Sale also lost her sympathy for the wretched stragglers: 'The camp followers having been the bane of this unfortunate army, they [the British column] hoped to move off quietly and leave them behind; but no sooner did they start, then they found that all who were able to stand were accompanying them.'[46] The camp followers did not suddenly spring forth from the loins of the sepoys. The lady seemed to forget that they were sent with the consent of the Governor-General to keep the sepoys 'anchored' in the foreign country. Sadly, the doomed Hindustanis still looked to their officers and troops for some protection, but the surviving English officers were concerned about their own lives more than anything else by this stage.

Thus, on 11 January, General Elphinstone, his deputy Brigadier Shelton and few other English officers handed themselves over to Akbar Khan as hostages to save their lives, abandoning the few hundred surviving camp followers and troops. They pretended that they had gone to 'confer' with Akbar Khan, but Lady Sale honestly records that the previous day the General 'had received a note in cypher from Capt. Conolly, warning him that Akbar Khan had quitted Cabul, with the avowed intention of getting into his hands the person of the General, and all the married [English] people with their families.'[47] The General, instead of being cautioned, used the information to pass himself into the hands of Akbar Khan. While Indian camp followers starved and shivered in the Afghan mountains, the General and his officers enjoyed 'good pillau and other dishes, as also tea ... and they formed a circle round it, and all [Akbar Khan and the English officers] ate out of the same dish.'[48]

Sita Ram, though shocked, was still sympathetic: 'To everyone's amazement, [the General] agreed to go to [Akbar Khan's captivity], but with the example of Burnes and "Macnaten" before him, what could he expect.'[49] Burnes and Macnaghten, of course, were slaughtered in the open by the Afghans a few months back.

The General and his officers placed themselves safely in Akbar Khan's lap, two days after securing a promise from Akbar Khan that he 'would not favour the desertion of the [Indian] troops; and he [Akbar] promised that all going over to him should be shot ... One of the Mission chuprassies [Indian civil official] was caught in the act of going off, and shot.'[50]

Akbar Khan, of course, knew that the English valued their own lives more than those of their colonial subjects. He wanted to ensure safe passage for his father, who was in India still, and correctly calculated that taking more English hostages would be the best way to achieve this. The next day, he confidently told the General that he would 'bring every European away in safety ... but he would not allow a single Hindostanee to follow.'[51]

The General, on 12 January, smuggled out a message to the remnants of the 44th, the European regiment, 'urging them to make a run for it. The 200 remaining men did this that same night.'[52] However, not without the inconvenience of 'the camp followers, who were still numerous, crowded upon them as usual.'[53] Sita Ram had attached himself to the 44th Regiment in this final push to break through the Jagdalak pass. The Afghans now blocked the pass with barriers, and slaughtered the followers and soldiers alike. The cavalry galloped through and over the infantry in the hope of securing their own retreat through the pass and to Jalalabad. Some infantrymen fired at their own cavalry thus fleeing.

In the melee, Sita Ram 'was struck down by a jezail ball on the side of my head. After this I knew nothing until I found myself tied crossways upon a horse which was being led rapidly away from the fighting towards Kabul. I now learned that I was being taken there to be sold as a slave. I begged to be shot, or have my throat cut, and abused the Afghans in Pushtu and in my own language. Many a knife shook in its sheath, but my captor could not prevent me speaking, and as the fear of death had no effect on me he threatened to make me a Moslem on the spot if I did not keep quiet.'[54]

While Sita Ram was being carried towards Kabul, the remnant of the column emerged out of the Jagdalak pass, and when they reached Gandamak, the scene of Woollen's painting, the force consisted of twenty officers, fifty men of the 44th, six of the horse artillery, and four or five sepoys. Three hundred wretched camp followers still continued to trail after them. This was the final outcome of the Army of the Indus's Kabul garrison, which had comprised close to 20,000 men, women and children a week earlier. Just about 1.5 per cent of the Indians from the Kabul garrison were last seen alive at Gandamak, compared to almost 20 per cent of the Europeans who left Kabul on 6 January. The disaster fell primarily on the hapless Indian sepoys and their families, and about 500–600 European soldiers and officers perished too. The imperial hierarchy was not just a matter of status and pay; the Afghan disaster proved that it placed the value of some lives above others. Despite this, the impact of the Afghan resistance levelled the imperial hierarchy to some extent in the end.

This is the background to the 'stand' at Gandamak, where the survivors of the 'advance guard' of the Kabul garrison had assembled in a rush to escape to Jalalabad. The remaining 300 camp followers were not reported alive thereafter, and the Afghans showed no mercy to the Europeans on the hill either.

VI

The camp followers who were not killed immediately by the Afghans, or were not healthy enough to be sold as slaves, had a miserable end. Lady Sale, now safely ensconced in Akbar Khan's camp, was transported with the General, accompanying English officers and their families through the Afghan countryside. She records:

> We also passed a cave at small distance, in front of which were some dead bodies and many bones strewed about: and, from the blood close to its entrance, there is every reason to believe that the inhabitants were supporting nature by devouring each other. I saw three poor wretches crawling on hands and knees just within the cave: but all we had to bestow upon them was pity, not unmingled with horror at the evidence of cannibalism but too apparent. These miserable creatures called to us for that relief which we had it not in our power to afford; and we can only hope that their sufferings were speedily terminated by death.[55]

The English hostages were eventually rescued by a subsequent 'Army of Retribution' sent to restore the ruined dignity of the Empire. Thousands of Indians were not so lucky, as most of the able-bodied Indians were sold into slavery, with 'men sell[ing] for forty-six rupees, and women for twenty-two rupees each.'[56]

The rescue of hostages focused on English prisoners, and unfortunately Sita Ram, like many other sepoys, was left to fend for himself. The resilient Sita Ram 'did not become a Mahommedan but strove to bear up against [his] hard fate' as a slave of one Osman Beg. Initially, he lived in hope of rescue, but soon learnt that the English had come, burnt Kabul and left for India with the English prisoners. He bribed one Ahmad Shah, a caravan trader, with a promise to pay 500 rupees for carrying him to India. He was almost caught on the road to Ghazni, when his master's caravan appeared opposite him, moving in a different direction. Sita Ram covered his face, and seeing his master from a distance 'at once determined to use the pistol which I had been given, either against him or myself, rather than be taken back into slavery'.[57] Fortunately, Sita Ram was unnoticed, and finally arrived at Ferozepore in October 1843.

Sita Ram was in for a further shock on his arrival at the cantonment. The brigade major at the cantonment told him that 'the Government would not pay as much as 500 rupees, or indeed anything, for my ransom!'[58], leaving him at the mercy of Ahmed Shah. He borrowed 250 rupees from a subedar, and on the subedar's testimonial, the brigadier major finally paid the balance, after making Sita Ram sign a promissory note. Finally, Sita Ram was a free man. The ransom was eventually reimbursed but Sita Ram's salary for the period he was in slavery in Afghanistan was not paid 'as there were no accounts to show how many months' arrears of pay were due to me, or to any others of Shah Shuja's Levy'.[59] He did manage to join another regiment as havildar.

The Afghan retreat of 1842 had a very deep impact on the psyche of the sepoys. The Bengal Army was never the same. The bond of trust between the sepoy and the officer was stretched too thin. No wonder that all the native regiments that were in Afghanistan mutinied in 1857. Despite the sepoys' stoicism and forbearance, some Europeans in India and England tried to find scapegoats in the sepoys, to explain the disaster which was not at all of their making. Brigadier Nott, the only senior officer who came out of the Afghan campaign with credit to his name, keeping his regiment at Kandahar safe, and then marching back via Kabul, wrote to his daughter: 'I have now several times seen European troops under fire with sepoys alongside of them, and, believe me, the more I see of sepoys, the more I like them; properly managed, they are the best troops in the world. Some John Bulls would hang me for saying this.'[60]

Sir Henry Lawrence, one of the finest observers of the events in Afghanistan, summed up the impact of the campaign thus:

> At Caubul, we lost an army, and we lost some character with the surrounding states. But I find that by far our worse loss was in the confidence of our Native soldiery. Better had it been if our harassed troops had rushed on the enemy, and perished to a man, than that surviving sepoys should be able to tell the tales they can of what they saw at Caubul ... when it is not the Hindustani (most exposed to cold, and least able to bear it) who clamours for retreat and capitulation, but the cry is raised by the men (British) he has been accustomed to look up to and to lean upon.[61]

The Afghan campaign costed fifteen million pounds[62] — a multiple of the combined GDP of India and the UK at the time — all borne by Indian taxpayers. This was a tragic war, paid for by starving Indian peasants, for the massacre of 20,000 of their own countrymen in a foreign land, to fulfil the fantasies of a few imperialists. Not a needle moved in Afghanistan, Dost Mohammad was back in power, and the murderer of the British Envoy, Akbar Khan, appointed his Wazir. What bigger indictment of imperial hubris than this?

Despite this disaster, the British Empire invaded Afghanistan in 1878–80 on a similar unwise strategy and logic, spearheaded by the Indian Army. After securing initial victories, the British made the mistake of leaving a Resident Envoy in Kabul. The Envoy, Sir Louis Cavagnari, was guarded by a small contingent, numbering about seventy-five, of the Guides, an Indian regiment. The Afghans surrounded the Residency, and the Guides gave a good account of themselves but they were hopelessly outnumbered. Most of the Guides died in repeated sorties to protect the Residency, and when the Envoy was also killed in one of the charges, the Afghans asked the remaining twelve Indians to surrender, saying they had no quarrel with them.

Having seen the pusillanimity of the British Army officers in the first war, when the Envoy was murdered in open sight of the garrison, and expecting the same this time round, the Afghans were in for a surprise this time. The Afghans shouted that no English are left alive in Kabul, and that if the Guides laid down their arms, they would be spared. The Guides, led by Jemadar Jewand Singh, had a final consultation. Then, to the absolute shock and befuddlement of the Afghans, the Guides charged at the hordes surrounding the Residency. Every single one of the Guides sold their lives as dearly as possible, and eventually fell under Afghan knives or bullets. Jewand Singh personally killed eight of the enemy, and by the end of the day, 600 of the enemy lay dead around the bodies of the Guides.

This 'last stand' is in contrast with the 'last stand at Gandamauck', which formed the subject of Wollen's hagiographic painting in 1898, receiving no such memorial despite being more recent.

VII

The Indian Army continued to undertake successful campaigns in Asia and Africa for the rest of the nineteenth century, and once garrisoned Malta and Cyprus during the 1878 Russian crisis. The last successful campaign before the Great War was against the Boxer rebels in China during 1900-01, followed by a brief campaign to intimidate the Tibetans in 1903. In addition, the Army was continuously engaged in the North-West Frontier against the Pathan tribes.

However, the Great War involved the Indian Army at an unprecedented scale. More than 1.1 million Indians served outside India, the majority of them in Mesopotamia. The Mesopotamia campaign was the biggest engagement of the Indian Army outside India in its history, and it was only matched during WW2 in the Burma theatre. In Mesopotamia, after initial successes, the British Army suffered a crushing defeat in 1916 at the hands of the Ottoman Army. This was the most humiliating defeat for the British Army after the first Afghan war. Almost all the callousness towards Indian lives, poor planning, terrible supplies and equipment, and gross underestimation of their enemies—demonstrated during the first Afghan war—was repeated during the campaign preceding the defeat and surrender at Kut-al-Amara in Mesopotamia in April 1916.

In many ways, the Mesopotamia campaign up to the Kut disaster is a sad reflection of the British strategy of 'war on the cheap' using Indian resources that had worked so well until then, and its limitations. The Empire's exploitative economic model using Indian revenues to pay for its global military reserve, its unequal treatment of its subjects, and its hubris, all collapsed into the humiliating defeat at the hands of the Ottoman Army in 1916. The Indian Army, subsequently better supplied—as a hue and cry arose in England on the discovery of the murderous wastage of lives—eventually went on to defeat the Ottoman armies in the Middle East, securing a resounding victory by 1918. However, that seemed like an age away in late 1915 and 1916.

To understand the structural drivers of the Kut disaster, we need to understand the economic underpinnings of the British Empire in India for the preceding two centuries. At the start of the eighteenth century, India was a much larger economy, almost ten times that of the UK, and an average Indian's income was three-quarters that of a British person. By the start of the Great War, Britain had overtaken India as an economy, and the average British person was five times richer than the average Indian.[63] The revenue base of India to finance an army was ten times higher than that of Britain in 1700; but by the beginning of the Great War, it was lower than Britain. The other European powers had also grown correspondingly richer in comparison to India over this period. Therefore, despite almost half of the Indian revenue base being spent on maintaining the British Indian Army, the absolute amount of the army budget had declined in comparison to Britain and other European powers. With much larger economies at the start of the twentieth century, Britain and other European countries could afford a correspondingly larger military budget in absolute terms, even if they spent a smaller percentage of their revenues on defence, compared to India. Britain, benefitting from the imperial reserve based in India, spent a much lower portion of its GDP on defence, compared to the European powers.

The consequence of this was that the Indian Army at the start of the twentieth century was poorly equipped in comparison to other armies, let alone European armies; even if the morale and motivation of its soldiers was second to none. The Indian economy had been destroyed by colonial exploitation, and could not afford to equip an army capable of taking on other global powers. When the war started, the British home army budget was expanded massively, but no such capacity existed in India, because already the majority of the revenue went to military expenditure. The standing army in India had served its purpose of a global reserve in numerous conflicts of the previous century, but its funding had to be drastically expanded if it was to face modern powers in the Great War.

No such budgetary support was provided to enhance the Indian Army's capability at the start of the Great War. Over the next four years, the demands on the Indian Army expanded significantly; and from a standing army of 150,000 soldiers with a role limited to defending Indian frontiers from 'minor' enemies, it expanded to almost 1.5 million men, fighting on a global scale.

When the Indian Lahore and Meerut Divisions landed in Europe in October 1914 to avert disaster on the Western Front, the inadequate supplies and equipment were quickly evident; crucially to the French, who treated their imperial subjects in the army much better. Being close to Britain, the deficiencies were made up in a few months. However, the Indian Army in Mesopotamia would not have the same good fortune, as they were not exposed to the mirror gaze of the French, or indeed to their fellow countrymen in India. They were treated as expendable, and suffered depredations and death at an immeasurable scale that could have been avoided if the financial burden of the Indian Army had been fairly shared with the British exchequer historically. It had been borne on the backs of poor Indian peasants, who could not afford to equip their soldiers better from their limited resources, as they themselves survived almost at the subsistence level.

Despite India's abysmal fiscal situation and poverty, it contributed almost £214 million from Indian revenue towards the Great War, including a £100 million 'free gift to the mother country'.[64] This was more than twice the annual revenue of the Government of India.[65] To put it in perspective, it would be similar to the UK Government today subsidizing another country's war effort by contributing 1,600 billion pounds — almost 80 per cent of its current annual GDP.

However, returning to 1914, the Indian Army was grossly underequipped for a modern war. Its transport was based on mules, it was armed with old rifles, and artillery was almost non-existent. Medical services and hospital equipment belonged to the nineteenth century. Aircraft were unknown. The cavalry still operated on the 'silladar' system, where the trooper bought a membership of a cavalry regiment by down payment, and supplied his own horse and equipment. The Indian soldiers still used weapons inferior to the European soldiers.

All this was the consequence of the parsimony of the British government in London. It was obvious to everyone except Whitehall that the Indian Army was a strategic global reserve for the safety and security of the whole British Empire, as its numerous expeditions over the last century had proved. As such, it should have been paid and equipped accordingly; if needed, from the revenues of the British exchequer. However, that would have upset the 'gravy train' that the Raj in India was. India's most regular and significant financial contribution to the mother country was the maintenance of a standing army at zero cost to the British exchequer. The British excuse was that the Indian Army was for India's defence and so must be funded exclusively by Indian taxes. This made it awkward to use this army outside India.

What proves this point is that the British strategic planners were reluctant to deploy the Indian Army—especially against white enemies—outside India. The peril of the Western Front, when the British Army was about to be thrown into the English Channel, forced the reluctant use of Indian soldiers in Europe. Thereafter, it was clear to the war planners in London that it would be impossible to run and win a global war without the resources of India.

Thus, by November 1914, when war was declared on Ottoman Turkey, almost 5,000 men of the Indian Army—more than 80 per cent of whom were Indians—landed at Basra, with medical support that could cater to no more than a few hundred casualties. Reinforcements would expand this army to 12,000 in the next few months, and thereafter by the end of the war, almost 600,000 Indians would serve in this theatre. The largest number of casualties suffered by the Indian Army was also in Mesopotamia, especially the unfortunate ones who landed there up to 1916.

Before the tragic turn of events in 1916, the 6th Poona Division in Mesopotamia was one of the rare earliest successes in the Great War. It captured Basra, secured the Gulf and the oil supplies, sufficiently intimidated the local Arabs and Persians, and pushed the Ottoman armies 435 miles back to the edge of Baghdad, at Ctesiphon. This was achieved in the extremely harsh weather of Iraq, without adequate transport and supplies, and reflects on the level of motivation of the Indian Army and its soldiers.

However, despite being fully aware of the limited equipment and supplies and knowing the risks, the British civil and military leaders overplayed their hand. The successes in driving the Turks from their southern positions spurred ideas of capturing Baghdad. The Viceroy in India confided in a friend, 'I hope to be the Pasha of Baghdad before I leave India!'; reflecting the hubris and blurred visions of grandeur at the cost of Indian soldiers. Every mile advanced north was stretching the supply lines of an already ill-equipped army, which had been winning so far with its motivation, fighting not just against the Turks but also the landscape and the climate.

VIII

After retreating for a year, the Turks were well entrenched at Ctesiphon, some nineteen miles south of Baghdad, and more than 300 miles away from Basra, the base of the British Indian Army in Mesopotamia. The 6th Indian Division, comprising 13,700 fighting men led by Lieutenant General Townshend,[66] attacked Ctesiphon on 22 November 1915. Of this force, British troops were approximately 2,750 and the remaining 11,000 were Indians. One of the many surprises of the Great War was the performance of the Ottoman Army. British leadership underestimated the fight

Turks gave in defending their homes and country. They might not have been as rich as Britain and France, but their equipment—supplied by the German Army—was far better than the Indian Army's.

At Ctesiphon, the Indian Army was outnumbered and outgunned, and the tide turned. The Turks not only repulsed the attack at Ctesiphon, they now pursued the British Indian Army south, which suffered severe casualties, and was almost without any medical support. The British strategy was premised on continued success, and made no allowance for a defeat and retreat pursued by a determined enemy. Even if a reverse had been factored in, the medical resources were abysmal. There was no adequate field hospital, provision was made only for a few hundred casualties, and animal wagons were used as ambulances.

The result was a slaughter, as much by the negligence and absence of transport and medical facilities as by Turkish bullets. Sisir Sarbadhikari, a medical assistant with the Bengal Ambulance Corps, writes in his diary of the day: 'We left behind those who were badly wounded. They couldn't stand let alone walk. When they saw that we were leaving they began to weep, and who could blame them? ... We tried to reassure them by saying that we would send transport for them soon.'[67]

While injured Indian soldiers were left behind, two British officers with fractured legs were fortunate to be picked by Sarbadhikari's team and transported on stretchers to steamers for onward transport to Kut-al-Amara; Sarbadhikari continues to describe the fate of the men next day:

> On all sides, the corpses of men and animals. In some places they seemed to be in each other's arms; in some places men had been pinned under animals and were lying there, groaning ... In some places men were hanging from the wires; some were dead (they were the lucky ones) and

some were still alive. Here was a severed hand hanging from the wire; there a foot. One man was hanging on the wires with all his entrails tumbling out. In some trenches four or five men had died with their limbs thrown over each other—Turkish, Hindustani, British, Gurkha, all mixed up together ... One man's limb in another man's stomach, another's in someone's eye, that's how they were lying—and in the midst of this some were still alive—bringing them out was impossibly difficult.[68]

The casualties—estimated to be 4,300 by Townshend—forced the 6th Division's retreat to Kut-al-Amara, ninety miles south on the Tigris river. Here, Townshend decided to make a stand, and the Turks laid siege to the town.

By now, the Indian 3rd and 7th Divisions had been diverted from the Western Front in Europe to Mesopotamia. They arrived in early January, sans all the good equipment that they used on the Western Front for a year against the Germans. They were just as ill-equipped for the fight that lay ahead as the besieged 6th Division at Kut. Both the divisions were immediately thrown into relieving Kut, without establishing supply lines, and without adequate medical facilities. The prospect of surrender of the 6th Division at Kut was unimaginable for the war leaders in London, especially to an Oriental enemy, as was the effect it would have on the prestige of the Empire.

With primitive light artillery, the relief force had no chance against the well-entrenched Turkish machine guns. The repeated efforts to relieve Kut failed over the next three months, at a very heavy cost to the Indian soldiers. Once again, the unbearable suffering and death was caused more due to lack of supplies, almost non-existent medical support and poor generalship. The injured Indian soldiers were left out in the cold for there weren't enough stretchers or ambulances to transport them to the field hospital and subsequently 220 miles to Basra, from where the seriously maimed could be sent to Bombay hospitals. While lying in the cold, the soldiers were frequently murdered by the Arab tribes, who stole clothes from their bodies. The ambulances were rickety, springless two-wheel carts pulled by mules or horses. Travelling in them was so painful for those with broken limbs that many soldiers dragged themselves to the edges of these carts and threw themselves out. They preferred to crawl to the field hospital three miles away from the front line. Even when they reached the field hospital, only a lucky few got any treatment. The hospitals had just 250 beds, while the number of wounded swelled quickly to 4,000 and kept rising. Dead and dying wounded soldiers lay outside the hospital in the mud, with their wounds infested with maggots, and bodies drowned in their own excreta.

Even in such desperate conditions, the imperial hierarchy ensured that the white soldiers and officers received priority in medical treatment at the field hospital, and then during the steamer and barge river transport back to Basra on the Tigris. The European wounded were given covered areas on the steamers while Indians lay on bare decks. The last vestiges of dignity were stolen from the Indian soldiers on these steamers and barges, as they lay exposed, drenched under winter rain, while their European counterparts were sheltered. One British officer described the arrival of the injured Indian soldiers on medical transports to Basra:

> The patients were so huddled and crowded together on the ship that they could not perform the offices of nature clear of the edge of the ship and the whole of the ship's side was covered with stalactites of human faeces ... We found a mass of men huddled up anyhow—some with blankets and some without ... they were covered in dysentery and dejecta generally from head to foot.[69]

While soldiers were dying in agony, General Nixon, Townshend's superior and Theatre Commander, lied to Whitehall in a letter: 'Wounded satisfactorily disposed of, many likely to recover ...'[70] S.L. Menezes aptly observes that disposal was death, and the recovery was that of corpses. Repeated efforts to relieve Kut led to almost 30,000 casualties, 8,000 of whom were dead, mostly Indians.[71] However, the Turks did not release their stranglehold over the town and the 6th Division.

The circumstances of those who were besieged in Kut were no better. Freezing temperatures, lack of clothing and blankets, inadequate medical arrangements, and unrelenting shelling from the Turks made life hell for the besieged. To add insult to injury, the British troops continued to get preferential treatment in all basic necessities throughout the siege, which reflects in the much lower mortality of white troops compared to Indians. The worst was the lack of adequate food, and consequent malnutrition and starvation, which killed almost half of the Indian soldiers in the camp. Captain Kalyan Mukherjee, a doctor with the 6th Division, writes:

> After three months with very little to eat the troops are starving ... Of what use is medicine now? There is nothing to eat ... With nothing to give them, how can we help? Apart from that, there are no medicines left either ... What we went through during the siege is beyond description. When we came here, after our defeat at Ctesiphon, our [reference to Indians] numbers were 10/11 thousand; now it is less than half that. It's horrifying![72]

The Turks continued to tighten their squeeze on the town, and incessant bombardment added to the misery of the troops. Sarbadhikari describes:

One shell, instead of bursting above, hit a sepoy who was lying in bed, in one of the tents; it took off half his face before burying itself. The man rose to his feet as he was dying and then fell to the ground. His eyes, nose and mouth were all gone, there were only holes in his face, spouting blood. The sight was so ghastly that it created terror amongst others in the tent.[73]

It appears that hunger was the worst killer. The town's limited food supply was particularly short on grains, vegetables and lentils, the basic source of protein for vegetarian Indian soldiers. The soldiers could neither change nor bathe, and had to wear just one set of clothes. As a result, 'Everybody was covered with lice. They would swarm all over us ... For lack of meat or fresh vegetables, scurvy broke out.'[74]

Even for those soldiers who took meat, the fresh and tinned supplies ran out. The garrison now started to consume its pack animals, including horses. This was a particularly sensitive issue for Hindu soldiers who did not eat meat, and even for those who ate meat, horse and mule meat felt taboo. Those who did not accept horsemeat now continued to starve and deteriorate. Townshend resorted to quoting the Imam of Jama Masjid in Delhi and other 'leading' pundits and granthis that horsemeat was not objectionable. Most remained unmoved, as 'they declared that every village pundit would be against them on their return to India and that, in consequence, no one would give them their daughters to marry'.[75]

Most Indian troops continued to subsist on flour and plants picked from the orchards and river bank, abstaining from horsemeat. Their condition deteriorated further, and many of them succumbed to jaundice, pneumonia and dysentery, for their immunity had degenerated due to poor diet. Under severe duress and threats of demotion for the Indian VCOs, many Indian soldiers did come around to accepting horsemeat by mid-April. However, it was too late by then. Many Hindus stuck to their prejudice, and preferred to die than eat 'forbidden' meat. Some pre-empted their death from starvation by walking down to the Tigris, standing with folded arms and waiting for a Turkish soldier's bullet to end their agony. The stoutly devout preferred a steel bullet in their chest to the flesh of another living being in their mouth. Thus ended their journey in this material world, on the banks of the ancient river of Mesopotamia, far from their homes, but true to what they considered to be their faith.

While his troops suffered, General Townshend fudged his reports about the supply situation to force an early relief. He reported lower supplies than what they had. This only led to more casualties for the relieving Indian divisions, without any success. He used the signallers to send messages to his family and friends but not to troops' families. He asked for a promotion during the siege, and asked permission if he could escape to fight another day, abandoning the besieged division. In a sorry reminder of the conduct of General Elphinstone and Shelton in Afghanistan in 1842, he sent ingratiating messages to the Turkish commander besieging his troops. When he surrendered along with the 6th Division on 29 April, he luxuriated in the hospitality of his captors, while his troops suffered forced marches, starvation and death. He first went to Baghdad, then to Constantinople and subsequently stayed at a villa on Halki Island in the Marmara Sea as an 'honoured guest' of the Turks, after having lied to his troops that he was leaving them to secure their repatriation. He even arranged with the Turkish commander to transfer his pet dog to Basra, from where it was transported to Britain to join its master, while more than two-thirds of his troops taken prisoner would die in captivity.

On 29 April 1916, General Townshend with his garrison of 2,750 British troops, 6,500 Indian troops, 227 British officers and 204 Indian VCOs surrendered to Khalil Pasha, the Turkish Commander.[77] Most of the British troops had survived the defeat at Ctesiphon and the ensuing siege, while almost 30 per cent of Indians had perished.[77] It would be convenient to blame the rejection of horsemeat by the Indians for this high mortality. The truth is that the structural inequalities of the imperial hierarchy, which remained in place during the siege, as British officers were in charge, jeopardized the life chances of Indians. Indians received inferior medical facilities, accommodation, supplies and food, leading to their reduced chances of survival. Nikolas Gardner quotes a study that indicates the number of Indians who died in Kut was ten times higher than the British.[78] This disparity is also validated by Kalyan Mukherjee's testimony above.

In Turkish captivity, the suffering of Indian troops intensified, but the big change was that the British troops also now suffered in equal measure, as Turkish maltreatment ignored the imperial hierarchies maintained by the British officers so far. The Turks separated the 400 or so British and Indian officers from the other ranks, and sent them ahead by river and motor transport to Turkey, where they spent the rest of the war. It rankled some British officers that Indian VCOs were being treated similarly to them. Major Sandes did not lose the chance to explain to the Turks that 'Indian officers ... were always inferior in rank to British officers'.[79] He writes matter-of-factly, 'Our first business was naturally to get separate accommodation for the Indian officers.'[80] Even in the worst of circumstances, imperial hierarchies continued to add insult to the injuries of Indian VCOs.

If the British officers were discriminating against VCOs, the soldiers were no different. Sarbadhikari recounts that on steamers to Baghdad, the white soldiers now turned to the usual scapegoating:

> The white or British soldiers are behaving very badly with the black or Indian sepoys; they're even beating them!

They say it is because of the Indians that they lost at Kut! It's unimaginably vile. The astonishing thing is that even when complaints are taken to the British officers, they do nothing. The whites are sitting in comfort in the lower deck, every one of them has space to sleep. We're on the upper deck—there's no roof over our heads, and we scarcely have enough space to sit.[81]

Such discrimination between whites and Indians was to be short-lived, as soon they would all be subject to extremely harsh conditions in Turkish captivity. As in the Afghan campaign of 1842, the blade and brutality of the enemy (Afghans and Turks) would bring about a sad even-handedness in the fate and circumstance of the Indian and British soldiers of the Empire.

IX

British and Indian prisoners arrived in Baghdad on steamers in May, spent two months there, and went from Baghdad to Samara on trains on 19 July.[82] From Samara, the prisoners were forced to march to prisoner camps in Ras al-Ain, which currently is in Syria, bordering Turkey. This gruelling 500-mile+ distance was covered over forty-six days on foot. The route included: Samara—Tikrit—Sangat—Hammam Ali—Mosul—Tell Kaaf—Nisibeen—Ras al-Ain.[83] Meanwhile, the approximately 400 officers continued on some form of transport into Turkey, avoiding the terrible fate of the soldiers.

A number of accounts describe the horrors of the forced march from Samara to Ras al-Ain. The burning heat of the Mesopotamian summer amid the sands during the day, lack of food, and dysentery and disease were compounded by the atrocities of the prisoners' guards. Those who were too weak to walk were simply left behind, to die of starvation or to be eaten by animals or have their throats slit by the local tribes. Many prisoners were described as delirious skeletons walking and mumbling to themselves, their eyes sunken, and faces pale. Sarbadhikari's recollection of the march was the cruel shouts from their guards: 'haidi haidi', meaning hurry up, in the middle of the night, which marked the start of a forced march. The prisoners were flogged, whipped, knifed, shot and stoned by the local Iraqi civilians as well as the Turkish guards. Their clothes, boots and other belongings were ripped off from them.

Sarbadhikari describes these atrocities in a very stoic, matter of fact way in his diary. The most evocative narrative from late August is the fate of the Armenians, who were facing unspeakable cruelty at the hands of the local population and Turkish military. Early in August, when they reached Mosul, Sarbadhikari learnt that the Hindu and Sikh soldiers would be separated from the Muslim and British soldiers, and sent to work on the rail line at Ras al-Ain. Ras al-Ain was also the area where most of the Armenian concentration camps were located. The Hindu soldiers assumed that being neither Europeans nor co-religionists of Turks, they would be treated worse off. When they learnt that the camps they were being sent to would be shared with the Armenians, it only confirmed their fears, as now they felt they were being singled out to suffer the same fate as the Armenians. The soldiers had started to see the signs of the atrocities towards Armenians during their march from late August onwards, even before reaching Ras al-Ain. No wonder the feeling of a shared plight led to bonds of sympathy as the 'underdogs' of the imperial system on all sides.

Muslim Indian soldiers did get slightly better treatment during their captivity. The Hindus and Sikhs were worse off, and British prisoners certainly suffered more than they had before the surrender to the Turks. However, the discrimination between British and Indian soldiers continued into the prisoner camps. Sarbadhikari mentions the higher rate of pay from Red Cross and Relief funds to the white soldiers compared to the Indian soldiers, and also better provisions — sugar instead of molasses, for instance. However, the Turks seemed to have treated both the British and Hindu/Sikh soldiers equally badly, with some exceptions permitted by human bonds and circumstances.

Sarbadhikari's first encounter with the Armenians came around 18 August, when he met two rosy-cheeked Armenian boys, eight to ten years old. Sisir writes 'we understood that the Turks had slaughtered their father and older brothers; where their mother was, they did not know.'[84] On 23 August, he came across a small village that looked 'pretty as a picture' from a distance. When he entered the village, it was empty; and it dawned on him that this was an Armenian village before 'men had been slaughtered and the women and children driven away'.[85] Sarbadhikari cautiously walked to a well in the village, and did not dare to drink as 'there were Armenian corpses rotting in many of them'.[86] Sarbadhikari does not describe himself as being witness to the Turkish soldiers committing these atrocities, and at one place suggests that local inhabitants — Kurds, Chechens and others — were responsible for these cruelties towards the Armenians, and not the regular Ottoman soldiers. However, it is difficult to see how local inhabitants could have carried out such a murderous campaign against a vast population of civilians with an army amidst them, unless they had at least their tacit support.

After seeing a number of burnt-down villages, Sarbadhikari and his fellow prisoners reached Ras al-Ain on 2 September via Nisibeen. Here the prisoners were ordered to work on the Istanbul to Baghdad railway. Sarbadhikari describes how the 'prisoners would be taken to work barefoot on the line, in snow. They would get frostbite at first and then the flesh would fall off and the wounds would turn gangrenous.[87] They were housed in Bedouin tents, exposed to the elements of nature, with limited rations given only once in three days, and asked to collect camel dung to cook their food, as there was no firewood, and no trees to get branches from.

Typhus decimated the Indian prisoners at Ras al-Ain from November onwards, when Sarbadhikari was luckily sent to Aleppo to accompany very seriously ill patients to the hospital there. The Aleppo hospital was a unique oasis in the sea of misery that drowned the Armenians. Here many of the staff were Armenians, including the doctor who ran the ward in which Sarbadhikari was. This doctor, Saghir Effendi, receives praise from Sarbadhikari on account of his care for the patients and his good nature. Sadly, Dr Saghir Effendi was 'sent to the firing line' in January 1917, and Sarbadhikari was 'saddened to learn of this' and vowed to never 'forget his kindness'.[88] We will never know for what offence the poor doctor was killed; perhaps he just annoyed an officer, perhaps he was picked at random, just to add to the numbers of dead and dying.

Sarbadhikari also mentions an Armenian woman called Marum: 'How well she looked after us!' Sadly, her kindness did not credit her in the eyes of the authorities and she was dismissed from service soon. It must have been harrowing for the Armenian staff to work in the Aleppo hospital, knowing fully well that only a few miles away members of their community were being killed in the camps. Sarbadhikari and other Indian troops remained sympathetic to the Armenians throughout their stay, and did what they could to 'share their sorrows'.

Sisir Sarbadhikari became close friends with an Armenian called George at Aleppo hospital. George was from Diyarbakir and his family was all killed; he somehow managed to escape. George was given the job of cleaning toilets, and lived in a corner of the hall where the toilets were located. On cold evenings Sisir and George 'used to sit and warm [themselves] at [George's] brazier, and then [they] would talk'.[89]

Sarbadhikari's stay at Aleppo hospital came to an end in June 1917, and he stayed in a number of camps before landing at the German-administered hospital in Nisibeen. Before ending in Nisibeen, he describes that the city of Mardin, 'in the interior of Armenia', was 'empty … there were no people in it'.[90] Most likely the inhabitants were killed or forcibly displaced. On his arrival at Nisibeen hospital, Sarbadhikari describes himself as the only prisoner of war; the rest were 'Armenian mohajers (refugees); they were all women, only one had a little boy with her'.[91]

In the camp, Sisir developed close and empathetic relationships with the Armenians, and became intertwined with their fate. One Armenian woman, whom Sisir calls 'old Mary', surmised affectionately that Sisir ended up joining the war because he lost his mother, and if his mother was alive 'she would not have let [him] go [to the war]'.[92] He became close friends with two Armenian 'boys': Ilyas, a fifteen-year-old from a 'well-off' background from Erzurum, and Yakob, a twenty-year-old from a 'very ordinary' family from 'further south'. Ilyas developed a stronger bond with Sisir and other Indians, as he came to depend on them. 'Ilyas looked on Bhola and me like older brothers,' writes Sisir, 'and we too loved him like a younger brother.'[93]

Ilyas's parents, elder brother and sister were dragged out of their Erzurum home by the Turkish Army and forced to march alongside other Armenians from the surrounding region. At one stage, the men were separated from the women and children 'to go to a separate camp'. The Armenians by now knew that there were no separate camps, and that the menfolk would be killed. Sarbadhikari describes the parting scene for Ilyas' family: '… there was much weeping and many tears, the women clung on to the men and would not let them go. But what could come of that? The men were dragged by force, Ilyas's father and brother among them. The next day one male from that group managed to escape, bringing back the news that all the men had been killed. He had himself been badly wounded ... After a few hours he succumbed to his wounds.'[94] The women and children were subsequently abandoned to forage for themselves. Ilyas became separated from his mother and sister, and ended up in Nisibeen.

Sarbadhikari did not see the killing of Armenians himself, but he writes what Sachin, another Indian in the Ras al-Ain camp, described to him: 'A group of Armenians was made to stand up, their hands were tied, and their throats were slit one by one.'[95] Sachin was at the Ras al-Ain camp earlier than Sarbadhikari, and many Armenians were killed there.

Returning to the Nisibeen hospital camp, Sarbadhikari was soon joined by other Indian, British and Russian POWs, including Bhola, his friend who was separated before Sisir moved to Aleppo.

By mid-1917, the camp residents realized that the tide of war was turning in the Middle East, with Baghdad wrested by the Indian Army in March 1917, and the Ottoman Army in a defensive retreat. This unnerved the Armenians in the camps even more, especially after the German withdrawal, as it was feared that the Turks would slaughter the remaining Armenians, and would not even spare the women. The Germans had provided a degree of protection to the Armenians who managed to stumble into these camps.

Instead of waiting to risk an encounter with retreating Turkish forces, the Nisibeen Armenians planned a secret escape in August 1918 to safer refuges. The degree of mutual trust and affection with Sisir and other Indians meant that Ilyas did not depart without taking his leave. He confided in Sisir and his comrades the plan to escape. Sisir describes:

> Ilyas came to us one night ... What he whispered, after waking us, was this: For a few days [the Armenian mohajers] had been conferring in secret on matters such as how best they might escape to places that were now under Russian or

British control ... Now their destination had been decided on—where it was Ilyas did not yet know. They would flee that night, horses had been arranged. He had come to take his leave of us.[96]

Sisir Sarbadhikari describes the emotional farewell, and the parting scene with their fraternal concern for Ilyas' safety and well-being:
Whatever warm clothing we had between us we gathered together and gave to Ilyas—the poor fellow had hardly any clothes ... He held me tight! None of us could say a word; nor was there any need for anything to be said ... In the dead of night Ilyas left. We never saw him again ... Did he manage to reach home? Did he find his mother and his sister?'[97] Sisir continues to ponder over Ilyas and his family's fate, and later in the book he writes: 'I still think of [Ilyas]. A boy of fourteen or fifteen; a really good fellow. Did he manage to get back to Erzurum in the end? Or did he die on the way? What happened to his mother and sister?'[98]

Within a few weeks, as the British Indian Army advanced north, the Germans decamped, leaving the POWs and Armenians to their own fate. The Armenians panicked, fearing that the Turkish Army would get to them before the British Indian forces. Sarbadhikari mentions: 'The greatest terror is amongst the poor Armenians. Old Mary, Dudu, Haiganoush, Jarohi all of them are crying out loud, asking: what will happen to us now?'[99] Sarbadhikari continues to worry about the fate of the Armenians and writes in early November 1918:

> I'm overjoyed at the thought of going back home, but in the midst of that I am despondent at the thought of the [Armenian] mohajers and their fate. We've worked together for so many days; we've shared sorrow and joy. They have become like our own. I wonder, even if the Turks don't kill

them, what will they find when they get home? Who will they return to? Who knows if they even have any homes left?[100]

X

While the Armenians lamented their fate, the POWs were fortunate to be told suddenly on 17 November that a train would come for them that night. Sarbadhikari and his four friends entered a wagon that night for the onward journey. Before departure, they heard the whispers of Yakob—the other young Armenian teenager in the camp—asking them to take him in. This obviously was a dangerous proposition because they had not yet reached the safety of the British Indian Army's territory. Had they been found hiding an unauthorized Armenian, they could have been targeted by the Turks, or would likely have faced disciplinary action from British authorities. Initially, Sarbadhikari and his friends refused Yakob, citing the dangers for him and them in letting him hide in their wagon. Sarbadhikari describes Yakob's response, and what they did: 'But Yakob was stubborn, he began to weep. He said the blame would be his alone; if the Turks caught him then there was nothing to be done; he would die anyway if he remained in Nisibeen; if he was going to die then he might as well make an attempt to get away. In the end we let him in. It was only the four of us in that wagon ... Had there been anyone else we wouldn't have dared.'[101] Sarbadhikari and his friends hid Yakob under the bench for two nights and a day, before he got off at a station and took his leave saying 'he would be all right from there on'.

Sarbadhikari, with the rest of the Indian POWs, arrived at Tripoli in today's Lebanon on 26 November, and proceeded to board a ship on 4 December, destined for Port Said. Before they could embark, there occurred one of the most moving events of this saga between the Indians and Armenians. This involved a camp follower named Jumman and a young Armenian boy. Sisir narrates:

> When we were marching from Mosul [in 1916], Jumman saw an Armenian child on the banks of a stream near Ras al-Ain and picked him up. His mother must have died, and his father must have been killed ... Jumman took on the responsibility of looking after the boy and named him Babulal. He used to call Jumman 'Baba' [father].[102]

Jumman cared for Babulal like his own child in the concentration camp of Ras al-Ain for two years, and Babulal learned to speak Hindi. Having developed a paternal bond, Jumman now wanted to bring Babulal with him to India as an adopted son. However, they faced an issue in Tripoli:

> Before embarking on the ship to Suez Jumman was told that he would not be allowed to bring Babulal with him. An Armenian padre [priest] came to take Babulal away. But why would Babulal go to him? He made a huge fuss and cried up a storm of tears; and Jumman wept too, holding to the boy. In the end Jumman was allowed to take Babulal home with him.[103]

Although the 'shared sorrow' and empathy with the plight of the Armenians ran deep, the Indian POWs' bonds were not limited to Armenians. On a few occasions, the Indian POWs also developed strong empathy for some of the Turkish guards. Sarbadhikari writes about some of the Turkish soldiers he met in Aleppo hospital: 'One thing they always said was this: What are you going to gain from this war? Why are we cutting each other's throats? You live in Hindustan, we live in Turkey, neither of us have ever met, we have no quarrel with each other, but at the behest of a couple of men we've become enemies overnight.'[104]

Sarbadhikari mentions another story at the Aleppo hospital, which is equally moving and describes the circumstances of Turkish soldiers at the time:

> There was a Turkish soldier in our ward, about thirty years of age, he had been wounded in the fighting. With him was a pretty young girl, of about five or six. Her name was Farida. She used to play with all of us. The soldier had no one at home to leave his daughter with, so he took her with him when he went to fight—he brought her to the hospital too. During the fighting he would leave her in some safe place in the care of one of his comrades ... [One day] I asked him: Kardesh, if you had been killed in the fighting what would have happened to your daughter? He smiled and said 'Allah bilior'—or 'only Allah knows' ... I never saw this Kardesh looking gloomy. And the girl? She was always cheerful, busy playing.[105]

The bonds developed between Armenian prisoners and Indian POWs is one of the most moving episodes of the First World War. Far from home, suffering indescribable cruelties and hardships, the human bond that developed across language, religion and civilization is a treasure and testimony to the deep humanity of both the sepoys and their mohajer friends.

The Indian survivors of the Ottoman prisoner camps reached India in 1919. They had suffered a harrowing fate, and one of the worst death rates of any army and campaign during the First World War. Of the original 13,700 British and Indian soldiers of the 6th Division that fought the Turks at Ctesiphon and subsequently surrendered at Kut, only 3,000 survived by the end of the war, a mortality rate of 78 percent.[106] This is double the mortality rate of the Battle of the Somme, considered one of the deadliest on the Western Front during WW1. What is more instructive to note is that while most of the British deaths occurred in Turkish prisons, the Indian soldiers died at almost the same rate in Kut under British supervision as in Turkish prison camps.[107] The Leader of the Opposition in the House of Commons, Edward Carson, summed up: 'This terrible business has been conducted with criminal negligence.'[108] The Mesopotamia Commission, reporting in 1917, confirmed the same.

Eventually, the Indian soldiers, who predominantly composed the British Indian Army in the Middle East, defeated the Ottoman armies. However, popular British culture remembers the First World War in the Middle East for the escapades of Lawrence of Arabia, which was a mere side show. The Mesopotamia campaign, like the first Afghan campaign, was a tragedy that befell Indian soldiers. While almost all the Indian soldiers and their families perished in Afghanistan in 1842, the 1916–18 experience of the 6th Division shows not much had changed in imperial attitudes and hierarchies when disaster struck in campaigns outside India. The inferior status of Indians in the Empire affected not just the pay and service conditions, but also the mortality of their soldiers.

Chapter Nine

Defenders of the Faith

We have sold our military duty for 11 rupees a month but we haven't sold our religion.[1]
—A sepoy from the Western Front

I

COLONIALISM WAS AND CONTINUES TO BE A BRUTAL DESTROYER of lives and cultures. Living in the twenty-first century, when it appears to be all behind us, it is easy to forget what colonialism did to the cultures, civilizations and populations who suffered it. Huge swathes of land in North America, Australia and New Zealand have had their native inhabitants wiped out, except a handful. In places like South America, while native populations survived physically, their cultures and faiths have been lost, homogenized into the western-European Christian cultural ambit. The climate and geography prevented the same fate in Africa, except for the small southern and eastern tips of the continent. The fate of these populations was well summarized in a native American chief's words:

> We are now about to take our leave and kind farewell to our native land, the country the Great Spirit gave our Fathers, we are on the eve of leaving that country that gave us birth, it is with sorrow we are forced by the white man to quit the scenes of our childhood ... we bid farewell to it and all we hold dear.[2]

It is not an exaggeration to think that India and its ancient civilization once risked the same fate. The physical elimination of a densely populated civilization was impossible, even if it was hopelessly divided in the mid-eighteenth century. The fact that its faiths and cultures did not meet the fate of the natives in Latin America is a fortunate outcome. To this outcome, India owes a great debt to its sepoys, who—in spite of being in the pay of foreigners—were steadfast to the faith of their ancestors. This dawned upon the British colonizers in India very early. However, there were efforts to homogenize the soldier into the colonial master's faith and beliefs. These efforts were rejected outright by the sepoys, who zealously guarded their religious beliefs, frequently at the cost of their lives.

In this devotion to their respective faiths, both Hindus and Muslims were alike. The British slowly came to understand this. Respect for the sepoys' religious beliefs came to be an article of faith in the British Indian military leadership. Reaching there was not a smooth road though; it passed through a number of mutinies, culminating in the 1857 rebellion, which almost destroyed British rule in India. While the sepoy nursed a number of grievances, the immediate spark to the 1857 Mutiny in the Bengal Army was the callous introduction of cartridges greased with cow and pig fat. The sepoy considered this an assault on his faith, and responded with violent subversion of military authority.

We saw in an earlier chapter that the sepoy saw no contradiction between his faith, and the military employment outside his faith.

On the contrary, his faith enjoined him to do his duty as a soldier to whoever employed him. Historically, we saw Hindus in Muslim military service and vice versa, performing their professional obligations with utmost loyalty. Thus, leading Rajput principalities of north-west India were the key mansabdars under the Mughals. There definitely was a sense of affiliation to one's faith, but the obligation to be loyal to their patron was of equal importance. As long as the employer did not interfere with his faith, the sepoy would serve with dedication. In his worldview, the obligation to defend his right to practise his faith ranked above all others, even surpassing his family, in some cases. We saw numerous examples of repeated jauhars and sakas—the ritual self-immolation and suicide by women and men respectively—during the middle and early modern ages. In all these acts, the dedication to one's faith was kept above the family and life, two of the dearest things to a man. Thus, by anchoring their lives in the faith of their ancestors, the sepoy ensured that India's essence, its culture that is so centred around its ancient system of beliefs, was ushered into a post-colonial world more or less intact. Of course, the English language, Western style of dress and other changes were adopted, but finely accommodated within the language of ancient faiths practised within this land. Given his pivotal position as the foundation of British military power, the sepoy thus was instrumental in saving India's soul.

In the matter of respecting the sepoy's faith, the British followed a similar pattern as with the status of native officers, and a general attitude toward Indian culture and civilization. The British in the seventeenth century were acutely aware of the deep and ancient civilizational heritage of India, and were dazzled by its riches. This attitude continued while their rule did not look very old till the late eighteenth century. However, from the late eighteenth century onwards, a sense of superiority started to creep into the British mind in India. The days of being a supplicant were more than half a century behind. The territorial gains made were immense, and the wealth it brought swelled heads both in India as well as back home in England. The native officer, who was a critical ally in the initial decades of the 1740s and 1750s, came to be seen as someone who could be dispensed with. The sepoy, with his eccentric belief system, was similarly embraced initially with open arms, if not heart, in the early days of EIC rule. The attitude towards Indians as colonial subjects started to seep into the British attitude towards their sepoys too. The sepoy reacted to any real or perceived onslaught on his faith. The lesson was learnt by the British authorities, but it took some time and a number of mutinies. In this chapter, we will review a number of incidents that illustrate how sensitive the Indian soldier was to defend his religious beliefs. Simultaneously, we will also learn how his employer came to be an even firmer and dogmatic believer in maintaining the sepoy's religious autonomy, as an essential part of their mutual contract.

II

In seventeenth- and early-eighteenth-century India, the English were no different from other people who would seek safety and comfort in the company of their co-religionists, in a land so far away from home. While the seething mass of humanity in India belonged to an alien faith for an Englishman, there was a tiny minority of mixed Portuguese and Indian heritage, widely known as Topasses. The Topasses were Christians, and mostly hailed from Goa, the small Portuguese colony on the west coast of India. They were heavily employed by the EIC in guard duties, but their absolute numbers were limited. This pool of recruits was barely sufficient for a small guard force of a few hundreds permitted by the Mughal authority to foreign traders. The EIC made the most of the Topasses as their cultural background was amenable to the English. Precisely because they were culturally close to the

English, they were alienated from the rest of the Indians. This seemed to be a desirable outcome, actively encouraged by the English. For example, in 1748, the Topasses in the Madras garrison were rewarded with higher pay compared to their brethren at Fort St. David for wearing 'stockings and shoes' like Europeans. The Topasses were a permanent fixture of the EIC factories throughout the seventeenth and early eighteenth century. Thus, almost half of the Bombay Regiment in 1670 was classed as 'white Portuguese' or Topasses.[3] In 1737, the Topasses outnumbered the Europeans at the Bombay garrison: 449 European sailors, 299 European soldiers and 817 Topasses. As late as February 1747, the number of Topasses was twice that of 100 Europeans at the Fort St. David garrison.[4]

The war against the French, Chanda Sahib and Siraj-ud-Daulah required thousands of sepoys. Not only was the Topasse recruitment pool limited in size, its value in a wider military conflict was unproven. When it came to the war with Indian princes and the French, the EIC relied on the traditional sources of recruitment for Indian soldiers from the fighting classes: Jats, Rajputs, Pathans, etc. Different they were in cultural terms, but they served the purpose assigned to them. There was a high degree of tolerance towards their 'native' habits in the nascent years of the EIC Army in India. Even while they were trained and drilled in the European style, the sepoy 'lived apart, cooked apart, ate apart, after the fashion of his tribe. No one grudged him his necklace, the ear-rings, the caste marks on his forehead, or the beard which lay upon his breast.'[5]

In fact, the British were fascinated by the strongly held beliefs and prejudices of these fighting men. The thought of hiring a mere mercenary that would sell his service to the highest bidder was not a comforting one. The British wanted to believe in, and rightly discovered, that the men they hired had deeper motivations and ideals. There lay the fundamental contradiction of the British

Army's Indian recruitment strategy. Their cultural and religious differences—while a cause of caution and concern—were at the core of the sepoy's moral universe. Any attempt to subvert it was futile. So, a quiet acquiescence at the least, if not an active encouragement of their religious beliefs and prejudices, was pursued by the British. This was a wise policy in the early years of EIC rule in India.

The Muslim soldiers' beliefs concerned avoidance of pork in their diet, and of pig fat and pig leather in any product, of keeping a beard, and taking leave on the holy days of Eid and Muharram; but the high-caste Hindu soldiers took the observance of rituals to another level. Many of the Hindu recruits in the Bengal Army during the late eighteenth and early nineteenth century were Brahmins from Awadh and Bihar. The cow is a sacred animal for Hindus. While most Hindus strictly avoided beef, and any product made of cow leather or fat, the Brahmins avoided meat altogether. The Brahmins insisted on cooking separately, so their utensils were not touched by non-Hindus and lower-caste men. The Brahmins drew their own water from the well, and even a shadow of a non-Hindu on their food meant it was not fit for consumption. Each day, they had to take a ritual bath and pray long enough to break the heart of any sergeant-major. For most Hindus, serving beyond the borders of the Indus or going on a sea journey were considered to be ritually polluting. Wearing a sacred thread about his torso and 'tilak' mark on his forehead was a jealously guarded privilege for the Hindu sepoy. Serving in lands predominated by non-Hindus, such as Afghanistan, would mean loss of caste status for a Brahmin, which could only be regained at great expense and effort. Some of these prejudices, especially on foreign travel, sharing of food and water, and a ritual bath each day, came to be relaxed from the nineteenth century onwards; especially as the recruitment ground for the British Army moved to north-west India. The Sikhs, Jats and other classes had a more relaxed approach on the strict caste-related rituals. Nevertheless, in the matter of diet, even as late as WW2, arrangements were made to strictly comply with the soldier's faith.

The British obsession with recruiting men of a high caste and from the north started very early, and only got worse over time. Only during periods of great crisis did the recruitment extend to wider sections of the population. During the crisis in Madras in the 1740s, in the Bombay Army during the Maratha wars, and of course during WW1 and WW2, when there were insufficient men from the 'right' caste and class, the recruitment net was cast wider. As soon as the crisis passed, the doors closed for the 'lower'-caste men. This was true of the Tamils and Tilangas during the 1740s and the 1750s, of Mahars hired during the Anglo–Maratha wars, and eventually the Marathas themselves. Not to speak of the various 'other classes' hired during WW1, which were demobilized after the war.

In those early days, it was the idiosyncrasies of the sepoy that appealed to the EIC officials. The sepoy—especially a caste Hindu—would not harm an animal out of respect for the sanctity of life, but would kill a man in a fairly fought battle. The same sepoy would accept pay and orders from his English officer, but would not countenance even a glass of water touched by the same officer, let alone food. One episode illustrates this grudging admiration that underlined the relationship between the early sepoys and European officers. James Skinner, son of an English officer and Rajput mother, and founder of the celebrated Skinner's Horse cavalry regiment, recounts an episode when he found a Brahmin subedar dying of thirst and wounds in the battlefield. Skinner offered some water to the dying subedar, to which the subedar replied in a faint voice, 'My caste, Sir! My caste!', and refused the water from a European hand. Skinner persisted and pressed the water on the subedar again, saying, 'We are alone. No one will see you.' The dying subedar shook his head, and said, 'God sees me!'

and departed from this world a thirsty man. Skinner exclaims, 'What is to be done with such men?'[6]

Such men are to be recruited in their ranks, and that is precisely what the EIC officers did. Warren Hastings had a particular penchant for filling the sepoy ranks with native social elites, and particularly high-caste Hindus. By 1789, Lord Cornwallis informed London that most of the Bengal Army's sepoys are 'Bramins [sic] and many other of their higher casts.'[7] By the end of the eighteenth century, the Bengal Army was a predominantly Hindu army. The Madras Army was less exclusive but still aspired to recruit high-caste Hindus. Captain James Oliver of the 7th Battalion of the Madras infantry claimed in 1783 to have recruited 'a number of good men and of superior cast'.[8] The Bombay Army was perhaps the most heterogeneous, but even there a general order from the Commander-in-Chief (C-in-C) in 1797 forbade enlisting men who had 'lost their cast, who are of a mean and disgraceful cast or who may be of depraved characters'.[9]

For those who were recruited to the EIC ranks, the British officers had come to guard against any intrusion upon their religious and social arrangements. One such officer, who served in India for forty years, observed:

> Treated kindly, [one might] rest assured of their devoted attachment; But [one] must not interfere in their religion, nor in their prejudice regarding caste. Any wrong done to them on these points [could not] be atoned for by apologies or expressing of regret.[10]

Army administrators were acutely aware of the peculiarity of the native sepoy's character. A number of concessions were made to the sepoy so he could practise and guard his faith, in what he understood to be the ritually correct way. In fact, the feelings of the sepoy were foremost in the minds of the EIC officials, when legislating for the wider population. The British frequently take credit for banning in 1829 the self-immolation of widows (sati) on their husband's funeral pyre. However, before legislating to this effect, Governor-General William Bentinck had taken the precaution to conduct a wide consultation with the native officers and sepoys to ensure they would not be opposed to it. The practice of sati had no wide support in nineteenth-century India, and both the sepoys as well as the emerging middle-class intellectuals like Raja Ram Mohan Roy were keen to prohibit the small number of such cases. The point to note is that the British did not have the courage to act on what they thought was a sensitive social practice without being sure that the sepoy's religious and social sensibilities would not be offended.

III

The English of the eighteenth century, such as Warren Hastings, were prudent to leave the religious practice and belief of Hindus to 'the Being who has so long endured it and who will in his own time reform it'.[11] While the attitude of EIC officials was tolerant, if not outright indulgent, towards the religious beliefs of sepoys in the eighteenth century, change started to be visible in the early nineteenth century, when the British felt more confident of their hold in India. Let us survey the changing British attitudes towards Indians, before reviewing specific incidents when the sepoy's beliefs contradicted EIC military rules, and how the sepoys reacted. While experienced and wise army administrators always acted with caution so as to humour the sepoys' religious beliefs, there was a marked change in the British attitude towards Indian civilians. When the arrogance and sense of superiority started to seep into British minds, the civilian population faced it first. However, the sepoys, coming from the same society, could not remain unaware of this, even if it did not impact them directly.

By the second quarter of the nineteenth century, many of the British officials in India belonged to the evangelical movement. They believed that they were in India on a divine mission ordained by Providence. Their sense of superiority developed after most native powers were defeated, with the 'bulwark of Hindustan'— the Bharatpur Fort—also breached in the 1826 Anglo–Jat war. Men like James Thomasson, the Lieutenant-Governor of North-West Provinces, were convinced that the natives of Hindustan would be converted to the true faith by the Lord 'in His own good time'. Not all were content to leave matters in the Lord's hands. Many wanted to take a more active role in the Lord's work, despite government policy guarding against it for fear of upsetting the native army. They were indignant with the authorities for allowing 'heathen practices' and public holidays on Hindu and Muslim festivals. Worse still, the participation of the troops to provide a guard of honour when Indian princes celebrated the festivals of their faith made many of them feel affronted. In India, tradition held that the management of the religious establishments was a responsibility of the ruler. The EIC had adopted this responsibility initially, and managed a number of Hindu temples, especially the famous shrine of Jagannath at Puri. Under pressure from the evangelist opinion at home and in India, the Government handed the management of Hindu and Muslim places of worship to people of the respective faiths in 1839. To many Indians, this appeared to be a denial of patronage to the religious beliefs of a majority of the subjects.

This disappointment at denial of patronage of their religious places was compounded by the view of the government's tacit support of Christian missionaries, and ultimately turned into distrust, with many coming to view Europeans as being bent on subverting native faiths. Missionary activity gathered momentum in public places, even hospitals, prisons and markets. Many missionaries were prone to preach Christ's message in the markets, often accompanied by the police. Not only did they preach their message, they often ridiculed the 'heathen' beliefs of Hindus. Sir Syed Ahmed indicates there was a widespread belief that 'the Government appointed missionaries and maintained them at its own cost'.[12] From markets, the missionary moved to classrooms; not just in missionary schools, but government schools too. Sir Ahmed notes that the missionaries posed questions like 'Who is your God? Who is your redeemer?'[13] to impressionable young minds. Rev. Gopinath Nandi, a Bengali convert, also mentions that junior native civil officials, such as patwaris (village accountants), were compelled to hear the Gospel during their training, and were furnished with a copy of the New Testament to carry home.

Even prisons were a target for harvesting souls. Nandi admits that with the blessings of the district magistrate, 'The prisoners in the jail were also daily instructed in Christianity ... and every Sabbath morning the Gospel was preached by me.'[14] The order to remove personal brass 'lotas' carried by Hindus to fetch water and food—because one was used as a weapon against an English officer in a prison in one instance—caused much grief to the prisoners and families. Eating from earthenware, even china plates, was a sure way to ritual defilement. In 1845, a new regulation introduced common messing in the jails. This was seen as a blatant attempt by the government to destroy the caste of the devout. Most Hindus, whether in prison or outside, cooked their own food and ate strictly within their caste groups. The communal dining arrangement, though practical, would offend the religious sensibilities of all caste Hindus.

Against this background, the government passed the Caste Disabilities Removal Act in 1850, which enabled converts to inherit their ancestral property. The act had no use for a Muslim convert, who was forbidden to inherit the property of an infidel. Hinduism being a non-proselytizing faith, had nothing to gain from it. The obvious conclusion reached by most Indians was that the act was designed to encourage Christian converts.

All this fuelled the suspicion that the government was waiting for the right opportunity to convert the whole population by force. In this charged environment, a missionary, Mr E. Edmond, sent a widely circulated letter from Calcutta in 1855, which appeared to most Indians as evidence of the government's true intention of making them all Christians. The letter, which was considered the height of indiscretion even by the British authorities, suggested that as the new modes of transport and communication were bringing various parts of society together, and as the structure of society was being modified by these advances, it was high time that earnest attention should be given to the question 'whether or not all men should embrace the same system of Religion'.[15] The letter was posted to all the officers of the state. If there was any proof needed of the firangi's (foreigner's) true intention, this was it, in the public mind. The denials issued by the Lieutenant-Governor were of no use, as people identified most Englishmen with the government.

Thus, throughout the second quarter of the nineteenth century, the Indians suspected a hidden plot by the European government to assault the faith of their ancestors. The sepoy could not have been unaware of these views, even if there was no direct attempt to undermine his religious practice and belief. As it happened, the sepoy was one of the closest Indians to the Europeans, in social and physical proximity in the cantonments. While great restraint was advised by the army administrators to their officers on matters related to the sepoy's faith, occasionally overzealous officers, or unintended errors, led the sepoy to fear for his faith. In all such instances, the sepoy reacted without any hesitation, and with a strength of purpose and belief that reinforced to the British that the cost of tampering with the sepoy's faith was prohibitive. Next, we will survey a number of incidents that made the sepoy concerned about his employer's intentions regarding his faith, and how each time he set matters straight.

IV

The years between 1799 to 1805 transferred the EIC from being one of the competing powers in India to the position of 'paramount' power. The sepoy and their English comrades were too busy fighting to think of anything else, during these years. The victories over Tipu Sultan, who died fighting at Seringapatam in 1799, and Scindia and Bhonsle at Assaye and Laswari in 1803, were only interrupted by the stubborn resistance of the Jats at Bharatpur in 1805. In all these fights the sepoy was at the forefront, so much so that Napoleon disparagingly called the Duke of Wellington—who led the southern campaigns—'the Sepoy General'. When the fighting ended in 1805, the British turned their attention to reforming the sepoy's appearance, to make him look more like a European soldier. The sepoy, ever sensitive about his faith, saw a plot to convert him in the new regulations concerning his appearance and uniform.

It all started with an order in November 1805 from the Madras Presidency Commander-in-Chief, Sir John Cradock. Confident from his alleged consultations with some permissive ulemas and Brahmins, and with the approval of the young and inexperienced Governor William Bentinck,[16] the C-in-C went ahead with this provocative prescription regarding sepoy's uniform. From now on, the sepoy was asked to replace his Indian turban with a round hat, which would be adorned with a feather and a leather cockade. The sepoy was also asked to wear leather stockings. This was followed by another order in early 1806:

> ... that a native soldier shall not mark his face to denote his caste, or wear ear-rings when dressed in his uniform ...

every soldier of the battalion shall be clean-shaven on the chin ... also that uniformity shall ... be preserved in regard to the quantity and shape of the hair on the upper lip.[17]

The pattern of the soldier's turban had been debated, and given 'every consideration which a subject of that delicate and important nature required' by a Military Board in 1797. The delicacy and importance seemed lost on Sir Cradock, who asked a major to draft the order, got it approved by a colonel, signed it himself and sent it out. All the wisdom and caution of the likes of Warren Hastings seemed to have been lost on the C-in-C. Only a naïve commander could have played with the sentiments of his sepoys so crudely, if he had any understanding of their character.

There were so many objections to this innocuous-sounding prescription, that it is difficult to know where to start. First of all, the round hat was associated with the Europeans and native converts, who wore it to mark themselves as 'topi-wallahs' or 'hat-wearers'. The leather in the cockade was sacrilege for most Hindus, and a Muslim could never be sure it wasn't made of the prohibited pig skin. Surely, this was a clever technique designed by the 'topi-wallah' to secretly convert the sepoy! Today topi-wallah started with the head gear, tomorrow he would come after the sepoy's right to wear the sacred thread or celebrate Eid! More importantly, how would the leather-cockade-wearing sepoy face his family and friends, in whose eyes he will be an outcast. The mark on a Hindu sepoy's forehead was his manifestation of having gone through the sacred rites, and a reflection of the sect he belonged to. Without it, he would be no different from a 'topi-wallah' or a 'firangi'. The earrings were worn as symbols of childhood rituals for a Hindu, removing them would defile the status thus obtained. Most soldiers took pride in their luxurious moustaches, and Muslims in the subcontinent treated the beard as a reflection of their faith. All in all, this was a badly concocted order, without much forethought, and bound to cause anxiety to the sepoys across the Presidency.

The rumour mill in the bazaars gathered steam.

> Surely it was significant that cross-belts were an essential part of the uniform? Every sepoy was marked with the cross! And what was that strange implement suspended from the cross-belts? A turn-screw? That is what they say—but it looks very like a cross. And leather—why must a soldier wear leather round his neck and on his hat? And have you heard that in Ceylon a colonel marched his whole regiment to church and made them sit through the service? And that a shipload of padres has just arrived from England to convert you? And that the English have sprinkled all the salt in the bazaars with the blood of cows and pigs?[18]

It was widely said by the sepoys and townsmen: 'We shall next be compelled to eat and drink with the outcast and infidel English, to give them our daughters in marriage, to become one people, and follow one faith.'[19]

Something had to be done. Their faith enjoined them to stop this blatant assault on their beliefs and practices. In May 1806, a company of the 2nd Battalion of the 4th Madras Native Infantry stationed at Vellore Fort refused to wear the new hat, without overt aggression, but firmly. The commanding officers were harsh in their response, and threatened reprisals if the unit did not comply. Eleven Hindus and ten Muslims gathered the courage to stand forth and resist. They were immediately arrested and sent to Madras for trial, escorted by a squadron of a British cavalry regiment. They were tried, and two of them—one Hindu and one Muslim—were sentenced to 900 lashes each. They bore the brutal punishment on their backs, and were thereafter discharged from service. Their bodies and careers destroyed, they straggled away to their villages to tell the story of their courage to their families and neighbours. Their consolation lay in their righteous conduct, and securing their prospects in the afterlife. The other nineteen were sentenced to 500 lashes each, but at this stage they seemed to have compromised to utter some words of apology, which avoided the punishment being carried out. The battalion for the moment appeared subdued, and was transferred from Vellore to Madras.

The rumblings of dissent continued, nonetheless. Disaffection started to spread to other regiments and stations. In June, Cradock started to realize the folly of his actions, and wrote to the Governor, Lord Bentinck, that he was willing to rescind the order. The Governor, however, refused to yield to the palpable pressure, as he and his Council, in the first place, had approved the order. The right thing to do would have been to placate the sepoys by changing the orders, and showing signs of conciliation. Wisdom was in short supply with the Council and its young Governor. Both sides having set on opposing courses, conflict seemed inevitable.

Vellore continued to simmer all the while. The fortress of Vellore had about 400 European soldiers and 1,500 sepoys. One of the sepoys, Mustafa Beg, on 17 June told his colonel that the sepoys were plotting to murder the Europeans. His story was referred for investigation to some Indian officers, who were part of the conspiracy themselves. Mustafa Beg was censured and put in confinement.

Around 2.30 a.m. on 10 July 1806, Sergeant Cosgrave of the European regiment heard a 'trampling of feet'. He yelled for the sentry, but received a volley from the sepoys in response. The mutiny and the bloodshed were in full swing. The sepoys in their pent-up anger and frustration took revenge upon the European soldiers and officers, shooting them in the barracks and bungalows. Within a few hours, 130 Europeans lay dead or dying within the fort premises, cut down by the swords or spears or shot by the guns of angry sepoys. The remaining European survivors ran to take cover in a bastion above the main gateway, where they barricaded themselves, and prayed for relief from the nearby garrisons. Vellore Fort was in the hands of the sepoys and the tiger-striped flag of Tipu Sultan was raised on the ramparts, accompanied by the cries of 'Din! Din! [Faith! Faith!]'. This war cry was a call to defend one's faith.

Incidentally, along with the troops, Tipu's sons and widows along with their retainers were kept as pensioners in Vellore Fort. Some officials later tried to implicate Tipu's sons in fomenting the rebellion, but no such evidence was ever found. At best, it seemed like the enthusiastic retainers joined in when the pandemonium began, and tried to exploit the situation for their gains. It seems that sepoys who mutinied had no grand plan in their mind before acting, either. The act of resistance was more important for them than the outcome. No strategic leadership was available, and Tipu's sons did not step forward to lead. The poor leadership from the native princes had in the first place led the sepoy to the employment of a foreign power, which was at least able to maintain some order in the realm. During the Vellore mutiny, and in the 1857 Revolt, the political leadership again failed to lead sepoys towards a coordinated strategic effort. Disorder soon spread throughout the fortress.

Some Europeans, who were outside the fort when the mutiny started, managed to send a message for help to Arcot, the closest British outpost. All the while, the mutineers failed to organize the defences, and did not even man the ramparts. The outer door of the fort was not shut immediately. When the relief party of about 1,000 British soldiers and some Madras cavalry arrived in the morning by around 9 a.m., the mutineers were caught off-guard. Colonel Gillespie, who lead the relief force from Arcot, found the fort poorly defended by the sepoys, and the group of Europeans entrenched above the gate. He brought light siege guns with him, which, if the sepoys had barricaded the gates, would not have been very effective. The right course, if the sepoys had been led properly, was to have barricaded the fort gates, man the ramparts, starve the Europeans above the gate, and wait for news of their heroic resistance to spread. There was much agitation in the sepoy ranks of the Madras Presidency, and had the Vellore mutineers held out for longer, it is very likely that other stations would have joined the mutiny. Unfortunately, the lack of leadership, poor strategic planning, and general indiscipline meant that these would remain mere hopes for the rebels.

Colonel Gillespie attracted the attention of the Europeans above the gate, who pulled him up with a makeshift rope of belts and clothes. From there, Gillespie directed the siege, and managed to clear the surrounding of the inner gates, before blowing them with the siege guns. The outcome from here was not in doubt. The relief force was sufficiently large in number, and once the fort gates were breached, they poured in with their weapons blazing fire. The reprisals were equally brutal, and within hours about 350 sepoys and natives were killed. Later, the ringleaders were tried, and six were blown away by guns, five shot by muskets, eight hanged, five transported, and the regiments they belonged to were disbanded.

The mutiny failed, but the sepoys made their point. On matters of faith, they would brook no compromise. As on many other occasions, they had no 'grand designs', but acted on the spur of the moment. The sepoy might be a mercenary, true to his salt, but he could not place the salt above his faith. The primary duty of the man who held arms was protection of his faith. In this, the sepoy would be uncompromising. If the leather cockade had been needlessly and insensitively mandated as his uniform, he would throw away the uniform that defiled his faith, and lowered him in the eyes of his countrymen and families. Both Hindus and Muslims held devout men of the other's faith in high esteem, but looked down upon those who were not true to their ancestral religious beliefs, even if they were alien to their own. It was a tragedy that the Madras Governor and the C-in-C did not understand this fundamental trait of the sepoy's character.

While Vellore Fort was subdued, disturbances were reported from Hyderabad, Nundidroog, Bangalore, Bellary, Pallamcottah and Wallajahbad. The situation was explosive, and barely under control. Finally, the Council and the Governor came to their senses, and did what they ought to have done a few months back. The order regarding headgear and dress, which had caused so much unnecessary bloodshed, was finally quashed on 17 July. The Governor issued a proclamation denying any intention to subvert the sepoy's faith. On 24 September, a general order prohibited 'all unauthorised alterations in dress, or interference with the native soldiers in regard to their national observances'.[20] While no evidence was found of Tipu's family's involvement in the incitement of the mutiny, they were transferred out of Vellore to Calcutta as a matter of precaution.

A tense calm prevailed, but the rumblings continued. Not taking any chances, the Company Directors decided to sack the Madras Governor and the C-in-C. Lord Bentinck and Sir Cradock, whose provocative actions caused the trouble in the first place, were recalled to England. Their obstinacy in insisting upon 'objectionable' uniform, despite the sepoys' representations, was taken by the sepoys as proof of their intent to make them Christians. Whether or not this was their real aim, their fellow English officers also recognized:

> However strange it may appear to Europeans, I know that the general opinion of the most intelligent natives in this part of the country is, that it was intended to make the sepoys Christians.[21]

The episode was a clear warning to the British authorities of the dangers of missionary activity. While broadly the message was registered, there would continue to be incidents that excited the sepoys' minds. In each such instances, the sepoy did not shirk from his duty to set the limit for the authorities' conduct.

V

One issue that caused continuous friction between the Hindu sepoy's belief and military requirement was passage by sea, and travel beyond the Indus. Over the period of a century between the mid-eighteenth and mid-nineteenth centuries, the sepoys gradually overcame this prejudice, but not before a number of violent incidents and mutinies. The strict caste rules required the Hindu sepoys to make sure that the water they drank and used for their daily ablutions was not touched by non-Hindus or 'unsuitable'-caste men. Equally, to avoid ritual pollution, they had to make sure they cooked their vegetarian food themselves, and the cooking pots and utensils were made of brass and maintained separately.

In a foreign land, the risks of their eatables, water and general belongings coming into contact with non-Hindus was of course very high. Nor could separate cooking facilities be provided on a sea journey. Their water casks on the ship had to be maintained separately. If separate cooking was impossible, the sepoy would have to survive on parched gram, sugar and raw flour. These were huge inconveniences on their own. When mixed with the peril of ritual pollution by coming in contact with the 'mlechhas' (foreigners), the sepoy was extremely reluctant to travel by sea or go beyond the Indus. The added complication of having lost their caste, which could only be regained by propitiating the Brahmins at great expense, meant they could easily be ruined by a foreign expedition.

Thus, a contingent of sepoys who were destined for Madras from Bengal in 1768 by sea, refused to go beyond Vizagapatnam. They threatened to take control of the ships, and run them ashore unless allowed to disembark. The army yielded, and they were allowed to march from Vizagapatnam to Madras over land. A later enquiry established that 'from the horrid inconsiderate ... [and] cruel management of last embarkation to the Deccan, not a Gentoo [would] ever venture on board a ship again'.[22] This turned out to be the case for a very long period. In 1781, when 5,000 Bengal sepoys were marched to aid their beleaguered Madras compatriots against Hyder Ali and Tipu, they took eight months via land. By sea, it would not have taken more than a fortnight. The Bengal sepoy, henceforth was not required to cross the sea, except on voluntary basis. In 1795, the commanding officer of the 15th Battalion assured the sepoys 'of every indulgence being shown to their prejudices of caste in laying in water and provisions'[23] *if* they agreed to volunteer for Malacca.

Even in the Madras Army, where the soldiers were less strict about sea travel, the authorities took no chances. Thus, when in 1775, the 9th Battalion of the Madras Infantry was to travel from Anjengo to Bombay by sea, the commanding officer was anxious to make sure 'there are several large pots or kettles besides earthen vessels provided in every vessel for the various casts'.[24] Thus, the sepoy had both the sanction of religion and force of law with him to not travel by the sea.

The war with Burma broke out in 1824, and the Madras regiments were insufficient for the conflict. The government decided to send some of the Bengal infantry units, and asked the 47th, 26th and 62nd battalions to march from Mathura to Barrackpore, before an onward journey to Burma. The Bengal sepoy had no objection to marching overland through Assam and Arakan, but a sea voyage was in violation of his faith and contract. The three units reached Barrackpore in July 1824. While at Barrackpore, it was decided that the 47th would march ahead of the other two units, and was asked to purchase its own bullocks to transport their heavy baggage in late October. It was widely known that bullocks were in short supply because of recent government purchases. In any event, it was unfair to expect sepoys to succeed in this purchase, when the government itself had failed. No wonder that rumours started to gain ground that once the sepoys failed to purchase bullocks, they would be told that there was no alternative but to embark from the Chittagong port.

Whether or not that was the intention of the government, the communication was very poor. The commanding officer, Colonel Cartwright, tried to mollify the troops by offering loans for the purchase of bullocks, and ultimately agreed to make the payment on their behalf. However, the seeds of distrust were sown. There was a stalemate, and the sepoys in a body refused to purchase the cattle. The C-in-C Sir Edward Paget was informed of the mutiny. He arrived on 1 November at midnight, followed by a large force the next morning—two European infantry regiments, horse artillery, the Governor-General's bodyguard and the 68th Native Battalion—to deal with the situation.

The sepoys represented that the Muslim subedar-major had threatened to forcibly embark them on the ship from Chittagong. That they had heard five companies of sepoys had been obliged to embark already. They pointed out that their faith did not allow them to embark, and that they had actually pledged themselves to that effect with Ganges water and tulsi (sacred basil). Paget tried to assure them that they would never be asked to travel by ship without their consent, and he would be 'ready to listen' if they laid down their arms. The sepoys by now had lost all trust, and surrounded as they were by threatening European infantry, they refused to lay down arms. Meanwhile, twenty sepoys from the 26th Battalion and two companies of 62nd Battalion also joined the mutinous 47th.

The simmering situation on the parade ground exploded on 2 November, and some of the mutineers seized the colours of the 26th Regiment and destroyed it. Suddenly, the C-in-C ordered the two artillery guns, which were so far hidden behind the European regiments, to open fire on the mutineers. A number of mutineers were blown to smithereens, a considerable number fled, and eighty were taken prisoner. It was later found that the mutineers' muskets were not loaded, and they were merely making a point in defence of their position. A court martial was conducted the same day, and the ringleaders hanged. The 47th was disbanded, and its name removed from the army list.

For a moment it seemed like discipline had been enforced. However, the cruelty of opening artillery fire stealthily, while the sepoys did not even load their weapons, remained in their collective memory. That a Brahmin was killed in defence of his faith made the event all the more abhorrent. Unknown to the European officers, the mutineers became martyrs in the eyes of the sepoys. The sepoys planted a banyan tree—sacred to Hindus—next to the water tank where one of the Brahmin ringleaders was hanged. Thirty-two years later, in the heat of the 1857 Mutiny, the Calcutta newspaper, *The Englishman*, recorded:

> This tree, a sacred banyan, is pointed to by the Brahmins and others to this day, as the spot where an unholy deed was performed, a Brahmin hanged! ... his [the Brahmin's] brass 'pootah' or worshipping utensils ... were carefully preserved and lodged in the quarter guard of the [Barrackpore] regiments ... These relics, worshipped by the sepoys, have been, for thirty-two years, in the safe keeping of regiments ... passed through the hands of 233,600 men, and have served to keep alive, in the breasts of many, the recollection of a period of trouble, the scene of a mutiny, and its accompanying swift and terrible punishment.[25]

Such bloody memories remained in the collective psyche of the sepoys, and would contribute to the resentment that burst out into the bloodshed and mutiny of 1857. The sepoy, on his part, reiterated his commitment to his beliefs, and many sacrificed their lives and livelihoods to uphold the principle.

VI

While the evangelists were making their presence felt in the bazaars, schools, hospitals and prisons, the authorities managed to keep them away from the sepoys, just about. The attitudes that pervaded the British in India could not have been hidden from the Indian soldiers. There were mutinies related to the 'batta' as we saw in an earlier chapter, but largely, the sepoy soldiered on, annexing Punjab and Sind, after recovering from the disaster of the Afghanistan campaign.

In 1855, while Mr Edmond wrote his infamous circular enjoining 'all men to embrace the same system of religion', an incident at Bolarum should have warned the British government of the dangers of such efforts. Brigadier Colin Mackenzie, the most senior British officer at the Bolarum station, ran for his life from his compound to his house, chased by the sowars of a cavalry regiment under his overall command:

> A man [sowar] sprang from behind another who was beating a drum, and struck him [Mackenzie] a violent blow with a sword on the head. Sabre cuts followed in rapid succession; one cut, six inches long, penetrated the skull, another severed the outer bone of the left arm; a third cut the deltoid to the bone; two others took off the middle finger of the right hand, and severed all the tendons and bones at the back of it … finding … that to stand there was to be murdered, [Mackenzie] at last turned and made

for the house. Streaming with blood from no less than ten wounds ... he actually outran his pursuers, though they were after him like a pack of hungry wolves. As he mounted the steps of his new house, one or two overtook him, and gave him two tremendous gashes on the back, one of them eleven inches long. A Chaprasi and servant shut the door of the house after him.[26]

This was in the evening of Friday, 21 September. Something was clearly wrong with the 3rd Cavalry regiment, to which the assailants were easily identified as belonging. Captain Orr, commandant of the 3rd Cavalry, was in the brigadier's house, along with Mrs Mackenzie and a few other guests. Captain Orr sent for Jemadar Muhammad Huseyn, who took some time to arrive. Apprehensive of what was happening and might follow, Mrs Mackenzie asked the jemadar one question that she knew would strike the right chord: 'Is the regiment faithful to its salt?'[27] The jemadar 'looked at her without making salaam, or giving any reply. She laid her hand on his arm, and repeated the question, when he turned away.'[28] Even in the middle of the full-blown mutiny, the jemadar could not bring himself to face his officer's wife, when questioned if his comrades have remained true to their salt.

What led to the otherwise loyal sowars (cavalrymen) launching a murderous attack on their Divisional Commander? The trouble started with the brigadier issuing an order on Thursday, 20 September, that 'No processions, music, or noise will be allowed, on any account whatever, from twelve o'clock on Saturday to twelve o'clock Sunday night.'[29] Sunday, 23 September, was the tenth day of Muharram, the final day of the annual Shia Muslim festival, when tazias or processions are carried out. Sunni Muslims and Hindus would also sometimes join in the procession on the final day, in solidarity and out of customary behaviour. The order was a gross injury to the feelings of the devout, not least because—as Governor-General Dalhousie later mentioned—it 'put forward the Mohurram in direct conflict with the Christian Sabbath, and so introduced a religious element into the prohibition.'[30]

The order was withdrawn the next day, on 21 September, but the damage had already been done. The withdrawal order was not well publicized, and the latent fears and apprehensions played their part in the minds of the sowars. It is clear that the sowars had reasons to suspect the brigadier's intent. Setting aside Lord Dalhousie's observations on the indiscretion of the order passed by Brigadier Mackenzie, his association with a converted Christian—Aga Muhammad Khan—provided plenty of fodder to the sowars' suspicions.

Aga Khan, an Afghan of Persian extraction, was credited with saving the life of Shah Shuja's son in Kabul during 1842, when the Afghan hordes fell upon and destroyed the British forces, and ended Shuja's brief reign. Having made enemies of his countrymen, Aga Khan escaped to India, and met Mackenzie in the Ludhiana cantonment. Mackenzie seemed to have taken a liking to Aga Khan, and took him under his wing. The brigadier clearly was in a 'spiritual' conversation with Aga as 'they had for some time been in the habit of reading the Persian Testament together'.[31] Influenced by a severe illness, and more likely by the brigadier's persuasion,

> [Aga Khan] declared himself a Christian, and was baptized on the 23rd October 1853. The Bibi, his wife, followed his example in November 1854. On Mrs Mackenzie's return to India, they, in April 1855 (accompanied by the mother of the Bibi, a bigoted old Mussalmani), rejoined the Brigadier at Bolarum, on exactly the same footing as formerly, save that the tie of friendship was naturally much strengthened by the new community of faith and of feeling.[32]

Not content with finding his path to the Lord, Aga Khan attempted to spread the word to his Muslim brethren. On one occasion, he, along with a catechist,

> went to the Bazar close to the cavalry lines, and had some discussion with those assembled. At first everything was friendly; but at last some of the party got angry, and the catechist refusing to retire, he and Aga Muhammad were pushed and pelted ... This was the sum total of the Aga's intercourse with the Rissalah [cavalry regiment] but they hated him as a converted Moghul.[33]

The brigadier was harbouring a Muslim convert to Christianity in open sight of the cavalry lines, who were devout Musalmans. It is a wonder that the brigadier remained unharmed for the last five months, ever since Aga and his family appeared in Bolarum.

Smarting under the orders of the previous day, unclear about the revision of the prohibitory order, and unwilling to wait till 23 September, the tenth day of Muharram, a group of sowars decided to act on the evening of Friday, 21 September. A small party of young lads took out a procession, with the usual noise and shouts, and the standards of their faith in their hands. Two mounted sowars from 3rd Cavalry accompanied them. They came round to the front of the brigadier's garden, which was situated next to the main road of the cantonment. Hearing the noise, the brigadier went out to confront the sowars, despite Mrs Mackenzie's warning: 'Oh, you don't know how dangerous they are at the time of the Muharram.' An argument ensued, and the brigadier proceeded to seize the standards from the hands of two men of the party. A sowar, later identified as Bilund Khan, now came forward and remonstrated: 'My flags are as dear as my life.' The brigadier wrested his sword from his hand, and with it struck a blow across the head of Bilund Khan. The brigadier's personal guard now intervened, and the small group making up the procession withdrew briefly.

This was the point of no return. Not only was the Muharram procession interrupted, the standards were seized, and it seems that Mackenzie delivered the first blow. Bilund Khan, furious with Mackenzie's conduct, rushed to the cavalry lines, 'threw his turban on the ground, and gathered the whole regiment by the war cry of "Din! Din! [Faith! Faith!]"[34] This, as noted before, was a call to defend one's faith, which was in danger. In response, a number of sowars unsheathed their swords, rushed to Brigadier Mackenzie's house, and broke through the compound gate. This was the background to the murderous attack on Mackenzie that fateful Friday night, when he ran and hid for safety inside his house.

The dark of the night, and a lie by one faithful orderly—Gufoor Khan—saved Mackenzie's life. Gufoor Khan told the assailants that the brigadier was dead, and his family had fled to the residency, after the assailants failed to find them in a frantic search of the front quarters. The sowars of the 3rd Cavalry that night attacked a number of other Europeans, before the alarm bugle was sounded. On hearing the alarm bugle, 'the whole of the 3rd Infantry flew to arms, many of them throwing their belts over their undress [arming themselves while naked or half-clothed]', and their approach restored order.

A tense calm prevailed the next day, but the disturbance continued in the lines. On Sunday, 23 September, in contrast to Mackenzie's orders blocking the Muharram procession, the Europeans had to cancel the Sunday service. An irate European later fumed:

> The remainder of Sunday passed over quietly, but with one omission, which a sense of our national dignity ... ought imperatively to have forbidden. No public worship took

place that day; the mutineers thus having the satisfaction of putting a stop to all the religious observances of their officers ... and had the acting authorities had a befitting sense of British honour, it would have been performed as usual.[35]

The government of the most powerful empire in the world could not afford its European officers the safety of a Sunday church service. Such was the effect of the sepoy and sowar's conviction, when it came to matters of faith. After an enquiry, the government made conciliatory gestures. Brigadier Mackenzie, who managed to survive the attack, was asked to go on indefinite leave, effectively ending his military career. The 3rd Cavalry went unpunished; except for its officers, who—barring two—were dismissed. Two Hindu officers of the infantry guard were also dismissed, the enquiry finding their response not robust enough.

Finally, in January 1856, Governor-General Lord Dalhousie was constrained to reiterate the cardinal principle of the British government policy:

> '...never to interfere with the religious observances of the Natives of India.'[36]

As we will see next, neither did the native soldiers believe this assertion to be sincere, nor was it strictly observed by the British officers, leading to the worst bloodshed India had seen for centuries.

VII

The ominous summer of 1857 destroyed the finest standing army in Asia. Some say this was inevitable, but even so the speed of events surprised everyone. Within two years, almost all units of the

Bengal Army—the largest of the three Presidency armies—would be disbanded. A new Bengal Army would be recruited from the peoples of north-west India. The old recruitment ground of Bihar and Awadh would be out of favour. After all, many blamed the hard-held prejudices of Brahmins, Muslims and Rajputs of this region for the destruction of the Bengal Army. With hindsight, it is clear that the sacrifice of the sepoys was not in vain. They had genuine fears of what the Company's government was conspiring with the help of padres. The mistrust had been growing for almost half a century. It burst forth into a military mutiny, which would turn into a full-scale rebellion with the participation of the peasants, rajas and city dwellers alike. Such large-scale destruction of life and property had never been seen before. British sources put the numbers of the dead around 100,000, many believe it was millions. The truth will never be known.

The violence was preceded by a sense of helplessness in the minds of peasants and sepoys alike. An old man told Dr Lowe, a British officer, before the storm broke:

> The jungles, sahib, the trees, the rivers, the wells, all the villages, and all holy cities belong to the Sircar; they have taken all—everything very good, what can we do?[37]

An old villager might have felt helpless, but the sepoy was the sword arm of the government. He had the ability, and the duty, to act in defence of his faith. In this, he was never found wanting, and 1857 would be no different.

The first gunshot of the Mutiny was fired by a young Brahmin sepoy—Mangal Pandey—whose name is etched in the memory of most Indians. Late in the afternoon on Sunday, 29 March 1857, Mangal Pandey, a sepoy of the 34th Bengal Native Infantry, appeared on the parade ground of Barrackpore cantonment, which is fifteen miles from Calcutta. Mangal Pandey armed himself with both his musket and his talwar (curved sword). He was wearing his regimental red jacket, and a dhoti instead of the regulation pantaloons. He paced up and down the parade ground in agitation, and exhorted his fellow sepoys:

> Why are you not getting ready? It is for our religion ... Come out you bhainchods (Hindustani term of abuse, meaning someone who commits incest with his sister), the Europeans are here. From biting these cartridges, we shall become infidels. Get ready, turn out all of you.[38]

His fear of becoming an infidel was driven by the new cartridges that sepoys were supposed to bite open.

Sergeant-Major James Hewson now arrived on the scene, and Mangal Pandey instantly fired at him, but missed the shot. While Hewson was taking cover, the Adjutant, Lieutenant Baugh, rode onto the ground on his horse, which was shot from beneath him by Pandey, who had actually aimed at Baugh. A Muslim sepoy, Sheikh Paltoo, extricated Baugh from the dead horse, and Baugh fired at Pandey with his pistol, but missed. While Pandey was loading his musket, both Hewson and Baugh now rushed at him with their swords, and shouted for help from the sepoys at the quarter guard. The guards were unmoved, and Pandey proved to be no easy win. He stopped loading his musket, unsheathed his sword, and gave serious wounds to both Europeans. Only when Sheikh Paltoo held him by his waist, were Hewson and Baugh able to escape with their lives.

What happened thereafter confirmed that this Brahmin's son had resolved to renounce the pleasures of this world. The government had contrived to turn him into an apostate, and he would sacrifice his life as a mark of protest. When he was surrounded by a number of British officers, charging towards him on horseback, including Major-General John Bennett Hearsey, the commanding officer of Barrackpore, Pandey once again enjoined the fellow sepoys 'to defend and die for their religion and caste'. As a final act of resistance, he turned his musket upon himself, and pulled the trigger with his toe. The bullet made a 'deep graze, ripping up the muscles of his chest, shoulder and neck, and he fell prostrate.'[39] He was immediately arrested, and given medical attention to revive him. He was tried by court martial on 6 April, and sentenced to death by hanging. The sentence was carried out on 8 April.

He made a resolute stand when faced with the court martial. He did not repent, or betray any of his comrades, and when asked, 'Did you act on Sunday last by your own free will, or were you instructed by others?' Pandey insisted, 'Of my own free will. I expected to die.' Did he load his own musket to save his own life? 'No, I intended to take it.'[40] Ishwari Pandey, the jemadar of the quarter guard that showed no energy to assist the English officers was also tried, and hanged on 18 April. The government tried to make an example of this strict punishment by disseminating the news of their hanging to all the main cantonments within the Bengal Army. Thus, Delhi cantonment was due to hear the details of the sentence on 11 May, but all hell broke loose before that.[41]

VIII

Mangal Pandey's agitation was driven by the cartridges he and his fellow sepoys feared were an instrument to destroy their religion. In 1856, the new Enfield rifle was issued to the European soldiers in the Indian Army, and was slated to be extended to the sepoys too. The Enfield rifle, which was to replace the Brown Bess musket, used a cartridge that was greased with animal fat, and required the cartridge to be bitten to tear it open before inserting it into the barrel. There had been suspicions that the fat used was sourced from cows or pigs, and the British averments that it used mutton fat were disbelieved. In any event, mutton was also objectionable to many Hindus, although not as much as beef and pork. Many later accounts do not deny that the grease originated from an 'objectionable source', especially what was produced in England. Even the grease produced in India undoubtedly contained cow fat, and probably also pig fat, as mutton was far more expensive, and the contractors, who were not instructed to prohibit cow or pig fat, would supply the cheapest.

Fortunately, the new cartridges had not been issued across the whole of the native army. Equally, there was no certainty that no sepoy to date handled the cartridge containing objectionable fat. We will never know the truth, but the fear of ritual pollution was real. Musketry depots were set up at Dum-Dum (near Calcutta), Ambala and Sialkot to train a few sepoys from each unit in the new weapon. At Dum-Dum, a low-caste lascar taunted a high-caste sepoy that caste would end soon as sepoys would be forced to bite the cartridges containing the fat of pigs and cows. Mason explains the effect on high-caste Hindus and Muslims as though 'a Catholic were asked the same time to profane a sacrament and to touch excrement with his lips.'[42] The news spread like wildfire, and the Dharma Sabha of Calcutta heard the story and sounded the alarm. Soon, English officers also knew the damaging stories circulating in and outside the cantonments, and the existential danger these stories posed to the government.

On 22 January 1857, sepoys from a detachment of 70th Native Infantry on musket practice at Dum-Dum Depot reported their concerns to their commanding officer. The Lieutenant immediately understood the gravity of the situation, and escalated their concerns to the commander of the depot, who in turn informed General Hearsey, the divisional commander. Even though the C-in-C was away, the matter was escalated to the military secretary of the Governor-General. The military secretary acted promptly, and on 27 January reached Dum-Dum, and told the sepoys that they were free to use their own grease of oil and beeswax. He also telegraphed the Adjutant-General to immediately issue a general order across all stations that sepoys were free to use their own grease. The Adjutant-General hesitated, because a general order might raise doubts in the mind of sepoys about cartridges they have already used, even if they did not contain the objectionable fat. They might have been right, but the doubts already existed, general order or no order. The general order eventually was issued that only European soldiers were to use the new cartridges with grease. The sepoy would be free to grease his cartridges with vegetable oil and beeswax, and he was also allowed to break open the cartridge with his fingers, instead of teeth.

Not making the announcement was equally fraught; but the announcement having been made in an environment of distrust, many took it as a sign that a sinister plot to break the faith of native sepoys was on track, and had been accidentally discovered and stopped. From here on, the suspicion seems to have extended to *any* cartridge, not just the greased cartridges. The sepoys often refused to use cartridges that they had been using for a long time, and had no trace of animal fat. The background of missionary activity in preceding years, the disaffection in the countryside and the fears of the sepoy about his religion all played a part. Alongside the cartridge affair, a number of rumours about the English plot to convert Hindus and Muslims started doing the rounds. An anonymous letter sent in March to Major H.W. Matthews, commanding the 43rd Regiment at Barrackpore, ran as follows:

> We will not give up our religion. We serve for honour and religion ... You are the masters of the country. The Lord Sahib [Lord Canning, the Governor-General] has given orders, which he has received from the Company, to all commanding officers to destroy the religion of the country. We know this ... The officers in the Salt Department mix up

bones with the salt. The officer in charge of ghee [clarified butter] mixes up fat with it; this is well known ... the Sahib in charge of sugar burns up bones and mixes them in the syrup the sugar is made of; this is well known ... the senior officers have ordered rajas, noblemen, landowners, money-lenders, and peasants all to eat together and English bread has been sent to them; this is well known ... throughout the country, the wives of respectable men, in fact all classes of Hindus, on becoming widows are to be married again; this is known. Therefore we consider ourselves as killed.[43]

The letter added cartridges to the list of grievances, and emphasized the unanimity of all sepoys in the station. This was broadly the view held by the native soldiers of the Bengal Army across stations.

In this charged atmosphere, the first act of insubordination occurred at Berhampore, which is 100 miles north of Barrackpore. Here was only one battalion of infantry—the 19th—and some cavalry and artillery, but no British troops. Barrackpore was the larger cantonment, and four native battalions—the 2nd, 34th, 43rd and 70th—were stationed there. On 28 February, there was to be an ordinary parade of the 19th Regiment at Berhampore. The regiment was anxious, as they had heard rumours about the cartridges. The regiment was issued percussion caps the night before the parade, and cartridges were to be issued on the parade ground next day. The battalion refused to accept the percussion caps, as by now they suspected the cartridges given the next day would also be laced with objectionable fat. Their commanding officer, Colonel Mitchell, went to the lines, assembled the native officers, and threatened that if the regiment refused the cartridges—made more than one year ago—on the parade ground '[he] will take them to Rangoon or China, where they will suffer many privations and all die.'[44] This was clearly unwise, as it added the threat of crossing the sea to the sacrilege of touching cow fat, both abominable to the sepoys. The sepoys took his anger as a sign that his trick had been found out before it could be carried out.

He went back to his bungalow, and issued orders for a general parade—to include cavalry and artillery—alongside the 19th the next morning. This was with an intent to use the cavalry and artillery as a check upon the infantry battalion. The sepoys now feared that the next morning they would be forced to bite the cartridges at gunpoint, using the cavalry and artillery. They did not wait till morning. After heated discussions, they took their muskets, loaded them and rushed out to the parade ground, where they stood, not knowing what to do next. Their intention was still not violent. Colonel Mitchell immediately came on the scene, and ordered cavalry and artillery on to the parade ground, too. He summoned the native officers and reasoned with them. The native officers warned him that the presence of cavalry and artillery was taken as a grave threat by the sepoys, and must be cleared off the field, before the sepoys would return to their lines. The Colonel's order to the sepoys to lay down arms was ignored, and finally he had to withdraw both cavalry and guns without the sepoys disarming. He also countermanded his order of a general parade the next morning. Once the threat of violence was removed, the native officers managed to reason with the sepoys, who started to move away with their weapons. The next morning, the parade—without cavalry and artillery—went peacefully.

Unquestionably, there had been a mutiny at midnight in Berhampore, and the incident had to be reported to the government. The government resolved to disband the 19th Regiment, but thought it unsafe to do it in Berhampore, without the presence of a European regiment. The closest European regiment, the 84th Foot, was summoned from Rangoon, and arrived on 20 March. It was this battalion to which Mangal Pandey was referring when he said 'the Europeans are here'. When the European battalion arrived, the 19th, which had been in suspense over its fate for a month, was asked to march to Barrackpore.

The authorities decided to disband the 19th at Barrackpore on 31 March. The men of the 19th were not told their fate, but complied, and marched to Barrackpore without any incident. The arrival of the European regiment, the 84th Foot, had caused considerable alarm among the sepoys. It was rumoured that the whole division at Barrackpore would be forced to bite the abominable cartridge under threat of violence from the 84th. The 19th had already become martyrs in the eyes of their brother sepoys. As Surendra Nath Sen said: 'Their [the 19th's] only offence was loyalty to their faith and a faithless government was on that account going to inflict on them the greatest humiliation that a soldier could suffer.'[45]

It was while the 19th was at Baraset, eight miles away, that Mangal Pandey fired the first shot of the Mutiny, two days before the scheduled disbandment of the 19th. The disbandment of the 19th occurred peacefully on 31 March, in the presence of artillery as well as the 84th Foot Regiment. Mangal Pandey's regiment, the 34th Native Infantry, was disbanded at Barrackpore on 4 May. On the surface, things appeared to settle, but the trouble was not over. It soon spread westward. Not least because the news of Mangal Pandey's hanging and the disbandment of regiments now circulated across the various army stations in North India. The conflict was soon to explode wider.

Before we narrate what occurred next, it would be appropriate to mention the indiscretion of the commanding officer of the 34th Native Infantry, Colonel Wheeler. This regiment was the most disaffected at the Barrackpore station, and Wheeler amply contributed to their disquiet. Wheeler was 'terribly given to preach' according to Lady Canning. Wheeler himself freely admitted:

> As to the question whether I have endeavoured to convert Sepoys and others to Christianity, I would humbly reply that this has been my object, and I conceive is the aim ...

of every Christian ... that the Lord would make him the happy instrument of converting his neighbour to God, or, in other words, of rescuing him from eternal destruction.[46]

It is not clear if he managed to save any sepoy's soul from eternal destruction, but he surely destroyed his regiment. As was the case in Bolarum two years earlier, the missionary zeal of the likes of Mackenzie and Wheeler was living proof to the sepoy of the government's intention to destroy his religion.

IX

The next scene of this saga unfolded in Meerut, about forty miles northeast of Delhi. As we saw, the disbanded regiments straggled home westwards, telling the tales of the firangi's evil designs to make them Christians, and how they bravely resisted and paid the price with their livelihoods. The government also made sure the disbandment order was read out at every military station, not realizing that they were making heroes of the disbanded men in the eyes of their comrades.

Meerut cantonment was quite different from Barrackpore. The European and Indian troop numbers were more evenly matched; the 3rd Cavalry was mainly Muslim, and the Europeans had the edge of artillery. At Meerut were stationed about 2,000 European troops, and between 2,000–2,500 sepoys and sowars. The native regiments included the 3rd Cavalry, 20th Native Infantry and 11th Native Infantry. The European units included a cavalry regiment, the 6th Dragoon Guards (Carabiniers), one infantry regiment, the 60th Rifles, and both horse and foot artillery. Therefore, Meerut looked like the last place to harbour a mutiny. But the summer of 1857 was full of surprises.

On 23 April, Colonel Smyth, the commanding officer of the 3rd Cavalry, ordered a parade the next morning, of only a select ninety skirmishers (soldiers stationed ahead or next to a larger body of troops) from his regiment. Smyth was not particularly popular with his men, and most contemporary accounts term him as 'obstinate and self-opinionated'. This man decided to show the picked ninety skirmishers how to use the cartridges without biting them, and thus proving once and for all that the fears of defilement were irrational. He must have found encouragement in the false belief among some of the Europeans that Muslim troops were not prone to the 'superstitions' of Hindus on the subject. So far, most affected regiments were composed of Hindus, including the 19th, disbanded recently at Barrackpore.

Quite why the regiment, which had never been issued the new cartridges, and had been happily using the old ones so far, thus needed to be 'enlightened' is beyond rational understanding. Perhaps Smyth wanted to make a point; perhaps he thought the Muslims could be aligned against the prejudiced Hindus, no one will ever know for sure. What is known is that the order caused much consternation. All the sowars asked the same question: If nothing is wrong, why we are fixing it? Very likely there is a hidden plot!

Soon, it was clear that on the subject of cartridges, Hindus and Muslim soldiers formed a united front. Captain Edmund Craigie, one of the officers in the 3rd Cavalry, sensed the danger, and urged the adjutant:

> Go at once to Smyth, and tell him that the men of my troop have requested in a body that the skirmishing tomorrow morning may be countermanded, as there is a commotion throughout the native troops about cartridges, and that the regiment will become 'budnam' [get a bad name/lose honour] if they fire any cartridges. I understand that in all six troops a report of the same kind is being made. This is a most serious matter, and we may have the whole regiment

in mutiny in half-an-hour if this be not attended to. Pray don't lose a moment, but go to Smyth at once.[47]

Smyth paid no heed. He went ahead with the parade the next morning, and exhorted the ninety men that the new regulations were perfectly compliant with their scruples. The sowars had taken a solemn oath the night before not to touch the abominable cartridges. Smyth's exhortations failed to convince the sowars, and all but five refused to accept the cartridges. The parade was broken, and the faint hope that the cartridge affair would blow away was dashed. 'Oh! Why did you have a parade?' lamented divisional commander General Hewitt later. 'My division has kept quiet, and if only you had waited another month or so, all would have blown over.'[48]

A dilemma stared the authorities in the face. There was open defiance of military orders, and while the action to enforce discipline would be risky, not acting was equally fraught. The eighty-five sowars were brought to a court martial and all were sentenced to ten years of prison with hard labour, though the youngest eleven saw their sentence reduced to five years. In the meantime, at Lucknow, Henry Lawrence disarmed the 7th Irregular Awadh battalion, who had refused cartridges on 3 May and were threatening to kill their officers. The 34th, Mangal Pandey's regiment, was disbanded on 4 May at Barrackpore.

A punishment parade was staged on 9 May, ostensibly to make an example of the grave consequences of disobedience. This was to misfire badly. T. Rice Holmes recounts:

> On the morning of 9th May, beneath a sunless sky darkened by rolling storm-clouds, the whole brigade was assembled to see the culprits disgraced. Stripped of their uniforms, these miserable felons were handed over to the smiths, who riveted fetters on their arms and legs.[49]

It seems that the smiths took time in doing their work, and for almost an hour the rest of the troops witnessed the humiliation of their comrades in silence. This must have stung badly, as the prisoners had not done anything 'depraved or wicked'. They had stood firm to their faith, and for that they were being deprived of their livelihood and liberty. The presence of European troops with loaded rifles on the ground, while native troops were deprived of ammunition, just about averted immediate disaster. Finally, the condemned men were marched away from the parade ground. As they were being marched away, some of them hurled abuses and their boots at Colonel Smyth; the boots had been removed to fix the iron fetters on their legs. The convicts were lodged in the civil jail under a sepoy guard. The parade was dismissed.

The effect of seeing iron chains on the bodies of their comrades can only be imagined. Perhaps an honourable dismissal—like of the 19th at Barrackpore—might have looked more proportionate. The long prison sentences, topped by the humiliation of iron fetters, tilted the balance of just conduct away from the government. What happened in the native lines over the next twenty-four hours can only be speculated upon. By now, the civilian population had also become aware of the goings on.

Seeing honourable sowars thus hauled in chains, and their comrades watching helplessly, incensed the people in the bazaar. The courtesans in the bazaar reportedly taunted the sowars that evening that they were 'not man enough', having let their comrades be thus humiliated. There were rumours that 2,000 more fetters were waiting in the prison for those who would not give up their religion: the fanatical government was unlikely to stop with the eighty-five condemned. A life with honour and faith seemed impossible. However unreasonable their fears might appear to us today, this feeling was widely shared by sepoys across the Bengal Army in 1857. The same day, Sir Henry Lawrence wrote to the Governor-General:

> Last night I held a conversation with a Jemadar of Oude artillery ... and was startled by the dogged persistence of the man ... in the belief that for ten years past Government has been engaged in measures for the forcible, or rather fraudulent, conversion of all the natives ... When I told him of our power in Europe ... he replied he knew we had plenty of men and money, but that Europeans were expensive, and that therefore we wished to take Hindoos to sea to conquer the world for us ... 'You want us all to eat what you like that we may be stronger and go anywhere.' He gave us credit for nothing. He often repeated, 'I tell you what everybody says.' The Jemadar was a person of good character.[50]

One of the officers of the 3rd Cavalry, Lieutenant Hugh Gough, was warned by a native officer of his troop that a general mutiny of all native troops would occur the next day in Meerut. Colonel Smyth, on receiving this information chided the subaltern for 'listening to such idle words'. Brigadier Archdale Wilson also paid no heed to the warning. The dawn of 10 May arrived without any untoward occurrence. The long summer day dragged on in the native lines as well as in European quarters.

Suddenly around 5 p.m., a cook-boy ran to the native lines warning that the European infantry and artillery were on their way to arm themselves. It later turned out that the European soldiers were on their way to the Sunday church parade. Whether or not there was a concerted ploy by sepoys to rebel, they thought they had been caught unawares by the menacing Europeans. The time for action was upon them, lest the fetters be put on their limbs too shortly, for none would contemplate forsaking their religion. Perhaps out of panic, perhaps as an act of self-preservation, or perhaps as part of a well-rehearsed plan, the sowars of the 3rd Cavalry mounted their horses, and instantly galloped towards the city gaol. There they arrived, many of them without uniform, to release their fettered comrades from the prison.

While the 3rd Cavalry was on its way to the prison, the 20th Native Infantry occupied the parade ground, after seizing their muskets. They were shortly joined by the 11th Native Infantry, which appeared restrained for the moment. At the parade ground, the European officers tried to reason, cajole and threaten the sepoys to maintain order. Most sepoys were still uncertain of their future course, and had not attacked their officers by that point. The situation was on a knife-edge, when a sowar of the 3rd Cavalry rode by, shouting that the Europeans were coming. Suddenly, all hell broke loose. One young recruit from the 20th Infantry shot Colonel John Finnis, the commanding officer of the 11th Infantry, and Finnis died instantly. There was some uncertainty in the minds of the 11th, and it seems there was some aggressive posturing against 20th, but Finnis's death seemed to have decided matters for them. Certain that they would not escape the blame for the murder of their commanding officer, the 11th also threw their lot behind the mutinous 20th. All native troops, except for a few loyal sowars and sepoys, were now ranged against the government.

From there on, the various accounts, even if true, are difficult to fit into a coherent chronology. It was absolute chaos all around. Gough, who reached the sepoy lines shortly after the killing of Finnis, described the scene in front of his eyes:

> The huts on fire, the sepoys ... having seized their arms and ammunition, dancing and leaping frantically about, calling and yelling to each other, and blazing away into the air in all directions—absolutely a maddened crowd of fiends and devils, all thirsting for the blood of their officers, and of Europeans generally.[51]

Whether or not they were thirsting for the 'blood of their officers and Europeans', the sepoys seemed to have exercised great restraint on this account. Neither the 11th Infantry nor the 3rd Cavalry harmed their officers, as Gough later testified: 'Indeed I may say that not a single officer's life was taken by our own men.'[52] Many simply asked their officers to remove themselves from harm's way, 'To their credit be it said the men did not attack us, but warned us to be off, shouting that the Company's Raj was over for ever!'[53]

By now, the natives of Meerut had joined the sowars and sepoys, turning the mutiny into a general revolt against the Company's government. There were some unscrupulous elements in the bazaar, joined by the prisoners who escaped the prison. Undoubtedly, they committed great acts of violence, murder and pillage on the Europeans. Sepoys did not join in these violent acts, and many tried to save the Europeans.

Mackenzie hurried back from the parade ground with a troop of loyal sowars to check upon the safety of his sister, who was the wife of Captain Edmund Craigie, another officer. A violent mob had surrounded their house, baying for blood and vengeance. Neighbouring rows of European houses were ablaze, many inhabitants murdered. Sensing there was no way for safety except an appeal to the honour of his troopers, Mackenzie writes he

> ... determined on a desperate stroke. I ... brought the ladies down to the door of the house, and calling to me the troopers commended their lives to their charge ... Like madmen they threw themselves off their horses and prostrated themselves before the ladies, seizing their feet and placing them on their heads, as they vowed with tears and sobs to protect their lives with their own.[54]

The ties of salt, though menaced by mistrust, were easily bound with an appeal to the honour of the men.

The Europeans were frozen with fear. Despite numbering close to 2,000, and with the advantage of artillery, their response was wanting. By the time the 60th Infantry and Dragoons came looking for the sepoys in the native lines, all had moved on. Instead of pursuing and engaging the mutineers, the European troops were ordered to their lines for the safety of European lives. The leadership was much to blame. John Rotton says, 'In truth, our military authorities were paralysed. No one knew what was best to do, and nothing was accordingly done.'[55]

The mutineers did not appear to have a grand plan either. The resolute ones did not stay around at Meerut. Most made their way to Delhi, which was just forty miles away. Delhi seemed the obvious choice of destination, even if the mutiny was not pre-planned. Delhi was an important military station, with three native regiments, no European troops and the largest ammunition store in north India. More important, it was the ancient capital, the seat of prestige, and the old Mughal Emperor, Bahadur Shah Zafar, resided in the Red Fort, even if he had no real power. The mutineers straggled in small groups over the night of 10 May and the next day to Delhi. No attempt was made by Europeans to engage them.

X

Early next morning, a group of twenty sowars from the 3rd Cavalry shouted from below the palace window in Delhi, clamouring for an audience with Emperor Bahadur Shah Zafar. The eighty-one-year-old man was living a peaceful retirement on a pension, which his courtiers pretended was a tribute from the Company. The sowars were told to move away by the head of the palace guards, who added they were showing disrespect to the Emperor, while standing opposite the royal ladies' apartments. The sowars moved south in the direction of what is now known as the Rajghat gate. Within a few minutes, Zafar noticed smoke from within the walls, and he could see the Meerut sowars and sepoys were within the walls of the fort, and more filing in.

The Emperor stayed aloof for the best part of the day, while more and more rebellious troops poured in, joined by the fanatic elements from within the city. The rebels put to sword any Christians—white or Indian—they found within the city. In the late afternoon, they started filing into the Diwan-e-Khas (Hall of Private Audience) of the Emperor. Camping in the inner quarters, their leaders sent a message to the Emperor that they had 'come to fight for our religion and to pay our respects to His Majesty'. The Emperor would still not oblige, and the massed soldiers 'commenced firing their muskets, pistols and carbines in the air, making a great clamour'.[56] The Emperor finally appeared, and asked the soldiers to not make noise. When they stopped firing, he asked their officers to present their case. The officers explained:

> They had been required to bite cartridges, the use of which deprives both Hindus and Mahomedans of their religion, as the cartridges were greased with pork and beef fat, that they accordingly had killed the Europeans at Meerut, and had come to claim his protection.[57]

Zafar argued, 'I have neither troops, magazines or treasury. I am not in a condition to join anyone.' The soldiers replied, 'Only give us your blessing. We will provide everything else.'[58] Surrounded by armed, angry and clamouring soldiers who would not take no for an answer, the Emperor finally gave in, and blessed the revolt. The mutiny of sepoys—which at best escalated to a small revolt with Meerut residents joining in—now transformed into a national struggle. At midnight, a salvo of twenty-one rounds fired from the fort guns announced to the world that Timur's descendant had assumed the reins of his forefathers' Empire. Simultaneously, to hedge his bets, Zafar despatched a camel rider with a letter to the Lieutenant-Governor at Agra, conveying the arrival of mutinous sepoys, and asking for help to restore order.

The three native regiments in Delhi soon joined the rebels. Most British residents were either killed or fled. One by one, almost all the regiments of the Bengal Army either mutinied or were disbanded across the Hindustan. In Punjab alone, the Company disbanded 30,000–40,000 sepoys as a precaution. In an environment of mistrust, John Lawrence, Governor of Punjab, summed up the dilemma facing both the government and the sepoys:

> The misfortune of the present state of affairs is this. Each step we take for our own security is a blow against the regular Sepoy. He feels this, and on his side takes a further step, and so we go on, until we disband or destroy them, or they mutiny and kill their officers.[59]

The Madras Army remained unaffected, while there were minor conflagrations in the Bombay Army. Everywhere in north India, the disbanded or mutinous soldiers aligned themselves to the local princes. Thus, Begum Hazrat Mahal and her son Birjis Qadir at Lucknow, Nana Saheb at Kanpur, Rani Lakshmi Bai at Jhansi, and the old lion, Kunwar Singh in Bihar, became leaders of the rebellious troops in their respective regions.

It is beyond the purpose of our study to write a complete history of the Mutiny, which would require a separate text to do it justice. Of interest to us are the circumstances leading up to the Mutiny, and what drove the sepoys. As we have seen, it was the fear for their faith that led sepoys to this rebellion. Eventually, with the help of the new recruits from Punjab, Gurkhas from Nepal and the loyal Madras and Bombay troops, the Company recovered its control over Hindustan. The Sikhs were a steady source of recruitment for the Company. The Sikhs did not relish the prospect of a Mughal overlord who had so tormented their gurus in the seventeenth and early eighteenth centuries. They also saw this as an opportunity to get even with the purabiyas, who had destroyed the Sikh Empire less than ten years earlier.

There were some moving instances of Hindu–Muslim unity during the 1857 rebellion. Thus, on 1 August on the festival of Eid, in respect of Hindu beliefs, while Delhi was under siege, the Emperor declared:

> No cows were to be killed within the city during the festival of the Eid, and if any Mahommedan should do so he would be blown away from a gun; and whoever, on the part of a Musalman helped to kill a cow, would also be killed.[60]

This dashed the hopes of the English who had expected 'a grand row in the city'. In Lucknow, the Hindu rebels went around in groups crying 'Bum Mahadev', called Birjis Qadir from the palace, embraced him, and said, 'You are Kanhaiya [Krishna].'[61]

The sepoys neatly summarized their reasons for fighting against the Company, while they retreated into Nepal in the final phases of their fight, in a petition to Maharaja Jang Bahadur of Nepal. Having explained the circumstances arising in Meerut, they went on to add:

> The reason, that the sowars of the said Cantonment were put into jail, was that we should be frightened into biting the new cartridges; on this account we and all our countrymen having united together, have fought here and there with the British for the preservation of our faith ... we have been compelled to make war for two years and the Rajahs and Chiefs who are with us in faith and religion, are still so,

and have undergone all sorts of trouble; we have fought for two years in order that our faith and religion may not be polluted. If the religion of a Hindoo or Mussalman is lost, what remains in the world?[62]

The sepoys seem charitable in their assessment of the support of the 'Rajahs and Chiefs' above. The fact is that the leadership failed the soldiers. The old Bahadur Shah in Delhi was not up to the task. A reluctant leader, he betrayed their cause, being in league with the Company throughout the siege. As poor political leadership had led them in the eighteenth century into the pay of foreigners, poor leadership again could not capitalize on the opportunity the sepoys presented to free the country. The government of India was assumed by the Crown in 1858 from the EIC.

However, in so far as their objective was to protect their faith, and put a stop to the missionary activity, they were spectacularly successful. The Mutiny dashed all hopes of making the Indian population Christian. From now on, the British authorities would carefully guard against any overt missionary activity, and no further interference in the religious practices of Hindus or Muslims would be allowed. Queen Victoria's proclamation of 1858 avowed not to disturb the religious beliefs of the Indians:

> We disclaim alike the Right and Desire to impose our Convictions on any of Our Subjects. We declare it to be Our Royal Will and Pleasure that none be in anywise favoured, none molested or disquieted, by reason of their Religious Faith or Observances; but that all alike shall enjoy the equal and impartial protection of the Law; and We do strictly charge and enjoin all those who may be in authority under Us that they abstain from all interference with the Religious Belief or Worship of any of Our Subjects on pain of Our highest Displeasure.[63]

On this matter, the British Raj did keep its promise till the end.

Separated as we are from the incidents by more than one-and-a-half centuries, the fears of the sepoys might look like products of a fertile imagination. The Raj's non-interference in Indians' faith after 1858 is no evidence that earlier designs of aligning the ruler's faith with that of the ruled did not exist. One has only to look at the Prime Minister Lord Palmerston's statement in 1855:

> Perhaps it might be our lot to confer on the countless millions of India a higher and holier gift than any mere human knowledge.[64]

The line drawn by the sepoys in their blood led to the volte-face three years later by the highest British authority, and was firmly respected. In fact, if anything, the British Raj was overzealous in protecting the religious identities of its soldiers from 1858 onwards. Thus, the strict observance of Sikh religious symbols, including turban, beard, etc., in many ways strengthened the Sikh identity. The missionaries were kept at a distance from the soldiers.

During WW1, when Sir Walter Lawrence, the Commissioner for Indian troops, found that a missionary had handed a Bible to a sepoy recovering at the Brighton hospital, he was furious and banned any kind of religious books brought by the visitors. He wrote to Kitchener, 'We cannot be too careful, as if it got abroad that any attempt has been made to proselytise men who are sick and wounded there would be great trouble.'[65]

When he discovered that the YMCA in France had been distributing letter-writing paper with a Christian inscription to the sepoys, he immediately warned the War Office. The YMCA was restrained, as no one wanted to risk an impression that attempts were being made to convert the sepoys. The British made a point to widely advertise the separate dining arrangement for Hindu and Muslim soldiers at the Western Front, including separate butchers slaughtering animals as per their religious customs. In Mesopotamia, the 45th Sikh Regiment marched in Mesopotamia with the Guru Granth Sahib leading them.

To some it might appear as small consolation to a subjugated race. To generations of Indian sepoys, this was the core of their being. Especially in the nineteenth century, religion was a reference point to the lives of most Indians. Ironically, the atheist Karl Marx's description of religion as the 'general theory of this world, its encyclopaedic compendium, its logic in a popular form, its spiritualistic point d'honneur, its enthusiasm, its moral sanction, its solemn complement, its universal source of consolation and justification'[66] pretty much summarizes why it mattered to the soldiers of the British Indian Army. The preservation of their faith over centuries of foreign rule is to the credit of the Indian soldiers of the Raj.

Chapter Ten

With Faith towards Freedom

But I am certain from what I have heard from a very wide variety of people here, British and Indian, that the best thing to do is to cut our losses.[1]

—Sir G. Cunningham

I

During the 1950s, Britain fought a brutal war to maintain its hold over Kenya. Tens of thousands of Kenyans were killed, maimed and raped. Britain used concentration camps and fighter planes to overpower the Mau-Mau rebellion. At the same time, Britain also resolutely fought against fighters in Malaysia, leaving thousands dead. These engagements lasted till the end of the decade, and proved that Britain's appetite for Empire was strong and alive at the time. Yet, in 1947, Britain was in such a tearing hurry to get out of India that the Viceroy Lord Mountbatten advanced the previously stated date of departure by almost a year, to 15 August 1947.

The usual narrative about the decolonization process in India remains ambiguous to date. From the Indian perspective, the narrative has been centred on the nationalist movement led by the Indian National Congress. From the British perspective, the arguments range from the economic 'costs' of the Empire, and the shift in political opinion at home after the war.

The Indian nationalist movement had been active since the early part of the twentieth century, without any discernible impact on the will of British leadership to continue ruling India. The 'Quit India Movement' of 1942 was brutally crushed, and most Congress leaders were incarcerated throughout the war.

As we reviewed in the first two chapters, the most significant economic contribution of India to the Empire was the maintenance of an army that did not cost the British exchequer, and that would have been impossible to maintain without the revenue and human resources of India. This was proven repeatedly, and especially during the two global wars. This underlying fact had not changed at the end of the war. In addition, Indian revenues provided highly paid expat jobs for countless British civil servants, and a number of valuable business enterprises in India were owned by the British.

Political opinion at home was near unanimous across both the Conservatives and Labour when it came to the Empire. It was not just Churchill who was doggedly averse to 'preside over the liquidation of the British Empire'. The Labour Home Secretary in Churchill's government, Herbert Morrison, compared the idea of giving freedom to the colonies with 'giving a child of ten a latch-key, a bank account and a shot gun'.[2] Morrison was Deputy Prime Minister in Clement Attlee's Labour government that had to concede freedom to India. So far as the sociocultural attitudes are concerned, forget 1947, even in 2014, 59 per cent of respondents in a YouGov poll thought the Empire was 'something to be proud of' and 34 percent said 'they would like it if Britain still had an empire'.[3]

As late as 1940, Viceroy Lord Linlithgow wrote to the Secretary of State: 'I am not too keen to start talking about a period after which British rule will have ceased in India. I suspect that that day is very remote and I feel the least we say about it in all probability the better.'[4]

All pronouncements of progressive self-government, whether during WW1, or subsequently, were insincere. The new capital city of the Raj—New Delhi—was inaugurated in 1931 at huge expense and it was widely perceived to be the signal of British intention to stay for centuries. We also saw that the pace of 'Indianization' of the Indian Army before WW2 was so slow that it would have been at least a century before the Indian Army would be entirely officered by Indians. 'Indianization' was seen by most British authorities as the inherent threat to British control of the Indian Army. The 'Indianization' scheme completion could be fairly assumed as the proxy for the date when the British thought they would depart from India. As late as 1939, this date was decades—if not a century—away.

To understand the reason behind the volte-face in 1946-47, we must look at the fundamental pillar that underpinned the strength of British rule in India—its Indian Army. So long as the Indian Army was faithful, nothing could shake the British Raj. In 1946, this confidence in the loyalty of the Indian Army towards British rule started to evaporate. Once it was clear that the Indian Army could not be relied upon to continue supporting the Raj, the British headed to the exit gate in earnest.

In this chapter, we will review the circumstances and forces that led to the change in the consciousness of the sepoy. The Indian Army at the end of the Second World War was very different from six years earlier. Besides the obvious increase in size to almost 2.5 million, the number and proportion of Indian officers increased dramatically. From a few hundred Indian commissioned officers in 1939, the number of Indian commissioned officers by the end of the war rose to 15,000 — three times the size of the peacetime strength of the Indian Army officer cadre. Most of the 30,000 or so British officers were conscripts, and were about to take their discharge soon. All Indian commissioned officers were volunteers. Whether the British authorities liked it or not, the Indian Army was going to have a predominantly Indian officer cadre going forward. Unless, of course, most of the Indian commissioned officers were to be demobilized. Those who have seen the US experience in post-Saddam Iraq are well aware of the effect of disbanding the entire well-trained officer cadre of an army. It was one thing to demobilize illiterate peasant soldiers, as was done at the end of WW1. It was a totally different prospect to demobilize well-educated Indian officers who had nationalist sympathies. This dilemma did not present any easy solutions.

Besides the change in composition, something else happened to the Indian Army during the war. A sizeable number of Indian soldiers joined the Indian National Army (INA) formed by Subhas Chandra Bose, and fought for the freedom of India against British and allied forces. Militarily, their success was limited, but their story had a huge moral impact. During the war, the British tried their best to keep the INA story hidden from the rest of the army and Indians. However, at the end of the war, many of these soldiers (by now prisoners of the Raj) started to arrive in India. The British government, in a stroke of poor judgement, decided to try these men for high treason, and opened the trial at the historic Red Fort in Delhi. This was presumably to give them exemplary punishment. However, the furore that this ill-judged act of policy created in the Indian Army and civilian population shook the foundations of the Raj. Within six months, the fear of mutiny and memories of the 1857 bloodshed forced the decision within Whitehall to grant India its freedom.

II

That the Indian sepoys were the foundation of the British Indian Army and the Raj was plain to both the British and the Indians who wished to see them leave. By the early twentieth century, a nationalist movement started to take shape across India. This movement was not lead by the princes and rajas, the traditional Indian leaders. The movement instead germinated within the professional classes: lawyers, teachers, students, many of them educated in English. A new type of leader emerged, which today we know as a 'politician'. It would have been natural for this leadership to suborn the loyalty of the sepoys to help achieve the freedom of India. However, there remained a big disconnect between the worldview of the peasant soldier from Punjab and that of the nationalist leaders.

The soldier was inspired by the personal conduct of his officers, and had a limited worldview that believed in giving his due to the lawful government, whose 'salt' he had eaten. He could see that the British were aliens to his faith, but this line was drawn well, and respected by the British scrupulously. Secure in his faith, and entrenched in the tradition of generations of loyal service, he felt little need for overthrowing his allegiance to the Raj in favour of the politicians. The nationalist leaders, despite occasional exhortations, did not succeed in subverting the loyalty of the sepoy. In 1921, Mahatma Gandhi had written, 'It is sinful for anyone, either soldiers or civilians, to serve this Government which has proved treacherous to the Mussalmans of India, and which has been guilty of the inhumanities of the Punjab.'[5]

The illiterate peasant soldier from Punjab could not relate to the exhortations of the apostle of non-violence. All this would change during the Second World War, when Bose took great personal risks, to inspire and lead the soldiers in an attempt to free India.

Before we get to the story of Bose and his INA, it is apt to remember that there were earlier attempts to align the sepoy to the nationalist cause. The Ghadr movement during the First World War actively tried to subvert the loyalty of Punjab soldiers. The counterintelligence of the Raj crushed the rebellion.

However, one man's efforts to free India by military means during the First World War deserves due credit. That man was Raja Mahendra Pratap Singh, scion of Hathras, a minor Jat principality in western Uttar Pradesh. Mahendra Pratap Singh's ancestor, Thakur Daya Ram, had measured swords with the EIC in 1817, just before the Pindari War. Hathras Fort was reduced by the 'most powerful assemblage of artillery to date' in Hindustan but Daya Ram refused to surrender. His descendant, Mahendra Pratap, resolved on raising an army to free India. On 20 December 1914, at the age of twenty-eight, he renounced his family in the cause of the nation, and headed to Germany. Before leaving, he went to take leave of his wife, a princess from the principality of Jind. He later wrote in a characteristically stoic fashion:

> It proved to be the last leave taking. My wife died in 1925. She was lying and weeping. I never saw before my wife weeping thus. I asked her not to weep. I tried to console her. I saw my tiny son asleep. My daughter too was in bed. It was night, and the newly arrived electric light was somehow very dim and pale.[6]

Pratap met with the Kaiser in Berlin, and addressed the Indian prisoners of war in the Camp Crescent Moon, outside Berlin. From the camp, he chose five Afridi soldiers who had defected to the Germans from the Western Front. These five, including Jemadar Mir Mast, the brother of Victoria Cross awardee Mir Dast, would accompany Pratap on his journey to Kabul from Berlin in 1915. Pratap met with the Ottoman Sultan in Constantinople, and accompanied by some German and Turkish officers, after a perilous journey across Persia, arrived in Kabul during September 1915.

With hindsight, it seems he was six months too early to depart from Berlin. In April 1916, the Kut garrison surrendered to the Turks, who took 6,750 Indian and 2,750 English soldiers as prisoners. Had he waited out 1915 in Berlin or Istanbul, he could have had the chance to try the loyalty of the Indian soldiers taken prisoner at Kut. A force numbering close to 7,000 is a totally different prospect than the five Afridis, whose primary interest was in reaching home than India's freedom. But this was not to be.

Pratap arrived at Kabul to welcoming drumbeats and fanfare, and was received by Afghan King Habibullah with open arms. The negotiations with Habibullah on supporting an army to help Pratap invade India from the western front were protracted, but eventually unproductive. The wily Afghan asked Pratap and his German and Turkish mission to 'spread out your wares before me so I can choose whatever I like and leave whatever I do not need'.[7] He eventually chose to stay neutral, and put paid to the high hopes of Pratap, the Germans and the Turks. Habibullah's father was placed on the Afghan throne with the help of the British Indian Army in 1880 after an Afghan civil war, and he was loath to gamble his throne. While Habibullah prevaricated, Pratap declared the first 'Provisional Government of India' on 1 December 1915, with himself as its President and Maulana Barkatullah as its Prime Minister. The Provisional Government was backed by Germany and Turkey, and reached an agreement that the Central Powers would ensure its recognition from all their allies after the war. The principle of Indian government by the Indians as the legitimate government of India was recognized by Germany and Turkey.[8]

All their hopes were dashed in January next year, when Habibullah openly declared that he would stay neutral. Pratap was declared a fugitive by the British, and accused of high treason. He could finally return to India in 1946, when independence for India had been announced. Tragedy struck his family in his absence, who were hounded by the British government, and his estate was confiscated for a period. His wife died of grief in 1925, and his young son also died within a year of Pratap's return to India. The son was a year old when Pratap left India, and unfortunately Pratap could not spend even a year together with him on his return.

Though this attempt failed, it served as a reminder to both Indians and the British that the fight for India was as much a fight for the heart and mind of the sepoy. It would fall on Bose to take this fight to its conclusion, when an opportunity arose during the Second World War.

III

Not since Raje Shivaji raised the standard of revolt against Aurangzeb in the seventeenth century did India possess a leader of the stature, vision and ability to have effected an alteration in the course of its history. All this was to change when Bose was born to a Bengali Hindu family in 1897 in Cuttack, Orissa. Like Raje Shivaji, Bose was to later confound his tormenters by escaping from their prison, and lead an inspiring fight for liberation from tyranny. Many in India believe there was a touch of the divine in the life of both these men, even if separated by more than two-and-a-half centuries.

The ninth child in a family of fourteen siblings, Bose was born to Janakinath and Prabhabati in a moderately wealthy family. At a young age, he was tormented by what he saw around himself, and aged fifteen, asked his mother in a letter:

> Will the condition of our country continue to go from bad to worse—will not any son of Mother India in distress, in total disregard of his selfish interests, dedicate his whole life to the cause of the Mother?[9]

He studied at Cambridge, and plunged into Gandhi's Indian freedom movement in 1921, after qualifying but resigning from the coveted Indian Civil Service.

His views got him in trouble with the Raj soon, and he was imprisoned in late 1924, without any charges, and transported to Mandalay jail in Burma. Thereafter, he spent eleven of the next sixteen years in either jail, or exile, or both; before leaving India for his final mission in January 1941. While the authorities did everything to cage him, his popularity climbed with the masses.

When his health deteriorated badly in prison in 1932, he was allowed to leave for Europe in February 1933 for treatment at his own expense, effectively sending him into exile. Bose headed to Vienna, and for the next three years travelled extensively within Europe in support of the Indian cause, and met his future wife, Emily Schenkl. He was arrested on his return to India in 1936, and was released in March 1937. He secretly married Emily on 26 December 1937 during a brief visit to Europe.

The next year, Bose was elected President of the Indian National Congress with Gandhi's backing. The Mahatma's non-violent path was in radical contrast to Bose's proposed programme that did not rule out any method—violent or otherwise—for India's freedom. Their political relationship soured. Despite his growing differences with the Mahatma, Bose contested and defeated Gandhi's proposed candidate for the Congress Presidency the next year in January 1939. It was the first time in two decades that Gandhi's authority was challenged within the Congress. The Mahatma now resorted to passive non-cooperation, and Bose was forced to resign as President in April 1939, and also barred from senior Congress office for three years.

The Second World War was declared, and India was made a party by the Viceroy, Lord Linlithgow, in September 1939, without any consultation with the Indians. Bose vehemently opposed India being dragged into an imperial conflict, and finally saw the opportunity that he had long waited for. While organizing a procession against the Holwell memorial, which he termed as 'an unwanted stain on the memory of Nawab [Siraj-ud-Daulah]', Bose was arrested on 2 July 1940. This memorial was installed by the British in memory of English prisoners who died in the 'Black Hole' of Calcutta, the blame for which was incorrectly placed on Nawab Siraj-ud-daulah, who was defeated by Clive at Plassey in 1757 in a treacherous battle.

Bose was transferred to house arrest on 5 December after his hunger strike, as the government did not wish to have his death on its hands. From this house arrest, he escaped on the night of 16 January 1941, in the guise of a Pathan, leaving his jailors shocked and baffled. In a daring journey, Bose escaped into Afghanistan on 26 January, leaving British intelligence and the Viceroy red-faced. To make up for their loss, British intelligence asked its representatives in Istanbul and Cairo 'to wire what arrangements they could make for his assassination'.[10] Fortunately, the Russians, who were not yet at war with Germany, cooperated with the Italians and Germans to allow safe passage to Bose through Soviet Russia. His enemies' plan to kill him in the Middle East failed. On 2 April 1941, Bose flew into Berlin from Russia, and Emily joined him shortly thereafter.

Crisis leads to strange bedfellows. Thus, the arch-imperialist, Churchill, found himself joining hands with Stalin in 1941. Bose's efforts to seek help from Adolf Hitler were in the same vein. To be sure, there was no love lost between Bose and the Nazis. He was aware of the reprehensible views Hitler held about Indians, and that in 1941 Hitler was still hoping to come to an understanding with Churchill. The old adage of your enemy's enemy is your friend guided him. While Germany fought Britain, this was where he hoped to get support for his plans to free India. For a long time, Bose had believed that by aligning the loyalty of Indian soldiers of the Raj with the cause of India's freedom, he could undermine the

British hold over India. His initial plan was to raise an army from Indian PoWs captured in North Africa, and invade India with the help of the USSR through Afghanistan. On 22 June 1941, Hitler attacked the USSR, and this dashed all hopes of invading India through Russia.

Bose continued to represent India's case for freedom to the German political and military leadership, and gained many Indian adherents who were stationed in Europe. In his meeting with German Foreign Minister Joachim von Ribbentrop on 29 April 1941, Bose made plain the feelings in India against Fascists who were 'striving to dominate other races'. Bose's first meeting with a senior German minister was not particularly cordial.

Bose inaugurated the Free India Centre on 2 November 1941 in Berlin. The Centre became a hub of free-India activities, and a number of Indians in exile joined. In December 1941 and January 1942, Bose began the process of recruiting Indian PoWs in Germany into the Indian Legion. Bose had limited success in the early days, for while the sepoys were inclined to respond to his message, the subedars and jemadars did their best to prevent sepoys joining the Legion. Eventually, around 4,000 of the Indian captives in German and Italian prisons agreed to join the Indian Legion.[11]

One of the first directives Bose issued to the Indian Legion was to ensure that the class- and religion-based battalion system under the British was dismantled. He mixed Hindu, Muslim and Sikh soldiers even at the platoon level, and the result 'contrary to the original doubts was surprisingly good'. Bose believed it was better to have fully committed volunteers than half-motivated soldiers in his Indian Legion. He would have preferred a higher number of Indian prisoners join the legion, but was not entirely unhappy with the outcome. Abid Hasan, whom Bose entrusted the task of recruiting Indian soldiers, left an insightful account of issues faced:

> Let us suppose there were some people so loyal to the British they would never join. There were people like that ... A few were hesitating to join because they had taken the oath very seriously ... They didn't want to break the oath they had taken over the Gita, the Koran or the Gurugranth ... A major part of them were worried about their families ... Another was that they had opposed and fought against the Germans. To join hands with the enemy—went against the thinking of a soldier.[12]

Despite their reservations, Bose's personality deeply impacted the soldiers. In autumn 1942, Bose spoke to a crowd of Indian soldiers near Dresden, and Gita Mookerjee, who was present, later recounted:

> He spoke in Hindustani and we circled round him, and as he warmed up I saw how the whole audience was coming under his spell and how they were listening with the greatest attention to every word that fell from his lip. When he finished, this audience of about four hundred men had almost acquired a new life, a new animation, and there was a new excitement among the men, who had mostly come to the meeting out of sheer curiosity. Dozens of Jats, Sikhs, and Pathans, many of them veterans of frontier wars, came crowding towards us and asked us to enrol them.[13]

The Indian Legion was trained in Germany but did not have a chance to fight while Bose was in Europe. After his departure, the Legion did fight against the Allies in late 1943 and 1944.[14] It would fall upon another army, which Bose would raise later, to fight for India's freedom directly.

The fall of Singapore—the largest British outpost in Southeast Asia—to a Japanese force on 15 February 1942 opened a more realistic strategic route for Bose. The war with the USSR had frustrated his plans to invade British India from the north-west. He saw the immense possibilities ahead, and in his first open broadcast to India said:

> The fall of Singapore means the collapse of the British Empire, the end of the iniquitous regime which it has symbolized and the dawn of a new era in Indian history. Through India's liberation will Asia and the world move forward towards the larger goal of human emancipation.[15]

In the meantime, Bose was dealing with the chicanery of Hitler, who repeatedly balked at making a public declaration in support of India's freedom. Bose simultaneously also guarded against any impression that he endorsed the totalitarian ideologies of Hitler, Mussolini or the Japanese. In a broadcast on 1 May 1942, he set the record straight, stating that he was 'not an apologist of the Tripartite Powers' and did not see it as his task 'to defend what they have done or may do in future'.[16]

Bose started to pester the German leadership to help him travel to Asia, from where he would launch his armed effort to free India. Hitler's distrust of Japan, and the lack of coordination between the Tripartite powers frustrated his plans. On 29 May 1942, Bose had a tense meeting with Hitler. Without flinching, Bose raised the matter of Hitler's anti-Indian racist remarks in *Mein Kampf* and asked for a clarification for the Indian nation. Hitler evaded a direct reply, and said something to the effect that he did not think 'passive resistance' of the Indian pattern was a strategy for the German Reich. Bose again pressed him into an open declaration in support of India's freedom, to which Hitler replied with a long monologue on the virtues of political and military realism, and German economic support for India post war. Nevertheless, he supported Bose's proposal to travel to Asia, and promised logistical support via submarine. The officers translating had a tough time, and they had to tone down some of Bose's responses into diplomatic language. Bose wasn't pleased with the meeting or impressed by Hitler. Bose later dubbed Hitler 'baddha pagal' ('raving mad' in Bengali) to his compatriots.[17]

It would be many months before Hitler's promise of logistical support to transport Bose to Asia would materialize. In the meantime, Bose and Emilie's daughter Anita was born on 29 November 1942. After persistent bickering between the Germans, Italians and Japanese, and two failed plans to transport Bose via air, Bose finally boarded a German submarine at Kiel on 9 February 1943. For this long and perilous journey to Southeast Asia, he chose Abid Hasan as his companion. On 28 April, Bose and Hasan were transferred to a Japanese submarine, in the Indian Ocean, 400 nautical miles off the coast of Madagascar. On 6 May, Bose and Hasan safely disembarked at Sabang, Indonesia, and headed to Tokyo in a small Japanese combat aircraft, accompanied by Colonel Yamamoto. British intelligence, although aware their enemy was on the move, was not specific enough to allow an identification and attack on the submarines he travelled in. Bose reached Tokyo in mid-May and was lodged at the Imperial Hotel on arrival. Very soon, Bose would be on his way to Singapore to meet the soldiers who would fight together with him to free India.

IV

The previous year, the British garrison at Singapore—90,000 strong—surrendered to a much smaller Japanese force on 15 February 1942. Two days later, on 17 February, 50,000 Indians of all ranks were separated from the British and handed over to the Japanese at the Farrer Park race course. A British officer, Colonel J.C. Hunt, told them that from now on they should conduct themselves according to Japanese instructions, and left. Captain Shanawaz Khan would later comment that they were 'handed over like cattle by the British'. The Indians were then addressed by

Major Fujiwara, a Japanese officer tasked with organizing Indian soldiers to fight the British, Pritam Singh of the India Independence League, and finally by Captain Mohan Singh. Mohan Singh had recently accepted Fujiwara's entreaties to help organize the Indian National Army (INA) from the captive Indian soldiers. Fujiwara was able to convince Mohan Singh that the Japanese truly believed in the cause of India's freedom. Mohan Singh spoke to convince the gathered soldiers, and later wrote:

> I ... asked the soldiers to raise hands if any one from amongst them would like to volunteer to join this force and fight for the liberation of his country. There was a spontaneous response from all the soldiers. Along with the raising of hands, thousands of turbans and caps were hurled up in the air ... soldiers jumped to their feet ... with prolonged shouts of 'Inquilab Zindabad' (Long Live the Revolution).[18]

A large majority of the soldiers and officers present agreed to join the INA. Almost 250 medical officers, and 150 combatant officers (100 Viceroy's Commissioned Officers and 50 Indian Commissioned Officers) joined the INA in Singapore.[19] This compares to just one VCO in the Indian Legion in Germany. The proportion of Indians agreeing to join the INA was much higher than those who agreed to join the Indian Legion in Germany. One of the main factors was the much higher proportion of ICOs in the Malayan theatre compared to North Africa.

As we saw in earlier chapters, the recruitment of ICOs gathered pace during the war. In an underestimation of Japanese and Indian fighting capability, the British sent most of the Indianizing units—the units that had a higher number of Indian commissioned officers—to the Malaya theatre to fight the Japanese. The Germans were considered too formidable to be confronted by Indianizing units, so very few units in North Africa had Indian ICOs. The ICOs, of course, were educated, had a wider worldview and had nationalist sympathies. This precisely was the reason the British schemed for forty years to keep a ceiling on the number of Indians in the commissioned ranks. Once the ceiling was broken, its impacts would be felt immediately.

British military intelligence was worried about the thousands of ICOs being recruited each year: 'It is certain that the majority are nationalist in outlook.'[20] An Indian officer in Malaya observed that of Indian commissioned officers 'about 60 per cent are nationalists and desire an early independence for India. The remaining 40 per cent are in a general way dissatisfied with British rule in India but hold no strong views.'[21] Despite obvious concerns, the lack of manpower was so acute that there was no alternative to hiring Indians into commissioned ranks, which would eventually transform the British Indian Army.

Captain Mohan Singh was a young officer, with no political experience or clout. Early in the year, he had told Fujiwara that 'Indians living in Asia would rise if a revolutionary such as Bose could be persuaded to come to Asia to lead the movement.'[22]

Meanwhile, Raja Mahendra Pratap had moved to Japan during the decade leading up to WW2 to garner Japanese support for India's freedom. Pratap founded the 'India Executive Board' in 1941, with Rash Behari Bose (another revolutionary from Pratap's generation) as his deputy, in Japan. Pratap, with his uncompromising attitude, fell out with the Japanese on their role in a future invasion of India. Pratap was put under effective 'house arrest' by the Japanese in early 1942 due to those disagreements. It now fell upon Rash Behari Bose to provide political leadership to the Indian freedom movement in the East. Rash Behari was nominated President of the India Independence League (IIL), an Indian umbrella political organization dedicated to securing Indian independence from colonial rule, with charge over the INA.

Mohan Singh and Rash Behari differed in their strategy on dealing with the Japanese, whom Mohan Singh suspected of wanting to use the INA. By the end of 1942, he fell out with the Japanese on the point of the independence of the INA from the Japanese Army and its war objectives. Rash Behari dismissed Mohan Singh, who in turn released a pre-drafted order dissolving the INA. Mohan Singh was arrested by the Japanese, and was in confinement for the rest of the war. Both the IIL and the INA were in dire straits by the end of the year, and the clamour for the Japanese to facilitate Bose's arrival increased. This was the background in which Bose arrived in Tokyo in May 1943.

However, by now the tide of the war was turning in the Allies' favour. The battle for the Atlantic went in the favour of the Allies, and with the Enigma code broken, German U-boats were being sunk regularly. The German and Italian forces in North Africa surrendered in May 1943, and the Allies would soon launch an invasion of Italy. On the Eastern front, Germans suffered a crushing defeat at Stalingrad, where 90,000 survivors of the German 6th Army surrendered in January 1943. The Kursk offensive during the summer of 1943 was also a failure, and Germany could never launch a strategic offensive against the USSR after that. On the Pacific front, the Japanese lost four fleet carriers at the Battle of Midway in June 1942; by June 1943, the US Navy felt ready to launch an offensive against the Pacific islands of New Guinea and Solomon.

V

Despite setbacks, Japanese morale was high when Bose reached Tokyo. In Japan, Bose found support and warmth that was absent in Nazi Germany. He met with Prime Minister Tojo in June, who declared that Japan would do 'everything possible' to help the cause of Indian independence.[23] Enthused by this clear support, Bose appeared in a press conference on 19 June, and thundered:

> The hour has struck, and every patriotic Indian must advance towards the field of battle. Only when the blood of freedom-loving Indians begins to flow will India attain her freedom.[24]

Here finally was a leader who spoke the language that the peasant soldier from Punjab could understand. That he was putting his own life in danger, and his talk was not a mere boast, made him even more credible in the soldier's eye.

Bose arrived in Singapore with Rash Behari, who presented him to the cheering IIL representatives on 4 July as 'best, noblest, the most daring, and the most dynamic in the youth of India'.[25] Thus the baton was passed from Mahendra Pratap and Rash Behari's generation to Bose, without rancour. The next day, Bose appeared in military uniform in front of some 12,000 INA soldiers. The soldiers were enthralled when he told them:

> For the present, I can offer you nothing except hunger, thirst, privation, forced marches and death. But if you follow me in life and in death—as I am confident you will—I shall lead you to victory and freedom.[26]

Bose renamed the INA the 'Azad Hind Fauj' (Independent Indian Army), and gave its soldiers the battle cry 'Chalo Delhi' (Onward to Delhi).

After the speeches and rallies, Bose and his comrades sat down to the serious business of organizing a fighting force. The incidents of late 1942 had reduced the strength of the INA to 12,000. Bose's charisma raised it back to 40,000. Many wavering and passive soldiers now joined in droves, in response to the call by their 'Netaji' (Dear Leader). To the soldiers, Bose added 18,000 civilians of Tamil origin, termed non-martial by the British, to train and fight alongside the soldiers from the north-west. He also raised a women's battalion, and named it after Rani Jhansi, the heroine of the 1857 Revolt.[27]

On 21 October, Netaji proclaimed the formation of the Provisional Government of Free India, and on 24 October his Government declared war on Great Britain and the USA. Bose fulfilled his promise to set foot 'on the holy soil of India before end of this year' by arriving in Port Blair, capital of Andaman and Nicobar Islands, on 29 December. The islands were wrested from the British by the Japanese earlier. Some of India's greatest revolutionaries and freedom fighters suffered in the prison on these islands, known as 'kala pani' (black water). Bose paid tribute to the revolutionaries, and compared the opening of the gates of the Cellular Jail to the storming of the Bastille. Bose also founded the Azad Hind Bank, and raised US$60 million from Indian expats in Southeast Asia. Such was his magnetism that many of the rich gave millions, and many of the poor all they had, housewives often donating their personal jewellery and life savings.

Bose's army comprised three fighting divisions with approximately 30,000 soldiers, and support units involved in intelligence and field propaganda. In early 1944, 12,000 INA soldiers of the First Division, headed by Major General Mohammad Zaman Kiani, spearheaded the march towards the Indian border at Imphal and Kohima. The Second Division was stationed in north Malaya, and the Third Division in Johor (close to Singapore) in reserve. The plan was to invade India from the Burma frontier, and march into Assam and Bengal. Bose was confident that once his army marched into Bengal, there would be a general uprising in support of his force, and thus the British Raj in India would be broken. The 12,000 soldiers of the INA First Division and 84,000 Japanese confronted 155,000 well-entrenched British forces at the Burma–India border.

Bose also had to continuously argue with the Japanese for an independent role for his army, for the Japanese saw the Indian troops in a supportive propaganda function. The Japanese strategic objective was to prevent a counteroffensive from British forces in India to reconquer Burma. The INA's objective was to catalyse a civilian uprising against the British Raj. Despite Japanese forces vastly outnumbering the INA, Bose wanted that 'the first drop of blood on Indian soil should be that of a member of INA.'[28] The Japanese supply lines were thinly stretched in Burma and Malaya. There was no air support, and the hopes were pinned on raiding the 'Churchill rations'—supplies of the British Army—once the Japanese and INA forces conquered Imphal and Kohima within the Indian frontier. The INA was even more poorly supplied compared to the Japanese units.

The task before the INA forces was extremely difficult. The distance from Singapore to Imphal at the India–Burma border is more than the distance between London and Tehran. Bose's army had to march across this difficult terrain, described by General Slim as 'some of the world's worst country, breeding the world's worst diseases, and having for half the year the world's worst climate.'[29]

Despite all the challenges, the INA First Division carried the fight onto Indian soil on 18 March 1944. The order of the day from Bose thrilled his soldiers:

> There, there in the distance—beyond that river, beyond the jungles, beyond those hills—lies the promised land—the soil from which we sprang—the land to which we shall now return. Hark! India is calling—India's metropolis Delhi is calling—three hundred and eighty million of our countrymen are calling. Blood is calling to blood. Get up, we have no time to lose. Take up your arms. There, in front of you, is the road that our pioneers have built. We shall march along that road. We shall carve our way through the enemy's ranks—or if God wills, we shall die a martyr's

death. And in our last sleep we shall kiss the road that will bring our Army to Delhi. The road to Delhi is the road to Freedom. Chalo Delhi (Onwards to Delhi).[30]

Contrary to Bose's advice, Japanese General Mutaguchi decided to lay siege to Imphal in April 1944. The Japanese gambled on capturing Imphal, instead of bypassing it and Kohima to take control of the railhead at Dimapur further north, which would have enabled movement deeper into Indian territory. The Japanese priority was to neutralize the British forces in Imphal and Kohima so they could not launch an offensive into Burma. Bose's objective was to reach the Assam delta and Bengal plains as quickly as possible to foment rebellion, and the population was receptive. The Nagas, the main tribe around Kohima, welcomed INA soldiers with open arms. They told Shah Nawaz that they didn't want to be ruled by the British or the Japanese: 'All that we would like to have is our own Raja, Netaji Subhas Chandra Bose.'[31]

In April, the INA unfurled the Indian tricolour on Indian soil at Moirang, a few miles short of Imphal. General Mutaguchi thought he had caught a big fish with his siege of Imphal, but it turned out to be a crocodile. The British garrison was adequately supplied by British and American warplanes. The Japanese supply lines in the meantime broke down. Supplying Imphal from the port city of Singapore was like supplying an army a few hundred miles east of Moscow from London. It was only possible via air support, given the poor tracks and treacherous ground conditions.

At this stage of the war, Japan could not spare aircraft for the Burma theatre, as the American Navy was soon to attack the Mariana Islands, from where the B-29 American bombers could bomb mainland Japan. The Pacific fight was proving to be existential for Japan. As a consequence, the Allies had an air superiority of ten to one in the Burma theatre. To make things worse, the rains came early that year, and turned the fighting ground of INA and Japanese forces into muddy slush. More soldiers died of malaria and starvation than of enemy bullets. The situation turned into a stalemate in May and June, with the British side well supplied and stocked, while the INA and Japanese resorted to eating grass, and fish caught from the streams. The INA First Division was about to be decimated due to lack of food and supplies.

On 10 July, the Japanese informed Bose that there was no alternative but to withdraw from the Imphal theatre, and on 18 July, Major General Kiani ordered all units of First Division to retreat into Burma. The soldiers showed great courage and stoicism during this retreat, even if Bose was deeply saddened by their sufferings. In their worst days, when Bose came to meet the retreating men in Mandalay, Abid Hasan recounts: 'Sikhs oiled their beards, the Punjabi Muslims, Dogras and Rajputs twirled their moustaches and we the indiscriminates put on as good a face as we could manage.'[32]

While the INA had retreated from the Imphal theatre, its fight was not yet over. Peter Fay observes, 'It was the battling with no hope along the Irrawady, not the battling with high hope about the Manipur basin that justified the freedom army (INA) and gave it in the end such moral leverage.'[33] However, by now it was a fight of men and muscle against iron and fire. The British counteroffensive organized under General Slim's 14th Army. Slim's 14th Army was exceptionally well equipped, with anti-malarial medicines, air force support, excellent firepower, and overwhelmingly superior numbers. The 14th Army was the largest army in the world at the time, with almost one million men under its command. Despite such odds, Bose joined his forces in Burma in January 1945 to fight this battle. The American B-29 bombers were bombing INA positions indiscriminately by now, and in February they mercilessly razed to the ground the INA hospital close to Rangoon. The hospital was clearly marked with a Red Cross sign.

Commanded by Gurbaksh Singh Dhillon, Prem Kumar Sahgal and Shah Nawaz, INA soldiers fought courageously in Burma. Bose himself was once trapped at Meiktila, from where he broke out with gun in hand. A great majority of INA soldiers died fighting at Imphal and Kohima, and during the retreat through Burma. Surrounded by superior armour, air power, and grossly outnumbered, many chose death over defeat. But, as Leonard Gordon observes, in numbers, supplies and weapons, they were dwarfs among giants. They fought bravely in particular actions as the Japanese were retreating, but their numbers were relatively small. Despite their patriotic fervour, they could not have altered the outcome of the war. Finally, Prem Kumar Sahgal became a prisoner of war on 29 April 1945; Shah Nawaz Khan and Gurbaksh Dhillon were captured on 18 May by the advancing 14th Army.

Bose remained unfazed, and on the eve of his departure from Burma, he addressed his soldiers:

> The future generations of Indians, who will be born not as slaves but as free men because of your colossal sacrifice, will bless your names and proudly proclaim to the world that you, their forebears, fought and suffered reverses in the battles in Manipur, Assam, and Burma, but through temporary failure you paved the way to ultimate success and glory.[34]

On his final march out of Burma, Bose ensured that the 100 or so girls in the Rani Jhansi battalion from Malaya reached safely back to their homes. Pursued by British infantry and fighter planes, in this long march through jungles, many of his compatriots later observed that Bose appeared intent on sacrificing his life in a last stand. However, strongly advised by all the military and civilian officers, who urged him to keep himself alive to fight another day, he returned to Singapore via Thailand and Malaya.

Japan surrendered on 15 August, after the horrific nuclear bombings of Hiroshima and Nagasaki on 6 and 9 August. Against his wishes, Bose reluctantly accepted the collective opinion of his comrades to leave Singapore for 'Russia, if possible'. Bose conceded it would be an 'adventure into [the] unknown'. Bose left Singapore on 16 August, and reached Taipei in the early afternoon of 18 August in a small Japanese aircraft, via Bangkok and Saigon. The aircraft carrying Bose crashed shortly after takeoff from the Taipei airport. That evening, this great son of India breathed his last in the hospital at Taipei. Habib Rahman was the only Indian with Bose in the plane, and was with him in his last moments. Rahman recounted the final message from Bose before he fell unconscious:

> Habib, my end is coming very soon. I have fought all my life for my country's freedom. I am dying for my country's freedom. Go and tell my countrymen to continue the fight for India's freedom. India will be free, and before long.[35]

On 23 August, the Japanese announced the death of Bose. The nation was stunned and grief stricken. The poet and freedom fighter, Sarojini Naidu, gave voice to that grief on 29 August: 'His [Bose's] proud, importunate and violent spirit was a flaming sword forever unsheathed in defense of the land he worshipped with such surpassing devotion. A greater love hath not man than this, that he lay down his life for his country and his people.'[36]

As we shall see, his death was not in vain.

Many British narratives written after the war, even by otherwise balanced observers, disparage the role and performance of the INA in the war. If one reads the British intelligence reports, Japanese military reports, and narratives of the INA participants, a different picture emerges. Even if we discount the first-hand narrative from the INA participants, the British intelligence noted at the time:

> A measure of courage cannot be denied to the leaders of INA front-line units in Burma in 1945 when ... they faced up to British equipment, tanks, guns, and aircraft with rifles and bullock-carts and empty stomachs.[37]

Much is made of some INA soldiers surrendering during the Burma campaign. This needs to be seen in perspective. By 2 October 1944, a British intelligence report documents: '[Just] 700 of the INA have come into our hands since the end of February 1944, and the rest have retired with the Japanese forces.'[38]

Until the Japanese rout and surrender in 1945, the INA men fought with tenacity. 'What did you mean, you people,' General Gracey would ask Prem Sahgal after his capture, 'by going on fighting? We had armor, artillery. You chaps had nothing. But instead of surrendering, you fought. It was madness.'[39]

Nevertheless, the INA was not unique in some of its soldiers deciding to surrender. Less than three years earlier, a 90,000-strong British garrison at Singapore had surrendered to a Japanese force of 23,000. The British surrendered, and so did the Japanese and Germans during WW2, depending on the fortunes of each fighting side in various theatres.

Victory or defeat alone does not account for the dedication of men fighting in an army. The outcome of war is dependent on a number of complex factors, including motivation, fighting strength, equipment, strategy and tactics. It was clear that the INA was lacking in equipment and supplies, and strategy was tightly controlled by the Japanese, even if Bose fought with them to amend it. The INA was vastly outnumbered by the British 14th Army. It more than matched them when it came to the motivation and commitment of the fighting men. The extremely high death rate of INA soldiers, when compared to all other armies fighting in WW2, proves that the men tried their best to cover for the inadequacies in supply, equipment, etc. The INA death rate estimates—including those killed in action and from disease and starvation—range around 40 per cent of the total strength.[40] Even unsympathetic accounts estimate a death rate of 32 per cent.[41] This compares to a death rate of 5.2 per cent for Britain and the Commonwealth, and 8 per cent for Britain alone[42] in WW2. The comparable death rates for Soviet, German and US armed forces was 31 per cent, 29 per cent and 2.5 per cent respectively.[43]

The INA soldiers paid the price of freedom with their blood, with every second soldier sacrificing his life for the cause. It speaks for itself that the number of Indian soldiers dying for the British side in WW2 was approximately the same as of those who died under INA flag opposing the British. The Indians fighting on the British side numbered 2.5 million, those who formed the INA were no more than 60,000. The INA might have lost the battle, but it was soon to win the war for the hearts and minds of Indian soldiers and civilians alike. The tale of its sacrifice and courage would dismantle the Raj in the coming months.

VI

On 24 July 1943, Clive Branson, an English soldier with considerable empathy for Indians, was interrogated by his Major at Ahmadnagar station in India. The Major had caught a letter Clive wrote to his wife on 18 July, which seemed problematic enough to warrant censorship and escalation to 'higher up than the Major'. The part of the letter that made the Major paranoid was:

> Chandra Bose is in Singapore and broadcasts as the 'Commander-in-Chief of the Army of Liberation'. He has already spoken of paratroops to be dropped in Indian clothes and appealed to the peasantry to give them cover.[44]

The Major bluntly asked Clive where he received the information, and if he listened to Bose's broadcasts? Clive was upbraided and told that the authorities knew what he was from his military documents, and warned that he didn't seem to have enough work to do. Clive was a member of the Communist Party in the UK, and sympathized with the plight of Indians under the Raj.

Such was the paranoia of the British government about Bose and his INA that heavy censorship was in place throughout the war against reporting about them. When the war ended, the censorship was lifted. In any event, there was no way to hide the arrival of 20,000 or so surviving INA soldiers, who were now being brought in batches as prisoners to India. Bose was dead, but his soldiers were living proof of his Herculean efforts.

Confident in their victory over Germany and Japan, the British now turned to the critical matter of military discipline in the Indian Army. But now they were confronted with huge numbers. Twenty-thousand INA prisoners couldn't all be tried and executed without serious implications, but they were all guilty, in the eyes of the British, of the ultimate crime of high treason and waging war against the King. The prisoners were kept in various stations across India. The remaining members of the Indian Legion from Germany were also transferred to India, and dealt with in the same vein as INA prisoners.

Unable to force discipline on such large numbers, the Army brass now came up with a disingenuous scheme to lighten their burden. The prisoners were divided into 'white', 'grey' and 'black' categories. Whites were deemed 'innocent', blacks as hardcore mutineers to be tried for their crimes, and greys in between. Greys were not to be tried but discharged from service; only whites were to be reinstated. About 17,500 fell into grey and black, and the majority of them were gradually discharged without trials. The Army top brass announced on 27 August that: 'Leaders who appeared consciously to have embraced the Japanese or German cause' would be tried for treason, the punishment for which was death.[45] Confident that once again the sepoy would see the justice of punishing his comrades for mutiny, about 600 INA prisoners were scheduled to be court-martialled.

Somehow, in the euphoria of victory, the government now seemed to have overreached. Not content with the usual behind-the-door trials, the Raj wanted to make an example of these 600 mutineers for the public too. So, the Commander-in-Chief decided to conduct the trials in public at the Red Fort in Delhi. He could not have chosen a more sensitive nerve to press. Just a few months back, Bose had vowed to unfurl the Indian flag on the ramparts of the Red Fort. It was here that the mutineers in 1857 made a stand against the British, and united under the old Emperor Bahadur Shah Zafar.

As the discharged INA soldiers reached their villages—having paid the price of freedom with their livelihoods—their stories spread rapidly. By early November, 3,000 had been released, and by December releases were averaging 600 per week. The press whipped up a fervour in favour of the INA men, whether released or facing trial. The Congress politicians who had spent a good part of the war in prison now wholeheartedly threw themselves in the defence of those on trial. The country could not have enough of the stories of these men who shed blood under Bose's command to free their motherland. In the light of public pressure, by 2 November, the government reduced the number to be tried to 125.[46]

The first trials opened on 5 November. To be tried were a Hindu, a Muslim and a Sikh: Captain P.K. Sahgal, Captain Shah Nawaz, and Lt Gurbaksh Dhillon. The Army brass could not have made a more maladroit choice, which united all the three religions of the country. The best legal minds in the land came to defend their case, led by Bhulabai Desai. Nehru donned his lawyer's robes for the first time in decades, despite having warned during the war that he would fight Bose with 'sword in hand' if he came to India with the Japanese. The trial gripped popular imagination. People bought INA memorabilia, Bose's pictures, copies of his speeches, biographies of the officers, and intently read the trial details. Students and housewives, workers and farmers, all now came to hear the uncensored story of how Bose and his daredevils allied with the Japanese to rid the country of its foreign occupiers.

The Viceroy Wavell was disgusted at this 'hero worship of traitors'[47] but he could do little about it by now. The Raj planned to make an example of these three officers, perhaps like Mangal Pandey in 1857, who was unceremoniously hanged from a tree. Instead, the men on trial would soon turn out to be more like the ninety sowars at Meerut, whose iron fetters had sparked the mutiny. The army of 1945 was a totally transformed entity compared to 1857. The illiterate peasant VCOs lead the mutinous Bengal Army in 1857, with not a single officer who had experienced independent command of more than a platoon before. Now there were 15,000 Indian commissioned officers with extensive field experience. Together with 2.5 million Indian troops, they had fought and defeated Germans, Japanese and Italians, they were nationalistic in outlook, and their sympathies were with the INA prisoners.

The Intelligence Bureau report of 20 November is perceptive:

> The situation in respect of the INA is one which warrants disquiet. There has seldom been a matter which has attracted so much Indian public interest and, it is safe to say, sympathy ... The general line of the nationalist case is that the men of INA were actuated by patriotic motives and the demand is made that none shall be punished.[48]

The report lamented that 'Army men (Indian soldiers of the Raj) on leave from Assam and Burma had not troubled enough to make their feeling known,'⁴⁹ and, that 'it is equally clear that this particular brand of sympathy cuts across communal barriers'. The report warned about the appearance of 'threatening posters' against Europeans and, that 'some respect for anonymous warning of this character has resulted from experience gained in earlier terrorist movements' which targeted Europeans. The report noted that Patel wanted the INA to form the 'nucleus of the new Indian Army', which might be an 'indication of the lines on which his mind is travelling'. The report mentioned efforts to recruit disbanded INA men and officers by Congress 'in the time of emergency'. After summarizing that 'dangerous possibilities exist which merit very careful consideration', the report ominously warned that the 'threat to the security of the Indian Army is one which it would be unwise to ignore'.⁵⁰

Public patience soon ran out. There were large agitations in Delhi, Calcutta, Mumbai and Karachi. Calcutta descended into violence on 21 November. The students and members of the Forward Bloc (Bose's group within Congress), wrote Bengal Governor Casey to the Viceroy, 'worked up to a state bordering on hysteria by previous propaganda in favour of the INA'.⁵¹ In the riots that raged for two days, 33 were killed and 400 were injured. The dead included an American soldier, and half the injured were police, soldiers or the fire brigade. The most startling feature, according to Casey, was that 'crowds when fired on largely stood their ground or at most only receded a little, to return again to the attack.'⁵² He was worried that the 'technique of the mob is improving' and expected matters to deteriorate 'with the return to India of persons trained in sabotage, like the members of the INA'.⁵³

While Calcutta was on fire, other provinces were equally unsettled. Reports came from the various governors warning the Viceroy about the dangers of proceeding with the INA trials. The spectre of the 1857 Mutiny started to trouble the Central Provinces

Governor, Sir Twynam. He had recently read reports related to the 1857 Mutiny, and worriedly noted that even units which were thought to be perfectly loyal suddenly turned against their European masters. He felt that the mood now was not different to that of 1857. He was 'uneasy as to the attitude which Indian troops may adopt if called upon to fire on mobs'.[54] He added that 'a slight uneasiness remains in my mind when I envisage the possibility of the Province being completely denuded of British troops'.[55] He admitted that the Europeans are 'undoubtedly unsettled'. Finally, he pointed to the difficulty of administering his province 'if the present "hymn of hate" leads to the retirement of any substantial proportion of this handful of [European] officers'.[56]

The North-West Frontier Province Governor, Sir Cunningham, was more forthright in his suggestion. He wanted the C-in-C to 'at once announce that, as Indian opinion is opposed to the trial of these persons, he wipes the whole thing out and takes no further proceedings against anyone'.[57] He admitted that stopping trials at this stage would be 'tantamount to surrendering to threats'[58] but believed the 'best thing to do is to cut our losses'. Finally, he regretted that the opportunity to shoot the INA men in Rangoon or Singapore was gone.

The most critical view was that of the Punjab Governor, as most soldiers came from that province. He believed that if the government carried out the death sentences against the INA members on trial, it would 'face unparalleled agitation, more widespread than in 1919 and 1942'.[59] He recommended that any death sentences imposed should be immediately commuted, and that no further trials should be held except for cases involving extreme brutality against fellow prisoners who did not join the INA. He advised that the charges of treason and waging war against the King should be dropped in future trials, as the 'INA are popular heroes, and the treason charges will only increase their popularity'.[60] He summed up with the observation that the army was 'generally sympathetic towards [the INA]'.[61]

Fortunately, the recommendations from the Punjab government were adopted substantially, and a communique to this effect was issued on 1 December. This meant that the ever-shrinking list of trial candidates now included just four more men, beyond the three currently on trial. Dhillon, Shah Nawaz and Sahgal—or any trial candidate for that matter—would not receive the death sentence. Pending further investigations, Wavell now estimated that no more than twenty to fifty would ever reach trial. This was a remarkable volte-face from the announced policy in August. Auchinleck in particular, since 1942, had been an ardent supporter of reintroducing the death penalty within the British army for cowardice and desertion of soldiers regardless of their origins, let alone deserters who subsequently fought on the side of the enemy or were guilty of brutality.[62]

To support his decision, British Commander-in-Chief Field Marshal Auchinleck cited evidence:

> There is no general resentment in the Indian Army against the INA. There are reasons to believe that Indian officers of the three services would ... approve the proposed limitation of trials ... The evidence reaching us now increasingly goes to show that the general opinion in the Army is in favour of leniency.[63]

Wavell, in turn, grudgingly supported this line, and added a warning in his letter to the Secretary of State: 'In Delhi, large handwritten posters in red ink recently appeared threatening death for "twenty English dogs" for every INA man executed.'[64] Wavell also admitted that the INA trials 'constitute a threat to the morale of the Indian Army'.[65]

The capitulation by the colonial authorities helped temporarily halt INA-related violence on the streets. A tense calm prevailed but the Europeans were very apprehensive by now. The Madras Governor wrote to the Viceroy:

> Europeans, particularly in Ootacamund, are getting very jumpy indeed and I hear about people who had intended staying on for a year or so more wanting to get passages earlier for fear of serious disturbances, mutiny, etc. This sounds unjustifiably alarmist, but it is quite a widespread feeling.[66]

On the same day as the communique regarding the limitation of the trial, Auchinleck sent a chilling assessment of the military situation to the Chiefs of Staff in London. He warned about the large quantities of unlicensed arms throughout India, and that discharged and demobilized soldiers would use them, especially INA men who had some experience in the 'technique of anti-British leadership'.[67] He admitted that the Congress–INA campaign must have had an unsettling effect on the armed forces, and that most Indian officers were nationalists and prone to 'over persuasion' by Congress propaganda around the INA. He expected a 'well organised revolution by next spring', and expressed doubts as to the continued loyalty of the armed forces.

He highlighted that the Europeans were likely to become victims of mob violence. He planned to concentrate vulnerable Europeans around main protected airfields, so they could be easily evacuated, but admitted that all such persons at risk could not be protected. He asked for all transport aircrafts in India to be placed at his disposal to deal with the emergency, but confessed the numbers were inadequate.

Having established reasonable doubt as to whether the Indian Army could be relied upon during the expected 'revolution', Auchinleck spelt out the consequences:

> The British Armed Forces now available are not likely to be able to control the internal situation or to protect essential communications, nor would any piecemeal reinforcement of these forces be of much avail. To regain control of the situation and to restore essential communications within the country, nothing short of an organized campaign for the reconquest of India is likely to suffice. It is not possible now to compute the air and land forces required for such a campaign, but they would inevitably be very large as, if the Indian Armed Forces are not prepared to support Government, they will almost inevitably actively oppose it.[68]

Auchinleck then went on to outline the impossible dilemma for the Army brass in London. Reinforcements from Britain in small numbers would be ineffective, and despatch of large-scale formations would do 'more harm than good in that it would show lack of confidence in the Indian Armed Forces and might well precipitate a crisis which we must do everything to avoid'.[69] To drive home his point, he made a request that he himself would have known could not be granted. He asked a rhetorical question about the 'possible strength of these reinforcements [from Britain]', and how long they might take to reach India from the time he sent his request. To keep up the charade, he suggested that any despatch of forces must be done under total secrecy and deception or else it might 'aggravate the present extremely delicate situation'.[70]

Auchinleck followed up on 22 December, in response to queries from London. The Chiefs of Staff wanted to know if there were parts of the Army more prone to mutiny than others. Auchinleck admitted that on this point all classes and regions of the Army were equally susceptible. He added that 'Indian officers who are mostly nationalist are spread throughout the Indian Armed forces except in Gurkha units,'[71] and hastened to add 'but Gurkhas are Hindus and not necessarily immune to Congress propaganda'.[72] He warned that if 'some units mutinied news would spread rapidly and mutiny might become general even if in some cases half-hearted'.[73] The fact that the INA trials had united the masses and the Indian soldiers was plain to see. Nehru observed in late December:

> It [the INA trial] has broken the impenetrable barriers that separated earlier the Government-controlled Indian Army and public opinion ... The trial has brought the two closer. It is apparently clear that the Government army also shares the feelings and aspirations of the country.[74]

It was under the threatening clouds of mutiny that the first INA trials concluded on 3 January 1946. Dhillon, Sahgal and Shah Nawaz were found guilty of waging war against the King, sentenced to transportation for life, but the sentence was immediately commuted. The three were discharged without any punishment, and walked out to the tumultuous welcome of cheering supporters outside the Red Fort. The men were swept off their feet, and paraded around the streets of Old Delhi on people's shoulders. A crowd of almost 100,000 came out to greet them, and people clamoured to shake their hands, and feed them sweets. They were the heroes of the nation, the surviving link and symbol of Bose's effort and sacrifice.

Their victory parades continued in Delhi, Lahore and other cities. Crowds begged for their autographs, and thrust garlands around their necks, wherever they went. 'The arrival of three "heroes" in Lahore,' grumbled the Punjab Governor, 'gave rise to a continual orgy of extravagant welcomes, speeches and entertainments.'[75] What disturbed the Governor most was the 'attendance of Indian Army personnel in uniform at meetings held in honour of the INA accused'.[76] Dhillon would later recount:

> People wanted to see us, hear us speak and garland us. They had gone mad with joy of our release. Young girls cut their fingers with razor blades and applied blood to our foreheads instead of vermillion.[77]

The subsequent trials were a low-key affair. A short 2 May announcement declared the end of prosecutions, and the release of any INA personnel remaining in custody, who had not yet been convicted. Just twelve INA men were ever sentenced on lower charges. Even these twelve were released on 15 August 1947 as part of a general amnesty, thanks to an agreement brokered between Mountbatten and Nehru.[78]

It was plain to many that the release, without any penalty, of Dhillon, Shah Nawaz and Sahgal was a capitulation by the military authority. One British officer averred that the Army top brass was displaying 'suppliant posteriors seductive to the foot of insolence'.[79] The authority and legitimacy of the Raj was crumbling under the weight of popular sentiment that Bose and his soldiers inspired.

VII

An immediate crisis might have been averted by the release of the INA officers, but the disaffection in the armed forces continued, not least because the formal announcement ending INA trials was not out yet. In a lengthy post-mortem of his decision to limit the INA trials, Auchinleck told British officers, 'Any attempt to enforce the sentence on three officers would have led to chaos in the country at large and probably to mutiny and dissension in the Army.'[80] He stated the urgent need for disposing of the remaining INA men at the earliest possible moment in the hope that 'the whole affair may have a reasonable chance of being forgotten'.[81] Having admitted that every Indian commissioned officer was a nationalist, he summed up that his objective was 'to maintain the reliability, stability and efficiency of the Indian Army for the future, whatever Government may be set that up in India'.[82] The military head of the Raj in India now anticipated a new government to be set up in India. If London was a bit behind in comprehending the changed situation, the events within a week of Auchinleck's report would bring them around to his view that the current regime was unsustainable.

It seems that the Indian sailors who manned the Royal Indian Navy (RIN) ships transferring INA prisoners from Rangoon and Singapore to India were infected by the stories of their heroism. Earlier, ratings were frequently reprimanded by their officers for using the ships' wireless to listen to Bose's speeches. 'The life of a rating was hard,' wrote Biswanath Bose, a sailor on one of the RIN ships:

> Sailors found some leisure while on duty, like greasing the parts and barrels of the various types of guns ... and started some idle talks with their colleagues ... In many such talks, Netaji and INA topics figured prominently which gradually became the prime talk in almost all such occasions.[83]

The trouble started on the HMIS *Talwar*, a shore establishment in Bombay whose ratings went on a hunger strike on 18 February 1946 to protest against their commanding officer's racist jibes. The authorities arrested the leading protesters for the 'alleged act of conspiracy, writing politically motivated slogans on the wall, and exciting others to follow them'.[84] By evening, the news of the disturbance on HMIS *Talwar* spread to other ships and shore establishments. As the excited ratings started to convene at various ships, the British officers were 'moving out of the ships and establishments which they belonged to for fear of being killed'.[85]

The key demands of the ratings included freeing the INA and HMIS *Talwar* prisoners, and 'last but not the least [for the British to] Quit India immediately'.[86] The ratings hoisted Congress's tricolour flag 'over the mast in their respective ships and set fire to the Union Jack in utter disgust'. The ratings next day marched into Bombay, and workers, students and farmers joined them. Violence followed and is recounted by Biswanath Bose:

> Incidentally one white man was instantly hit on the head by a hockey stick by one of the marchers on the way and he later died in the hospital ... The ratings bagged the first booty of a white man and a European. This news spread everywhere in no time and the British subjects and/or Europeans went underground or disappeared from the very scene suddenly.[87]

Biswanath adds that people welcomed the ratings 'by stretching out their arms and kissed [sic] them on their cheeks in full solidarity ... What an affectionate welcome! What a marvellous scene! What a dialogue! Everyone greeted the ratings by saying "Jai Hind" and the ratings replied in the same manner repeating "Jai Hind".' The marchers stop-searched the British officers and civilians and asked them to 'shout "Jai Hind" and "Subhas Bose ki Jai", only then they were allowed to go, with a hard kick before they leave'.[88]

Two British fighter aircrafts approached the ships harbouring mutineers but they were 'once seen disappeared by the anti-aircraft guns firing from HMIS *Assam* immediately and none returned thereafter'. The sailors were determined to give battle. Eventually, eighty ships and 20,000 sailors were to participate in the mutiny. The most worrisome for the authorities was the realization that 'Maratha troops could not be used. Actually they had refused to fire against their own brothers in the Navy'.[89]

On the evening of 19 February, the news of the Bombay mutiny reached Karachi harbour. The next day, ratings on HMIS *Bahadur* went on strike, shouting slogans and 'jeering the colours being hoisted'. There were intense parlays between the ratings of the five ships in Karachi during the day and the night. The next morning, on 21 February, sailors from HMIS *Himalaya* and HMIS *Chamak* also joined the strike. Just after breakfast, trouble broke out on the parade ground when the ratings 'disrupted the hoisting ceremony of Union Jack, tore it into pieces and re-hoisted Tricolour flag on the mast of HMIS *Bahadur*'.[90] The ratings from three ships now decided to march to Karachi. In the meantime, ratings on HMIS *Hindustan* evicted their British officers and seized the ship. The British soldiers fired on the *Bahadur*, *Himalaya* and *Chamak* sailors to prevent them marching to Karachi. In response, the sailors from Hindustan trained their 'Oerlikon' anti-aircraft gun on the British troops and threatened to open fire on them if they blocked their comrades from reaching the city.

More than 200 were killed in the Bombay clashes. The Karachi sailors were overpowered after a gunfight, although ensuing riots claimed eight more civilian lives in the city. Eventually, Vallabh Bhai Patel, the Congress leader in Bombay, intervened to broker peace between the mutinous sailors and the government. Most of the demands of the sailors were accepted. The irony of the staunch opponent of the Raj mediating on its behalf with the soldiers was not lost on anyone. For decades the Raj had used the soldiers to subdue and contain Congress's mass movement successfully. Now the same Congress was called upon to save the Raj from its own soldiers. The writing on the wall was clear, this time to the authorities in London as well. If there was any doubt left, Nehru's statement that it was not a breach of discipline for an Indian soldier to refuse to quell riots was taken to be 'incitement to mutiny' by the Bombay Governor.[91]

The acts of individual and collective insubordination continued in the various branches of the armed forces. The trouble spread to the army in Jabalpur, where angry signalmen defied orders, broke free from the barracks, and held meetings in the town. Indian airmen at many stations went on strike in support of their navy and INA comrades. There was disturbance in an infantry battalion in Santa Cruz, Bombay. Two Pioneer units in Calcutta disobeyed orders, and assaulted their British officers. These were the known incidents. Eventually, in a vast country like India, we will never fully know the extent of incidents of the sepoys', sailors' and airmen's insubordination. More than outright mutiny, one can only imagine the impact of the harsh and threatening looks, the words said and unsaid, and what the British officers 'felt' in an environment when their authority over the men was declining rapidly. Eventually, around 400 sailors were discharged, and no punishment beyond this could be enforced.

The ratings later lamented the lack of support from the political leaders to carry their struggle to a logical and violent conclusion. Mahatma Gandhi openly reproached the sailors for 'setting a bad and unbecoming example'. He also issued a general warning to Indians: 'The rulers have declared their intention to quit. Let not the action be delayed by a moment because of the exhibition of this distressful unrest.'[92]

As the mutinous sailors and seething civilians swarmed the streets of Bombay against the Raj on 19 February, a momentous announcement was made in London. The Attlee government decided to send a Cabinet Mission to India, whose key task was to agree 'the method of framing a constitution for a self-governing, independent India.'[93]

The Mission was led by Pethick-Lawrence, India Secretary, and included Stafford Cripps, the unofficial 'India specialist' in the Cabinet, and A.V. Alexander, First Sea Lord. In a note dated 4 March 1946, Pethick-Lawrence sought clarification from Attlee, ahead of the Mission's meeting with the King prior to departure for India. Pethick-Lawrence averred in the note:

> Clearly, however, he [King George VI] ought to be informed that we are prepared to contemplate a settlement on the basis that India will not remain within the Empire, and as this will affect the King's title I presume that his approval is necessary.[94]

In another note to Attlee on the same date, Pethick-Lawrence shared the top-secret communication he had sent to the Viceroy in India. That communication had effectively informed the Viceroy of the British Government's intention to 'arrive at any arrangement for the granting of independence and self-government to India'[95] with certain pre-conditions. Prime Minister Attlee added his agreement to Pethick-Lawrence's second note on 5 March, and remarked on the same day: 'I told him [King George VI] that the basis of our negotiations was necessarily based on the Cripps offer which gave India to choose her future, which might be independence. He [the King] did not dissent from this.'[96]

The British Prime Minister agreed to the Secretary of State's note proposing India's freedom, and communication of the same to the Viceroy and the C-in-C in India. King George VI agreed. If there was any doubt, on 15 March in the House of Commons, Attlee himself announced 'complete independence' as one of the objectives of this Mission.[97]

This dramatic change in British policy came about in less than a month, indeed within a week of the naval mutiny. Just a week before the naval mutiny, Sir Stafford Cripps sent a letter dated 10 February that sufficiently annoyed Nehru due to the ambivalence of the language used in relation to India's future. Nehru replied on 5 March, noting that he found 'a strange reluctance to use the word "independence"' in Cripps's communication. He resented that the word 'self government' was used in the old way and 'that rubs people up the wrong way'. He dismissed the old references to 1942, saying that 'India has changed vastly during this interval of four years. We have to deal with a new situation, an urgent situation, and to deal with it finally.'[98] In the three weeks between Nehru receiving Cripps's letter and writing his reply, India had changed.

The firm announcement of a date by which the British would leave India was delayed for another eleven months, mostly due to disagreements between the main Indian political parties. Even so, the focus of British officials in India from March 1946 onwards was the safety of their European population and a withdrawal that did not jeopardize their life and limb. Eventually, on 20 February 1947, the date of independence was set to be 'no later than June 1948'. It was advanced to 15 August 1947, almost a year, to avoid any risk to the safety of the Europeans in India.

Thus, Indian soldiers, after two centuries of bondage, secured India her freedom.

Notes

Introduction

1. I cover my grandfather's war service and the unexpected end of his army career in Chapter 2 of the book.
2. Sir Chhotu Ram was the revenue minister of undivided Punjab, and the co-founder of the National Unionist Party, which kept both the Congress and the rabid communalism of the Muslim League at bay. In those years, this truly secular political alliance of the Hindus, Muslims and Sikhs of Punjab appeared to be a bulwark against the divisions and hatred. Despite their loss at the elections, the Muslim League activists continued to agitate, intimidate and threaten the senior leaders of the Unionist Party in Lahore. It is but a matter of conjecture that if the Unionist Party had not buckled under the communal surge of 1946, after Chhotu Ram's demise in 1945, the inhabitants of South Asia might have had a different future.

Chapter One

1. Niall Ferguson, 'Niall Ferguson on Belief', *Big Think* (4 January 2008), https://bigthink.com/videos/niall-ferguson-on-belief.
2. Niall Ferguson, *Empire: How Britain Made the Modern World* (London: Penguin Books, 2007); William Wilberforce, speaking in the House of Commons in 1813: 'Our religion is sublime, pure and beneficent. Theirs

is mean, licentious and cruel. Of our civil principles and conditions, the common right of all classes to be governed, and punished by equal laws, is the fundamental principle ... Of theirs, the essential and universal pervading general character is inequality, despotism in the higher classes, degradation and oppression in the lower.' in *Substance of the Speeches of William Wilberforce, Esq. on the Clause in the East-India Bill for Promoting the Religious Instruction and Moral Improvement of the Natives of the British Dominions in India, on the 22d of June, and the 1st and 12th of July, 1813* (London: J. Hatchard, J. Butterworth, and Cadell and Davies, 1813), 54.

3 Pankaj Mishra, 'Watch This Man', *London Review of Books 33*, no. 21 (3 November 2011), https://www.lrb.co.uk/the-paper/v33/n21/pankaj-mishra/watch-this-man; Shashi Tharoor, *An Era of Darkness* (New Delhi: Aleph Book Company, 2016); Utsa Patnaik and Shubhra Chakravarti, eds., *Agrarian and Other Histories: Essays for Binay Bhushan Chaudhari* (New Delhi: Tulika Books, 2019), cited in Jason Hickel, 'How Britain Stole $45 Trillion from India', *Al Jazeera* (19 December 2018), https://www.aljazeera.com/opinions/2018/12/19/how-britain-stole-45-trillion-from-india.

4 Some empires, like the vast but short-lived Mongol Empire, encompassing almost all of Eurasia, and even the First French Empire under Napoleon, could not extract much economic advantage for the metropole from their periphery.

5 The East India Company (EIC), the predecessor of British Crown rule in India, was granted its charter on 31 December 1600 by Queen Elizabeth I, establishing the company and granting it monopoly over trade 'into the Countries and Parts of Asia and Africa', and into and from 'all the Islands, Ports, Towns, and Places of Asia, Africa, and America', or any of them, beyond 'the Cape of Bona Esperanza, to the Streights of Magellan', in East India Company, *A Collection of Charters and Statutes Relating to the East India Company* (London: Eyre and Strahan, 1817), i.

6 Quoted in V. Longer, *Red Coats to Olive Green: A History of the Indian Army* (New Delhi: Allied Publishers, 1974), 2.

7 A royal edict or grant.

8 S.L. Menezes, *Fidelity and Honour: The Indian Army from the Seventeenth Century to the Twenty-First Century* (New Delhi: Oxford University Press, 1999), 2.

9 Quoted in G.J. Bryant, *The Emergence of British Power in India 1600–1784: A Grand Strategic Interpretation* (Woodbridge: Boydell Press, 2013), 4.

10 The origin of the word sepoy lies in the Persian sipahi. Sepoy was used to denote an infantryman in the service of an Indian prince. The word thereafter came to be used for the Indian infantry soldiers of the EIC and the Raj in India.
11 Alex von Tunzelmann, *Indian Summer: The Secret History of the End of an Empire* (London: Simon & Schuster Books UK, 2012), 11.
12 B.N. Pandey, *The Break-Up of British India: Making of the Twentieth Century* (London: MacMillan Books, 1969), 1.
13 Sir Penderel Moon, *The British Conquest and Dominion of India*, Part 2 (New Delhi: India Research Press, 1999), 1050.
14 Ferguson, *Empire*, 216.
15 Ferguson.
16 Ferguson, 217-218; Philip Mason states, 'India has *always* been a desperately poor country; the peasant lives near the border of starvation' [italics mine], in Philip Mason, *A Matter of Honour: An Account of the Indian Army, Its Officers and Men* (London: Jonathan Cape Ltd, 1974), 410; a Raj-era Government of India (GoI) publication observes, 'Judged not by the splendour of individuals but by the prosperity of the people India was then, and still is now, a poor country,' in *India's Contribution to the Great War* (Calcutta: Superintendent Government Printing, 1923), 150.
17 Angus Maddison, *The World Economy: A Millennial Perspective*, (Paris: OECD Publications, 2001), 263.
18 Utsa Patnaik, cited in Hickel, 'How Britain Stole $45 Trillion from India'.
19 Cited in Menezes, *Fidelity and Honour*, 12-13.
20 Tharoor, *Era of Darkness*, 24.

Chapter Two

1 Lord Salisbury, the future Prime Minister of the United Kingdom, said in Parliament in 1867 that India was 'an English barrack in the Oriental Seas from which we may draw any number of troops without paying for them', quoted in Sir Charles Lucas, ed., *The Empire at War*, (London: Oxford University Press, 1921), 1:56-57.
2 A music-hall parody during the Victorian era on the subject of using Indian troops for British defence. Cited in *Oxford Dictionary of Quotations*, 2nd ed. (London: Oxford University Press, 1953), 11, n. 9.
3 In 1700, the UK had about 1.7 per cent of the world population and its future colony—India—was almost nineteen times that at about 32.1 per cent (Bolt et al., Maddison Project Database, 2018). This imbalance

remained till the Empire collapsed in the wake of Indian independence in 1947. In 1820, the Indian population was ten times that of the UK, and just before Indian independence, it was eight times. The populations of other colonies (Australia, New Zealand, Canada, etc.) were too small to make any difference, even if you could argue they were more aligned with the metropole due to racial connection.

4   France, Britain's main rival during empire building, had a population 2.5 times that of the UK in 1700, and 1.5 times in 1820. Not before 1899 would Britain be able to match the French population. In contrast, France's metropole and colonial population was almost evenly balanced. In 1921, the Indian population was seven times that of the UK's, while that of French colonies was a bare 1.5 times that of France. (Statistique générale de la France, 'La IIIe République, 1919–1940', in *le Code Officiel Géographique*.)

5   Ferguson, *Empire*, 35.

6   Cited in Cathal J. Nolan, *Wars of the Age of Louis XIV, 1650–1715: An Encyclopedia of Global Warfare and Civilisation* (Westport: Greenwood, 2008), i.

7   Cited in Ian Beckett, *Ypres: The First Battle 1914* (Abingdon: Routledge, 2006), 38.

8   John Childs, 'The Restoration Army 1660–1702', in *The Oxford History of the British Army*, David G. Chandler and Ian Beckett, eds. (Oxford: Oxford Paperbacks, 1996), 63.

9   Childs, 63.

10 David Chandler, 'The Great Captain-General 1702–1714', in *The Oxford History of the British Army*, David G. Chandler and Ian Beckett, eds. (Oxford: Oxford Paperbacks, 1996), 75.

11 David Gates, 'The Transformation of the Army 1783–1815', in *The Oxford History of the British Army*, David G. Chandler and Ian Beckett, eds. (Oxford: Oxford Paperbacks, 1996), 132.

12 Gates, 138.

13 Peter Burroughs, 'An Unreformed Army? 1815–1868', in *The Oxford History of the British Army*, David G. Chandler and Ian Beckett, eds. (Oxford: Oxford Paperbacks, 1996), 168.

14 E.W. Sheppard, *A Short History of the British Army* (London: Constable, 1959), 264.

15 Charles Ross, (ed.), *Correspondence of Charles, First Marquis of Cornwallis* (London: Murray, 1859), 1:316.

16 Cited by J.W. Kaye, in 'The Crisis in India', *North British Review* 27 (Edinburgh: Murray and Gibb, August–November 1857), 259.

17 Philip Mason, A *Matter of Honour: An Account of the Indian Army, Its Officers and Men* (London: Jonathan Cape Ltd, 1974), 386.

18 Ferguson, *Empire*, 180.
19 Mason, *Matter of Honour*, 242.
20 Longer, *Red Coats to Olive*, 51.
21 Alan J. Guy and Peter B. Borden, eds., *Soldiers of the Raj: The Indian Army 1600-1947* (London: National Army Museum, 1997), 352–356; Tharoor, *Era of Darkness*, 27.
22 Mason, *Matter of Honour*, 341.
23 *India's Contribution to the Great War* (Calcutta: Superintendent Government Printing, 1923), 263.
24 *India's Contribution to the Great War*, 265.
25 Mason, *Matter of Honour*, 411.
26 *India's Contribution to the Great War*, 176.
27 Santanu Das, *India, Empire, and First World War Culture: Writings, Images and Songs* (Cambridge: Cambridge University Press, 2018), 11.
28 Charles Trench, *The Indian Army and the King's Enemies 1900–1947* (London: Thames and Hudson, 1988), 300–303.
29 'Second World War (1939–1945)', Making Britain, The Open University, http://www.open.ac.uk/researchprojects/makingbritain/content/second-world-war-1939-1945. This appears to exclude the Indian National Army soldiers who fought against the British Empire during WW2.
30 Oral Archives, no. 2/6, BL OIC, http://www.open.ac.uk/researchprojects/makingbritain/content/second-world-war-1939-1945
31 Tharoor, *Era of Darkness*, 28.
32 Mason, *Matter of Honour*, 410.
33 Tharoor, *Era of Darkness*, 27-8.
34 Ferguson, *Empire*, 360, 247, 360, 377-8.
35 Government of UK, Report of the Indian Statutory (Simon) Commission, vol. 1 (London: 1930), 362, British Library: IOR/V/26/261/17
36 David Omissi, *The Sepoy and the Raj: The Indian Army, 1860–1940 (Studies in Military and Strategic History)*, (London: Palgrave MacMillan, 1998), 232.
37 Translates to 'Red Battalion', owing to the red coat uniform of the Indian soldiers.
38 The ratios are derived using figures provided by Omissi, *The Sepoy and the Raj*, 133, and *The Oxford History of the British Army*, 132, 164; Ferguson, *Empire*, 171, 247.
39 *India's Contribution*, 79-80.
40 *India's Contribution*, 79-80.
41 Daniel P. Marston and Chandar S. Sundaram, eds., *A Military History of India and South Asia: From the East India Company to the Nuclear Era* (Bloomington: Indiana University Press, 2008), 102.

42 George Orwell, *Burmese Days* (New York: Harper, 1934), 68-9.
43 Interview between the author and his grandfather in the 1990s.

Chapter Three

1 Omissi, *The Sepoy and the Raj: The Indian Army, 1860–1940 (Studies in Military and Strategic History)* (London: Palgrave MacMillan, 1998), 133.
2 Omissi, *The Sepoy and the Raj*, 133.
3 Geoffrey Parker, *The Military Revolution: Military Innovation and the Rise of the West, 1500–1800*, (Cambridge: Cambridge University Press, 1996), 23.
4 Michael Howard, *War in European History* (Oxford: Oxford University Press, 2009), 29.
5 Geoffrey Parker, *The Thirty Years' War* (London: Routledge Books, 1997), 200.
6 William Irvine, *The Army of the Indian Mughals: Its Organization and Administration* (London: Luzac & Co., 1903), 61.
7 'The Speech of Edmund Burke on Moving His Resolutions for Conciliation with the Colonies, March 22, 1775', Eighteenth Century Collections Online, Text Creation Partnership (ECCO-TCP) (3 May 2022), https://quod.lib.umich.edu/e/ecco/004895777.0001.000/17:3?page=root;size=100;view=text.
8 Niccolao Manucci, *Storia Do Mogor 1653–1708, vol. 2, translated by William Irvine* (London: John Murray, 1907), 320. 'They began their pillage by breaking in the great gates of bronze which it had, robbing the valuable precious stones and plates of gold and silver, and destroying what they were not able to carry away. Dragging out the bones of Akbar, they threw them angrily into the fire and burnt them.'
9 Cited in Waldemar Hansen, *The Peacock Throne: The Drama of Moghul India* (Delhi: Motilal Banarsidas, 1986), 28.

Chapter Four

1 V. Longer, *Red Coats to Olive Green: A History of the Indian Army* (New Delhi: Allied Publishers, 1974), 4-5, 11.
2 Jon Wilson, *India Conquered: Britain's Raj and the Passions of Empire* (Delhi: Simon & Schuster India, 2016), 49.
3 Sanjay Subrahmanyam, 'Un Grand Derangement: Dreaming an Indo-Persian Empire in South Asia, 1740–1800', *Journal of Early Modern History* 4, no. 3-4 (2000): 357-8.

Notes

4 William Dalrymple, *The Anarchy: Corporate Violence, the East India Company and the Pillage of an Empire* (New Delhi: Bloomsbury Books, 2019), 49.
5 Longer, *Red Coats to Olive*, 17-18. The peons were ill-disciplined local levies while sepoys were Indian soldiers, trained and armed in the European style, per Orme.
6 Sir Penderel Moon, *The British Conquest and Dominion of India, Part One 1745–1857* (Delhi: India Research Press, 1989), 17.
7 Longer, *Red Coats to Olive*, 19.
8 Philip Mason, *A Matter of Honour: An Account of the Indian Army, Its Officers and Men* (London: Jonathan Cape Ltd, 1974), 78.
9 Mason, 78.
10 The initial battalions had varied numbers of sepoys, but later the fixed approximate size of a sepoy battalion was 800–1,000.
11 Colonel G.B. Malleson, *The Decisive Battles of India from 1746 to 1849*, (London: W.H. Allen & Co., 1885), 73.
12 Mason, *Matter of Honour*, 63; Amiya Barat, *The Bengal Native Infantry: Its Organisation and Discipline, 1796 to 1852* (Calcutta: Firma K.L. Mukhopadhyay, 1962), 8.
13 Henry Dodwell, *Sepoy Recruitment in the Old Madras Army* (Madras: Superintendent Government, 1922), 11.
14 Channa Wickremesekera, *'Best Black Troops in the World': British Perceptions and the Making of the Sepoy, 1746–1805* (Delhi: Manohar Books, 2002), 135.
15 P.E. Roberts, *History of British India* (Delhi: Oxford University Press India, 1978), 160.
16 Brian Robson, 'The Organization and Command Structure of the Indian Army from its Origins to 1947', in *Soldiers of the Raj: The Indian Army 1600–1947* (London: National Army Museum, 1997), 10. Assuming 800 sepoys per battalion.
17 G.J. Bryant, 'The Early Years of the East India Company's Armies to c 1800', in *Soldiers of the Raj*, 31.
18 The size of a company was approximately 80–100 sepoys.
19 Wickremesekera, *'Best Black Troops in the World'*, 110.
20 Wickremesekera, 105.
21 Wickremesekera, 106.
22 Captain Dalton, cited in S.C. Hill, *Yusuf Khan: The Rebel Commandant* (London: Longman, Greens and Co., 1914), 11.
23 Major Stringer Lawrence, quoted by Mason, *Matter of Honour*, 72.
24 Dalton, cited in Hill, *Yusuf Khan*, 11.
25 S. Muthiah, 'The Ballad of the Khan Sahib', *The Hindu* (6 March 2018).

Chapter Five

1. 'Eating salt' was a common term for 'receiving pay'. The expression harked back to the time when salt was used as currency.
2. Shah Wali Khan of Ambala Cavalry Brigade, writing from the Western Front in France to Zaman Ali in Punjab during March 1916. Life is meant for his family, and death for his King and the Faith. Cited in David Omissi, *Indian Voices of the Great War: Soldiers' Letters, 1914–1918* (Gurgaon: Penguin Books, 2014), 168.
3. Omissi, *Indian Voices*, xiii, 3. The Lahore Division arrived in Flanders on 21 October 2014, and the Meerut Division reached St. Omer on 21 October.
4. Omissi, 2.
5. Shrabani Basu, *For King and Another Country: Indian Soldiers on the Western Front, 1914–1918* (London: Bloomsbury Paperbacks, 2015), xxi.
6. Lt Col. Merewether and Sir Frederick Smith, *The Indian Corps in France* (London: John Murray, 1918) 33.
7. Merewether and Smith, *The Indian Corps*, 35.
8. Sita Ram Pandey, *From Sepoy to Subedar*, James Lunt, ed. (London: Papermac, 1988). There has been some dispute about the authenticity of this account. Some historians suggest that it might have been written by an English officer, as the original Awadhi manuscript has not been traced. My own reading of the account led me to believe that it is broadly an authentic account, although no doubt embellished in the translation, especially where it credits English soldiers and officers with extraordinary fighting capabilities, and their honourable conduct in war, as if those qualities were unknown to an old Indian soldier like Sita Ram.
9. Pandey, *Sepoy to Subedar*, 56-57.
10. Pandey, 57.
11. Pandey, 57-58.
12. More accurately, a 'Gandharva' marriage, meaning a love marriage per ancient customs.
13. Pandey, 64.
14. Pandey, 167-68.
15. Pandey, 168-69.
16. Dean Mahomet, *The Travels of Dean Mahomet: An Eighteenth-Century Journey through India*, Michael H. Fisher, ed. (Berkeley and Los Angeles: University of California Press, 1997).
17. This was the year in which Shahzada Shah Alam made a failed attempt on the city of Patna, which was also Raja Ram Narain's capital.

18 This battalion was recruited by Robert Clive in late 1757 from the Bhojpur countryside, when he came to subdue Ram Narain after the Battle of Plassey. Ram Narain was executed on the orders of the renegade Nawab Mir Kasim in 1763, before Mir Kasim escaped into Awadh to form an alliance against EIC. Shitab Rai succeeded Ram Narain as the Raja of Bihar and deputy to the EIC's recently restored Bengal Nawab, Mir Jafar. The 3rd Bengal Infantry Battalion was placed by the EIC to assist Shitab Rai in revenue collection from rebellious zamindars. The government of Bengal and Bihar was now firmly in the EIC's grip, and the EIC forces assisted Raja Shitab Rai in revenue collection.
19 Mahomet, *The Travels of Dean Mahomet*, 37-38.
20 Mahomet, 38.
21 Mahomet, 39.
22 Mahomet, 42.
23 Pandey, *Sepoy to Subedar*, 4.
24 Pandey, 4-5.
25 Pandey, 5.
26 Pandey, 6.
27 Pandey, 6.
28 C-o-C Colonel Richard Smith's letter, dated 2 November 1768, in Bengal Secret and Military Consultations (BSMC), India Office Library (17 November 1768), quoted in Mahomet, *Travels of Dean Mahomet*, 15.
29 Cited by His Divine Grace A.C. Bhaktivedanta Swami Prabhupada, *Bhagavad-Gita: As It Is* (Mumbai: The Bhaktivedanta Book Trust, 1986), 105–108.
30 Cited in Norman Ziegler, 'Evolution of the Rathore State of Marwar: Horses, Structural Change and Warfare', in Karine Schomer, ed., *The Idea of Rajasthan: Exploration in Regional identity* (Columbia: South Asia Publications, 1994), 2:205-06.
31 Velcheru Narayana Rao, David Schulman and Sanjay Subramaniyam, *Symbols of Substance: Court and State in Nayaka Period Tamilnadu* (Delhi: Oxford University Press, 1992), 236. These examples are also covered in Channa Wickremesekera's fine work, *'Best Black Troops in the World': British Perceptions and the Making of the Sepoy, 1746–1805* (Delhi: Manohar, 2002).
32 Nizamuddin Ahmad, Brajindranath De, trans., *The Tabaqat-i-Akbari of Khwajah Nizamuddin Ahmad*, (Calcutta: Royal Asiatic Society of Bengal, 1939), 3:366.
33 Ahmad, *The Tabaqat-i-Akbari*, 3:366.
34 Durgavati's daughter-in-law was the daughter of Rana Sanga of Mewar, the head of the Rajput confederacy of Rajputana.
35 Mirza Nathan, M.I. Borah, trans., *Baharistan-I-Ghaybi* (Gauhati: Government of Assam, 1936), 1:439-440.

36 Nathan, Borah, *Baharistan-I-Ghaybi*, 2:594, 599.
37 Philip Mason, *A Matter of Honour: An Account of the Indian Army, Its Officers and Men* (London: Jonathan Cape Ltd, 1974), 439.
38 Mason, 439.
39 Cited in Omissi, *Indian Voices*, 39.
40 Omissi, 126.
41 Omissi, 57-58.
42 Omissi, 126.
43 Omissi, 142.
44 Omissi, 142-143.
45 Omissi, 175.
46 Omissi, 35.
47 Omissi, 80.
48 Omissi, 85.
49 Omissi, 95.
50 Omissi, 295-296.

Chapter Six

1 Parliamentary Papers, 1852–53, vol. 31, no. 627, House of Lords, 240, British Library.
2 Letter from Bengal, 14 October 1830, *Military Letters Received from Bengal*, vol. 32, British Library, Oriental and India Office Collections, India Office Records (BL IOR).
3 V. Longer, *Red Coats to Olive Green: A History of the Indian Army* (New Delhi: Allied Publishers, 1974), 12.
4 Lt Col. W.J. Wilson, *History of the Madras Army*, quoted in Longer, *Red Coats to Olive*, 25.
5 Minutes of the Bengal Council, 8 August 1796, BL IOR.
6 S.L. Menezes, *Fidelity and Honour: The Indian Army from the Seventeenth Century to the Twenty-First Century* (New Delhi: Oxford University Press, 1999), 212.
7 Vedica Kant, *India and the First World War* (Delhi: Roli Books, 2014), 30. Kant estimates this to be roughly equivalent to Rs. 14,000 per month in today's terms.
8 Kant, 30. Kant estimates this to be Rs. 25,800 today.
9 Yasmin Khan, *The Raj at War: A People's History of the Second World War* (London: Vintage Books, 2015), 220.
10 Despatches to Bengal, 29 October 1828, *Military Despatches Sent to Bengal*, vol. 14A, BL IOR.
11 Amiya Barat, *The Bengal Native Infantry: Its Organisation and Discipline, 1796 to 1852* (Calcutta: Firma KL Mukhopadhyay, 1962), 137.

12 Alan J. Guy, 'People who will stick at nothing to make money'? Officers' Income, Expenditure and Expectations in the Service of John Company, c 1750–1840', in Alan J. Guy and Peter B. Borden, *Soldiers of the Raj*, 44.
13 Durgadas Bandopadhyaya, *Bidrohe Bangali* (Calcutta: Patra Bharati, 1924), 67-68.
14 Lieutenant-General John Briggs, A Letter on the Indian Army, Addressed to the Most Noble the Marquess of Tweeddale, May 1842 (London: Wm. H. Allen & Co., 1857), p. 13.
15 Maria Graham, *Journal of a Residence in India* (Edinburgh: G. Ramsay for A. Constable, 1812), 2.
16 Parliamentary Papers, 1831, vol. 5 (320A), House of Commons, Ap. 40, BL IOR.
17 Henry Lawrence to Canning, 2 May 1857; Foreign Department Secret Consultations, 18 December 1857, Consultation No. 564, National Archives of India, New Delhi.
18 Philip Mason, *A Matter of Honour: An Account of the Indian Army, Its Officers and Men* (London: Jonathan Cape Ltd, 1974), 201.
19 Oliver J. Jones, *Recollections of a Winter Campaign in India, 1857–1858* (London: Saunders and Otley, 1859), 122.
20 T.A. Heathcote, *The Indian Army: The Garrison of British Imperial India, 1822–1922* (London: David and Charles, 1974), 34. Mark Jacobsen also notes British troops cost four times Indian ones; Mark Jacobsen, 'The Indian Army and the Government of India, 1858–1947', in Alan J. Guy and Peter B. Boyden, *Soldiers of the Raj*, 87.
21 Longer, *Red Coats to Olive*, 188.
22 Unnamed author, *The Mutiny in the Bengal Army* (London: John Chapman, 1857), 6.
23 Menezes, *Soldiers of the Raj*, 116.
24 Heathcote, *The Indian Army*, 128.
25 John Jacob, *A Few Remarks on the Bengal Army and Furlough Regulations, with a View to Their Improvement, by a Bombay Officer [J. Jacob]. Repr., with Corrections*, (London: Smith Elder and Co., 1857), 8.
26 Bryant, *The East India Company and Its Army, 1600–1778* (London: University of London, 1978), 260-61.
27 T. Rice Holmes, *A History of the Indian Mutiny and of the Disturbances which Accompanied It among the Civil Population* (London: W.H. Allen & Co., 1891), 49.
28 Unnamed author, *The Mutiny in the Bengal Army*, 25.
29 Report of the Commission under Lord Peel on the Organization of the Indian Army, Appendix B to Appendix 54, Command 2516 (1859 Sess. 1), Parliamentary Command Papers, BL IOR.
30 Surendra Nath Sen, *The Military System of the Marathas* (Calcutta: Orient Longman, 1928), 110.

31 William Irvine, *The Army of the Indian Mughals: Its Organization and Administration* (London: Luzac & Co, 1903), 172.
32 Narendra Krishna Sinha, *Ranjit Singh* (Calcutta: A.R. Mukherjee, 1951), 157.
33 Irvine, *Army of the Indian Mughals*, 13.
34 Sen, *Military System of the Marathas*, 57.
35 Sinha, *Ranjit Singh*, 157.
36 W.G. Osborne, *Court and Camp of Runjeet Singh* (London: Henry Colburn, 1840), 83-84.
37 'Letter to Bengal, 11 April 1785', *Despatches to Bengal*, vol. 13, India Office, British Library.
38 *Parliamentary Papers, 1852-53*, vol. 31, no. 627, House of Lords, BL IOR, 175.
39 Irvine, *Army of the Indian Mughals*, 178-179.
40 Sen, *Military System of the Marathas*, 68-69.
41 Sinha, *Ranjit Singh*, 158.
42 Barat, *Bengal Native Infantry*, 31.
43 Barat, *Bengal Native Infantry*, 143-144.
44 Lieutenant-Colonel W.J. Wilson, *History of the Madras Army* (Madras: E. Keys, 1882), 2:103.
45 Capt. J. Williams, *An Historical Account of the Rise and Progress of the Bengal Infantry, from its formation in 1757 to 1796* (London: John Murray, 1817), 52.
46 Captain Arthur Broome, *History of the Rise and Progress of the Bengal Army* (London: Smith, Elder and Co., 1850), Vol. 1, p. 416.
47 Orderly Book, British Museum Additional Manuscripts, no. 6049, BL IOR, 90.
48 'Letter from Pemble to Bengal Council, 3 August 1764', Bengal Secret Department Record Proceedings (13 August 1764), BL IOR.
49 'Letter from Vantissrat to Munro, Ghyratty, 12 August 1764', Bengal Secret Proceedings (13 August 1764), BL IOR.
50 'Letter from Munro to Vansittrat, 16 September 1764', Bengal Secret Proceedings (24 September 1764), BL IOR.
51 Menezes, *Soldiers of the Raj*, 113.
52 Menezes, 113-114.
53 Surendra Nath Sen, *Eighteen Fifty-Seven* (New Delhi: The Publications Division, Ministry of Information and Broadcasting, Government of India, 1957), 18.
54 'Hunter to Adjutant General, Shikarpore, 21 June 1844', Bengal Foreign Secret Consultations, no. 146 (13 July 1844), BL IOR.
55 'Hunter to Adjutant General, Sukkur, 28 June 1844', Bengal Foreign Secret Consultations, no. 6 (23 November 1844), BL IOR.

56 'Commander-in-Chief to Governor General, Simla, 21 August 1844', Bengal Foreign Secret Proceedings (21 September 1844), BL IOR.
57 'Young before the Court of Enquiry, Ferojepore, 2 March 1844', no. 2, Bengal Military Consultations, no. 280 (22 March 1844), BL IOR.
58 'Young before the Court of Enquiry'.
59 'Assistant Surgeon before the Court of Enquiry, Ferojepore, 2 March 1844', Bengal Military Consultations, no. 280 (22 March 1844), BL IOR.
60 *The Friend of India* (24 March 1844), cited in Barat, *Bengal Native Infantry*, 265.
61 *Bombay Times* (26 March 1844), cited in Barat, 265.
62 This came to one shilling per day for a private ('The Long, Long Trail: Researching the Soldiers of the British Army in the Great War, 1914-1918', https://www.longlongtrail.co.uk/soldiers/a-soldiers-life-1914-1918/british-army-rates-pay-1914/), with twenty shillings equal to one pound, using the exchange rate at https://newworldeconomics.com//wp-content/uploads/2017/01/Foreign-Exchange-Rates-1914-1941.pdf.
63 Lt Col. R. Evans, *A Brief Outline of the Campaign in Mesopotamia* (London: Sifton Praed & Co, 1926), 68.
64 Sisir Sarbadhikari, *Abhi Le Baghdad* (Calcutta: Privately printed, 1957), cited by Amitav Ghosh, 'Shared Sorrows: Indians and Armenians in the Prison Camps of Ras al-'Ain, 1916–18', private blog, http://amitavghosh.com/blog/?p=5558 (5 February 2013).
65 Sarbadhikari, cited by Ghosh, 13.
66 Two shillings per day for a private (https://www.britishmilitaryhistory.co.uk/docs-services-royal-army-pay-corps/), using the 1939 exchange rate (https://newworldeconomics.com//wp-content/uploads/2017/01/Foreign-Exchange-Rates-1914-1941.pdf).
67 The British private, in his turn, was one of the lowest paid Allied soldiers. In 1944, for example, the US private was paid the equivalent of eight shillings three pence, compared to three shillings paid to the British private.
68 Ferguson, *Empire*, 347.
69 *The Times* (15 January 1849), cited in Barat, *Bengal Native Infantry*, 170-171.
70 C.B.W. Smith, *Florence Nightingale* (London: Constable, 1952), 48.
71 Omissi, *The Sepoy and the Raj*, 63.
72 James Ranald Martin, 'Report of the Sanitary Commission in India', 69, cited in Barat, *Bengal Native Infantry*, 172.
73 Nikolas Gardner, 'Morale of the Indian Army in the Mesopotamia Campaign: 1914–17', in Kaushik Roy, ed., *The Indian Army in the Two World Wars* (Leiden: Brill, 2012), 397.

74 Omissi, *The Sepoy and the Raj*, 63.
75 Khan, *The Raj at War*, 251.
76 Khan, *The Raj at War*, 251.
77 Cited by Shrabani Basu, *For King and Another Country: Indian Soldiers on the Western Front, 1914–1918*, (London: Bloomsbury Paperbacks, 2015), 151.
78 Lt Evans, *A Brief Outline of the Campaign in Mesopotamia*, 50.
79 Evans, 60-61.
80 Sisir Sarbadhikari, *Abhi Le Baghdad*, cited by Amitav Ghosh, 'On to Baghdad', blog, http://amitavghosh.com/blog/?p=4562.

Chapter Seven

1 *The Tribune*, British Library IOR, PNR, L/R/5/195 (3 September 1914): 838.
2 Sir Thomas Munro, cited by George Robert Gleig, *Life of Sir Thomas Munro* (London: John Murray, 1849), 249.
3 Minutes by the Governor-General and Commander-in-Chief on the Composition of the Army of India, 13 March 1835, Parliamentary Papers 1867 (500) LII.459, East India (European and Native Troops), BL IOR, 68.
4 Peter Mundy, *The Travels of Peter Mundy in Europe and Asia, 1608–1667* (Cambridge: Cambridge University Press, 1907), 2:256-7, 261, 287, 294–6.
5 Gentoos was a term used in the eighteenth century by Europeans to denote Hindus.
6 Ninth Report of the Committee of Secrecy (1773), House of Commons, BL IOR, 559-560.
7 Ninth Report, 550.
8 Bengal Military, Consultations, 9 August 1830, no. 1600, BL IOR.
9 Purabiya was a term used to denote the EIC's soldiers hired from Bihar and Awadh (today's eastern UP). The word purabiya means one who hails from the east.
10 Report of the Commission under Lord Peel on the Organization of the Indian Army, Command 2516, Parliamentary Command Papers, session 1(1859), BL IOR, 14.
11 Longer, *Red Coats to Olive Green: A History of the Indian Army* (New Delhi: Allied Publishers, 1974), 112.
12 Frederick Sleigh Roberts, *Forty-One Years in India: From Subaltern to Commander-in-Chief* (London: Richard Bentley & Son, 1897), 2:383.
13 Roberts, 442.

14 Sir Walter Roper Lawrence, *The India We Served* (London: Cassell and Company, 1928), 209.
15 Philip Mason, *A Matter of Honour: An Account of the Indian Army, Its Officers and Men* (London: Jonathan Cape Ltd, 1974), 391.
16 Mason, *Matter of Honour*, 318.
17 R.C. Butalia, *The Evolution of the Artillery in India: From the Battle of Plassey 1757 to the Revolt of 1857*, (New Delhi: Allied Publishers, 1999), 157.
18 Lt Col. W.J. Wilson, *History of the Madras Army* (Madras: E. Keys, 1882), cited in Longer, *Red Coats to Olive*, 46.
19 Mason, *Matter of Honour*, 144.
20 Mason, *Matter of Honour*, 144.
21 Longer, *Red Coats to Olive*, 112.
22 Longer, *Red Coats to Olive*, 123.
23 Wilson, *History of the Madras Army*, 1:72.
24 Channa Wickremesekera, *'Best Black Troops in the World': British Perceptions and the Making of the Sepoy, 1746–1805* (Delhi: Manohar Books, 2002), 120-121.
25 Michael Baldwin, 'Arming the Indian Army, 1857–1947', in Alan J. Guy and Peter B. Boyden, *Soldiers of the Raj*, 148.
26 Baldwin, 148.
27 T.A. Heathcote, *The Indian Army: The Garrison of British Imperial India, 1822–1922* (London: David and Charles, 1974), 55-56; Baldwin, *Soldiers of the Raj*, 148–160.
28 Sir Henry Lawrence, *Essays: Military and Political, Written in India* (London: Allen, 1859), 28.
29 Henry Davison Love, *Vestiges of Old Madras* (London: John Murray, 1913), 3:542-3.
30 Wilson, *History of the Madras Army*, vol. 1, cited in Longer, *Red Coats to Olive*, 78-9; OIOC Mss. Eur. B., BL IOR, 215:236.
31 *Quarterly Review* (May 1818), 391, cited by S.C. Hill, *Yusuf Khan: The Rebel Commandant*, ix.
32 Quoted in Hill, *Yusuf Khan*, 28.
33 Madras Select Committee Communications, 9 November 1758, OIOC P/C/53, 461, BL IOR.
34 Robert Clive to the East India Company, 8 March 1755, OIOC Misc Ltrs Recd, E/I/38, no. 120, BL IOR.
35 Mrs Kindersley, *Letters from the Island of Teneriffe, Brazil, the Cape of Good Hope and the East Indies* (London: J. Nourse, 1777), 209.
36 Holmes, *A History of the Indian Mutiny*, 49-50.
37 Pandey, *From Sepoy to Subedar*, 22.
38 Pandey, 23.

39 Lawrence, *Essays, Military and Political*, 28.
40 Lawrence, 479.
41 Pandey, *Sepoy to Subedar*, 172.
42 Frederick Cooper, *The Crisis in the Punjab, from the 10th of May Until the Fall of Delhi* (Lahore: Punjabee Press, H. Gregory, 1858), 201.
43 George Bourchier, *Eight Months' Campaign against the Bengal Sepoy Army during the Mutiny of 1857* (London: Smith, Elder and Co., 1858), 44.
44 'Proclamation, by the Queen in Council, to the Princes, Chiefs and People of India, 1 November 1858', British Library online, https://www.bl.uk/collection-items/proclamation-by-the-queen-in-council-to-the-princes-chiefs-and-people-of-india.
45 In the hierarchy, the India Secretary was superior to the Viceroy in India.
46 Cited in Daniel P. Marston and Chandar S. Sundaram, eds., *A Military History of India and South Asia: From the East India Company to the Nuclear Era*, 92.
47 Lord Curzon's Memorandum of 4 June 1900, para. 32, in GoI's confidential despatch no. 103 of 19 July 1900, in OIOC: L/MIL/17/5/1750, BL IOR.
48 DeWitt Elinwood, cited in Chandar S. Sundaram, 'Grudging Concessions: The Officer Corps and Its Indianization, 1817–1940', in Marston and Sundaram, eds., *A Military History of India and South Asia*, 93.
49 Amar Singh, in Susanne Rudolph and Lloyd Rudolph, eds., *Reversing the Gaze: Amar Singh's Diary, A Colonial Subject's Narrative of Imperial India* (Colorado: Westview Press, 2002), 117.
50 Singh, 117.
51 Singh, 117.
52 Singh, 158-159.
53 Cited in David Dilks, 'Achievement', *Curzon in India* (London: Hart-Davis, 1969), 1:240.
54 Singh, *Reversing the Gaze*, 264–266.
55 Singh, 280.
56 Correspondence re European War, part 1, *Hardinge Papers*, Cambridge University Library, 5:1, 103.
57 Rushbrook-Williams, *India in the Years 1917-1918: A Statement Prepared for Presentation to Parliament* (Calcutta: Government Printing Press, 1919), 19.
58 Philip Mason estimates the Indian Army commissioned officers' peacetime (1930s) strength to be 5,000 in Mason, *A Matter of Honour*, 511;

V. Longer offers a figure of approximately 3,000 Indian Army officers in 1939. V. Longer, *Red Coats to Olive Green*, 216.
59 Marston and Sundaram, eds., *A Military History of India and South Asia*, 96.
60 D.K. Palit, 'Indianisation of the Indian Army's Officers Cadre, 1920–1947', in *The Indo-British Review: A Journal of History* 16 (1989); Z. Masani, *Indian Tales of the Raj* (Berkeley: University of California Press, 1992), 90–93.
61 Cited in David Omissi, *The Sepoy and the Raj*, 172.
62 Omissi, 172.
63 Marston and Sundaram, eds., *A Military History of India and South Asia*, 97.
64 T.A Heathcote, *The Military in British India: The Development of British Land Forces in South Asia* (Barnsley: The Praetorian Press, 2013), 174.
65 Omissi, *The Sepoy and the Raj*, 185.
66 Omissi, 185.
67 Omissi, 184.
68 Longer, *Red Coats to Olive*, 238; Mason, *A Matter of Honour*, 511.
69 GoI, Defence Department, Official Communique, 17 June 1940, in OIOC: L/MIL/7/19112, BL IOR.
70 Anirudh Deshpande, *British Military Policy in India 1900–1945: Colonial Constraints and Declining Power* (Delhi: Manohar Books, 2005), 123; Menezes, *Soldiers of the Raj*, 367.
71 General C.J.E. Auchinlek to Leo Amery, 12 October 1940, in OIOC: L/MIL/7/19156, BL IOR.

Chapter Eight

1 Mohan Lal Kashmiri, *Life of the Amir Dost Mohammed Khan of Kabul*, vol. 1 (London: Longman, Brown, Green, and Longmans, 1846), 396–397.
2 Sita Ram was offered higher pay with havildar rank in Shuja's contingent. He readily agreed to leave his old regiment as he had lost chances of promotion due to a court martial he had to face related to a financial misdemeanour in which white officers were complicit, but he alone was punished as pay havildar.
3 Lady Sale, *A Journal of the Disasters in Affghanistan, 1841-42* (London: John Murray, 1843), 104.
4 Cited in Philip Mason, *A Matter of Honour: An Account of the Indian Army, Its Officers and Men* (London: Jonathan Cape Ltd, 1974), 184.

Fane refers to Sir Henry Fane, the C-in-C of the Bengal Army at the time.
5. Mason, 184.
6. Pandey, *From Sepoy to Subedar*, 88–91.
7. Barat, *The Bengal Native Infantry*, 231.
8. Major-General Sir Thomas Seaton, *From Cadet to Colonel: The Record of a Life of Active Service*, vol. 1 (London: Hurst and Blackett, 1866), 139.
9. Pandey, *Sepoy to Subedar*, 98.
10. Cited in Mason, *Matter of Honour*, 222.
11. Pandey, *Sepoy to Subedar*, 103.
12. Barat, *Bengal Native Infantry*, 232.
13. Sale, *A Journal of the Disasters*, 37.
14. Sale, 42, 46.
15. Journal of Captain Hugh Johnson, private collection, 16, in William Dalrymple, *Return of a King: The Battle for Afghanistan* (Delhi: Bloomsbury Books, 2012).
16. Sale, *A Journal of the Disasters*, 60.
17. Pandey, *Sepoy to Subedar*, 111.
18. Sale, *A Journal of the Disasters*, 61.
19. Sale, 63.
20. Sale, 89.
21. Sale, 90.
22. Sale, 90.
23. Sale, 100.
24. Cited in Sir Penderel Moon, *The British Conquest and Dominion of India, Part One 1745-1857* (Delhi: India Research Press, 1989), 537.
25. Moon, 537.
26. Sale, *A Journal of the Disasters*, 120.
27. Sale, 121.
28. Sale, 126.
29. Sale, 131-132.
30. Sale, 170.
31. Pandey, *Sepoy to Subedar*, 112-113.
32. Lady Sale, p. 85.
33. Ibid.
34. Sale, 185.
35. Sale, 207.
36. Patrick Macrory, *Signal Catastrophe: The Story of the Disastrous Retreat from Kabul, 1842* (London: Book Club Associates, 1972), 220.
37. Colin Mackenzie, *Storms and Sunshine of A Soldier's Life, 1825–1881* (London: Wentworth Press, 2016), 1:135.

38 Sale, *A Journal of the Disasters*, 229.
39 Sale, 230.
40 Lady Sale, p. 232.
41 Sale, 242-243.
42 Journal of Captain Hugh Johnson, in Dalrymple, *Return of a King*, 34.
43 Sir George Lawrence, *Reminiscences of Forty-Three Years in India* (London: John Murray, 1874), 156.
44 Sale, *A Journal of the Disasters*, 249.
45 Journal of Captain Hugh Johnson, in Dalrymple, *Return of a King*, 41.
46 Sale, *A Journal of the Disasters*, 260.
47 Sale, 260.
48 Sale, 265.
49 Pandey, *Sepoy to Subedar*, 114.
50 Pandey, 252.
51 Pandey, 271.
52 Pandey, 114.
53 Sale, *A Journal of the Disasters*, 274.
54 Pandey, *Sepoy to Subedar*, 115.
55 Sale, *A Journal of the Disasters*, 331.
56 Sale, 344.
57 Pandey, *Sepoy to Subedar*, 122-123.
56 Pandey, 124.
59 Pandey, 133.
60 Menezes, *Fidelity and Honour*, 65.
61 Menezes, 63.
62 Menezes, 66.
63 Angus Maddison, *The World Economy: A Millennial Perspective*, 261; Jutta Bolt et al., 'Rebasing "Maddison": New Income Comparisons and the Shape of Long-Run Economic Development', Maddison Project Working Paper, no. 10 (2018), Maddison Project Database, ver. 2018, www.ggdc.net/maddison.
64 *India's Contribution to the Great War*, 228.
65 *India's Contribution*, 296.
66 Lt Evans, *A Brief Outline of the Campaign in Mesopotamia, 1914–1918* (London: Sifton Praed & Co, 1926), 48.
67 Sisir Sarbadhikari, *Abhi Le Baghdad*, cited in Amitav Ghosh, 'On to Baghdad', blog, 12, https://www.amitavghosh.com/docs/On%20to%20Baghdad.pdf.
68 Sarbadhikari in Ghosh, 13.
69 Ron Wilcox, *Battles on the Tigris: The Mesopotamian Campaigns of the First World War* (London: Pen & Sword Military, 2006), 70.
70 Russell Brandon, *The Siege* (New York: The Viking Press, 1969), 129

71. Figures cited in George Morton-Jack, *The Indian Empire at War: From Jihad to Victory, the Untold Story of the Indian Soldiers in the First World War* (London: Little & Brown Publishing, 2018), 307.
72. Mokshada Debi, *Kalyan Pradeep: The Life of Captain Kalyan Kumar Mukherji I.M.S.* (Calcutta: Privately published, 1928), cited in Amitav Ghosh, 'At "Home and the World" in Iraq 1915–17', blog, 11–13, https://www.amitavghosh.com/docs/Home%20and%20the%20World.pdf.
73. Sarbadhikari, *Abhi Le Baghdad*, cited in Amitav Ghosh, 'On to Baghdad', blog, 18.
74. Sarbadhikari in Ghosh, 19.
75. H.C.W. Bishop, *A Kut Prisoner* (London: John Lane, 1920), 28.
76. Evans, *A Brief Outline of the Campaign in Mesopotamia*, 68; A.J. Barker, *The Neglected War: Mesopotamia 1914-1918* (London: Faber & Faber, 1967), 266, 286.
77. If we include the approximately 1,130 hospital patients in Kut as all being Indians and all fighting men, and assume they all survived after they were allowed to go to Basra, even then the death rate of Indian fighting soldiers up to the end of the Kut siege is 30 per cent, compared to the very small number of deaths amongst European soldiers. The numbers exclude the non-combatant Indians, on whom figures are very difficult to reconcile fully.
78. Nikolas Gardner, *The Siege of Kut-al-Amara: At War in Mesopotamia, 1915-1916* (Indiana: Indiana University Press, 2016), 156.
79. Major F.W.C. Sandes, *In Kut and Captivity with the Sixth Indian Division* (London: John Murray, 1919), 287.
80. Sandes, p. 285.
81. Sarbadhikari, *Abhi Le Baghdad*, in Ghosh, 'On to Baghdad', blog, 31.
82. Some accounts describe a foot march straight from Kut-al-Amara for some of the British and Indian captives.
83. The details of the dates and route are provided by Sisir Sarbadhikari in *Abhi Le Baghdad*. Cited in Amitav Ghosh, blog.
84. Sisir Sarbadhikari, *Abhi Le Baghdad*, cited in Amitav Ghosh, 'Shared Sorrows', blog, 9, https://www.amitavghosh.com/docs/Shared_Sorrows.pdf.
85. Sarbadhikari, in Ghosh, 9.
86. Sarbadhikari, in Ghosh, 9.
87. Sarbadhikari, in Ghosh, 12.
88. Sarbadhikari, in Ghosh, 12.
89. Sarbadhikari, in Ghosh, 16.
90. Sarbadhikari, in Ghosh, 16.
91. Sarbadhikari, in Ghosh, 17.
92. Sarbadhikari, in Ghosh, 17.

93 Sarbadhikari, in Ghosh, 19
94 Sarbadhikari, in Ghosh, 17-18.
95 Sarbadhikari, in Ghosh, 18.
96 Sarbadhikari, in Ghosh, 19.
97 Sarbadhikari, in Ghosh, 19.
98 Sarbadhikari, in Ghosh, 20.
99 Sarbadhikari, in Ghosh, 20.
100 Sarbadhikari, in Ghosh, 20.
101 Sarbadhikari, in Ghosh, 22.
102 Sarbadhikari, in Ghosh, 22.
103 Sarbadhikari, in Ghosh, 23.
104 Sarbadhikari, in Ghosh, 15.
105 Sarbadhikari, in Ghosh, 16.
106 David E. McNabb, *Oil and the Creation of Iraq: Policy Failures and the 1914–1918 War in Mesopotamia,* (London: Routledge Books, 2016), 123.
107 Out of the approximately 2,750 British soldiers in the 6th Division, 1,700 died in Mesopotamia. See Barker, *The Neglected War,* 286. This would imply a death rate of 62 per cent, and survival of 1,000 British soldiers and 2,000 Indian soldiers. McNabb mentions 3,000 combined survivors, British and Indian, in *Oil and the Creation of Iraq,* 123. Of the approximately 11,950 Indian soldiers from the 6th Division, 6,500 were taken prisoner at Kut, approximately 1,200 hospital patients in serious condition were released from Kut to proceed to Basra, and 2,000 of the prisoners survived by the end of the war. This implies almost 8,750 died, of which 4,500 in Turkish camps and 4,250 in the siege at Kut-al-Amara. The overall death rate of Indian soldiers was around 73 per cent, with a slightly higher mortality of Indians at Kut compared to Turkish camps. See Evans, *Brief Outline of the Campaign in Mesopotamia,* 68; Morton-Jack, *The Indian Empire at War,* 307. These numbers only include the fighting men, as figures for the Indian camp followers have not been possible to reconcile.
108 Morton-Jack, *The Indian Empire at War,* 312.

Chapter Nine

1 Attributed by Paul Walter from the Berlin Foreign Office to sepoys who deserted on the Western Front to join Germany. Cited in George Morton-Jack, *The Indian Empire at War: From Jihad to Victory, the Untold Story of the Indian Soldiers in the First World War* (London: Little & Brown Publishing, 2018), 208.

2   Charles Hicks, Tsalagi (Cherokee) Vice Chief, speaking of the Trail of Tears, 4 November 1838. Cited in George Henderson and Thompson Olasiji, *Migrants, Immigrants and Slaves: Racial and Ethnic Groups in America* (Lanham: University Press of America, 1995), 43.
3   Patrick Cadell, *History of the Bombay Army* (New York: Green & Co, 1938), 29.
4   Michael Edwardes cited in Percival Spear, *The Nabobs: a Study of the Social Life of the English in Eighteenth Century India*, (Oxford: Oxford University Press, 1963), 162.
5   J.W. Kaye, *The History of the Indian Mutiny*, G. B. Malleson, ed. (London: Longmans, Green and Co., 1909), 1:149.
6   Cited in Herbert B. Edwardes and Herman Merivale, *Life of Sir Henry Lawrence*, 50.
7   Lord Cornwallis to London, 6 November 1789, cited in Wickremsekera, '*Best Black Troops*', 100.
8   Cornwallis, cited in Wickremsekera, 102.
9   Cornwallis, cited in Wickremsekera, 104.
10 Colonel Pennington, cited in Barat, *The Bengal Native Infantry*, 174-175.
11 Warren Hastings, cited in Mason, *A Matter of Honour: An Account of the Indian Army, Its Officers and Men* (London: Jonathan Cape Ltd, 1974), 257.
12 Sir Syed Ahmed, cited in Sen, *Eighteen Fifty-Seven*, 9.
13 Ahmed, cited in Sen, 10.
14 Rev. M.A. Sherring, *The Indian Church during the Great Rebellion* (London: James Nisbett and Co., 1859), 184-85.
15 Cited in Sen, *Eighteen Fifty-Seven*, 15.
16 Governor Bentinck was thirty-two years old at the time.
17 Lt Col. W.J. Wilson, *History of the Madras Army*, 3:169-170.
18 Mason, *A Matter of Honour*, 239.
19 Cited in Moon, *British Conquest and Dominion of India*, 350.
20 Wilson, *History of the Madras Army*, 3:189.
21 Thomas Munro to William Bentinck, cited in Moon, *British Conquest and Dominion*, 352.
22 Committee of Secrecy, cited in Barat, *Bengal Native Infantry*, 35.
23 Bengal Military Consultations, 9 October 1795, cited in Wickremsekera, '*Best Black Troops*', 126.
24 Wickremsekera, 128.
25 Cited in Menezes, *Fidelity and Honour*, 109-110.
26 Unknown, *Narrative of the Mutiny at Bolarum in September 1855: For the Information of Brigadier Colin Mackenzie's Family and Private Friends* (Edinburgh: Murray and Gibb, 1857), 18.

27 Unknown, 21.
28 Unknown, 21.
29 Unknown, 6.
30 Unknown, 47.
31 Unknown, 10.
32 Unknown, 10.
33 Unknown, 10-11.
34 Unknown, 14.
35 Unknown, 28.
36 Unknown, 51.
37 Thomas Lowe, *Central India during the Rebellion of 1857 and 1858* (London: Longman, 1860), 326-327.
38 Richard Forster, 'Mangal Pandey', *The Columbia Undergraduate Journal of South Asian Studies* 1, no. 1 (Fall 2009), 10.
39 Forster, 11.
40 Forster, 24.
41 Mason, *Matter of Honour*, 279.
42 Mason, 266.
43 John Kaye, *A History of the Sepoy War in India* (London: W.H. Allen and Co., 1880), 1:639-40.
44 Sen, *Eighteen Fifty-Seven*, 47.
45 Sen, 49.
46 Kaye, *History of the Sepoy War*, 1:480-81.
47 George W. Forrest, *A History of the Indian Mutiny* (New Delhi, Asian Educational Services, 2006), 1:32.
48 Moon, *British Conquest and Dominion*, 686.
49 Holmes, *A History of the Indian Mutiny*, 97.
50 Herbert Edwardes and Herman Merivale, *Life of Sir Henry Lawrence* (London: Smith Elder, 1872), 2:322-23.
51 Hugh Henry Gough, *Old Memories* (Edinburgh: W. Blackwood and Sons, 1897), 27-28.
52 Gough, 39.
53 A.R.D. Mackenzie, *Mutiny Memoirs* (Allahabad: Pioneer Press, 1891), 12-13.
54 Mackenzie, 18.
55 John Edward Wharton Rotton, *The Chaplain's Narrative of the Siege of Delhi: From the Outbreak at Meerut to the Capture of Delhi* (London: Smith Elder and Co., 1858), 7.
56 Hakim Ahsanullah Khan, cited in William Dalrymple, *The Last Mughal* (Delhi: Bloomsbury Books, 2006), 172.
57 Ghulam Abbas, Bahadur Shah Zafar's vakil, cited in Dalrymple, *The Last Mughal*, 172.
58 Khan, cited in Dalrymple, 173.

59 John Lawrence, cited in Moon, *British Conquest and Dominion*, 696.
60 Charles Metcalfe, *Two Native Narratives of the Mutiny at Delhi* (Westminster: Archibald Constable & Co., 1898), 170.
61 Sayyid Kamaluddin Haider Husaini, Qaisar-ut-Tawarikh, cited in Rudrangshu Mukherjee, *Awadh in Revolt, 1857-58: A Study of Popular Resistance* (London: Anthem South Asia Studies, 2002), 87.
62 Abstract translation of an arzi (petition) from the rebel camp on the part of all the rebel officers and sepoys to Maharaja Jang Bahadur, cited in Mukherjee, 151.
63 'Proclamation by the Queen in Council to the Princes, Chiefs and People of India (Published by the Governor-General at Allahabad, November 1st 1858)', British Library, London.
64 Cited in Moon, *The British Conquest and Dominion*, 676.
65 Walter Lawrence Papers, BL/IOR/Mss Eur F 143, BL IOR.
66 Karl Marx, 'A Contribution to the Critique of Hegel's Philosophy of Right, Introduction', in Karl Marx, *Early Writings*, Lucio Colletti, ed. (London: Penguin Classics, 2004), 244.

Chapter Ten

1 Sir G. Cunningham, Governor of North-West Frontier Province, to the Governor-General of India, Viscount Wavell, in a letter dated 27 November 1945. *Wavell Papers*, in Nicholas Mansergh, ed., Transfer of Power, (London: HMSO, 1972), 6:546.
2 Ferguson, *Empire, How Britain Made the Modern World*, 354.
3 Will Dahlgreen, 'The British Empire Is "Something To Be Proud Of"', YouGov (26 July 2014), https://yougov.co.uk/topics/politics/articles-reports/2014/07/26/britain-proud-its-empire.
4 Moon, *British Conquest and Dominion of India*, 1092.
5 Mahatma Gandhi, in September 1921, cited in Sugata Bose, *His Majesty's Opponent* (Harvard: Harvard University Press, 2010), 51.
6 Raja Mahendra Pratap, *My Life Story* (Delhi: Low Price Publications, 2004), 36.
7 George Morton-Jack, *The Indian Empire at War: From Jihad to Victory, the Untold Story of the Indian Soldiers in the First World War* (London: Little & Brown Publishing, 2018), 317.
8 Dr Vir Singh, introduction to Raja Mahendra Pratap, *My Life Story*, xiii.
9 Subhas Chandra Bose to Prabhabati Bose, 1912, in Subhas Chandra Bose, *An Indian Pilgrim: An Unfinished Autobigraphy* (Delhi: Oxford University Press, 2007), 143.
10 Special Operations Executive (SOE) War Diary, 7 March 1941, HS7/217, The National Archives, Kew.

11 N. Ganpuley, *Netaji in Germany: A Little Known Chapter* (Bombay: Bharatiya Vidya Bhavan, 1970), 95.
12 Abid Hasan Safrani, cited by Leonard Gordon, *Brothers against the Raj: A Biography of Indian Nationalists Sarat and Subhas Chandra Bose* (Delhi: Rupa & Co., 2015), 457.
13 Gita Mookerjee, cited by Bose, *His Majesty's Opponent*, 226.
14 Hugh Toye, *The Springing Tiger: The Indian National Army and Subhas Chandra Bose* (London: Cassell Publishing, 1959), 74.
15 'The Fall of Singapore', Bose's broadcast on Azad Hind Radio, 19 February 1942, in Subhas Chandra Bose, Sisir Bose, ed., *Azad Hind: Writings and Speeches, 1941–1943* (Delhi: Anthem South Asia Studies, 2015), 67-68.
16 Bose, *His Majesty's Opponent*, 218.
17 Bose, 220-221.
18 Mohan Singh, *Soldiers' Contribution to Indian Independence: The Epic of the Indian National Army* (Delhi: Army Educational Stores, 1974), 108-9.
19 Srinath Raghavan, *India's War: The Making of Modern South Asia, 1939–1945* (London: Penguin Books, 2017), 283-284.
20 Weekly Intelligence Summary, 8 May 1942, L/WS/1/1433, Asian and African Collections (AAC), British Library, cited in Raghavan, 284.
21 Note by an Indian ECO, n.d. (c. 1 April 1943), L/WS/1/1576, AAC, cited in Raghavan, 284.
22 Fujiwara Iwaichi, Akashi Yoji, trans., *F. Kikan: Japanese Army Intelligence Operations in South-east Asia during World War II* (Hong Kong: Heinemann Asia, 1983), 89.
23 Bose, *His Majesty's Opponent*, 243.
24 Bose, 244.
25 M. Sivaram, *The Road to Delhi* (Tokyo: C.E. Tuttle & Co, 1967), 122-23.
26 Sivaram, *Road to Delhi*, 124.
27 Sugata Bose, *His Majesty's Opponent*, 246; Gordon, *Brothers Against the Raj*, 498.
28 Shah Nawaz Khan, *My Memories of INA and Its Netaji* (Delhi: Rajkamal Publications, 1956), 99-100, 110.
29 William Slim, *Defeat into Victory: Battling Japan in Burma and India, 1942–1945* (New York: Cooper Square Publishers, 2000), 169.
30 Subhas Chandra Bose, *Chalo Delhi: Writings and Speeches 1943–1945* (Kolkata: Netaji Research Bureau, 2007) 173–189.
31 Khan, *My Memories*, 155-156.
32 Abid Hasan Safrani and Sisir Bose, eds., *Men from Imphal* (Kolkata: Netaji Research Bureau, 1971), 7–9.

33. Peter Fay, *The Forgotten Army: India's Armed Struggle for Independence, 1942–1945* (Michigan: University of Michigan Press, 1995), 556.
34. Bose, *His Majesty's Opponent*, 292.
35. S.A. Ayer, *Unto Him a Witness: The Story of Netaji Subhas Chandra Bose in East Asia* (Bombay: Thacker & Co, 1950), 114, quoting Rahman in September 1945, telling Ayer of Bose's death.
36. Sarojini Naidu, *The Hindu* (29 August 1945), cited in Sugata Bose, *His Majesty's Opponent*, 305.
37. Gordon, *Brothers Against the Raj*, 81.
38. Bose, *His Majesty's Opponent*, 282.
39. Fay, *The Forgotten Army*, 354–358; Khan, *My Memories*, 218–220.
40. Leonard Gordon suggests a great majority of the INA died fighting, in Gordon, *Brothers against the Raj*, 515; Chandar S. Sundaram estimates the death rate for the INA First Division with 9,000 men fighting in Imphal and Arakan to range from 33 per cent to 44 per cent. Chandar S. Sundaram, 'The Indian National Army, 1942–1946: A Circumstantial Force' in Daniel P. Marston and Chandar S. Sundaram, *A Military History of India and South Asia*, 2007, p. 126; Brig. R.S. Chhikara (Retd), foreword to Kalyan Kumar De, *Netaji: India's Independence and British Archives* (Delhi: Garuda, 2020), vi. He estimates 30,000 INA soldiers died in the war, which would imply a death rate higher than 50 per cent.
41. Mason, *A Matter of Honour*, 517. Mason estimates 1,900 dead of the 6,000 INA First Division that went into action at Imphal.
42. There were 580,497 deaths including the Commonwealth as per the Commonwealth War Graves Commission Annual Report 2014-2015, 38. A total of 11,116,000 men, including the entire Commonwealth, were serving as per John Ellis, *World War II—A Statistical Survey* (New York: Facts on File, 1993), 253-54. For UK alone: 264,443 deaths and 3,300,000 serving. See Reg G. Grant, *World War II: Europe* (London: Gareth Stevens Publishing, 2004), 60; Carlo D'Este, 'The Army and the Challenge of War: 1939–1945', in David Chandler and Ian Beckett, eds., *Oxford History of the British Army*, 274.
43. G.F. Krivosheev, ed., *Soviet Casualties and Combat Losses in the Twentieth Century* (London: Greenhill Books, 1997), 85–87; Rüdiger Overmans, *Deutsche militärische Verluste im Zweiten Weltkrieg* (Berlin: Oldenbourg, 2000), 333–335; Michael Clodfelter, *Warfare and Armed Conflicts—A Statistical Reference to Casualty and Other Figures, 1500–2000* (North Carolina: Jefferson Books, 2002), 584.
44. Clive Branson, *British Soldier in India: The Letters of Clive Branson* (New York: International Publishers, 1945), 79, 86.

45 General Auchinleck to Field Marshal Viscount Wavell, New Delhi, 24 November 1945, 'Official Correspondence: India, January–December 1945', *Wavell Papers*, 374–78, cited in Transfer of Power, 6:530.
46 Konrad Mitchell Lawson, *Wartime Atrocities and the Politics of Treason in the Ruins of the Japanese Empire, 1937–1953*, PhD dissertation at Harvard University, 81, https://dash.harvard.edu/handle/1/9795484 .
47 Field Marshal Viscount Wavell to Lord Pethick-Lawrence, 27 November 1945, para 6, *Wavell Papers*, in Transfer of Power, 6:552.
48 Intelligence Bureau Secret Report, 20 November 1945, in Transfer of Power, 6:512.
49 Intelligence Bureau Secret Report.
50 Intelligence Bureau Secret Report.
51 Mr Casey, Bengal Governor to Viceroy Wavell, 2 January 1946, in *Wavell Papers* in Transfer of Power, 6:724.
52 Casey.
53 Casey.
54 Sir H. Twynam to Viceroy Wavell, 26 November 1945, in *Wavell Papers* in Transfer of Power, 6:542.
55 Twynam.
56 Twynam.
57 Sir G. Cunningham to Wavell, 27 November 1945, in *Wavell Papers*, January–December 1945, 383-84, in Transfer of Power, 6:546.
58 Cunningham.
59 Cunningham, 62-64; Proposal from Punjab Governor, 17 November 1945, enclosure to Auchinleck's letter to Viceroy Wavell, 24 November 1945, in *Wavell Papers*, January–December 1945, 374–78, in Transfer of Power, 6:530.
60 Cunningham.
61 Cunningham.
62 David French, 'Discipline and the Death Penalty in the British Army in the War Against Germany During the Second World War', *Journal of Contemporary History* 33, no. 4 (1 October 1998): 539-40.
63 Auchinleck's letter to Viceroy Wavell, 24 November 1945, in *Wavell Papers*, January–December 1945, 374–78, in Transfer of Power, 6:530.
64 Wavell to Lord Pethick Lawrence, 27 November 1945, in Transfer of Power, 6:552.
65 Wavell to Lord Pethick Lawrence.
66 Sir A. Hope to Wavell, 10 December 1945, in Transfer of Power, 6:631.
67 Auchinleck to Chiefs of Staff Committee, 1 December 1945, in Transfer of Power, 6:576.
68 Auchinleck, 1 December.
69 Auchinleck, 1 December.

70 Auchinleck, 1 December.
71 Auchinleck to Chiefs of Staff, 22 December 1945, in Transfer of Power, 6:673.
72 Auchinleck, 22 December.
73 Auchinleck, 22 December.
74 Report on Speech of 24 December 1945, Sarvepalli Gopal, ed., *Selected Works of Nehru* (New Delhi: Orient Longman, 1972–2010), 14:279-80.
75 Sir B. Glancy to Wavell, 16 January 1946, in Transfer of Power, 6:807.
76 Glancy to Wavell.
77 Gurbaksh Singh Dhillon, *From My Bones* (Delhi: Aryan Books International, 1988), 509.
78 Mason, *Matter of Honour*, 1173.
79 F.S. Tuker, *While Memory Serves* (London: Cassell & Co, 1950), 59.
80 General Auchinleck to Army Commanders, 12 February 1946, *Wavell Papers*, January 1946–March 1947, 60–67, in Transfer of Power, 6:939.
81 Auchinleck, 12 February.
82 Auchinleck, 12 February.
83 Biswanath Bose, *RIN Mutiny: 1946* (Delhi: Northern Book Centre, 1988), 10.
84 Bose, 27.
85 Bose, 20.
86 Bose, 20.
87 Bose, 20-21.
88 Bose, 30, 32.
89 Bose, 86.
90 Bose, 90.
91 Sir F. Mudie to Wavell, 27 February 1946, in Transfer of Power, 6:1071.
92 Moon, *British Conquest and Dominion*, 1144.
93 Moon, 1145.
94 Lord Pethick-Lawrence to Clement Attlee, 4 March 1946, in Transfer of Power, 6:1106–1108.
95 Draft of Directive of Cabinet Delegation by Sir Stafford Cripps, Appendix 1 to Record of Discussions at Chequers on 24 February 1946, in Transfer of Power, 6:1057–1064. The document was shared with Wavell on 26 February.
96 Minute by Mr Attlee, 5 March 1946, in Transfer of Power, 6:1106–1108.
97 V. Longer, *Red Coats to Olive Green: A History of the Indian Army* (New Delhi: Allied Publishers, 1974), 250-251.
98 Pandit Nehru to Sir Stafford Cripps, 5 March 1946, in Transfer of Power, 6:1107.

Bibliography

British Library, Oriental and India Office Collections, London

Military Letters Received from Bengal and India.
Military Despatches Sent to Bengal and India.
Parliamentary Papers (via onsite ProQuest Database).
Bengal Secret and Military Consultations.
Madras Select Committee Communications.
Oral Archives.
Orderly Book, British Museum Additional Manuscripts.
'Proclamation, by the Queen in Council, to the Princes, Chiefs and People of India'. 1 November 1858.
Government of India's Confidential Despatch.
Government of India, Defence Department, Official Communique.
Walter Lawrence Papers.
Wavell Papers.
Report of the Indian Statutory (Simon) Commission, 1930.
Transfer of Power, 1942–1947. Vol. 6.

The National Archives, Kew

Charles Cornwallis Papers.
Special Operations Executive (SOE) War Diary.

Cambridge University Library, Cambridge

Hardinge Papers.

National Archives of India, New Delhi

Foreign Department Secret Consultations.

Old Manuscripts

Manuscripts (including edited versions) containing first-hand descriptions of the events and facts included in my book.

Ahmad, Nizamuddin. *The Tabaqat-i-Akbari of Khwajah Nizamuddin Ahmad*. Translated by Brajindranath De. Calcutta: Royal Asiatic Society of Bengal, 1939.

Ayer, S.A. *Unto Him a Witness: The Story of Netaji Subhas Chandra Bose in East Asia*. Bombay: Thacker & Co., 1950.

Bose, Biswanath. *RIN Mutiny: 1946*. Delhi: Northern Book Centre, 1988.

Bose, Subhas Chandra. *Azad Hind: Writings and Speeches, 1941–1943*. Edited by Sisir Bose. Delhi: Anthem South Asia Studies, 2015.

—. *Chalo Delhi: Writings and Speeches 1943–1945*. Kolkata: Netaji Research Bureau, 2007.

—. *An Indian Pilgrim: An Unfinished Autobiography*. Delhi: Oxford University Press, 2007.

Bourchier, George. *Eight Months' Campaign against the Bengal Sepoy Army during the Mutiny of 1857*. London: Smith, Elder and Co., 1858.

Bibliography

Branson, Clive. *British Soldier in India: The Letters of Clive Branson.* New York: International Publishers, 1945.

Commonwealth War Graves Commission Annual Report, 2014-2015.

Cooper, Frederick. *The Crisis in the Punjab, from the 10th of May until the Fall of Delhi.* Lahore: Punjabee Press, H. Gregory, 1858.

Debi, Mokshada. *Kalyan Pradeep: The Life of Captain Kalyan Kumar Mukherji I.M.S.* Calcutta: Privately published, 1928. Cited in Amitav Ghosh (blog). https://www.amitavghosh.com/docs/Home%20and%20the%20World.pdf.

Dhillon, Gurbaksh Singh. *From My Bones.* Delhi: Aryan Books International, 1988.

Ganpuley, N.G. *Netaji in Germany: A Little-Known Chapter.* Bombay: Bharatiya Vidya Bhavan, 1970.

Government of India. *India's Contribution to the Great War.* Calcutta: Superintendent Government Printing, 1923.

Graham, Maria. *Journal of a Residence in India.* Edinburgh: G. Ramsay for A. Constable, 1812.

Iwaichi, Fujiwara. *F. Kikan: Japanese Army Intelligence Operations in Southeast Asia during World War II.* Translated By Akashi Yoji. Hong Kong: Heinemann Asia, 1983.

Jones, Oliver J. *Recollections of a Winter Campaign in India, 1857-1858.* London: Saunders and Otley, 1859.

Kashmiri, Mohan Lal. *Life of the Amir Dost Mohammed Khan of Kabul.* Vols. 1 and 2. London: Longman, Brown, Green, and Longmans, 1846.

Khan, Shah Nawaz. *My Memories of INA and Its Netaji.* Delhi: Rajkamal Publications, 1956.

Kindersley, Mrs. *Letters from the Island of Teneriffe, Brazil, the Cape of Good Hope and the East Indies.* London: J. Nourse, 1777.

Lawrence, Sir George. *Reminiscences of Forty-Three Years in India.* London: John Murray, 1874.

Lawrence, Sir Henry. *Essays: Military and Political, Written in India*. London: Allen, 1859.

Lawrence, Sir Walter Roper. *The India We Served*. London: Cassell and Company, 1928.

Lowe, Thomas. *Central India during the Rebellion of 1857 and 1858*. London: Longman, 1860.

Mackenzie, Colin. *Storms and Sunshine of A Soldier's Life, 1825–1881*. Vol. 1. London: Wentworth Press, 2016.

Mahomet, Dean. *The Travels of Dean Mahomet: An Eighteenth-Century Journey through India*. Edited by Michael H. Fisher. Berkeley and Los Angeles: University of California Press, 1997.

Marx, Karl. *Early Writings*. Edited by Lucio Colletti. London: Penguin Classics, 2004.

Merewether, Lt Col., and Sir Frederick Smith. *The Indian Corps in France*. London: John Murray, 1918.

Metcalfe, Charles. *Two Native Narratives of the Mutiny at Delhi*. Westminster: Archibald Constable & Co., 1898.

Mundy, Peter. *The Travels of Peter Mundy in Europe and Asia, 1608–1667*. Vol. 2. Cambridge: Cambridge University Press, 1907.

The Mutiny in the Bengal Army. London: John Chapman, 1857.

Narrative of the Mutiny at Bolarum in September 1855: For the Information of Brigadier Colin Mackenzie's Family and Private Friends. Edinburgh: Murray and Gibb, 1857.

Nathan, Mirza. *Baharistan-I-Ghaybi*. Vols. 1 and 2. Translated by M.I. Borah. Gauhati: Government of Assam, 1936.

Omissi, David, ed. *Indian Voices of the Great War: Soldiers' Letters, 1914–1918*. Gurgaon: Penguin Books, 2014.

Osborne, W.G. *Court and Camp of Runjeet Singh*. London: Henry Colburn, 1840.

Pandey, Sita Ram. *From Sepoy to Subedar*. Edited by James Lunt. London: Papermac, 1988.

Pratap, Raja Mahendra. *My Life Story*. Delhi: Low Price Publications, 2004.

Roberts, Frederick Sleigh. *Forty-One Years in India: From Subaltern to Commander-in-Chief*. Vol. 2. London: Richard Bentley & Son, 1897.

Ross, Charles, ed. *Correspondence of Charles, First Marquis of Cornwallis*. Vol. 1. London: Murray, 1859.

Rotton, John Edward Wharton. *The Chaplain's Narrative of the Siege of Delhi: From the Outbreak at Meerut to the Capture of Delhi*. London: Smith Elder and Co., 1858.

Rudolph, Susanne, and Lloyd Rudolph, eds. *Reversing the Gaze: Amar Singh's Diary, A Colonial Subject's Narrative of Imperial India*. Colorado: Westview Press, 2002.

Rushbrook-Williams, L.F. *India in the Years 1917-1918: A Statement Prepared for Presentation to Parliament*. Calcutta: Government Printing Press, 1919.

Safrani, Abid Hasan, and Sisir Bose, eds. *Men from Imphal*. Kolkata: Netaji Research Bureau, 1971.

Sale, Lady. *A Journal of the Disasters in Afghanistan, 1841-42*. London: John Murray, 1843.

Sarbadhikari, Sisir. *Abhi Le Baghdad*. Calcutta: Privately Printed, 1957. Cited in 'Shared Sorrows: Indians and Armenians in the prison camps of Ras al-'Ain, 1916–18'. Amitav Ghosh (blog). https://www.amitavghosh.com/docs/Shared_Sorrows.pdf.

Seaton, Major-General Sir Thomas. *From Cadet to Colonel: The Record of a Life of Active Service*. Vol. 1. London: Hurst and Blackett, 1866.

Sherring, Rev. M.A. *The Indian Church during the Great Rebellion*. London: James Nisbett and Co., 1859.

Singh, Mohan. *Soldiers' Contribution to Indian Independence: The Epic of the Indian National Army*. Delhi: Army Educational Stores, 1974.

Sivaram, M. *The Road to Delhi*. Tokyo: C.E. Tuttle & Co., 1967.

Slim, William. *Defeat into Victory: Battling Japan in Burma and India, 1942–1945*. New York: Cooper Square Publishers, 2000.

Tuker, F.S. *While Memory Serves*. London: Cassell & Co, 1950.

Wilberforce, William. *Substance of the Speeches of William Wilberforce, Esq. on the Clause in the East-India Bill for Promoting the Religious Instruction and Moral Improvement of the Natives of the British Dominions in India*. London: J. Hatchard, J. Butterworth, and Cadell and Davies, 1813.

Williams, Capt. J. *An Historical Account of the Rise and Progress of the Bengal Infantry, from Its Formation in 1757 to 1796*. London: John Murray, 1817.

Books

Bandopadhyaya, Durgadas. *Bidrohe Bangali*. Calcutta: Patra Bharati, 1924.

Barat, Amiya. *The Bengal Native Infantry: Its Organisation and Discipline, 1796 to 1852*. Calcutta: Firma K.L. Mukhopadhyay, 1962.

Barker, A.J. *The Neglected War: Mesopotamia 1914–1918*. London: Faber & Faber, 1967.

Basu, Shrabani. *For King and Another Country: Indian Soldiers on the Western Front, 1914–1918*. London: Bloomsbury Paperbacks, 2015.

Bose, Sugata. *His Majesty's Opponent*. Harvard: Harvard University Press, 2010.

Beckett, Ian. *Ypres: The First Battle 1914*. Abingdon: Routledge, 2006.

Bishop, H.C.W. *A Kut Prisoner*. London: John Lane, 1920.

Brandon, Russell. *The Siege*. New York: The Viking Press, 1969.

Broome, Captain Arthur. *History of the Rise and Progress of the Bengal Army*. Vol. 1. London: Smith, Elder and Co., 1850.

Bryant, G.J. *The East India Company and Its Army, 1600–1778*. London: University of London, 1978.

—. *The Emergence of British Power in India 1600–1784: A Grand Strategic Interpretation*. Woodbridge: Boydell Press, 2013.

Butalia, R.C. *The Evolution of the Artillery in India: From the Battle of Plassey 1757 to the Revolt of 1857*. New Delhi: Allied Publishers, 1999.

Cadell, Patrick. *History of the Bombay Army*. New York: Green & Co., 1938.

Chandler, David G., and Ian Beckett, eds. *The Oxford History of the British Army*. Oxford: Oxford Paperbacks, 1996.

Clodfelter, Michael. *Warfare and Armed Conflicts—A Statistical Reference to Casualty and Other Figures, 1500–2000*. North Carolina: Jefferson Books, 2002.

Dalrymple, William. *The Anarchy: Corporate Violence, the East India Company and the Pillage of an Empire*. New Delhi: Bloomsbury Books, 2019.

—. *Return of a King: The Battle for Afghanistan*. Delhi: Bloomsbury Books, 2012.

Das, Santanu. *India, Empire, and First World War Culture: Writings, Images and Songs*. Cambridge: Cambridge University Press, 2018.

Deshpande, Anirudh *British Military Policy in India 1900–1945: Colonial Constraints and Declining Power*. Delhi: Manohar Books, 2005.

Dilks, David. *Curzon in India*. Vol. 1, *Achievement*. London: Hart-Davis, 1969.

Dodwell, Henry. *Sepoy Recruitment in the Old Madras Army*. Madras: Superintendent Government, 1922.

Ellis, John. *World War II—A Statistical Survey*. New York: Facts on File, 1993.

Edwardes, Herbert, and Herman Merivale. *Life of Sir Henry Lawrence*. Vol. 2. London: Smith Elder, 1872.

Evans, Lt Col. R. *A Brief Outline of the Campaign in Mesopotamia*. London: Sifton Praed & Co., 1926.

Fay, Peter. *The Forgotten Army: India's Armed Struggle for Independence, 1942–1945*. Michigan: University of Michigan Press, 1995.

Ferguson, Niall. *Empire: How Britain Made the Modern World.* London: Penguin Books, 2007.

Forrest, George W. *A History of the Indian Mutiny.* Vol. 1. New Delhi: Asian Educational Services, 2006.

Gardner, Nikolas *The Siege of Kut-al-Amara: At War in Mesopotamia, 1915-1916.* Indiana: Indiana University Press, 2016.

Gleig, George Robert. *Life of Sir Thomas Munro.* London: John Murray, 1849.

Gopal, Sarvepalli, ed., *Selected Works of Nehru.* Vol. 14. New Delhi: Orient Longman, 1981.

Gordon, Leonard. *Brothers against the Raj: A Biography of Indian Nationalists Sarat and Subhas Chandra Bose.* Delhi: Rupa & Co., 2015.

Gough, Hugh Henry. *Old Memories.* Edinburgh: W. Blackwood and Sons, 1897.

Grant, Reg G. *World War II: Europe.* London: Gareth Stevens Publishing, 2004.

Guy, Alan J., and Peter B. Borden, eds. *Soldiers of the Raj: The Indian Army 1600–1947.* London: National Army Museum, 1997.

Hansen, Waldemar. *The Peacock Throne: The Drama of Moghul India.* Delhi: Motilal Banarsidas, 1986.

Heathcote, T.A. *The Indian Army: The Garrison of British Imperial India, 1822–1922.* London: David and Charles, 1974.

—. *The Military in British India: The Development of British Land Forces in South Asia.* Barnsley: The Praetorian Press, 2013.

Henderson, George, and Thompson Olasiji, *Migrants, Immigrants and Slaves: Racial and Ethnic Groups in America.* Lanham: University Press of America, 1995.

Hill, S.C. *Yusuf Khan: The Rebel Commandant.* London: Longman, Greens and Co., 1914.

Holmes, T. Rice. *A History of the Indian Mutiny and of the Disturbances which Accompanied It among the Civil Population*. London: W. H. Allen & Co., 1891.

Howard, Michael. *War in European History*. Oxford: Oxford University Press, 2009.

Irvine, William. *The Army of the Indian Mughals: Its Organization and Administration*. London: Luzac & Co., 1903.

Jacob, John. *A Few Remarks on the Bengal Army and Furlough Regulations, with a View to Their Improvement, by a Bombay Officer [J. Jacob]. Repr., with Corrections*. London: Smith Elder and Co., 1857.

Kant, Vedica. *India and the First World War*. Delhi: Roli Books, 2014.

Kaye, Sir John. *History of the Indian Mutiny*. Vol. 1. Edited by G.B. Malleson. London: Longmans, Green and Co., 1909.

—. *A History of the Sepoy War in India*. Vol. 1. London: W. H. Allen and Co., 1880.

Khan, Yasmin. *The Raj at War: A People's History of the Second World War*. London: Vintage Books, 2015.

Kolff, Dirk H.A. *Naukar, Rajput and Sepoy: The Ethnohistory of the Military Labour Market in Hindustan, 1450–1850*. Cambridge: Cambridge University Press, 1990.

Krivosheev, G.F., ed. *Soviet Casualties and Combat Losses in the Twentieth Century*. London: Greenhill Books, 1997.

Lawson, Konrad Mitchell. 'Wartime Atrocities and the Politics of Treason in the Ruins of the Japanese Empire, 1937–1953'. PhD diss., Harvard University, 2012.

Longer, V. *Red Coats to Olive Green: A History of the Indian Army*. New Delhi: Allied Publishers, 1974.

Love, Henry Davison. *Vestiges of Old Madras*, Vol. 3. London: John Murray, 1913.

Lucas, Sir Charles, ed. *The Empire at War*. Vol. 1. London: Oxford University Press, 1921.

Mackenzie, A.R.D. *Mutiny Memoirs.* Allahabad: Pioneer Press, 1891.

Macrory, Patrick. *Signal Catastrophe: The Story of the Disastrous Retreat from Kabul, 1842.* London: Book Club Associates, 1972.

Maddison, Angus. *The World Economy: A Millennial Perspective.* Paris: OECD Publications, 2001.

Malleson, Colonel G.B. *The Decisive Battles of India from 1746 to 1849.* London: W.H. Allen & Co., 1885.

Marston, Daniel P., and Chandar S. Sundaram, eds. *A Military History of India and South Asia: From the East India Company to the Nuclear Era.* Bloomington: Indiana University Press, 2008.

Masani, Z. *Indian Tales of the Raj.* Berkeley: University of California Press, 1992.

Mason, Philip. *A Matter of Honour: An Account of the Indian Army, Its Officers and Men.* London: Jonathan Cape Ltd, 1974.

McNabb, David E. *Oil and the Creation of Iraq: Policy Failures and the 1914–1918 War in Mesopotamia.* London: Routledge Books, 2016.

Menezes, S.L. *Fidelity and Honour: The Indian Army from the Seventeenth Century to the Twenty-First Century.* New Delhi: Oxford University Press, 1999.

Moon, Sir Penderel. *The British Conquest and Dominion of India, Part One and Two.* New Delhi: India Research Press, 1999.

Morton-Jack, George. *The Indian Empire at War: From Jihad to Victory, the Untold Story of the Indian Soldiers in the First World War.* London: Little & Brown Publishing, 2018.

Mukherjee, Rudrangshu. *Awadh in Revolt, 1857-58: A Study of Popular Resistance.* London: Anthem South Asia Studies, 2002.

Nolan, Cathal J. *Wars of the Age of Louis XIV, 1650–1715: An Encyclopedia of Global Warfare and Civilization.* Westport: Greenwood, 2008.

Omissi, David. *The Sepoy and the Raj: The Indian Army, 1860–1940 (Studies in Military and Strategic History)*. London: Palgrave MacMillan, 1998.

Orwell, George. *Burmese Days*. New York: Harper, 1934.

Overmans, Rüdiger. *Deutsche militärische Verluste im Zweiten Weltkrieg*. Berlin: Oldenbourg, 2000.

Oxford Dictionary of Quotations, 2nd ed. London: Oxford University Press, 1953.

Parker, Geoffrey. *The Military Revolution: Military Innovation and the Rise of the West, 1500–1800*. Cambridge: Cambridge University Press, 1996.

—. *The Thirty Years' War*. London: Routledge Books, 1997.

Pandey, B.N. *The Break-Up of British India: Making of the Twentieth Century*. London: MacMillan Books, 1969.

Prabhupada, His Divine Grace A.C. Bhaktivedanta Swami. *Bhagavad-Gita: As It Is*. Mumbai: The Bhaktivedanta Book Trust, 1986.

Raghavan, Srinath. *India's War: The Making of Modern South Asia, 1939–1945*. London: Penguin Books, 2017.

Roberts, P.E. *History of British India*. Delhi: Oxford University Press India, 1978.

Roy, Kaushik, ed. *The Indian Army in the Two World Wars*. Leiden: Brill, 2012.

Sandes, Major F.W.C. *In Kut and Captivity with the Sixth Indian Division*. London: John Murray, 1919.

Sen, Surendra Nath. *Eighteen Fifty-Seven*. New Delhi: The Publications Division, Ministry of Information and Broadcasting, Government of India, 1957.

Sen, Surendra Nath. *The Military System of the Marathas*. Calcutta: Orient Longmans, 1928.

Sheppard, E.W. *A Short History of the British Army*. London: Constable, 1959.

Sinha, Narendra Krishna. *Ranjit Singh*. Calcutta: A.R. Mukherjee, 1951.
Smith, C.B.W. *Florence Nightingale*. London: Constable, 1952.
Spear, Percival. *The Nabobs: A Study of the Social Life of the English in Eighteenth-Century India*. Oxford: Oxford University Press, 1963.
Tharoor, Shashi. *An Era of Darkness*. New Delhi: Aleph Book Company, 2016.
Toye, Hugh. *The Springing Tiger: The Indian National Army and Subhas Chandra Bose*. London: Cassell Publishing, 1959.
Trench, Charles. *The Indian Army and the King's Enemies 1900–1947*. London: Thames and Hudson, 1988.
Tunzelmann, Alex von. *Indian Summer: The Secret History of the End of an Empire*. London: Simon & Schuster Books UK, 2012.
Wickremesekera, Channa. *'Best Black Troops in the World': British Perceptions and the Making of the Sepoy, 1746–1805*. Delhi: Manohar Books, 2002.
Wilcox, Ron. *Battles on the Tigris: The Mesopotamian Campaigns of the First World War*. London: Pen & Sword Military, 2006.
Wilson, Jon. *India Conquered: Britain's Raj and the Passions of Empire*. Delhi: Simon & Schuster India, 2016.
Wilson, Lieutenant-Colonel W.J. *History of the Madras Army*. Vols. 1, 2 and 3. Madras: E. Keys, 1882.

Newspapers, Journals, Databases and Web Portals

Al Jazeera. https://www.aljazeera.com/.
Big Think. https://bigthink.com/.
Bolt, Jutta, Robert Inklaar, Herman de Jong and Jan Luiten van Zanden. Maddison Project Database, ver. 2018. https://www.rug.nl/ggdc/historicaldevelopment/maddison/.
The Bombay Times.

British Army website. https://www.army.mod.uk/.
'The British Empire Is "Something to Be Proud Of"'. YouGov, website of the government of UK. https://yougov.co.uk/topics/politics/articles-reports/2014/07/26/britain-proud-its-empire.
British Military History. https://www.britishmilitaryhistory.co.uk.
The Columbia Undergraduate Journal of South Asian Studies.
Eighteenth Century Collections Online. https://quod.lib.umich.edu/e/ecco/.
The Friend of India.
Ghosh, Amitav. Amitav Ghosh (blog). https://www.amitavghosh.com/.
The Hindu.
The Indo-British Review: A Journal of History.
Journal of Contemporary History.
Journal of Early Modern History.
'La IIIe République, 1919–1940'. *Code Officiel Géographique.* Statistique générale de la France. https://www.insee.fr/fr/information/2560452.
London Review of Books.
'Making Britain: Discover How South Asians Shaped the Nation, 1870–1950'. The Open University Database. https://www.open.ac.uk/researchprojects/makingbritain/.
New World Economics. https://newworldeconomics.com.
The North British Review.
The Quarterly Review.
The Times.
The Tribune.

Index

Abdali, Ahmad Shah, 36, 50, 59
Abyssinian campaign, 14
Adolphus, Gustavus, 26
Afghanistan, 11, 17, 103, 160–163, 165, 167, 169, 173, 181–182, 194, 206, 212, 267–268; attacks, 160, 175; campaign, 111, 162, 181–182, 196, 230; civilians ally with US and British, 160; knives, 170, 183; Persian siege of Herat in, 163; war, 14, 66, 151, 184
Afghans, 34–36, 47, 50, 55, 96, 161–162, 167–171, 173–176, 178–180, 182–183, 196
Africa, 3–4, 10, 207; campaign in, 183; soldiers, 62
agitation, 149, 154, 224, 237, 288, see also mutiny, rebellions, revolutions
Ahmed, Syed Sir, 217
aide-de-camp (ADC), 148
Akbar, 2, 32, 174, 178

Alam II, Shah, 54–57
Alexander, A.V., 297
Ali, Hyder, 54, 59, 62, 94, 97, 133, 227, 265
Ali, Muhammad, 40, 43–47, 62
Ambala, 104, 239
ambulances, 113, 189–190
Ambur, battle at, 43
American Navy, 278; soldier, 287
American War of Independence, 11
Anglo–Afghan war, first, 83
Anglo–Jat war, 216
Anglo–Maratha war, 13, 66, 133, 138; third, 13
Anglo– Mysore war, 97
Anglo–Sikh war in 1849, 119
Anwaruddin, 39, 43; killing of, 43
Apa Sahib, 66
Arcot, 43, 45–48, 60–61, 102, 223; garrison, 46
Armenians, 197–204; concentration camps, 197; mohajers, 200–202;

survivors, 161; victims, 161; village, 198; woman, 199–200
Army of Retribution, 103
'army of the Indus', 163
artillery, 26, 29, 58, 60, 125–126, 162, 186, 190, 229, 241–244, 248, 251, 263; regulation of, 126
Asia, 3, 17, 235, 270–271, 273; campaign in, 183
atrocities, 196–198, see also massacres
Attlee, Clement, 259, 297–298
Auchinleck, Claude, Gen., 16, 158, 289–291, 293–294
Aurangzeb, 31–33, 38, 265; death of, 32–33; letter to Azam, 33; rise of, 30; and temple destructions, 31
Australia, 4, 6, 157, 207
Austrian War, 11–12, 39
Awadh, 35, 53, 54, 56–58, 74, 99, 103, 118–119, 212, 236, 246
Aylmer, General, 114
'Azad Hind Fauj' (Independent Indian Army), 275, see also Indian National Army (INA)

Baghdad, 113–114, 187–188, 194–196, 201; Indian prisoners in, 196
Bahadur, Banda, 33
Bahadur, Jang, 254
Baker, Godfrey Evan, 72–73
Bala Hisar Fort, 169
Balfour, Arthur, 4
Balparveshi, 96
Baluchis, 118; brigands, 165; knives, 166
Barkatullah, Maulana, 264

Barrackpore cantonment, 227, 229, 236, 238, 240–241, 243–247
Basra, 113, 187–188, 190–191, 194
battalions, 22–23, 26, 50, 52–53, 57, 60, 101, 103–107, 126, 129, 132–134, 220, 222, 241–242
Battle of Buxar, 56–57, 119, 132–133
Battle of Chamkaur, 32
Battle of Ctesiphon, 113
Battle of Helsa, 55
Battle of Midway, 274
Battle of Plassey, 52
Baugh, Lt., 237
bazaars, 221, 230, 247, 250
Beg, Mustafa, 222
belief system, 62, 71; and Hindu sepoys, 226, see also faith
Bengal, 35–36, 38–39, 48–57, 81, 99–100, 111, 118–119, 122, 130, 132, 276; province of, 54, 132
Bengal Ambulance Corps, 189
Bengal Army, 55–58, 72, 74, 90–91, 103–104, 107–108, 117, 119–120, 138, 163–164, 214, 236; Kindersley on, 133; rebellion and disintegration, 21; sepoys, 53, 56, 103, 167, 227
Bengal Native Infantry, 66, 105–106, 119, 171–172, 176, 236, 243
Bengal Presidencies, 89, 129
Bentinck, William, Lord, 89, 116, 215, 219, 222, 225
Berhampore, 241–242
Best, Thomas, Capt., 2
Bharatpur, 13, 66, 138, 219; fall of, 162
Bharatpur Fort, 216
bharatvarsha, 109
Bhutan campaign, 14

Bihar, 48, 52, 71, 100, 119, 212, 236, 253; zamindars, 54
black commandant, 60, 129, 132–133, 135
Boer War, 142–143
Bolarum, 230, 232–233, 244
Bombay, 37, 49, 57, 122, 126, 169, 227, 294–297; clashes, 296; garrison, 57, 211; mutiny, 295
Bombay Army, 14, 57, 103, 110, 123, 132–133, 163–164, 167, 213–214, 253
Bombay Regiment, 211
bombers, 279; B-29 American, 278–279
Bose, Subhas Chandra (Netaji), 22, 49, 261–262, 265–271, 273–282, 284–286, 293; army, 276–277; arrest of, 267; and Hitler, 267; as President of INC, 266; reaching Taipei, 281; in Singapore, 283; speeches, 294; in Tokyo, 274
Bose, Anita, 271
Bose, Biswanath, 294–295
Bose, Rash Behari, 273–275
Boxer Rebellion, 18, 143–145, 183
Branson, Clive, 283
Brighton Hospital, 84–85, 256
Britain, 3–7, 9–12, 16–21, 25, 184–186, 188, 194, 258–259, 276, 283, 291; loosing America in 1781, 11; over Kenya, 258
British: colonial possessions, 4; defence expenditure, Ferguson on, 19; exchequer, 16, 18, 186–187, 259; forces, 93, 97, 108, 110–111, 124–125, 128–129, 156, 161, 195–197, 223, 232; Imperial allies, 160; military intelligence, 273; officers, 84, 122–123, 130, 132, 138, 140, 142, 146–148, 152–154, 158, 175, 194–195, 235–237, 293–294, 296–297; re-conquer Delhi, 119; surrender at Kut-al-Amara, 108; troops, 18, 93, 108, 110, 128, 141, 188, 192, 194–195, 288, 296
British Army, 10–11, 20, 143, 145, 152, 183–184, 187, 212, 277
British Empire, 1–2, 5, 7–9, 12, 14, 20, 23, 110, 116, 182, 184, 186
British Expeditionary Force (BEF), 63
British Indian Army, 2, 12, 14, 16, 20, 24–25, 58, 66, 83, 115, 139, 144, 147, 185, 188–189, 202–203, 206, 257, 262, 264, 273; in Singapore, 22
British Raj, 14, 115, 129, 141–144, 154, 158, 256, 260, 276, 277; Ferguson on, 14
brutality, 33, 49, 196, 288–289
Bryant, Gerald, 94
Bulkley, Lieutenant, 131
Burke, Edmund, 32
Burma, 11, 16, 30, 162, 227, 266, 277–280, 282, 286; campaign, 282; theatre, 22, 112, 184, 278; wars, 14; war with, 227
Burma–India border, 276
Burns, Alexander, Sir, 168
Bussy, Marquis de, 39, 45, 47–48, 50, 54
Buxar, 56–57, 100, 119, 127, 132–133

Caillaud, Maj., 55
Caley, Maj., 106–107

camp: Crescent Moon, 263; Indian, 162, 177; Nisibeen hospital, 201; Ras al-Ain prisoner, 196–198, 200–201, 203–204
Canning, Lady, 243
Canning, Lord, 124, 240
capitulation, 182, 289, 293
Carnac, Major, 55
Carnatic wars, 13
cartridges, 100, 127, 208, 237–242, 245–246, 252, see also guns; rifles
Cartwright, Col., 228
Casey, Gov., 287
caste, 68, 86–88, 120, 213–214, 217, 219, 226–227, 238–239; Brahmins, 50, 119, 212, 219, 226, 229, 236; high-caste, 214, 239; kshatriyas, 77–78, 81; related rituals, 213
Caste Disabilities Removal Act in 1850, 217
casualties, 113, 187–191, 194
Cavagnari, Louis, Sir., 182
cavalry, 26, 28–29, 85–86, 123, 126, 178, 233–235, 241–242, 244–245, 248–251
Cavalry regiment, 231
Central Legislative Assembly (CLA), 152
Chandarnagore, 38; French garrison, 51
Child, Josiah, Sir, 38
children and women, 160, 169; sold as slaves, 176
China, 11, 18, 143–145, 183, 241
China Wars, 14, 142
Christianity, 217, 233, 243, see also missionaries

Christians, 210, 218, 225, 232, 244, 252
Churchill, Winston, 4
civil jail, 247
Clive, Robert Capt., 5, 7, 20, 46–47, 50–55, 57–58, 61, 97, 118–119, 130–131, 267, 283–284: and Mir Jafar, 52, 54; to relieving Ali, 46
Cobbe Scheme, 152
code of conduct, 77, 82, 102. See also discipline
colonialism, 207
colonies, 6, 259
Commander-in-Chief (C-in-C), 25, 28, 30, 101, 103–107, 137–138, 214, 219–221, 225, 227–229, 238–241, 243–244, 249, 283, 285
commissariat fort, 170
Company Army, 129, 163
conflicts, 11, 19, 35–36, 39, 47, 49, 55, 68, 80, 222, 227
Congress–INA campaign, 290
Congress of Vienna in 1814-15, 3
Conolly, Capt, 177
'no conscription,' 12
Constantinople, 194, 263
coolies, 145, 147, 151
Coote, Eyre, 55
co-religionists, 33, 197, 210
Cornwallis, Lord, 13, 133, 214
Cosgrave, Sergeant, 222
cost of maintenance, 92–93
court martial, 93, 105, 107, 229, 238, 246, see also trials
Cradock, John, Sir, 219–220, 222, 225
Craigie, Edmund, Capt., 245, 250
Creagh, O'Moore, Gen., 148
Crimean War, 11, 127

criminals, 10
Cripps, Stafford, Sir, 298
Crown's rule, 5, 13, 17, 22, 98, 255, see also British Empire
cruelty, 197, 229
Ctesiphon, 113, 187–188, 192, 194, 205
Cunningham, G. Sir, 258, 288
Curzon, George, Lord, 4, 142, 147, 153

Dalhousie, Gov.-Gen. Lord, 232, 235
Dalton, Capt., 61
Dast, Mir, 263
Dayal, Prabhu, 85
Deccan sultanates, 31
deception, 104, 291
defence spending, 19
Defoe, Daniel, 10
Delhi cantonment, 238
Desai, Bhulabai, 285
despotism, 21, 301
dharma, 76–77
Dhillon, Gurbaksh Singh, Lt., 280, 285, 289, 292–293
disbanding, 106–107, 261
disciplining, 146
discrimination, 21, 98–100, 108, 111–112, 114, 143, 152, 156–157, 161, 196–197
disease, 24, 83, 111, 196, 283
disobedience, 246, 297
divisions and differences, 118
Dogra Company, 64–65
Dogras, 64–65, 85, 121, 279
Dragoon Guards (Carabiniers), 192, 244
Duke of Connaught, 15

Dunkirk, 16, 126
Dupleix, Joseph Francoise, 38–40, 42–43, 45, 47–48
Durgavati, Rani, 80–81
Durlabh, Rai, 51
Durrani, Ahmad Shah, 35
Dutt, Shri, 87

East Africa, 14, 16
East India Company (EIC), 2, 12–13, 20, 24, 36–38, 42, 46–49, 51–57, 59–62, 68–69, 71, 90–91, 94–100, 117–120, 138–139, 162–163, 210–216, 255, 263; armies, 20, 24, 66, 69, 120, 125, 138, 211
Eden Commission, 126
Edmond, E., 218, 230
Effendi, Saghir, 199
Egypt, 11, 14–16
Elphinstone, Lord, 126, 169, 174, 176–177, 194
Emilie, 271
Emperor of Hindustan, 13, 30, 35
Empires, 2, 9, 30–31, 162
English: factory, 2, 38; prisoners, 180, 267; prisoners at Fort William, 49; women, 112, 176
English East India Company, 58
entertainment, 92, 125
equal pay demands, 93, 108
Esher Committee, 152
Ethiopia, 11, 16
European(s), 28–29, 46–47, 59, 125–127, 136, 166, 170–173, 178–179, 184–185, 211, 222–225, 234, 237, 244–245, 248–252, 287–290, 295; officers, 60, 94, 129, 131–135, 168, 213, 229, 235,

249; regiment, 58, 72, 76, 161, 170, 178, 222, 228–229, 242–243; sailors, 211; trading companies, 12, 24, 35–36; troops, 17, 24, 50, 56, 58, 99–100, 102, 127, 133–134, 163–164, 166, 170–171, 238, 247–248, 251
executions, 32–33, 47, 52, 102, 105, 284, 289
exploitation, 19, 185, see also discrimination

faith, 31, 82–83, 118, 120, 207–210, 214, 216, 218–221, 223–224, 227–229, 232–236, 247, 253–255, 257–258, 262
Farrukhsiyar, 34, 38
Ferguson, Niall, 1, 5, 9, 14, 19, 110
Ferozepore, 106, 163, 181
festival: Eid, 212, 254; Muharram, 212, 231, 233–234
Finnis, John, Col., 249
Flanders, 15, 63–64
Foot Regiment, 25, 29, 243
forced marches, 196–197, 275
Forde, Colonel, 53
fortifications, 29, 49
Fort Louis, 38
Fort St. David, 37–38, 40–42, 44, 46, 53, 55, 127, 211; French siege of, 40, 42–43
Fort St. George, 37–38, 40–41, 130
Fort St. George Council, 127
Fort William, 37–38, 49–51
Forward Bloc, 287
French, 12–14, 38–46, 48–51, 53–55, 57, 60–62, 99, 102, 130–131, 138, 186, 211; army/forces, 40, 45, 48, 53–55, 62, 147; Army Corps to, 15; captured the Fort of Gingee, 45; companies, 41–42; pursued Muhammad Ali, 46; siege of Madras, 53, 61; surrendered Pondicherry, 55; trading company, 38; trading post, 38, 51
French–British rivalry, 12
Frere, Bartle, Sir, 124
Fujiwara, 272–273

Gandhi, Mahatma, 262, 266, 297
GDP, 19, 90, 185
Gentoos, 119, 227
George, Lloyd, 153
George V, King, 86
George VI, King, 297–298
Germans, 11, 63–65, 190, 201–202, 263–264, 267–269, 271–272, 274, 282–284
Germany, 263–264, 267–269, 272, 274, 284; Army of, 188; Grenadier battalions, 64
Ghadr movement, 262
Ghazees, 172
Ghazni, 166, 181
Ghilzai tribes, and 37th Native Infantry, 176
Gillespie, Colonel, 223–224
Gobind Singh, Guru, 33, 84
golandauz, 125
Goldney, Capt., 107
Gordon, Leonard, 280
Gough, Viscount, 89, 96, 105, 249–250
Great War. See World War I
grievances, 100, 102, 104, 106, 130, 134–135, 208, 241
gulf, 1, 88–89, 93, 127, 187
gunners, 131; Indian, 126

guns (see also rifles), 26, 46, 79, 101–102, 125–127, 176, 222–224, 229, 242, 252, 294–295; anti-aircraft, 295; Oerlikon anti-aircraft, 296; Turkish machine, 190
Gurkhas, 66, 78, 86, 121–122, 162, 189, 253, 291; regiment, 93, 108; war, 14
Guru Granth Sahib, 257

Habibullah, 264
Hamilton, George, Lord, 142
hangings, 36, 62, 189, 224, 229, 238, 243, 286, see also executions
Hanuman, jamadar, 74
Hasan, Abid, 268, 271, 279
Hastings, Warren, 5, 98, 214–215, 220
Hathras Fort, 263
havildars, 60, 90, 99, 132, 135, 171–172, 181
healthcare, 110, 112, 114; and Indian soldiers, 112
Hearsey, John Bennett, Maj.-Gen., 237, 239
Heber, Bishop, 1
Her Majesty's Native Indian Land Forces (HMNILF), 142–143, 150
Heron, Alexander, Col., 130
Hewitt, General, 246
Hewson, James, Serg.-Maj., 237
Hindu–Muslim unity, 254
Hindus/ Hindoos, 30–31, 117–118, 166, 212, 215–217, 220–221, 224, 229, 231, 239–241, 245, 248, 252, 255–256, see also castes; faith
Hiroshima and Nagasaki, bombings of, 281
Hitler, Adolf, 3, 267–268, 270–271

HMIS Assam, 295
HMIS Bahadur, 295–296
HMIS Chamak, 296
HMIS Himalaya, 296
HMIS Hindustan, 296
HMIS Talwar, 294
Holwell, John, 49
horrors, 101, 180; of forced march, 196
horse artillery, 179, 228
hospitals, 76, 84, 87, 111–113, 191, 198, 205, 216, 230, 279, 281, (see also healthcare); Aleppo, 198–199, 204; French, 149; Kitchener, 112; in Nisibeen, 199
hospital ships, 113
House of Timur, 32, 34
Hughes, Capt., 145–146
human bonds, 197, 205
Hunt, J.C., Col., 104–105, 271
Hunter, Com. Maj.-Gen., 104–105
Huseyn, Jemadar Muhammad, 231
Hydar, Ghazidin, 74
Hyderabad, 35, 37, 40, 42–45, 48, 50, 54, 57, 118, 225

Imad-ul-Mulk, 54–55
imperial: army, 33, 123; authorities, 32, 150, 161; memorial in Delhi, 15; systems, 161, 197; wars, 6
Imperial Cadet Corps (ICC), 142–143, 147, 150
Imperial State Troops (ISTs), 143–145, 148
Imphal, 276–278, 280; theatre, 279
imprisonments, 105, see also prisoners
independence, 11, 19, 35, 130, 264, 274, 298–299

India–Burma border, 277
India Independence League (IIL), 272–275
Indian: airmen, 296; military college, 141; nationalist movement, 259; officers, 42, 65, 129, 140, 144, 146–147, 152–155, 157–158, 195, 222, 289–291; taxes, 18, 187; taxpayers, 18–19, 182
Indian Armed Forces, 291
Indian Army, 13–19, 21, 23–24, 116, 120, 124–125, 139–140, 142–145, 147–148, 150–154, 157–158, 182–188, 260–261, 289–290, 292–293; at Basra, 187; cavalry in Europe, 86; conquest of Jawa, 14; diversity in, 120; international expedition of, 14; in London, 120; Mason on payment for, 18; role in Imperial defence, 18; as 'strategic imperial reserve,' 13, 17; suffering of, 16
Indian Civil Service (ICS), 139
Indian Commissioned Officers (ICOs), 150, 156–157, 260–261, 272–273, 293
Indian Empire, 3, 7, 21, 153, 162
Indianization, 139–141, 151–159, 260, 272
Indian Lahore Division, 185
Indian Legion, 268–269, 284, in Germany, 272
Indian Military Academy (IMA), 156–157
Indian National Army (INA), 22, 261–262, 272–279, 281–290, 292–293; 'Chalo Delhi,' 275, 278; comrades, 281, 297; death rate, 282–283; First Division, 276–277, 279; flag, 283; forces, 22–23, 275–278, 280, 282–285; front-line units in Burma, 282; hospital, 279; memorabilia, 286; prisoners, 284–286; releasing officers of, 293; trials, 287, 289, 292–293
Indian National Congress (INC), 141–142, 259, 266
Indians, as inferiors, 146, see also discrimination
Indian women vs English women, 174, 176
industrial revolution, 3, 6–7
Infantry, 103, 106–107; battalion, 29, 74, 102, 105, 108, 135, 242, 297; regiment, 161, 244, 178; units, 26, 125
'Inqilab Zindabad,' 272
insubordination, 23, 40, 100–101, 107, 151, 241. See also disobedience; discipline
intermediaries, 59, 155
invasions, 162–163, 273–274
Iraq, 16, 188, 261; theatre, 22
Irregular Awadh battalion, 246
Irvine, William, 95
Isouf Cawn, 61
ISTs. See Imperial State Troops
Italy, 16, 274

Jacob, John, 93
Jagdalak pass, 178–179
jagir system, 28, 97
Jahan, Shah, 38
Jahanara, 38
Jahangir, 2
Jajau, 34
Jamaica, 11

Index

James II, King, 38
Jang, Salabat, 48
Japanese Army, 157, 160, 269, 271, 274, 277, 279, 282
Jasjee, 145–146
Jats, 28, 31–35, 50, 78, 86–87, 118, 121, 123, 211, 213, 219, see also peasant rebellion
'jauhar,' 65, 80–81
Java, 14, 103
'jawhar,' 81–82
jemadars, 59–60, 64–65, 69, 73–74, 90, 92, 129, 132, 134, 140, 144, 231, 248
Jemaul Sahib, 130–131, 134
Jennings, Capt., 99–100
'jewel in the crown', 2–3, 9
jiziya, 31
Jodhpur Lancers, 143–144, 147
Jung, Muzaffar, 35, 43–46; Afghans killing of, 47
Jung, Nasir, 43–45; assassination of, 45–46; summoned Muhammad Ali, 44
Jung, Salabat, 47–48, 50, 54

Kabul, 35, 66, 68, 70, 83, 162-164, 167-168, 172, 175, 179, 181–183, 232, 263–264; garrison, 168, 174, 179; with Uzbek retainers, 172
Kaiser, 3, 83, 263
'kala pani' (black water), 276
Kandahar, 163, 166–169, 181
Karachi sailors, 296
Khalsa Army, 108, 120
Khan, Aga, 232–233
Khan, Aga Muhammad, 232–233
Khan, Akbar, 173–178, 180, 182
Khan, Alivardi, 35, 48–49

Khan, Bakht, 138
Khan, Bilund, 233–234
Khan, Chin Qilich. See Nizam-ul-Mulk
Khan, Dost Mohammad, 95, 163, 167, 172–173, 182
Khan, Fateh Mahomed, 87
Khan, Gufoor, 234
Khan, Ibrahim, 81
Khan, Jemadar Sultan, 87
Khan, Kunar, 85
Khan, Mahfuz, 40, 43
Khan, Mohammad Akbar, 172
Khan, Nizam Ali, 57
Khan, Qasim, 81–82
Khan, Shah Nawaz, 280
Khan, Shah Wali, 63
Khan, Shanawaz, Capt., 271
Khan, Taj, 81
Khan, Wazir, 33
Khan, Yasmin, 90
Khan, Yusuf, 53, 61–62, 130, 134; rebellion of, 131
Kiani, Mohammad Zaman, Maj. Gen., 276, 279
Kindersley, 133
King's Commissioned Indian Officers (KCIOs), 150, 152, 154–157
King's Commissioned Officers (KCOs), 140, 142, 150–152, 154–156
Kipling, Rudyard, 1
Kitchener, 256
Kohima, 276–278, 280; Nagas of, 278
Kursk offensive, 274
Kut-al-Amara, 108–109, 114, 160, 184, 189–190, 192, 195, 205, 264

Lakshmi Bai, Jhansi Rani, 253, 276, 280
Lally, French Commander, 53, 55, 62
Lal Paltan battalion, 20, 50
lascars, 125
Lauriston, Jean Law de, 51
Lawrence, Henry, Sir, 92, 129, 135, 182, 246–247; death of, 136
Lawrence, John, 253
Lawrence, Stringer, Maj., 41–43, 125, 127
Lawrence, Walter, Sir, 122–123, 256
Linlithgow, Viceroy Lord, 259
Longer, V., 92
Lord Clive's Fund, 97
loyalty, 21, 23, 79, 82, 85, 88, 115, 117, 120, 260, 262, 264, 267

Macaulay, Lord, 1
Mackenzie, Colin, Brig., 172, 230–235, 244, 250
MacMunn, 122
Macnaghten, William Lord, 167–169, 174–175, 178
Macrory, Patrick, 175
Madras, 37, 40, 42–44, 49, 53, 57, 61–62, 122, 125–126, 131, 221–222, 227; cavalry, 223; contingent for Manila, 17; restoration to British, 42
Madras Army, 14, 48, 60, 122–123, 125, 132–133, 163, 214, 227, 253
Madras Council, 49–50, 131
Madras Native Infantry, 53, 102, 106–107, 161, 227; battalion of, 102, 214

Madras Presidency, 90, 129, 131, 219, 224
Madurai, 61–62
Mahal, Begum Hazrat, 253
Mahars, 213
Mahmud II, Sultan, 80
Mahomet, Dean, 71–74
Mal, Suraj, 35, 50, 265
Malaya, 14, 16, 273, 277, 280
Malayan theatre, 272
Malcolm, John, Sir, 130, 136
Marathas/ Mahratta, 28, 31, 33–35, 41, 43, 47, 55, 59, 78, 83, 118, 122; army, 28, 96; invasions, 118; military commanders, 28; raids, 36; wars, 13, 66, 133, 138, 213
Mariana Islands, American Navy attacking, 278
Martial Races of India, The, 121
Mason, Philip, 13, 18
massacres, 35, 168, 173
Matthews, Major H. W., 240
Maurice of Nassau, 25
Mauritius, 11, 40
McMunn, George, 121
Medical services/support, 111, 113, 186–187, 189–190
Meerut, 63, 68, 106, 147, 157, 185, 244, 248, 250–252, 254, 286; cantonment, 244
Menezes, S.L., 191
Merewether, Col., 65
Mesopotamia, 15, 82–83, 113, 149, 161, 183–184, 186–188, 190, 194, 257; campaign, 111, 183–184, 206; Commission, 205; Ottoman armies in, 15; theatre, 111
Metcalfe, Charles, Sir, 13

Index

military: contractors, 59; Hindus in Muslim, 209; human resources, 9; labour market, 59, 94–95; revolution, 25, 30
military-political system, 25
Mir Jafar, 51–56, 97, 99; Miran as son of, 55
Mir Kasim, 55–57, 99
Mir Madan, 52
missionaries, 216–218, 226, 240, 255–256
mistrust, 58, 116, 124, 137, 236, 250, 253
Mitchell, Col., 241–242
Moghul, Mirza, 138
Montagu–Chelmsford, 149
Moormen, 119
morale, 85, 152, 166, 170, 185, 289
Morrison, Herbert, 259
Moseley, Lt.-Col., 104–105
Moslems, 123, 179
motivations, 22, 62, 64, 71, 83–84, 88, 117, 162, 185, 188, 282
Mountbatten, Viceroy Lord, 258
Mughal Empire, 12, 28, 30–36, 38, 40, 47, 59, 95, 117, 209–210; armies of, 28, 35, 59, 129
Mukherjee, Kalyan, Capt., 192, 195
Mundy, Peter, 118
Munro, Hector, Maj., 56–58, 99, 101, 136
muskets, 25, 41, 124, 127, 137, 224, 229, 237–238, 242, 249, 252; Brown Bess, 238; depots, 239
Muslims/Mahommedan/Musalmans, 117–119, 121, 217, 220–221, 224, 228, 233, 236, 239–240, 244–245, 254–255, 262, 268; soldiers as, 78, 81, 197, 212, 245, 256
Mutaguchi, Gen., 278
mutineers, 68, 99, 101, 223, 229, 235, 251, 285, 298
Mutiny/Revolt 1857, 17, 20–21, 23, 98, 100, 102–103, 107–108, 117, 119–121, 124–128, 130, 137, 208, 223, 229–230, 242–244, 247, 250–253, 285–287, 290–293, 298
Mysore, 59; force, 47

naiks, 60, 90, 99, 107, 132
Nandi, Gopinath, Rev., 217
Napoleon, 3, 11, 14, 219; war against, 20
Narain, Ram, 52–55
Nathan, Mirza, 82
Nationalist: leaders, 154, 157, 262; movement, 21, 117, 259, 262
native: artillery units, 125–126; battalions, 56, 101, 228, 241; gunners, 125–126; infantry, 127, 171–172, 176, 239, 243–244, 249; officers, 53, 60, 62, 129–137, 144, 166, 209–210, 215, 241–242, 248; Nightingale on troops of 111; ruling elite, 31; sepoys, 53, 59, 102, 117, 125, 240; soldiers, 89, 94, 97, 111, 115, 125, 127, 182, 219, 225, 235, 241; troops, 58, 111, 116, 127, 245, 247–249
Nawab /nabobs, 5, 57, 40–41, 43, 50–53, 56, 62, 92, 99–100, 102, 267
Nawab of Arcot, 48, 102
Nawab of Bengal, 36, 38, 49–50, 52, 55–56

Index

Nawab of Carnatic, 39–40, 43–45; French-installing, 44
Nawab of Murshidabad, 72
Nawaz, Shah, Capt., 278, 280, 285, 289, 292–293
Nazis, 142, 267
Nehru, Jawaharlal, 285, 292–293, 298
New Zealand, 4, 6, 11, 207
Nicholson, FM, 10
Nightingale, Florence, 110–111
Nine Years' War (1688–97), 10
Nisbeen Armenians, 201
Nixon, General, 191
Nizam, 35–37, 40–41, 43, 47, 58–59, 141
Nizam-ul-Mulk, 42–43, 47–48, 54
non-commissioned officers (NCOs), 140
non-violence, 262, 266, see also Gandhi, Mahatma
Norgate, J.T., Lt. Col., 66
North America, 3, 6, 11, 207
North-West Frontier, 183, 288
Nott, Brigadier, 167–169, 181

Oliver, James, Capt., 214
Omichand, 51
Oriental Seas, 14
Orme, Robert, 130
Orr, Capt., 231
Orwell, George, 21
Osborne, Capt., 95
Ottoman: army, 15, 82, 108, 160, 184, 187–188, 201; genocide, 161; prisoner camps, 205

Paget, Edward, Sir, 90, 228
Palmerston, Lord, 256
Paltoo, Sheikh, 237
Pandey, Mangal, 236–238, 242–243, 246, 286; hanging of, 238
Pandey, Sita Ram, Sub., 66–71, 74–75, 120, 135–136, 165–167, 170–171, 173, 178–181
Panipat, 55, 59
Panjam, Jarj, 83
Paradis, Louis, Capt, 40
Pasha, Khalil, 194
Pashtun tribes, 14
Patel, Vallabh Bhai, 287, 296
Patnaik, Utsa, 6
payments: 20, 28, 94, 96–97, 99, 104, 108–110, 168, 173, 228; allowances, 94, 96–97, 99, 103–105, 108, 110, 114, 137, 156, 170, 189; arrears, 94–98, 102, 181; batta issue, 89, 92, 98, 100, 102–106, 108, 230; and incentives, 92–93, 98; and Indian soldiers, 17, (see also discrimination); monetary compensation, 98, 110
peasant rebellion, 32, see also Jats
Peel Commission, 126
Pemble, Maj., 100
Persia, 16, 30, 35, 86, 263
Persia and Iran (PAI) force, 22
Persians, 34, 162–163, 187
Persian War, 14
Pert, Lilian, Nurse, 112
Pethick-Lawrence, 297–298
Pindaris, 67
pistols, 181, 237, 252
Plassey, 7, 52, 127, 267, see also Battle of Plassey
Pollock, Gen., 103
Pondicherry, 38–39, 42–45, 55, 131
Potsdam conference, 3

Index

prejudices, 121, 137, 193, 211–212, 214, 226–227
Prince of Wales, 15
prisoner camps, 196–197
prisoners, 49, 69–70, 108–109, 180, 196–198, 217, 247, 250, 261, 264, 267–268, 284–286, 288; in Baghdad, 196; division of, 284; flogging of, 197
Prisoners of Wars (POWs), 121, 201–205, 263, 268; compensation, 108; funds, 109
prize money, 92, 98–102, 165
punishment, 33–34, 102, 222, 229, 285, 292, 297; parade, 246
Punjab, 32–33, 35, 64, 85, 108, 117, 119–122, 163, 168, 253, 262; annexation of, 13

Queen Elizabeth I 2
Quit India movement, 259

race, 85, 87, 121, 139
RAF academy, 154
Rahman, Habib, 281
Rai, Shitab, 72
Rajaram of Sinsini, 32
Rajputana, 31
Rajputs, 50, 78, 80, 87, 119, 121, 211, 236, 279
Ram, Ananti, 69
Ram, Dawak, 86
Ram, Daya, 263
Ram, Duleep, 68, 75
Ram, Mansa, 84
Ram, Shiv, 87
Ranjit Singh, Guru, 95–96, 162–163, 265
Rao, Baji, 265

rations, 89, 92, 109, 111, 166, 170
Rawlinson, Commander-in-Chief, 153
Rawlinson, Henry, 92
Rawlinson Committee, 152
rebellion, 14, 20, 66, 117, 119, 137, 168–169, 208, 223, 253–254, 262; Indian, 11; Mau-Mau, 258
rebels, 32, 69–70, 224, 248, 252–253
recruitment, 11, 20, 39, 48, 121–122, 124, 211–213, 236, 253, 272; of Indian soldiers, 24; of 'martial races,' 121; pool, 11; strategy, 212
Red Cross Society, 109, 197, 279
Red Fort, 251, 292; trials, 285, see also trials
redress, 100, 135
regiments, 68–69, 105–108, 120–122, 133, 144–146, 166, 168, 170, 172, 175, 181, 221–222, 224, 229, 241–245; Indian, 149, 182; systems, 133, 135
relief funds, 197
religious beliefs and practices, 208, 210, 212, 215–216, 218, 255. See also caste
renunciation, 77, 80, 82
reorganization, 120, 129, 133, 135
revenue, 6–7, 19–20, 28–29, 57, 61, 72, 167, 184–186, 259; Indian, 17–18, 184, 186, 259
revolt, 252, 265, 276; of American settlers, 10
revolution, 25, 39, 158, 272, 290
revolutionaries, 276
rewards, 89
Reza Sahib, 46, 61

Rice Holmes, T., 134, 246
rifles, 63–65, 124, 127–128, 186, 244, 247, 282; Brown Bess, 127, 238; Lee-Enfield, 127–128, 238; Lee-Metford, 128; Martini-Henry, 128; Minié, 127
riots, 287, 296
ritual pollution, 226, 239, see also religious beliefs and practices
Roberts, Lord, 121–122, 141
Roe, Thomas, Sir, 2
Rotton, John, 251
Roy, Ram Mohan, 91, 139, 157, 215
Royal Indian Navy (RIN), 294
rumours, 52, 228, 240–241, 247
Russian crisis, 14, 183

sacrifice, 71, 84, 148, 236–237, 283, 292; of Indian soldiers, 148
Saheb, Nana, 253
Sahgal, P.K., Capt., 280, 282, 285, 289, 292–293
Sahib, Chanda, 43–47, 61, 90, 211
'saka,' 65, 80–82, 209
Sale, Lady, 164, 168–177, 180
Sale, Robert, 168
Sambhaji, public execution of, 32
Sandes, Maj., 195
Sandhurst, 140, 142, 151–152, 154–157
Sarbadhikari, Sisir, 109, 114, 189, 192, 195–204
sati, 215
Scindia, 138, 141, 219
Seaton, Thomas, 166
self-governance, 21, 140
self-government, 138, 157–158, 260, 298
Sen, Surendra Nath, 95, 243

sepoys: battalions, 53, 56–58, 73, 100–101, 125, 129, 132–133, 135; Bengal, 53, 56, 103, 167, 227; companies, 61, 72, 96, 131–133, 166, 228; Hindu, 103, 119, 212, 220, 226; Indian, 19–21, 90, 93, 100, 102, 108, 112, 115, 117, 124, 163–164, 257, 261; Madras, 53, 130; Nellore, 61; origin of 302n10; purabiya, 120
sergeants, 131–133, 135, 147
Seth, Jagat, 51
Seton, Bruce, Col., 113
Seven Years' War, 50
Shah, Ahmad, 180–181
Shah, Jahandar, 34
Shah, Nadir, 35, 39
Shahzada, 54–55
Shelton, Brig., 169, 172, 174, 194
Sheoran, Choudhary Raghbir Singh, 22–23
Shivaji Bhonsle, 31, 94–95, 219, 265; death of, 32
Shuja, Shah, 56, 66, 163, 167–169, 171, 173, 181, 232
Shuja-ud-Daulah, Nawab Wazir, 52, 56–57
Shureef, Mahommed, 170
Sialkot, 64, 239
Sikhs, 28, 32–33, 35, 59, 70–71, 78, 84, 118–121, 253, 269, 279, (see also under soldiers); kingdom, 120; regiment, 84, 257; religious symbols, 256; wars, 11, 66, 119
Silhadi, 80–81
silladar system, 186
Sind war, 103

Index

Singapore, 16, 22, 269–272, 275–278, 280–283, 288, 294; defeat, 160
Singh, Amar, 143–148, 150–152
Singh, Cheyt, 98, 133
Singh, Churaman, 34
Singh, Davedeen, 106–107
Singh, Dogra Jemadar Kapur, 64
Singh, Ganda, 85–86
Singh, Dhokul, Gen. 135
Singh, Gokula, 32
Singh, Gordhan, 86
Singh, Gulab, 87
Singh, Hurjee, 144
Singh, Jasji, 144
Singh, Jawahir, 138
Singh, Jemadar Chur, 84
Singh, Jemadar Ganda, 85
Singh, Jemadar Jewand, 183
Singh, Jemadar Kapur, 64–65, 71
Singh, Jeswant, 129
Singh, Jewand, 183
Singh, Kapur, 64–65
Singh, Kartar, 85
Singh, Keser, 130–131, 134
Singh, Kunwar, 253
Singh, Mahendra Pratap, 123, 144–147, 263–265, 273, 275
Singh, Mohan Capt., 272–274
Singh, Mokum, 67
Singh, Pritam, 272
Singh, Ram, 64, 107
Singh, Ranjit, 138
Singh, Zorawar, 150
Singhs, Jye, 129
Siraj-ud-Daulah, 49, 51–52, 211, 267
Sircar/Sirkar (British government), 66, 173, 236
Sirdars, 173

Skeen Committee, 152, 154
skills, 30, 78, 126, 133
Skinner, James, 213–214
slavery, 70, 180–181
Slim, General, 65, 244–248, 279
soldiers: abandoning of Indian, 160; Africa, 62; American, 287; Arab, 66; British, 16, 64, 93, 97, 108, 110–111, 124–125, 128–129, 156, 161, 195–197; English, 42, 264, 283; European, 17, 24, 50, 99–100, 102, 133–134, 164, 166, 170–171, 219, 222, 238, 240; French, 40, 62, 147; foot, 25, 29; Hindu, 193, 197; Hindu/Sikh, 197; Indian, 15–17, 20, 22, 24, 39, 64–66, 83, 111–113, 117, 160–162, 190–193, 197, 205–206, 210–211, 283; Muslims, 78, 81, 197, 212, 245, 256; Sikh, 120, 197, 268
Somaliland campaign, 14
South Africa, 11
Spanish war, 10
Sri Lanka, 14
standing army, 19, 27, 185, 187
subaltern, 133, 248
subedars, 59–60, 66, 72, 90, 102, 129–130, 132, 134–137, 140, 144, 213; Mughal, 35, 52; Nellore, 61–62, 131
Sudan, 11, 15–16; wars, 14
Sukkur, 105–106
Sultan, Tipu, 97, 133, 219, 223, 227
Sultanate of Mysore, 59
superiority, 25, 53, 209, 215–216
Syria, 16, 196

tactics, 25–26, 29–30, 39, 42, 62, 282

Tagore, Satyendra Nath, 139
Taliban, 160
Tanjore forces, 47
tax, 34
Teg Bahadur, Guru, 32
Thailand, 16, 280
Tharoor, Shashi, 7, 20
Theresa, Maria, 39
Thomasson, James, 216
Tibet expedition, 14
Timurid dynasty, 35
Tiruchirappalli (Trichinopoly), 44, 46
Tojo, 274
Topasses, 210; recruitment pool, 211
Townshend, Gen., 113–114, 188, 190–191, 193–194
training, 25, 39, 42, 89, 117, 124, 142–143, 148, 151, 155, 157
traitors, 68, 124, 286
treason, 52, 285, 288
Treaty of Aix-la-Chapelle, 42
Treaty of Westphalia, 27
Trevelyan, Charles, 1
trials, 63, 93, 146, 221, 261, 284–290, 292–293
Tricolour flag, 294, 296
Tripoli, 203–204
troops, Indian, 15, 17, 82, 110, 112, 124, 128, 193–195, 199, 286, 288; white, 24, 53, 93, 98–99, 102, 110–111, 140, 143, 192
Tunisia, 16
Tunzelmann, Alex von, 4
Turkey, 109, 195–196, 204, 264
Turkish: army, 189, 194, 197, 200, 202, 204; captivity, 195–196; maltreatment, 195; prison camps, 205; soldiers, 193, 198, 204

Turks, 83, 86, 113–114, 188, 190, 192, 194–198, 201–203, 205, 264
Turner, Major, 144–146
Twynam, Sir, 287

underdogs, 161, 197
UN Security Council, 3
untrustworthy, 124, 174
Uzbek retainers, 172

Vansittrat, Henry, 55
Vellore, 222; Fort, 221, 225; mutiny, 223–224
Viceroy's Commissioned Officers (VCOs), 140, 144, 151, 153–156, 193–195, 272, 286
Vijayvarghava, 79
Vincent, Major-General, 105
Vizagapatnam, 227
volunteers, 10, 21, 158, 171–172, 227, 261, 272

Waddy, Captain, 138
Wallenstein, Albrecht von, 26
war in Europe, 39
War Office, 18, 142, 256
Watson, Admiral, 50
Wavell, Viceroy, 286, 289
Wellington, 10, 219
Wheeler, Major, 105, 243–244
Whitehall, 186, 191, 261
Wilberforce, William, 1
Wilde's Rifles battalion, 64
Wilson, Archdale, Brig., 248
Wollen, William Barns, 161, 183
women and children, 68, 80–81, 160, 169, 174–176, 179–180, 198, 201, 209
Woolwich academy, 140, 154, 156

World War I, 15, 20, 22–21, 82, 90, 108, 111–112, 117, 121, 123, 129, 144, 148, 156, 158, 161, 183–188, 205, 213, 256, 260–263

World War II 9, 15–16, 18, 21, 110, 112, 114, 117, 124, 126, 157–158, 213, 260, 262, 282–283

Yamamoto, Col., 271
YMCA, 256
Young, Lt., 106–107

Zafar, Bahadur Shah, 34, 80–81, 138, 251–253, 255, 285
Ziegler, Norman, 78

About the Author

Ravindra Rathee started his career as a journalist with the *Times of India* in Delhi, writing on human rights and conflict resolution. After graduating from St Stephen's College in Delhi, he did an MA in politics at the University of Hull as a British Chevening Scholar. For the past two decades, he has worked as a banker. This is his first book, stemming from extensive research on the military life of his grandfather.